Readings in
BASIC MARKETING

Readings in

BASIC MARKETING

Edited by

E. Jerome McCarthy
Michigan State University

John F. Grashof
Temple University

Andrew A. Brogowicz
*University of Illinois
at Chicago Circle*

1978
Revised Edition

RICHARD D. IRWIN, INC.   Homewood, Illinois   60430
Irwin-Dorsey Limited   Georgetown, Ontario   L7G 4B3

ISBN 0-256-02050-7
Library of Congress Catalog Card No. 78–52940

Printed in the United States of America

1 2 3 4 5 6 7 8 9 0 ML 5 4 3 2 1 0 9 8

Preface

Just another readings book? No!

This collection of articles is intended as an educational tool to help enhance the beginning student's understanding of marketing. It has been designed to parallel the topical development of most introductory marketing books, in particular, E. J. McCarthy's *Basic Marketing, A Managerial Approach*. The articles contained in this collection were not selected just because they are popular, because their authors are popular, or because they happen to relate to the topical area. Rather, each article considered, was evaluated with the following criteria in mind:

1. The article should amplify or illustrate concepts introduced in the beginning marketing course, with an emphasis on *deepening* the student's understanding of these concepts rather than exposing him or her to more new concepts.
2. The article should be concise, readable, and within the scope of the beginning marketing student's understanding.
3. The article should make a specific contribution to the collection as a whole.
4. The article should provide a basis for class discussion.

Applying these criteria led to the selection of a variety of articles from more than a dozen different sources for the first edition of this book. When selecting the articles to be included in this revised edition, we relied heavily on comments from colleagues and students who had used the first edition. These inputs helped identify articles that had made important contributions to student understanding.

This edition contains 39 selections, 4 more than were in the first edition. Three of the four additional articles are in the last section, actually doubling the coverage of the macro-societal aspects of marketing. In total, 18 of the articles in the first edition were replaced with 22 new selections. These readings range from relatively theoretical selections from the *Journal of Marketing Research* to more pragmatic selections from sources such as *Business Week* and *The Wall Street Journal*. Some of the articles have become classics in the marketing literature while others, to our knowledge, have never been reprinted before. Two were written especially for this collection. While the number of articles has increased, the number of pages remains about the same as in the first edition because many of the new articles are shorter. It is our hope that this will provide increased flexibility and broader coverage and that the readings will lead to an interesting and fruitful educational experience for beginning marketing students.

The articles have been grouped into five major parts:

1. Introduction to Marketing.
2. Selecting Target Markets.
3. Developing Marketing Mixes.
4. Marketing Management in Action.
5. Marketing Reappraised.

To help guide the student through the readings, each part begins with a short introduction which presents an overview of the topics covered. In addition, each article is preceded by a brief introduction to help the reader focus on important aspects of the article.

Each reading in the collection is followed by a set of discussion questions that can serve as a check on the reader's understanding of key points contained in the article, while also providing a basis for class discussion. Most questions can be answered from the material contained in the article. Some questions, however—those indicated by an asterisk (*)—are broader in scope and relate concepts introduced in that particular article to concepts discussed in other articles. This integration of concepts from different readings can result not only in a deeper understanding of the concepts, but also in a heightened appreciation of the interrelationships among marketing variables.

The editors gratefully acknowledge the cooperation of the authors and journals who graciously consented to our reprinting their material. Most of the articles appear in their original versions. Occasionally, however, space constraints have made it necessary to shorten articles somewhat in order to expose the student to a broader array of authors, issues, and ideas. Where articles have been edited, we have tried to maintain the emphasis of the original article without distorting the meaning of an author's words. Of course, the original authors cannot be held fully accountable for the edited versions of their work which appear here. Interested readers are strongly encouraged to refer to the original article for complete exposure to an author's views and insights.

We hope the collection proves useful to both faculty and students. We do encourage your comments and suggestions. Responsibility for editorial errors or shortcomings in accomplishing our objective is ours.

April 1978

E. J. McCarthy
J. F. Grashof
A. A. Brogowicz

Contents

4. MARKETING MANAGEMENT IN ACTION   303

5. MARKETING REAPPRAISED   371

Part 1

Introduction to marketing

The roles of marketing within the firm and society are currently being reexamined. Scholars are studying the critical role marketing plays within the economy, the influence marketing techniques can have on nonprofit institutions, and the social responsibility marketers should demonstrate.

Most of the readings in this part were selected to illustrate current thought about marketing and its many roles. The articles present various points of view about marketing and its relationship to the firm and to society. These readings lay the groundwork for understanding the managerial approach to marketing, which will be the focus of most of the readings in this collection.

The concept of a marketing strategy and its importance to the survival of the firm are discussed by several of the authors. Reading 2, a case study of the development of the marketing strategy for P&G's Pampers, is of special note. This new-product success illustrated the application of the marketing concept.

The final two readings in Part 1 deal with the increasingly important area of business-governmental interaction. Reading 7, with the appliance industry postscript, points out that government involvement can be costly to business and therefore to consumers. The Business Week report in Reading 8 shows that failure to operate within limits of regulation can be personally expensive for overly aggressive managers.

1
Marketing's changing social relationships

William Lazer

What are the role(s) of marketing in our society? Lazer contends that marketing is a social institution whose role includes but also extends beyond the marketing activities of a firm. Recognition of this societal role provides a new perspective for examining the role of marketing tasks within a firm. Similarly, environmental factors such as changing life-styles and social norms can have considerable impact on the firm's marketing activities.

Marketing is not an end in itself. It is not the exclusive province of business management. Marketing must serve not only business but also the goals of society. It must act in concert with broad public interest. For marketing does not end with the buy-sell transaction—its responsibilities extend well beyond making profits. Marketing shares in the problems and goals of society and its contributions extend well beyond the formal boundaries of the firm.

The purpose of this article is to present some viewpoints and ideas on topics concerning marketing's changing social relationships. The author hopes to stimulate discussion and encourage work by others concerned with the marketing discipline, rather than to present a definitive set of statements. He first presents a brief discussion of marketing and our life style, and marketing's role beyond the realm of profit. This is followed by the development of some ideas and viewpoints on marketing and consumption under conditions of abundance, with a particular focus on changing consumption norms. The last section is concerned with changing marketing boundaries and emerging social perspectives.

MARKETING AND LIFE STYLE

Recent developments in such areas as consumer safety and protection, product warranties, government investigations, and a host of urban issues, including air and water pollution, and poverty, are stimulating thoughtful executives and academicians to pay increasing attention to marketing's fundamental interfaces with society. They highlight the fact that marketers are

Source: Reprinted with permission from the *Journal of Marketing,* published by the American Marketing Association, vol. 33 (January 1969), pp. 3–9. At the time of writing, William Lazer was a professor of marketing at Michigan State University.

inevitably concerned with societal norms and life styles of both our total society and societal segments. Since the American economy is a materialistic, acquisitive, thing-minded, abundant market economy, marketing becomes one of the cores for understanding and influencing life styles: and marketers assume the role of taste counselors. Since American tastes are being emulated in other parts of the world such as Europe, Japan, and Latin America, the impact of our values and norms reverberate throughout a broad international community.

Yet a basic difference exists between the orientation of the American life style, which is interwoven with marketing, and the life style of many other countries, particularly of the emerging and lesser-developed countries, although the differences are blurring. American norms include a general belief in equality of opportunity to strive for a better standard of living; the achievement of status and success through individual initiative, sacrifice, and personal skills; the provision and maintenance of a relatively open society with upward economic and social movement; the availability of education which is a route for social achievement, occupational advancement, and higher income. Yet, there are contradictory and conflicting concepts operating within this value system. One contradiction is seen in the conflict between concepts of equality for all on the one hand and the visible rank and status orderings in society. Another conflict much discussed today concerns the conflicts between the coexisting values of our affluent society and the pockets of poverty in the United States.

In their scheme of norms the majority of Americans, even younger Americans, exude optimism in the materialistic productivity of our society. They feel confident that the economic future will be much better than the present, that our standard of living and consumption will expand and increase, that pleasures will be multiplied, and that there is little need to curb desires. They are certain that increasing purchasing power will be made available to them.

This is not to deny the existence of discontent in our economy of plenty, or the challenging and questioning of values. There is evidence that some younger members are critical of our hedonistic culture, of our economic institutions and achievements. Questions have been raised about priorities of expenditures, and authority has been challenged. Various marketing processes and institutions have been attacked. But, by and large, there exists a general expectation of increasing growth, the availability of more and more, and a brighter and better future. As a result of this perspective, economic opportunities and growth are perceived not so much in terms of curbing consumer desires as is the case in many other societies, particularly in underdeveloped economies, but in increasing desires; in attempting to stimulate people to try to realize themselves to the fullest extent of their resources and capabilities by acquiring complementary goods and symbols. Whereas other societies have often hoped that tomorrow will be no worse than today, we would certainly be dismayed if present expectations did not indicate that tomorrow will be much better than today. Similarly, the emerging nations now have rising economic expectations and aspiration levels, and their life style perspectives are changing. They expect to share in the economic abundance achieved by highly industrialized economies.

The growth orientation which reverberates throughout the American society has its impact on our norms and on marketing practices. It is reflected in such marketing concepts and techniques as product planning, new product development, installment credit, pricing practices, advertising campaigns, sales promotion, personal selling campaigns, and a host of merchandising activities.

BEYOND THE REALM OF PROFIT

One of the next marketing frontiers may well be related to markets that extend beyond mere profit considerations to intrinsic values—to markets based on social concern, markets of the mind, and markets concerned with the development of people to the fullest extent of their capabilities. This may be considered a macro frontier of marketing, one geared to interpersonal and social development, to social concern.

From this perspective one of marketing's roles may be to encourage increasing expenditures by consumers of dollars and time to develop themselves socially, intellectually, and morally. Another may be the direction of marketing to help solve some of the fundamental problems that nations face today. Included are such problems as the search for peace, since peace and economic progress are closely intertwined; the renewal of our urban areas which is closely related to marketing development and practices, particularly in the area of retailing; the reduction and elimination of poverty, for marketing should have a major role here; the preservation of our natural resources; the reshaping of governmental interfaces with business; and the stimulation of economic growth. To help solve such problems, in addition to its current sense of purpose in the firm, marketing must develop its sense of community, its societal commitments and obligations, and accept the challenges inherent in any institution of social control.

But one may ask whether social welfare is consonant with the bilateral transfer characteristics of an exchange or market economy, or can it be realized only through the unilateral transfer of a grants economy? This is a pregnant social question now confronting marketing.

Business executives operating in a market economy can achieve the degree of adaptation necessary to accept their social responsibilities and still meet the demands of both markets and the business enterprise. At the very least, the exchange economy will support the necessary supplementary grants economy. Currently we are witnessing several examples of this.[1] The National Alliance for Businessmen composed of 50 top business executives is seeking

---

[1] For a discussion of this point see Robert J. Holloway, "Total Involvement in Our Society," in *Changing Marketing Systems,* Reed Moyer, ed. (Washington, D.C.: American Marketing Association, *1967 Winter Conference Proceedings,* December 1967), pp. 6–8; Robert Lekachman, "Business Must Lead the Way," *Dun's Review,* vol. 91 (April 1968), p. 11; and Charles B. McCoy, "Business and the Community," *Dun's Review,* vol. 91 (May 1968), pp. 110–11.

jobs in 50 of our largest cities for 500,000 hard-core unemployed; the Urban Coalition, composed of religious, labor, government, and business leaders, as well as several individual companies, is actively seeking ways of attacking the problem of unemployment among the disadvantaged; and the insurance companies are investing and spending millions for new housing developments in slum areas. It even seems likely that business executives, operating in a market environment, stimulated by the profit motive, may well succeed in meeting certain challenges of social responsibility where social planners and governmental agencies have not.

Governmental agencies alone cannot meet the social tasks. A spirit of mutual endeavor must be developed encompassing a marketing thrust. For marketing cannot insulate itself from societal responsibilities and problems that do not bear immediately on profit. Marketing practice must be reconciled with the concept of community involvement, and marketing leaders must respond to pressures to accept a new social role.[2]

The development of the societal dimensions of marketing by industry and/or other institutions is necessary to mold a society in which every person has the opportunity to grow to the fullest extent of his capabilities, in which older people can play out their roles in a dignified manner, in which human potentials are recognized and nurtured, and in which the dignity of the individual is accepted. While prone to point out the undesirable impact of marketing in our life style (as they should), social critics have neglected to indicate the progress and the contributions that have been made.

In achieving its sense of broad community interest and participation, marketing performs its social role in two ways. First, marketing faces social challenges in the same sense as the government and other institutions. But unlike the government, marketing finds its major social justification through offering product-service mixes and commercially unified applications of the results of technology to the marketplace for a profit. Second, it participates in welfare and cultural efforts extending beyond mere profit considerations, and these include various community services and charitable and welfare activities. For example, marketing has had a hand in the renewed support for the arts in general, the increasing demand for good books, the attendance at operas and symphony concerts, the sale of classical records, the purchase of fine paintings through mail-order catalogues, and the attention being given to meeting educational needs. These worthy activities, while sometimes used as a social measure, do not determine the degree of social concern or the acceptance of social responsibility.

A fundamental value question to be answered is not one of the absolute morality or lack of problems in our economic system and marketing activities,

---

[2] Among the recent articles discussing management's new social role are "Business Must Pursue Social Goals: Gardner," *Advertising Age*, vol. 39 (February 1968), p. 2; B. K. Wickstrum, "Managers Must Master Social Problems," *Administrative Management*, vol. 28 (August 1967), p. 34; and G. H. Wyman, "Role of Industry in Social Change," *Advanced Management Journal*, vol. 33 (April 1968), pp. 70–74.

as many critics suggest. Rather, it is one concerning the *relative* desirability of our life style with its norms, its emphasis on materialism, its hedonistic thrust, its imperfections, injustices, and poverty, as contrasted with other life styles that have different emphases. Great materialistic stress and accomplishment is not inherently sinful and bad. Moral values are not vitiated (as many critics might lead one to believe) by substantial material acquisitions. Increasing leisure time does not automatically lead to the decay and decline of a civilization. In reality, the improvement of material situations is a stimulus for recognition of intrinsic values, the general lifting of taste, the enhancement of a moral climate, the direction of more attention to the appreciation of arts and esthetics. History seems to confirm this; for great artistic and cultural advancements were at least accompanied by, if not directly stimulated by, periods of flourishing trade and commerce.

MARKETING AND CONSUMPTION UNDER ABUNDANCE

American consumers are confronted with a dilemma. On the one hand, they live in a very abundant, automated economy that provides a surplus of products, an increasing amount of leisure, and an opportunity for a relative life of ease. On the other hand, they have a rich tradition of hard physical work, sweat, perseverance in the face of adversity, earning a living through hard labor, being thrifty, and "saving for a rainy day." There is more than token acceptance of a philosophy that a life of ease is sinful, immoral, and wrong. Some consumers appear to fear the abundance we have and the potential life style that it can bring, and are basically uncomfortable with such a way of life.

Yet, for continued economic growth and expansion, this feeling of guilt must be overcome. American consumers still adhere to many puritanical concepts of consumption, which are relevant in an economy of scarcity but not in our economy of abundance. Our society faces a task of making consumers accept comfortably the fact that a life style of relative leisure and luxury that eliminates much hard physical labor and drudgery, and permits us to alter unpleasant environments, is actually one of the major accomplishments of our age, rather than the indication of a sick, failing, or decaying society. Those activities resulting in the acquisition of more material benefits and greater enjoyment of life are not to be feared or automatically belittled, nor is the reduction of drudgery and hard physical tasks to be regretted.

Some of the very fundamental precepts underlying consumption have changed. For example, consumption is no longer an exclusive home-centered activity as it once was; consumption of large quantities of many goods and services outside the home on a regular basis is very common. Similarly, the hard work and drudgery of the home is being replaced by machines and services. The inherent values of thrift and saving are now being challenged by the benefits of spending and the security of new financial and employment arrangements.[3] In fact, the intriguing problems of consumption must now receive the attention previously accorded to those of physical production.

In essence, our consumption philosophy must change. It must be brought into line with our age of plenty, with an age of automation and mass production, with a highly industrialized mass-consumption society. To do so, the abundant life style must be accepted as a moral one, as an ethical one, as a life which can be inherently good. The criteria for judging our economic system and our marketing activities should include opportunity for consumers to develop themselves to the fullest extent, personally and professionally; to realize and express themselves in a creative manner; to accept their societal responsibilities; and to achieve large measures of happiness. Abundance should not lead to a sense of guilt stemming from the automatic declaration of the immorality of a comfortable way of life spurred on by marketing practices.

In our society, is it not desirable to urge consumers to acquire additional material objects? Cannot the extension of consumer wants and needs be a great force for improvement and for increasing societal awareness and social contributions? Is it not part of marketing's social responsibility to help stimulate the desire to improve the quality of life—particularly the economic quality—and so serve the public interest?

In assessing consumption norms, we should recognize that consumer expenditures and investments are not merely the functions of increased income. They stem from and reflect our life style. Thus, new consumption standards should be established, including the acceptance of self-indulgence, of luxurious surroundings, and of non-utilitarian products. Obviously, products that permit consumers to indulge themselves are not "strict necessities." Their purchase does not, and should not, appeal to a "utilitarian rationale." For if our economic system produced only "utilitarian products," products that were absolute necessities, it would incur severe economic and social problems, including unemployment.

Yet some very significant questions may be posed. Can or should American consumers feel comfortable, physically and psychologically, with a life of relative luxury while they are fully cognizant of the existence of poverty in the midst of plenty, of practice of discrimination in a democratic society, the feeling of hopelessness and despair among many in our expanding and increasingly productive economy, and the prevalence of ignorance in a relatively enlightened age? Or, on a broader base, can or should Americans feel comfortable with their luxuries, regular model and style changes, gadgetry, packaging variations, and waste while people in other nations of the world confront starvation? These are among the questions related to priorities in the allocation of our resources, particularly between the public and private sectors

[3] Some aspects of the economic ambivalence of economic values are discussed by David P. Eastburn, "Economic Discipline and the Middle Generation," *Business Review,* Federal Reserve Bank of Philadelphia, July 1968, pp. 3–8.

and between the national and international boundaries that have been discussed by social and economic commentators such as Galbraith[4] and Toynbee.

These are not easy questions to answer. The answers depend on the perspective adopted (whether macro or micro), on the personal philosophy adhered to (religious and otherwise), and on the social concern of individuals, groups, and nations. No perfect economic system has or will ever exist, and the market system is no exception. Economic and social problems and conflicts will remain, but we should strive to eliminate the undesirable features of our market system. And it is clear that when abundance prevails individuals and nations can afford to, and do, exercise increasing social concern.

Toynbee, in assessing our norms and value systems (particularly advertising), wrote that if it is true that personal consumption stimulated by advertising is essential for growth and full employment in our economy (which we in marketing believe), then it demonstrates automatically to his mind that an economy of abundance is a spiritually unhealthy way of life and that the sooner it is reformed, the better.[5] Thus, he concluded that our way of life, based on personal consumption stimulated by advertising, needs immediate reform. But let us ponder for a moment these rather strong indictments of our norms and the impact of marketing on our value systems and life style.

When economic abundance prevails, the limitations and constraints on both our economic system and various parts of our life style shift. The most critical point in the functioning of society shifts from physical production to consumption. Accordingly, the culture must be reoriented: a producers' culture must be converted into a consumers' culture. Society must adjust to a new set of drives and values in which consumption, and hence marketing activities, becomes paramount. Buckminster Fuller has referred to the necessity of creating regenerative consumers in our affluent society.[6] The need for consumers willing and able to expand their purchases both quantitatively and qualitatively is now apparent in the United States. It is becoming increasingly so in Russia, and it will be so in the future among the underdeveloped and emerging nations. Herein lies a challenge for marketing—the challenge of changing norms and values to bring them into line with the requirements of an abundant economy.

Although some social critics and observers might lead us to believe that we should be ashamed of our life style, and although our affluent society is widely criticized, it is circumspect to observe that other nations of the world are struggling to achieve the stage of affluence that has been delivered by our

---

[4] John K. Galbraith, "The Theory of Social Balance," in *Social Issues in Marketing*, Lee E. Preston, ed. (Glenview, Ill.: Scott, Foresman and Company, 1968), pp. 247–52.

[5] "Toynbee vs. Bernbach: Is Advertising Morally Defensible?" *Yale Daily News*, Special Issue, 1963, p. 2.

[6] Buckminster Fuller, *Education Automation: Freeing the Scholar to Return to His Studies* (Carbondale, Ill.: Southern Illinois University Press, 1961).

economic system. When they achieve it, they will be forced to wrestle with similar problems of abundance, materialism, consumption, and marketing that we now face.

CONSUMPTION ACTIVITIES AND NORMS

The relative significance of consumers and consumption as economic determinants has been underemphasized in our system.[7] Consumption should not be considered an automatic or a happenstance activity. We must understand and establish the necessary conditions for consumption to proceed on a continuing and orderly basis. This has rich meaning for marketing. New marketing concepts and tools that encourage continuing production rather than disruptive production or the placement of consumer orders far in advance, or new contractual obligations, must be developed.[8] To achieve our stated economic goals of stability, growth, and full employment, marketing must be viewed as a force that will shape economic destiny by expanding and stabilizing consumption.

To date the major determinant of consumption has been income. But as economic abundance increases, the consumption constraints change. By the year 2000, it has been noted, the customer will experience as his first constraint not money, but time.[9] As time takes on greater utility, affluence will permit the purchase of more time-saving products and services. Interestingly enough, although time is an important by-product of our industrial productivity, many consumers are not presently prepared to consume time in any great quantities, which in turn presents another opportunity for marketing. The manner in which leisure time is consumed will affect the quality of our life style.

In other ages, the wealthy achieved more free time through the purchase of personal services and the use of servants. In our society, a multitude of products with built-in services extend free time to consumers on a broad base. Included are such products as automobiles, jet planes, mechanized products in the home, prepared foods, "throw-aways," and leased facilities. Related to this is the concept that many consumers now desire the use of products rather than mere ownership. The symbolism of ownership appears to take on lesser importance with increasing wealth.[10]

We live in a sensate culture, one which stresses materialism and sensory enjoyment. Consumers desire and can obtain the use of products and sym-

[7] George Katona, "Consumer Investment and Business Investment," *Michigan Business Review,* June 1961, pp. 17–22.

[8] Ferdinand F. Mauser, "A Universe-in-Motion Approach to Marketing," in *Managerial Marketing—Perspectives and Viewpoints,* Eugene J. Kelley and William Lazer, eds. (Homewood, Ill.: Richard D. Irwin, Inc., 1967), pp. 46–56.

[9] Nelson N. Foote, "The Image of the Consumer in the Year 2000," *Proceedings, Thirty-Fifth Annual Boston Conference on Distribution, 1963,* pp. 13–18.

[10] Same reference as footnote 8.

bols associated with status, achievement, and accomplishments. Material values which are visible have become more important to a broader segment of society, and marketing responds to and reinforces such norms. But our basic underlying value system is not merely the result of the whims of marketers—it has its roots in human nature and our cultural and economic environments.

The concept of consumption usually conjures a false image. Consumption generally seems to be related to chronic scarcity. It is associated with hunger, with the bare necessities of life, and with the struggle to obtain adequate food, shelter, and clothing.[11] It is associated with the perception of economics as the "dismal science," with the study of the allocation of scarce resources.

But, it has been noted that in the future consumption and consuming activities will occur in a society suffering from obesity and not hunger; in a society emerged from a state of chronic scarcity, one confronting problems of satiation—full stomachs, garages, closets and houses.[12] Such an environment requires a contemporary perspective and concept of consumption and con-sumers. It requires a recognition and appreciation of the importance of stimulating the consumption of goods. For consumers will find that their financial capabilities for acquiring new products are outstripping their natural inclinations to do so.

But what happens to norms and values when people have suitably gratified their "needs"? What happens after the acquisition of the third au-tomobile, the second color television set, and three or four larger and more luxurious houses? Maslow has noted that consumers then become motivated in a manner different from that explained by his hierarchy of motives. They become devoted to tasks outside themselves. The differences between work and play are transcended; one blends into the other, and work is defined in a different manner. Consumers become concerned with different norms and values reflected in metamotives or metaneeds, motives or needs beyond physical love, safety, esteem, and self-actualization.[13]

The tasks to which people become dedicated, given the gratification of their "needs," are those concerned with intrinsic values. The tasks are en-joyed because they embody these values. The self then becomes enlarged to include other aspects of the world. Under those conditions, Maslow maintains that the highest values, the spiritual life, and the highest aspirations of man-kind become proper subjects for scientific study and research. The hierarchy of basic needs such as physical, safety, and social is prepotent to metaneeds. The latter, metaneeds, are equally potent among themselves.

Maslow also makes a distinction between the realm of being, the "B-realm," and the realm of deficiencies, the "D-realm"—between the external and the practical. For example, in the practical realm of marketing with its

---

[11] Same reference as footnote 9.

[12] Same reference as footnote 9.

[13] Abraham Maslow, "Metamotivation," *The Humanist*, May–June 1967, pp. 82–84.

daily pressures, executives tend to be responders. They react to stimuli, rewards, punishments, emergencies, and the demands of others. However, given an economy of abundance with a "saturation of materialism," they can turn attentions to the intrinsic values and implied norms—seeking to expose themselves to great cultural activities, to natural beauty, to the developments of those "B" values.

Our society has reached the stage of affluence without having developed an acceptable justification for our economic system, and for the eventual life of abundance and relative leisure that it will supply. Herein lies a challenge for marketing: to justify and stimulate our age of consumption. We must learn to realize ourselves in an affluent life and to enjoy it without pangs of guilt. What is required is a set of norms and a concept of morality and ethics that corresponds to our age. This means that basic concepts must be changed, which is difficult to achieve because people have been trained for centuries to expect little more than subsistence, and to grid for a fight with the elements. They have been governed by a puritanical philosophy, and often view luxurious, new, convenient products and services with suspicion.

When we think of abundance, we usually consider only the physical resources, capabilities, and potentialities of our society. But abundance depends on more than this. Abundance is also dependent on the society and culture itself. It requires psychological and sociological environments that encourage and stimulate achievement. *In large measure, our economic abundance results from certain institutions in our society which affect our pattern of living, and not the least of these institutions is marketing.*

Advertising is the institution uniquely identified with abundance, particularly in America. But the institution that is actually brought into being by abundance without previous emphasis or existence in the same form is marketing.[14] It is marketing expressed not only through advertising. It is also expressed in the emphasis on consumption in our society, new approaches to product development, the role of credit, the use of marketing research and marketing planning, the implementation of the marketing concept, the management of innovation, the utilization of effective merchandising techniques, and the cultivation of mass markets. Such institutions and techniques as self-service, supermarkets, discount houses, advertising, credit plans, and marketing research are spreading marketing and the American life style through other parts of the world.

Marketing is truly an institution of social control in a relatively abundant economy, in the same sense as the school and the home. It is one of the fundamental influences of our life style. It is a necessary condition of our high standard of living. It is a social process for satisfying the wants and needs of our society. It is a very formative force in our culture. In fact, it is impossible to understand fully the American culture without a comprehension of marketing.

---

[14] David M. Potter, "People of Plenty" (Chicago, Ill.: University of Chicago Press, 1954), p. 167.

But, unlike some other social institutions, marketing is confronted with great conflicts that cloud its social role.

CHANGING MARKETING BOUNDARIES

We may well ask, what are the boundaries of marketing in modern society? This is an important question that cannot be answered simply. But surely these boundaries have changed and now extend beyond the profit motive. Marketing ethics, values, responsibilities, and marketing-government relationships are involved. These marketing dimensions will unquestionably receive increasing scrutiny by practitioners and academicians in a variety of areas, and the result will be some very challenging and basic questions that must be answered.

We might ask, for example, can or should marketing, as a function of business, possess a social role distinct from the personal social roles of individuals who are charged with marketing responsibilities?[15] Does the business as a legal entity possess a conscience and a personality whose sum is greater than the respective attributes of its individual managers and owners? Should each member of management be held personally accountable for social acts committed or omitted in the name of the business? Answers to such questions change with times and situations, but the trend is surely to a broadening recognition of greater social responsibilities—the development of marketing's social role.

Few marketing practitioners or academicians disagree totally with the concept that marketing has important social dimensions and can be viewed as a social instrument in a highly industrialized society. Disagreement exists, however, about the relative importance of marketing's social dimensions as compared to its managerial or technical dimensions.

The more traditional view has been that marketing management fulfills the greater part of its responsibility by providing products and services to satisfy consumer needs profitably and efficiently. Those adopting this view believe that as a natural consequence of its efficiency, customers are satisfied, firms prosper, and the well-being of society follows automatically. They fear that the acceptance of any other responsibilities by marketing managers, particularly social responsibilities, tends to threaten the very foundation of our economic system. Moot questions about who will establish the guidelines, who will determine what these social responsibilities should be, and who will enforce departures from any standards established are raised.

However, an emerging view is one that does not take issue with the ends of customer satisfaction, the profit focus, the market economy, and the economic growth. Rather, its premise seems to be that the tasks of marketing and

---

[15] For a discussion of the social responsibilities of executives, see James M. Patterson, "What are the Social and Ethical Responsibilities of Marketing Executives?" *Journal of Marketing,* vol. 30 (July 1936), pp. 12–15, and K. Davis, "Understanding the Social Responsibility Puzzle," *Business Horizons,* vol. 10 (Winter 1967), pp. 45–50.

its concomitant responsibilities are much wider than purely economic concerns. It views the market process as one of the controlling elements of the world's social and economic growth. Because marketing is a social instrument through which a standard of living is transmitted to society, as a discipline it is a social one with commensurate social responsibilities that cannot merely be the exclusive concern of companies and consumers.

Perhaps nowhere is the inner self of the populace more openly demonstrated than in the marketplace; for the marketplace is an arena where actions are the proof of words and transactions represent values, both physical and moral. One theologian has written, "the saintly cannot be separated from the marketplace, for it is in the marketplace that man's future is being decided and the saintly must be schooled in the arts of the marketplace as in the discipline of saintliness itself."[16]

In this context, marketing's responsibility is only partially fulfilled through economic processes. There is a greater responsibility to consumers and to the human dignity that is vital to the marketplace—the concern for marketing beyond the profit motive.

Academicians and executives will be forced to rethink and reevaluate such situations in the immediate future just by the sheer weight of government concern and decisions if by nothing else.[17] In the last year, there have been governmental decisions about safety standards, devices for controlling air pollution, implied product warranties, packaging rules and regulations, the relationship of national brands to private labels, pricing practices, credit practices, and mergers. There have been discussions about limiting the amount that can be spent on advertising for a product, about controlling trading stamps, about investigating various promotional devices and marketing activities. Such actions pose serious questions about marketing's social role. If we do not answer them, others will; and perhaps in a manner not too pleasing, or even realistic.

There need be no wide chasm between the profit motive and social responsibility, between corporate marketing objectives and social goals, between marketing actions and public welfare. What is required is a broader perception and definition of marketing than has hitherto been the case—one that recognizes marketing's societal dimensions and perceives of marketing as

---

[16] Louis Finkelstein, in *Conference on the American Character,* Bulletin, Center for the Study of Democratic Institutions, October 1961, p. 6.

[17] The reader can gain some insight into government concern from such articles as "Consumer Advisory Council: First Report," in *Social Issues in Marketing,* Lee E. Preston, ed. (Glenview, Ill.: Scott, Foresman and Company, 1968), pp. 282–94; Betty Furness, "Responsibility in Marketing," in *Changing Marketing Systems,* Reed Moyer, ed. (Washington, D.C.: American Marketing Association, *1967 Winter Conference Proceedings,* December 1967), pp. 25–27; Galbraith, same reference as footnote 4; Richard H. Holton, "The Consumer and the Business Community, in *Social Issues in Marketing,* Lee E. Preston, ed. (Glenview, Ill.: Scott, Foresman and Company, 1968), pp. 295–303; George H. Koch, "Government-Consumer Interest: From the Business Point of View," in *Changing Marketing Systems,* Reed Moyer, ed. (Washington, D.C.: American Marketing Association, *1967 Winter Conference Proceedings,* December 1967), pp. 156–60.

more than just a technology of the firm. For the multiple contributions of marketing that are so necessary to meet business challenges, here and abroad, are also necessary to meet the nation's social and cultural problems.

QUESTIONS

1. Identify the several roles, or potential roles, assigned to marketing by Lazer.
2. What are the dominant social norms and values of the United States and what demands do they place on the marketing system?
3. If businesses accepted Lazer's ideas, what specific changes might we expect in their marketing activities? How would profit be affected?
4. Should (and if so, how should) Lazer's analysis be modified if our young people must now live in and adjust to a world of shortages and growing austerity?
5. Should marketing accept the challenge suggested by Lazer: changing norms and values to bring them into line with the requirements of an abundant economy?
6. What are the basic assumptions in the United States regarding: freedom of choice with respect to production and consumption, the right to private property, and the responsibility of an individual for himself (vs. a societal responsibility for the individual)? Are these assumptions changing? What is the potential impact of any changes?

2
The Pampers story: A P&G success

Part of the social responsibility of marketing is to develop better ways for the members of society to meet their needs. This reprint from a Procter & Gamble consumer education booklet, Consumer Choice: The Driving Force of a Market Economy, *tells the story of the development and introduction of Pampers disposable diapers. It provides an overview of the marketing function and the activities of consumer goods firms in the United States. Further, it illustrates many of the problems of a firm attempting to serve consumers and shows how one firm successfully solved these problems.*

No one thought up Pampers, the disposable diaper, overnight. The process began when a loving grandfather was baby-sitting for his first grandchild, a job which, of course, included changing diapers. He decided that there had to be something better than cloth diapers, and that the disposable diapers then on the market weren't the answer.

While both the cloth diapers and the disposable diapers available met the need, neither did it very well. Cloth diapers meant laundering, folding, and the general nuisance of storing soiled diapers. The disposable diapers were not as absorbent as cloth and were not strong enough.

The grandfather, a consumer, was also a Procter & Gamble engineer. He knew his company was in business to solve consumer problems like this, so he brought his problem to his associates. He was persuasive enough to make the company want to verify his instincts. At this point, the company had to decide whether or not to try to develop a better way of diapering babies. Since Procter & Gamble, like every business and every individual, has limited resources and unlimited ways of using them, the company had to decide if diapering babies was a consumer need it could satisfy better than others.

Before embarking on a project that would cost millions of dollars, the men and women making decisions for Procter & Gamble had to be able to answer three basic questions:

1. Was there a *real consumer need* for an alternative method of diapering?
2. Did Procter & Gamble have the scientific and technological ability to develop the product?

Source: Reprinted with permission from *Consumer Choice*, an educational booklet prepared by the Educational Services Department, Procter and Gamble, Cincinnati, Ohio 45201, 1977.

3. Was the potential market for such a product large enough to offer some promise of making a profit?

To confirm that other consumers shared the engineer's need for an alternative diapering method, Procter & Gamble used consumer market research. Such research can take many forms: Interviews with consumers in their homes, telephone interviews, questionnaires, discussion groups. The objectives, however, are always the same: To discover what the consumers want by finding out how they use existing products, what they think of these products, and what their daily habits are. Procter & Gamble, for example, looks for clues in the interviews it annually conducts with more than a million consumers. These clues can help the company recognize a need that the consumers have not been able to verbalize.

In the case of Pampers, thousands of mothers were asked how they diapered their babies and how they felt about their current diapering methods and products. The consumer market research showed that mothers found the cloth diapers were uncomfortable for their babies. The cloth diapers bunched up, did not keep the babies dry enough, and required plastic pants which could irritate the baby's tender skin. Obviously, there was a real need for a better way of diapering, since this consumer problem involved more than just the messy task of storing and laundering soiled diapers.

QUESTION: CAN WE SELL IT AT A PROFIT?

The company had the expertise to develop the product since it had a good deal of experience inventing and manufacturing absorbent paper products like paper towels and facial and toilet tissue.

Now, P&G specialists in product research, engineering, marketing and advertising all began to examine the basic idea of a single-use, disposable diaper. Could it be made? How? Would it satisfy the consumer need? Could it be sold at a profit?

15 BILLION DIAPER CHANGES AREN'T HAY

All these questions were critical ones, but the final question—profit—was the most critical of all. In business, this is known as "the bottom line," because the last line of an accountant's column of figures shows the final results of a company's efforts—profit, or loss. If a company cannot make a profit, there is no incentive to develop a new product. Profits enable a company to stay in business.

Market opportunity—the potential size of a new market—is crucial in forecasting profit. A company has to have some promise of return on the millions of dollars required to develop a product from the idea stage through production. Procter & Gamble calculated that there were more than 15 billion diaper changes a year in the United States. This was certainly an impressive market, if an effective and efficient alternative method of diapering could be invented.

Such a market would lend itself to a mass produced product; one that could be produced in high volume but at a relatively low cost per unit. This was important because the company knew the new product would have to be sold at a price that could compete with cloth diapers, but at the same time provide some return (profit) on its investment.

Although each diaper sold would return only a tiny amount of the investment required, the return from millions of sales could make the effort worthwhile. Spreading huge research and investment costs over millions or billions of units of a product is an example of what economists call *economy of scale*.

In effect, Procter & Gamble had preliminary answers to the three basic questions mentioned earlier: (1) It found a *real consumer desire or problem;* (2) determined that it had the *technical capacity* to satisfy that desire or solve that problem; and (3) estimated there was a large enough *potential market* for such a product to justify the investment required to get the product from idea to mass-produced reality. In deciding that Pampers was a promising investment, Procter & Gamble had made its economic choice to go ahead.

STARTING PRODUCT DEVELOPMENT

The chain of action and reaction that began with the consumer was developing rapidly. The idea of a disposable diaper had reached the *product development* phase. Chemists and engineers were now assigned the task of inventing a product that would solve the problems consumers were encountering with their current diapering method.

The objective was to develop a product that would be comfortable for the baby to wear (better fit, keep baby drier than cloth), easy to store, disposable, and competitively priced with cloth diapers. The raw materials would have to be safe for babies and the environment in which these diapers would be disposed. After nine months of research, the product development team came up with a diaper pad for insertion in plastic pants. The pad, which used a special pleat for better fit, was absorbent and flushable.

The new disposable diaper was now ready for a pilot test, another form of market research. So a small supply of these unnamed diaper pads and plastic pants was made by hand and given free to parents in Dallas, Tex. Result? Dallas parents turned thumbs down on the product by an overwhelming majority!

What went wrong? The diaper was okay as far as comfort and absorbency were concerned, but the specialists forgot one thing: It gets very hot in Dallas. And while 80 to 90 percent of the babies up North were wearing elasticized plastic pants, Dallas parents weren't about to subject *their* babies to a Turkish bath.

So it was back to the drawing board.

Dallas consumers having spoken, it took another six months to develop a radically new diaper design. Scientists studied new materials and checked them thoroughly for human and environmental safety. Finally, six months later, a new diaper—changed to correct the Dallas problem—emerged. The company retained the things that Dallas parents liked about the diaper pad product—the special pleat for comfort and the absorbent materials for dryness. The new product also retained the disposability feature.

This time, however, plastic pants were replaced by a newly invented, thin sheet of plastic across the back that kept the moisture in but allowed some circulation to alleviate the hothouse effect of plastic pants. Another invention—a porous sheet between the baby and the absorbent material—allowed fluid to pass through to the absorbent material, but prevented most of it from coming back through. This kept babies drier and more comfortable.

ONGOING RESEARCH AND DEVELOPMENT

When the new product was ready for another tryout, 37,000 diapers were made by hand. This time, consumer reaction was overwhelmingly favorable. Parents liked the new diaper and said they would keep on buying it.

All the work needed to bring a product from idea to reality comes under the general category of research and development. This is a common activity in enterprises competing in the consumer marketplace. While work was going on to develop the disposable diaper, scores of other new products were going through similar research and development at Procter & Gamble, and at hundreds of other companies throughout the world. Only a small percentage of these new products would survive the rigorous tests.

At the same time, experiments were being conducted to find ways to improve existing products. This research and development was made possible because Procter & Gamble, and other companies, were able to earn a profit from other products that were already on the market.

TEST MARKETING A NEW PRODUCT

A product had been designed which appeared to meet consumers' needs for an alternative to cloth diapers. The next step was to introduce the product into the market to see if consumers really agreed that the product solved their problem effectively and efficiently. Despite the checks and rechecks that had already been made with consumers, the only way to determine if the product really solved the problem was to put it on sale under actual market conditions.

Pampers was a totally new product. All manufacturing up to this point had either been done by hand or on a small-scale manufacturing line, and raw materials had been purchased only in small quantities as needed. A decision to make the product available to consumers across the country would require constructing manufacturing facilities, purchasing equipment, hiring additional people, and contracting for huge quantities of raw materials. This would mean the expenditure of millions of dollars.

If, despite the research and testing, not enough consumers bought the product, the company would lose money and its capital investment in machinery would be lost.

To avoid gambling on such an investment, many companies first introduce a new product into a limited area called a *test market*. In a test market, a product that has already been proven safe and effective is put on sale in one or more selected cities with populations that correspond to the composition of the country as a whole. The product is sold exactly as though it were on sale nationally, with advertising, cents-off coupons, store displays, all of the modern mass marketing activities that could be used on a national scale to make consumers aware of the product.

The idea is to see if what looked good to the company, and to those consumers who tried the product for free in the preliminary research, still looks good to consumers under actual buying conditions. After the product has been in a test market for awhile, sales can be analyzed and projections made about the number of consumers who would buy the product if it were available nationally. Further market research can discover more about consumers' likes and dislikes, and perhaps lead to further product improvement.

P&G's completely redesigned diaper seemed to solve all the problems consumers had with cloth diapers. But before the company could move ahead with test marketing a lot of work still had to be done.

Engineers had to translate their thoughts and drawings into machines that could mass produce the new product in quantities sufficient to supply the test market, and with the same quality as the handmade versions. To do this, they had to invent a totally new manufacturing process. It took a year for P&G engineers to design and build a small-scale production line. The machinery, a complex array of metal, wires and pulleys, had to be adjusted and readjusted before the line began running smoothly enough to produce sufficient diapers for the test market. One hundred cases of the product were first given to consumers to try in their homes, to make sure that the machine-made ones were as satisfactory to consumers as the handmade ones had been.

PAMPERS, YES—DRI-WEES, NO

While engineering specialists were developing a way to make the product in quantity, with quality, and at high speed, the company's marketing groups were also busy in support of the new product.

Market researchers went back to the consumers for help in giving the new product a name. They tried all kinds of names—Tenders, Dri-Wees, Winks, Tads, Solos, Zephyrs—and, of course, the winner, Pampers. Those parents who were interviewed felt that Pampers best conveyed the feeling of tender, loving care that they gave their babies. The company agreed and thought it was a name that would be easily recognized and remembered.

P&G's newly named product also needed a package—so packaging experts worked toward a solution that would be the right size, protect the contents and attract the eye. Today's consumer products compete not only in meeting consumer needs, but also in visibility.

Other marketing specialists coordinated by an "advertising brand group"—a team set up to manage the total marketing of each product—began comparing what consumers had said they wanted with what the new product had to offer. Their job was to create advertising messages that would communicate these benefits effectively to potential consumers. At the same time, distribution experts were determining how to ship the product from the point of manufacture to the point of sale.

Still other technical experts and buying experts were searching for the best sources of supply, at the lowest prices, for the raw materials that they hoped would be needed in vast quantities. This points out another important economic fact—as the Pampers wheels began to turn, more jobs and more income were created not only for the company and its employes, but also for its suppliers and their employes, and *their* suppliers and *their* employes.

THE PRICING PROBLEM GETS STICKY

Accountants kept track of the costs that were being calculated by all the other groups: The cost of the raw materials and the cost of manufacturing and distributing the product. Each group had to estimate not only the cost of getting Pampers ready for the test market but also the cost of mass-producing Pampers if they were sold nationally. The accountants and the advertising brand group developed a price based on estimates of how many Pampers they could sell in terms of the total potential market (15 billion diaper changes every year) and how many people would use this new diapering method.

In its first test market (Peoria, Ill., in 1961), Pampers was offered for sale at a price of about 10 cents per diaper. This figure was based on the costs to produce about 400,000,000 diapers annually, which is the number of Pampers the company estimated could be sold nationally at the 10-cent price mass production would permit. However, a company always loses money in a test market because the product costs much more to produce in the small quantity needed than it does when it is finally in mass production.

The Peoria test was a major disappointment. Instead of the projected national sales level of 400,000,000 diapers, the Peoria test indicated that the most P&G could hope to sell was less than half this amount.

The company could not afford to invest any more capital in the equipment and machinery needed to mass produce Pampers if this was the best they could expect. But that's what test markets are for—to recheck what the consumer wants and alert the company to changes that need to be made in packaging, marketing, price, or even the product. The company could have moved ahead without the test market, but that could have meant the possible loss of the total investment made for national production and introduction of the product. As it was, P&G had already spent millions of dollars on a product that looked like a failure.

Market research soon found the trouble: Price. Consumers liked the disposable diaper idea, but they decided that 10 cents a diaper was too much to pay. .

HOW TO CUT COSTS OF A NEW PRODUCT

The trade-off of 10 cents of their resources for one disposable diaper wasn't worth it. Why hadn't P&G discovered this before? One reason was that consumers sometimes say they'll do one thing but actually do another. Also, consumer habits, needs, wants and priorities can change from day to day. At this point, test market research confirmed that parents who tried Pampers liked them, but not at the 10-cent price. Encouraged by consumer acceptance of the new product, but worried about the pricing problem, P&G turned to the challenge of bringing down that price.

Although Procter & Gamble found some additional ways to reduce the long-range costs of raw materials, production and delivery, the savings were nowhere near enough to enable the company to lower the price of Pampers. There was only one way to achieve the necessary savings while maintaining quality. That was to increase volume. If, instead of 400,000,000 diapers a year, Pampers could sell a billion diapers, they could be sold at 6 cents each.

The reasons are fundamental and apply to any mass-produced product. Certain costs, including administrative expenses and other indirect costs, would remain relatively fixed regardless of the number of diapers produced. If more than twice as many diapers were produced and sold, these fixed costs could be spread over the higher diaper volume, thereby reducing the *unit* cost. And with the increased volume, the company could exchange a higher profit per unit for a lower profit per unit, but make about the same *total profit*.

In terms of *price, supply* and *demand,* P&G's management was convinced that *demand* for Pampers at the lower price would be about double what it was at the higher price. The company revised its thinking about the quantity it would be willing to produce *(supply)*. P&G was now convinced that the increase in the number of units sold would make up for the lower income per unit at the lower selling price. After the Peoria experience, the risk appeared great, but the company's managers decided to take it.

The product was introduced in Sacramento, Cal., at the new price. Consumer response was immediate. At the new price, consumers began using Pampers regularly and not just for trips or under special circumstances. And they began making *repeat purchases* of Pampers.

Additional test markets were opened and Pampers continued to satisfy an increasing number of consumers. Production moved from the prototype line to eight lines in an existing company plant.

As consumer demand grew in each test market, the company made the decision to move Pampers into national distribution.

Soon, additional production facilities had to be built to keep the supply up with the demand. A plant was built in Pennsylvania, then in Missouri, California and Georgia. Each plant was a large investment for the company, but one it could afford to make because of expected return on the investment. More importantly, in terms of the total market system, each new plant represented more money being channeled into the local communities as payment for land, construction and wages. New jobs were created, and purchase orders went to hundreds of suppliers for goods and services.

WHY PRICE WAS HELD, DESPITE DEMAND

It took from 1966 to 1970, though, for all of this to happen. The demand was there, but it took a long time to build each manufacturing plant. Expansion into new geographical areas often had to wait until a new manufacturing facility was completed. For a time, the company was forced to allocate product to its customers, the supermarkets, to ensure fair distribution of the scarce commodity.

Despite the high demand and limited supply—a combination that generally pushes prices up—the company kept the price of Pampers relatively constant. Based on the Peoria test market experience, P&G knew that there would be a radical drop in sales of Pampers at a higher price—consumers had told the company what value they placed on the product, and the company had to live with that value.

By mid-1970—almost 20 years after one grandfather began to grumble—Pampers was available in enough quantity to satisfy demand throughout the U.S. The enormous investment of time, talent and personnel had earned success. By 1976, almost half the babies in the U.S. were wearing Pampers.

COMPETITION KEEPS US HOPPING

Pampers was a totally new product. It was the first to satisfy an unfilled consumer need. The company's response to that need and consumer reaction created a market for an entirely new product. Whenever this happens in a market economy, it is not long before other producers channel their resources, from products that are no longer satisfying a consumer need, into the new market. Such was the case with Pampers as other companies entered the market with related products. These companies asked themselves: Can we meet the consumer need that Pampers did, but more efficiently and effectively? Or is there a need or problem Pampers failed to see—on which we can capitalize?

Competition is generally regarded as the keystone of our market economy. Without competition, economies tend to stagnate. Through competition between producers for markets, retailers for customers, employes for jobs and promotions, most needs of people and society can be served. Fair competition in a free market benefits consumers by forcing manufacturers to organize and produce more efficiently in order to keep quality and value up and prices down. Competition forces companies to listen to consumers, and follow through with product improvements that will put, or keep, their product out in front in satisfying consumers' needs. P&G's ongoing efforts and investments in response to changing consumer concerns, and competition, are all part of the continuing chain of product design, development, marketing and improvement.

The 9,000 products sold in supermarkets make up the most competitive marketplace ever seen. Will Pampers survive against its new competitors?

The answer lies in a popular saying not formally considered one of the "laws" of economics—"build a better mousetrap, and the world will beat a path to your door." Pampers was successful because it was "a better mousetrap," the best one that could be made at the time. Since then, there have been several important improvements in Pampers to insure that the product continues to respond to the interests of consumers. New diaper sizes have been added, tape fasteners have replaced pins, new materials have been developed for even greater absorbency. Only by such continuing research and development can P&G hope to hold the major part of a market which it developed by filling a consumer need first effectively articulated by a new grandfather. Remember, its new competitors will be trying to improve their products, too.

BETTER MOUSETRAP WON'T ASSURE SUCCESS

The production of Pampers is growing more efficient and economical. As the engineers and manufacturing personnel gain experience with the new manufacturing process, they keep getting better at it, so that efficiency goes up while costs remain under control. So they hope, and expect, to keep ahead of the competition. Obviously, the competition hopes to go them one better.

Designing and producing a "better mousetrap" is only a part of the problem of product survival against competition. Nowadays, if one plans and builds a "better mousetrap" and doesn't tell anyone about it, it will only trap one's own mice. In the mass consumer market, there is only one effective way to tell people about your product, and that's *advertising*.

QUESTIONS

1. Why was P&G successful with the introduction of Pampers, while new products typically fail?

2. In marketing Pampers, P&G introduced a product that did not previously exist. Did P&G create a *need* for the product? If yes, what, specifically, was that need? If no, then what would you call, or how would you describe, the demand for a previously nonexistent product?

3. Some social critics are arguing against disposable products that consume irreplaceable resources. Was P&G's marketing of Pampers (a disposable product) to replace a reusable product (cloth diapers) a socially responsible decision? What criteria should be applied to evaluate the "social responsibility" of such a decision?

3
Broadening the concept of marketing

Philip Kotler and Sidney J. Levy

Marketing is an activity that goes considerably beyond the selling of diapers, soap, and steel. Kotler and Levy explain the value of the marketing concept for nonbusiness organizations and illustrate the application of marketing principles in such organizations. This article is placed here to help deepen (as well as broaden) your understanding of the marketing concept as it applies to both business and nonbusiness organizations. As you read the article, try to apply the concepts to organizations such as your school or church.

The term "marketing" connotes to most people a function peculiar to business firms. Marketing is seen as the task of finding and stimulating buyers for the firm's output. It involves product development, pricing, distribution, and communication; and in the more progressive firms, continuous attention to the changing needs of customers and the development of new products, with product modifications and services to meet these needs. But whether marketing is viewed in the old sense of "pushing" products or in the new sense of "customer satisfaction engineering," it is almost always viewed and discussed as a business activity.

It is the authors' contention that marketing is a pervasive societal activity that goes considerably beyond the selling of toothpaste, soap, and steel. Political contests remind us that candidates are marketed as well as soap; student recruitment by colleges reminds us that higher education is marketed; and fund raising reminds us that "causes" are marketed. Yet these areas of marketing are typically ignored by the student of marketing. Or they are treated cursorily as public relations or publicity activities. No attempt is made to incorporate these phenomena in the body proper of marketing thought and theory. No attempt is made to redefine the meaning of product development, pricing, distribution, and communication in these newer contexts to see if they have a useful meaning. No attempt is made to examine whether the principles of "good" marketing in traditional product areas are transferable to the marketing of services, persons, and ideas.

Reprinted with permission from the *Journal of Marketing,* published by the American Marketing Association, vol. 33 (January 1969), pp. 10–15. At the time of publication of this article, Philip Kotler and Sidney Levy were both professors of marketing at Northwestern University.

The authors see a great opportunity for marketing people to expand their thinking and to apply their skills to an increasingly interesting range of social activity. The challenge depends on the attention given to it; marketing will either take on a broader social meaning or remain a narrowly defined business activity.

THE RISE OF ORGANIZATIONAL MARKETING

One of the most striking trends in the United States is the increasing amount of society's work being performed by organizations other than business firms. As a society moves beyond the stage where shortages of food, clothing, and shelter are the major problems, it begins to organize to meet other social needs that formerly had been put aside. Business enterprises remain a dominant type of organization, but other types of organizations gain in conspicuousness and in influence. Many of these organizations become enormous and require the same rarefied management skills as traditional business organizations. Managing the United Auto Workers, Defense Department, Ford Foundation, World Bank, Catholic Church, and University of California has become every bit as challenging as managing Procter & Gamble, General Motors, and General Electric. These nonbusiness organizations have an increasing range of influence, affect as many livelihoods, and occupy as much media prominence as major business firms.

All of these organizations perform the classic business functions. Every organization must perform a financial function insofar as money must be raised, managed, and budgeted according to sound business principles. Every organization must perform a production function in that it must conceive of the best way of arranging inputs to produce the outputs of the organization. Every organization must perform a personnel function in that people must be hired, trained, assigned, and promoted in the course of the organization's work. Every organization must perform a purchasing function in that it must acquire materials in an efficient way through comparing and selecting sources of supply.

When we come to the marketing function, it is also clear that every organization performs marketing-like activities whether or not they are recognized as such. Several examples can be given.

The police department of a major U.S. city, concerned with the poor image it has among an important segment of its population, developed a campaign to "win friends and influence people." One highlight of this campaign is a "visit your police station" day in which tours are conducted to show citizens the daily operations of the police department, including the crime laboratories, police lineups, and cells. The police department also sends officers to speak at public schools and carries out a number of other activities to improve its community relations.

Most museum directors interpret their primary responsibility as "the proper preservation of an artistic heritage for posterity."[1] As a result, for many people museums are cold marble mausoleums that house miles of relics that soon give way to yawns and tired feet. Although museum attendance in the United States advances each year, a large number of citizens are uninterested in museums. Is this indifference due to failure in the manner of presenting what museums have to offer? This nagging question led the new director of the Metropolitan Museum of Art to broaden the museum's appeal through sponsoring contemporary art shows and "happenings." His marketing philosophy of museum management led to substantial increases in the Met's attendance.

The public school system in Oklahoma City sorely needed more public support and funds to prevent a deterioration of facilities and exodus of teachers. It recently resorted to television programming to dramatize the work the public schools were doing to fight the high school dropout problem, to develop new teaching techniques, and to enrich the children. Although an expensive medium, television quickly reached large numbers of parents whose response and interest were tremendous.

Nations also resort to international marketing campaigns to get across important points about themselves to the citizens of other countries. The junta of Greek colonels who seized power in Greece in 1967 found the international publicity surrounding their cause to be extremely unfavorable and potentially disruptive of international recognition. They hired a major New York public relations firm and soon full-page newspaper ads appeared carrying the headline "Greece Was Saved From Communism," detailing in small print why the takeover was necessary for the stability of Greece and the world.[2]

An anti-cigarette group in Canada is trying to press the Canadian legislature to ban cigarettes on the grounds that they are harmful to health. There is widespread support for this cause but the organization's funds are limited, particularly measured against the huge advertising resources of the cigarette industry. The group's problem is to find effective ways to make a little money go a long way in persuading influential legislators of the need for discouraging cigarette consumption. This group has come up with several ideas for marketing anti-smoking to Canadians, including television spots, a paperback book featuring pictures of cancer and heart disease patients, and legal research on company liability for the smoker's loss of health.

What concepts are common to these and many other possible illustrations of organizational marketing? All of these organizations are concerned about their "product" in the eyes of certain "consumers" and are seeking to find "tools" for furthering their acceptance. Let us consider each of these concepts in general organizational terms.

---

[1] This is the view of Sherman Lee, Director of the Cleveland Museum, quoted in *Newsweek*, vol. 71 (April 1, 1968), p. 55.

[2] "PR for the Colonels," *Newsweek*, vol. 71 (March 18, 1968), p. 70.

Products

Every organization produces a "product" of at least one of the following types:

Physical products. "Product" first brings to mind everyday items like soap, clothes, and food, and extends to cover millions of *tangible* items that have a market value and are available for purchase.

Services. Services are *intangible* goods that are subject to market transaction such as tours, insurance, consultation, hairdos, and banking.

Persons. Personal marketing is an endemic *human* activity, from the employee trying to impress his boss to the statesman trying to win the support of the public. With the advent of mass communications, the marketing of persons has been turned over to professionals. Hollywood stars have their press agents, political candidates their advertising agencies, and so on.

Organizations. Many organizations spend a great deal of time marketing themselves. The Republican Party has invested considerable thought and resources in trying to develop a modern look. The American Medical Association decided recently that it needed to launch a campaign to improve the image of the American doctor.[3] Many charitable organizations and universities see selling their *organization* as their primary responsibility.

Ideas. Many organizations are mainly in the business of selling *ideas* to the larger society. Population organizations are trying to sell the idea of birth control, and the Women's Christian Temperance Union is still trying to sell the idea of prohibition.

Thus the "product" can take many forms, and this is the first crucial point in the case for broadening the concept of marketing.

Consumers

The second crucial point is that organizations must deal with many groups that are interested in their products and can make a difference in its success. It is vitally important to the organization's success that it be sensitive to, serve, and satisfy these groups. One set of groups can be called the *suppliers*. *Suppliers* are those who provide the management group with the inputs necessary to perform its work and develop its product effectively. Suppliers include employees, vendors of the materials, banks, advertising agencies, and consultants.

The other set of groups are the *consumers* of the organization's product, of which four sub-groups can be distinguished. The *clients* are those who are the immediate consumers of the organization's product. The clients of a business firm are its buyers and potential buyers; of a service organization those receiving the services, such as the needy (from the Salvation Army) or the sick

---

[3] "Doctors Try an Image Transplant," *Business Week,* June 22, 1968, p. 64.

(from County Hospital); and of a protective or a primary organization, the members themselves. The second group is the *trustees or directors,* those who are vested with the legal authority and responsibility for the organization, oversee the management, and enjoy a variety of benefits from the "product." The third group is the active *publics* that take a specific interest in the organization. For a business firm, the active publics include consumer rating groups, governmental agencies, and pressure groups of various kinds. For a university, the active publics include alumni and friends of the university, foundations, and city fathers. Finally, the fourth consumer group is the *general public.* These are all the people who might develop attitudes toward the organization that might affect its conduct in some way. Organizational marketing concerns the programs designed by management to create satisfactions and favorable attitudes in the organization's four consuming groups: clients, trustees, active publics, and general public.

Marketing tools

Students of business firms spend much time studying the various tools under the firm's control that affect product acceptance: product improvement, pricing, distribution, and communication. All of these tools have counterpart applications to nonbusiness organizational activity.

Nonbusiness organizations to various degrees engage in product improvement, especially when they recognize the competition they face from other organizations. Thus, over the years churches have added a host of nonreligious activities to their basic religious activities to satisfy members seeking other bases of human fellowship. Universities keep updating their curricula and adding new students' services in an attempt to make the educational experience relevant to the students. Where they have failed to do this, students have sometimes organized their own courses and publications, or have expressed their dissatisfaction in organized protest. Government agencies such as license bureaus, police forces, and taxing bodies are often not responsive to the public because of monopoly status; but even here citizens have shown an increasing readiness to protest mediocre services, and more alert bureaucracies have shown a growing interest in reading the user's needs and developing the required product services.

All organizations face the problem of pricing their products and services so that they cover costs. Churches charge dues, universities charge tuition, governmental agencies charge fees, fund-raising organizations send out bills. Very often specific product charges are not sufficient to meet the organization's budget, and it must rely on gifts and surcharges to make up the difference. Opinions vary as to how much the users should be charged for the individual services and how much should be made up through general collection. If the university increases its tuition, it will have to face losing some students and putting more students on scholarship. If the hospital raises its charges to cover rising costs and additional services, it may provoke a reaction from the community. All organizations face complex pricing issues although not all of them understand good pricing practice.

Distribution is a central concern to the manufacturer seeking to make his goods conveniently accessible to buyers. Distribution also can be an important marketing decision area for nonbusiness organizations. A city's public library has to consider the best means of making its books available to the public. Should it establish one large library with an extensive collection of books, or several neighborhood branch libraries with duplication of books? Should it use bookmobiles that bring the books to the customers instead of relying exclusively on the customers coming to the books? Should it distribute through school libraries? Similarly the police department of a city must think through the problem of distributing its protective services efficiently through the community. It has to determine how much protective service to allocate to different neighborhoods; the respective merits of squad cards, motorcycles, and foot patrolmen; and the positioning of emergency phones.

Customer communication is an essential activity of all organizations although many nonmarketing organizations often fail to accord it the importance it deserves. Managements of many organizations think they have fully met their communication responsibilities by setting up advertising and/or public relations departments. They fail to realize that *everything about an organization talks*. Customers form impressions of an organization from its physical facilities, employees, officers, stationery, and a hundred other company surrogates. Only when this is appreciated do the members of the organization recognize that they all are in marketing, whatever else they do. With this understanding they can assess realistically the impact of their activities on the consumers.

CONCEPTS FOR EFFECTIVE MARKETING MANAGEMENT IN NONBUSINESS ORGANIZATIONS

Although all organizations have products, markets, and marketing tools, the art and science of effective marketing management have reached their highest state of development in the business type of organization. Business organizations depend on customer goodwill for survival and have generally learned how to sense and cater to their needs effectively. As other types of organizations recognize their marketing roles, they will turn increasingly to the body of marketing principles worked out by business organizations and adapt them to their own situations.

What are the main principles of effective marketing management as they appear in most forward-looking business organizations? Nine concepts stand out as crucial in guiding the marketing effort of a business organization.

Generic product definition

Business organizations have increasingly recognized the value of placing a broad definition on their products, one that emphasizes the basic customer need(s) being served. A modern soap company recognizes that its basic product is cleaning, not soap; a cosmetics company sees its basic product as beauty or hope, not lipsticks and makeup; a publishing company sees its basic product as information, not books.

The same need for a broader definition of its business is incumbent upon nonbusiness organizations if they are to survive and grow. Churches at one time tended to define their product narrowly as that of producing religious services for members. Recently, most churchmen have decided that their basic product is human fellowship. There was a time when educators said that their product was the three R's. Now most of them define their product as education for the whole man. They try to serve the social, emotional, and political needs of young people in addition to intellectual needs.

Target groups definition

A generic product definition usually results in defining a very wide market, and it is then necessary for the organization, because of limited resources, to limit its product offering to certain clearly defined groups within the market. Although the generic product of an automobile company is transportation, the company typically sticks to cars, trucks, and buses, and stays away from bicycles, airplanes, and steamships. Furthermore, the manufacturer does not produce every size and shape of car but concentrates on producing a few major types to satisfy certain substantial and specific parts of the market.

In the same way, nonbusiness organizations have to define their target groups carefully. For example, in Chicago the YMCA defines its target groups as men, women, and children who want recreational opportunities and are willing to pay $20 or more a year for them. The Chicago Boys Club, on the other hand, defines its target group as poorer boys within the city boundaries who are in want of recreational facilities and can pay $1 a year.

Differentiated marketing

When a business organization sets out to serve more than one target group, it will be maximally effective by differentiating its product offerings and communications. This is also true for nonbusiness organizations. Fund-raising organizations have recognized the advantage of treating clients, trustees, and various publics in different ways. These groups require differentiated appeals and frequency of solicitation. Labor unions find that they must address different messages to different parties rather than one message to all parties. To the company they may seem unyielding, to the conciliator they may appear willing to compromise, and to the public they seek to appear economically exploited.

Customer behavior analysis

Business organizations are increasingly recognizing that customer needs and behavior are not obvious without formal research and analysis; they cannot rely on impressionistic evidence. Soap companies spend hundreds of thousands of dollars each year researching how Mrs. Housewife feels about her laundry, how, when, and where she does her laundry, and what she desires of a detergent.

Fund raising illustrates how an industry has benefited by replacing stereotypes of donors with studies of why people contribute to causes. Fund raisers have learned that people give because they are getting something. Many give to community chests to relieve a sense of guilt because of their elevated state compared to the needy. Many give to medical charities to relieve a sense of fear that they may be struck by a disease whose cure has not yet been found. Some give to feel pride. Fund raisers have stressed the importance of identifying the motives operating in the marketplace of givers as a basis for planning drives.

Differential advantages

In considering different ways of reaching target groups, an organization is advised to think in terms of seeking a differential advantage. It should consider what elements in its reputation or resources can be exploited to create a special value in the minds of its potential customers. In the same way Zenith has built a reputation for quality and International Harvester a reputation for service, a nonbusiness organization should base its case on some dramatic value that competitive organizations lack. The small island of Nassau can compete against Miami for the tourist trade by advertising the greater dependability of its weather; the Heart Association can compete for funds against the Cancer Society by advertising the amazing strides made in heart research.

Multiple marketing tools

The modern business firm relies on a multitude of tools to sell its product, including product improvement, consumer and dealer advertising, salesman incentive programs, sale promotions, contests, multiple-size offerings, and so forth. Likewise nonbusiness organizations also can reach their audiences in a variety of ways. A church can sustain the interest of its members through discussion groups, newsletters, news releases, campaign drives, annual reports, and retreats. Its "salesmen" include the religious head, the board members, and the present members in terms of attracting potential members. Its advertising includes announcements of weddings, births and deaths, religious pronouncements, and newsworthy developments.

Integrated marketing planning

The multiplicity of available marketing tools suggests the desirability of overall coordination so that these tools do not work at cross purposes. Over time, business firms have placed under a marketing vice-president activities that were previously managed in a semi-autonomous fashion, such as sales, advertising, and marketing research. Nonbusiness organizations typically have not integrated their marketing activities. Thus, no single officer in the typical university is given total responsibility for studying the needs and attitudes of clients, trustees, and publics, and undertaking the necessary product development and communication programs to serve these groups. The university administration instead includes a variety of "marketing" positions such as dean of students, director of alumni affairs, director of public relations, and director of development; coordination is often poor.

Continuous marketing feedback

Business organizations gather continuous information about changes in the environment and about their own performance. They use their salesmen, research department, specialized research services, and other means to check on the movement of goods, actions of competitors, and feelings of customers to make sure they are progressing along satisfactory lines. Nonbusiness organizations typically are more casual about collecting vital information on how they are doing and what is happening in the marketplace. Universities have been caught off guard by underestimating the magnitude of student grievance and unrest, and so have major cities underestimated the degree to which they were failing to meet the needs of important minority constituencies.

Marketing audit

Change is a fact of life, although it may proceed almost invisibly on a day-to-day basis. Over a long stretch of time it might be so fundamental as to threaten organizations that have not provided for periodic reexaminations of their purposes. Organizations can grow set in their ways and unresponsive to new opportunities or problems. Some great American companies are no longer with us because they did not change definitions of their businesses, and their products lost relevance in a changing world. Political parties become unresponsive after they enjoy power for a while and every so often experience a major upset. Many union leaders grow insensitive to new needs and problems until one day they find themselves out of office. For an organization to remain viable, its management must provide for periodic audits of its objectives, resources, and opportunities. It must reexamine its basic business, target groups, differential advantage, communication channels, and messages in the light of current trends and needs. It might recognize when change is needed and make it before it is too late.

IS ORGANIZATIONAL MARKETING A SOCIALLY USEFUL ACTIVITY?

Modern marketing has two different meanings in the minds of people who use the term. One meaning of marketing conjures up the terms selling, influencing, persuading. Marketing is seen as a huge and increasingly dangerous technology, making it possible to sell persons on buying things, propositions, and causes they either do not want or which are bad for them. This was the indictment in Vance Packard's *Hidden Persuaders* and numerous other social criticisms, with the net effect that a large number of persons think of marketing as immoral or entirely self-seeking in its fundamental premises. They can be counted on to resist the idea of organizational marketing as so much "Madison Avenue."

The other meaning of marketing unfortunately is weaker in the public mind; it is the concept of sensitively *serving and satisfying human needs*. This was the great contribution of the marketing concept that was promulgated in the 1950s, and that concept now counts many business firms as its practitioners. The marketing concept holds that the problem of all business firms in an age of abundance is to develop customer loyalties and satisfaction, and the key to this problem is to focus on the customer's needs.[4] Perhaps the short-run problem of business firms is to sell people on buying the existing products, but the long-run problem is clearly to create the products that people need. By this recognition that effective marketing requires a consumer orientation instead of a product orientation, marketing has taken a new lease on life and tied its economic activity to a higher social purpose.

It is this second side of marketing that provides a useful concept for all organizations. All organizations are formed to serve the interest of particular groups: hospitals serve the sick, schools serve the students, governments serve the citizens, and labor unions serve the members. In the course of evolving, many organizations lose sight of their original mandate, grow hard, and become self-serving. The bureaucratic mentality begins to dominate the original service mentality. Hospitals may become perfunctory in their handling of patients, schools treat their students as nuisances, city bureaucrats behave like petty tyrants toward the citizens, and labor unions try to run instead of serve their members. All of these actions tend to build frustration in the consuming groups. As a result some withdraw meekly from these organizations, accept frustration as part of their condition, and find their satisfactions elsewhere. This used to be the common reaction of ghetto Negroes and college students in the face of indifferent city and university bureaucracies. But new possibilities have arisen, and now the same consumers refuse to withdraw so readily. Organized dissent and protest are seen to be an answer, and many organizations thinking of themselves as responsible have been stunned into recognizing that they have lost touch with their constituencies. They had grown unresponsive.

Where does marketing fit into this picture? Marketing is that function of the organization that can keep in constant touch with the organization's consumers, read their needs, develop "products" that meet these needs, and build a program of communications to express the organization's purposes. Certainly

---

[4] Theodore Levitt, "Marketing Myopia," *Harvard Business Review,* vol. 38 (July–August 1960), pp. 45–56. [See Reading 4.]

selling and influencing will be large parts of organizational marketing; but, properly seen, selling follows rather than precedes the organization's drive to create products to satisfy its consumers.

CONCLUSION

It has been argued here that the modern marketing concept serves very naturally to describe an important facet of all organizational activity. All organizations must develop appropriate products to serve their sundry consuming groups and must use modern tools of communication to reach their consuming publics. The business heritage of marketing provides a useful set of concepts for guiding all organizations.

The choice facing those who manage nonbusiness organizations is not whether to market or not to market, for no organization can avoid marketing. The choice is whether to do it well or poorly, and on this necessity the case for organizational marketing is basically founded.

QUESTIONS

1. Explain how your college could use Kotler and Levy's nine concepts to improve its effectiveness. Be specific.
2. What is the basic difference between business and nonbusiness organizations? How would nonbusiness organizations choose among attractive alternatives when applying the marketing concept?
3. If marketing techniques do lead to unnecessary consumption, as some have contended, then is it appropriate to use these tools in an even broader set of circumstances?
*4. Are the concepts that Kotler and Levy are discussing really any different from the usual marketing activities of a firm, as illustrated in the example of the development of Pampers (Reading 2)?

---

* Asterisk indicates question which relates concepts in this reading to those in other readings.

4
Marketing myopia

Theodore Levitt

Changing life-styles, social norms, and technology may affect the survival of a firm. In this well-known article, Levitt shows that the result of failing to recognize such changes can be failure of the firm or industry. He emphasizes that long-run survival requires (1) a clear understanding of the nature of the firm's business, and (2) top management ability to recognize and deal with change.

Every major industry was once a growth industry. But some that are now riding a wave of growth enthusiasm are very much in the shadow of decline. Others which are thought of as seasoned growth industries have actually stopped growing. In every case the reason growth is threatened, slowed, or stopped is *not* because the market is saturated. It is because there has been a failure of management.

FATEFUL PURPOSES

The failure is at the top. The executives responsible for it, in the last analysis, are those who deal with broad aims and policies. Thus:

The railroads did not stop growing because the need for passenger and freight transportation declined. That grew. The railroads are in trouble today not because the need was filled by others (cars, trucks, airplanes, even telephones), but because it was *not* filled by the railroads themselves. They let others take customers away from them because they assumed themselves to be in the railroad business rather than in the transportation business. The reason they defined their industry wrong was because they were railroad-oriented instead of transportation-oriented; they were product-oriented instead of customer-oriented.

Hollywood barely escaped being totally ravished by television. Actually, all the established film companies went through drastic reorganizations. Some simply disappeared. All of them got into trouble not because of TV's inroads but because of their own myopia. As with the railroads, Hollywood defined its business incorrectly. It thought it was in the movie business when it was

---

Source: Reprinted (with deletions) by permission of the publishers from Edward C. Bursk and John F. Chapman, eds., *Modern Marketing Strategy* (Cambridge, Mass.: Harvard University Press, 1964), pp. 24-48. Copyright © 1964 by the President and Fellows of Harvard College. At the time of writing, Theodore Levitt was a professor of marketing at the Harvard Business School.

actually in the entertainment business. "Movies" implied a specific, limited product. This produced a fatuous contentment which from the beginning led producers to view TV as a threat. Hollywood scorned and rejected TV when it should have welcomed it as an opportunity—an opportunity to expand the entertainment business.

Today TV is a bigger business than the old narrowly defined movie business ever was. Had Hollywood been customer-oriented (providing entertainment), rather than product-oriented (making movies), would it have gone through the fiscal purgatory that it did? I doubt it. What ultimately saved Hollywood and accounted for its recent resurgence was the wave of new young writers, producers, and directors whose previous success in television had decimated the old movie companies and toppled the big movie moguls.

There are other less obvious examples of industries that have been and are now endangering their futures by improperly defining their purposes. I shall discuss some in detail later and analyze the kind of policies that lead to trouble. Right now it may help to show what a thoroughly customer-oriented management *can* do to keep a growth industry growing, even after the obvious opportunities have been exhausted; and here there are two examples that have been around for a long time. They are nylon and glass—specifically, E. I. duPont de Nemours & Company and Corning Glass Works.

Both companies have great technical competence. Their product orientation is unquestioned. But this alone does not explain their success. After all, who was more pridefully product-oriented and product-conscious than the erstwhile New England textile companies that have been so thoroughly massacred? The DuPonts and the Cornings have succeeded not primarily because of their product or research orientation but because they have been thoroughly customer-oriented also. It is constant watchfulness for opportunities to apply their technical know-how to the creation of customer-satisfying uses which accounts for their prodigious output of successful new products. Without a very sophisticated eye on the customer, most of their new products might have been wrong, their sales methods useless.

Aluminum has also continued to be a growth industry, thanks to the efforts of two wartime-created companies which deliberately set about creating new customer-satisfying uses. Without Kaiser Aluminum & Chemical Corporation and Reynolds Metals Company, the total demand for aluminum today would be vastly less than it is.

Error of analysis

Some may argue that it is foolish to set the railroads off against aluminum or the movies off against glass. Are not aluminum and glass naturally so versatile that the industries are bound to have more growth opportunities than the railroads and movies? This view commits precisely the error I have been talking about. It defines an industry, or a product, or a cluster of know-how so narrowly as to guarantee its premature senescence. When we mention "railroads," we should make sure we mean "transportation." As transporters, the railroads still have a good chance for very considerable growth. They are not limited to the railroad business as such (though in my opinion rail transportation is potentially a much stronger transportation medium than is generally believed).

What the railroads lack is not opportunity, but some of the same managerial imaginativeness and audacity that made them great. Even an amateur like Jacques Barzun can see what is lacking when he says: "I grieve to see the most advanced physical and social organization of the last century go down in shabby disgrace for lack of the same comprehensive imagination that built it up. [What is lacking is] the will of the companies to survive and to satisfy the public by inventiveness and skill."[1]

SHADOW OF OBSOLESCENCE

It is impossible to mention a single major industry that did not at one time qualify for the magic appellation of "growth industry." In each case its assumed strength lay in the apparently unchallenged superiority of its product. There appeared to be no effective substitute for it. It was itself a runaway substitute for the product it so triumphantly replaced. Yet one after another of these celebrated industries has come under a shadow. Let us look briefly at a few more of them, this time taking examples that have so far received a little less attention.

Dry cleaning

This was once a growth industry with lavish prospects. In an age of wool garments, imagine being finally able to get them safely and easily clean. The boom was on.

Yet here we are 30 years after the boom started and the industry is in trouble. Where has the competition come from? From a better way of cleaning? No. It has come from synthetic fibers and chemical additives that have cut the need for dry cleaning. But this is only the beginning. Lurking in the wings and ready to make chemical dry cleaning totally obsolescent is that powerful magician, ultrasonics.

Electric utilities

This is another one of those supposedly "no-substitute" products that has been enthroned on a pedestal of invincible growth. When the incandescent lamp came along, kerosene lights were finished. Later the water wheel and the steam engine were cut to ribbons by the flexibility, reliability, simplicity, and just plain easy availability of electric motors. The prosperity of electric utilities continues to wax extravagant as the home is converted into a museum

---

[1] Jacques Barzun, "Trains and the Mind of Man," *Holiday*, February 1960, p. 21.

of electric gadgetry. How can anybody miss by investing in utilities, with no competition, nothing but growth ahead?

But a second look is not quite so comforting. A score of nonutility companies are well advanced toward developing a powerful chemical fuel cell which could sit in some hidden closet of every home silently ticking off electric power. The electric lines that vulgarize so many neighborhoods will be eliminated. So will the endless demolition of streets and service interruptions during storms. Also on the horizon is solar energy, again pioneered by nonutility companies.

Who says that the utilities have no competition? They may be natural monopolies now, but tomorrow they may be natural deaths. To avoid this prospect, they too will have to develop fuel cells, solar energy, and other power sources. To survive, they themselves will have to plot the obsolescence of what now produces their livelihood.

Grocery stores

Many people find it hard to realize that there ever was a thriving establishment known as the "corner grocery store." The supermarket has taken over with a powerful effectiveness. Yet the big food chains of the 1930s narrowly escaped being completely wiped out by the aggressive expansion of independent supermarkets. The first genuine supermarket was opened in 1930, in Jamaica, Long Island. By 1933 supermarkets were thriving in California, Ohio, Pennsylvania, and elsewhere. Yet the established chains pompously ignored them. When they chose to notice them, it was with such derisive descriptions as "cheapy," "horse-and-buggy," "cracker-barrel storekeeping," and "unethical opportunists."

The executive of one big chain announced at the time that he found it "hard to believe that people will drive for miles to shop for foods and sacrifice the personal service chains have perfected and to which Mrs. Consumer is accustomed."[2] As late as 1936, the National Wholesale Grocers convention and the New Jersey Retail Grocers Association said there was nothing to fear. They said that the supers' narrow appeal to the price buyer limited the size of their market. They had to draw from miles around. When imitators came, there would be wholesale liquidations as volume fell. The current high sales of the supers was said to be partly due to their novelty. Basically people wanted convenient neighborhood grocers. If the neighborhood stores "cooperate with their suppliers, pay attention to their costs, and improve their service," they would be able to weather the competition until it blew over.[3]

It never blew over. The chains discovered that survival required going into the supermarket business. This meant the wholesale destruction of their huge

---

[2] For more details see M. M. Zimmerman, *The Super Market: A Revolution in Distribution* (New York: McGraw-Hill Book Company, Inc., 1955), p. 48.

[3] Ibid., pp. 45–47.

investments in corner store sites and in established distribution and merchandising methods. The companies with "the courage of their convictions" resolutely stuck to the corner store philosophy. They kept their pride but lost their shirts.

Self-deceiving cycle

But memories are short. For example, it is hard for people who today confidently hail the twin messiahs of electronics and chemicals to see how things could possibly go wrong with these galloping industries. They probably also cannot see how a reasonably sensible businessman could have been as myopic as the famous Boston millionaire who 50 years ago unintentionally sentenced his heirs to poverty by stipulating that his entire estate be forever invested exclusively in electric streetcar securities. His posthumous declaration, "There will always be a big demand for efficient urban transportation," is no consolation to his heirs who sustain life by pumping gasoline at automobile filling stations.

Yet, in a casual survey I recently took among a group of intelligent business executives, nearly half agreed that it would be hard to hurt their heirs by tying their estates forever to the electronics industry. When I then confronted them with the Boston streetcar example, they chorused unanimously, "That's different!" But is it? Is not the basic situation identical?

In truth, *there is no such thing* as a growth industry, I believe. There are only companies organized and operated to create and capitalize on growth opportunities. Industries that assume themselves to be riding some automatic growth escalator invariably descend into stagnation. The history of every dead and dying "growth" industry shows a self-deceiving cycle of bountiful expansion and undetected decay. There are four conditions which usually guarantee this cycle:

1. The belief that growth is assured by an expanding and more affluent population.
2. The belief that there is no competitive substitute for the industry's major product.
3. Too much faith in mass production and in the advantages of rapidly declining unit costs as output rises.
4. Preoccupation with a product that lends itself to carefully controlled scientific experimentation, improvement, and manufacturing cost reduction.

I should like now to begin examining each of these conditions in some detail. To build my case as boldly as possible, I shall illustrate the points with reference to three industries—petroleum, automobiles, and electronics—particularly petroleum, because it spans more years and more vicissitudes. Not only do these three have excellent reputations with the general public and also enjoy the confidence of sophisticated investors, but their managements have become known for progressive thinking in areas like financial control, product research, and management training. If obsolescence can cripple even these industries, it can happen anywhere.

POPULATION MYTH

The belief that profits are assured by an expanding and more affluent population is dear to the heart of every industry. It takes the edge off the apprehensions everybody understandably feels about the future. If consumers are multiplying and also buying more of your product or service, you can face the future with considerably more comfort than if the market is shrinking. An expanding market keeps the manufacturer from having to think very hard or imaginatively. If thinking is an intellectual response to a problem, then the absence of a problem leads to the absence of thinking. If your product has an automatically expanding market, then you will not give much thought to how to expand it.

One of the most interesting examples of this is provided by the petroleum industry. Probably our oldest growth industry, it has an enviable record. While there are some current apprehensions about its growth rate, the industry itself tends to be optimistic. But I believe it can be demonstrated that it is undergoing a fundamental yet typical change. It is not only ceasing to be a growth industry, but may actually be a declining one, relative to other business. Although there is widespread unawareness of it, I believe that within 25 years the oil industry may find itself in much the same position of retrospective glory that the railroads are now in. Despite its pioneering work in developing and applying the present-value method of investment evaluation, in employee relations, and in working with backward countries, the petroleum business is a distressing example of how complacency and wrongheadedness can stubbornly convert opportunity into near disaster.

One of the characteristics of this and other industries that have believed very strongly in the beneficial consequences of an expanding population, while at the same time being industries with a generic product for which there has appeared to be no competitive substitute, is that the individual companies have sought to outdo their competitors by improving on what they are already doing. This makes sense, of course, if one assumes that sales are tied to the country's population strings, because the customer can compare products only on a feature-by-feature basis. I believe it is significant, for example, that not since John D. Rockefeller sent free kerosene lamps to China has the oil industry done anything really outstanding to create a demand for its product. Not even in product improvement has it showered itself with eminence. The greatest single improvement, namely, the development of tetraethyl lead, came from outside the industry, specifically from General Motors and Du-Pont. The big contributions made by the industry itself are confined to the technology of oil exploration, production, and refining.

* * * * *

Idea of indispensability

The petroleum industry is pretty much persuaded that there is no competitive substitute for its major product, gasoline—or if there is, that it will continue to be a derivative of crude oil, such as diesel fuel or kerosene jet fuel.

There is a lot of automatic wishful thinking in this assumption. The trouble is that most refining companies own huge amounts of crude oil reserves. These have value only if there is a market for products into which oil can be converted—hence the tenacious belief in the continuing competitive superiority of automobile fuels made from crude oil.

This idea persists despite all historic evidence against it. The evidence not only shows that oil has never been a superior product for any purpose for very long, but it also shows that the oil industry has never really been a growth industry. It has been a succession of different businesses that have gone through the usual historic cycles of growth, maturity, and decay. Its overall survival is owed to a series of miraculous escapes from total obsolescence, of last-minute and unexpected reprieves from total disaster reminiscent of the Perils of Pauline.

Perils of petroleum

I shall sketch in only the main episodes:

First, crude oil was largely a patent medicine. But even before that fad ran out, demand was greatly expanded by the use of oil in kerosene lamps. The prospect of lighting the world's lamps gave rise to an extravagant promise of growth. The prospects were similar to those the industry now holds for gasoline in other parts of the world. It can hardly wait for the underdeveloped nations to get a car in every garage.

In the days of the kerosene lamp, the oil companies competed with each other and against gaslight by trying to improve the illuminating characteristics of kerosene. Then suddenly the impossible happened. Edison invented a light which was totally nondependent on crude oil. Had it not been for the growing use of kerosene in space heaters, the incandescent lamp would have completely finished oil as a growth industry at that time. Oil would have been good for little else than axle grease.

Then disaster and reprieve struck again. Two great innovations occurred, neither originating in the oil industry. The successful development of coal-burning domestic central-heating systems made the space heater obsolescent. While the industry reeled, along came its most magnificent boost yet—the internal combustion engine, also invented by outsiders. Then when the prodigious expansion for gasoline finally began to level off in the 1920s, along came the miraculous escape of a central oil heater. Once again the escape was provided by an outsider's invention and development. And when that market weakened, wartime demand for aviation fuel came to the rescue. After the war the expansion of civilian aviation, the dieselization of railroads, and the explosive demand for cars and trucks kept the industry's growth in high gear.

Meanwhile centralized oil heating—whose boom potential had only recently been proclaimed—ran into severe competition from natural gas. While the oil companies themselves owned the gas that now competed with their oil, the industry did not originate the natural gas revolution, nor has it to this day greatly profited from its gas ownership. The gas revolution was made by newly formed transmission companies that marketed the product with an aggressive ardor. They started a magnificent new industry, first against the advice and then against the resistance of the oil companies.

By all the logic of the situation, the oil companies themselves should have made the gas revolution. They not only owned the gas; they also were the only people experienced in handling, scrubbing, and using it, the only people experienced in pipeline technology and transmission, and they understood heating problems. But, partly because they knew that natural gas would compete with their own sale of heating oil, the oil companies pooh-poohed the potentials of gas.

The revolution was finally started by oil pipeline executives who, unable to persuade their own companies to go into gas, quit and organized the spectacularly successful gas transmission companies. Even after their success became painfully evident to the oil companies, the latter did not go into gas transmission. The multibillion-dollar business which should have been theirs went to others. As in the past, the industry was blinded by its narrow preoccupation with a specific product and the value of its reserves. It paid little or no attention to its customers' basic needs and preferences.

* * * * *

Uncertain future

Management cannot find much consolation today in the rapidly expanding petrochemical industry, another oil-using idea that did not originate in the leading firms. The total United States production of petrochemicals is equivalent to about 2 percent (by volume) of the demand for all petroleum products. Although the petrochemical industry is now expected to grow by about 10 percent per year, this will not offset other drains on the growth of crude oil consumption. Furthermore, while petrochemical products are many and growing, it is well to remember that there are nonpetroleum sources of the basic raw material, such as coal. Besides, a lot of plastics can be produced with relatively little oil. A 50,000-barrel-per-day oil refinery is now considered the absolute minimum size for efficiency. But a 5,000-barrel-per day chemical plant is a giant operation.

Oil has never been a continuously strong growth industry. It has grown by fits and starts, always miraculously saved by innovations and developments not of its own making. The reason it has not grown in a smooth progression is that each time it thought it had a superior product safe from the possibility of competitive substitutes, the product turned out to be inferior and notoriously subject to obsolescence. Until now, gasoline (for motor fuel, anyhow) has escaped this fate. But, as we shall see later, it too may be on its last legs.

The point of all this is that there is no guarantee against product obsolescence. If a company's own research does not make it obsolete, another's will. Unless an industry is especially lucky, as oil has been until now, it can easily go down in a sea of red figures—just as the railroads have, as the buggy whip manufacturers have, as the corner grocery chains have, as most of the big movie companies have, and indeed as many other industries have.

The best way for a firm to be lucky is to make its own luck. That requires knowing what makes a business successful. One of the greatest enemies of this knowledge is mass production.

PRODUCTION PRESSURES

Mass-production industries are impelled by a great drive to produce all they can. The prospect of steeply declining unit costs as output rises is more than most companies can usually resist. The profit possibilities look spectacular. All effort focuses on production. The result is that marketing gets neglected.

John Kenneth Galbraith contends that just the opposite occurs.[4] Output is so prodigious that all effort concentrates on trying to get rid of it. He says this accounts for singing commercials, desecration of the countryside with advertising signs, and other wasteful and vulgar practices. Galbraith has a finger on something real, but he misses the strategic point. Mass production does indeed generate great pressure to "move" the product. But what usually gets emphasized is selling, not marketing. Marketing, being a more sophisticated and complex process, gets ignored.

The difference between marketing and selling is more than semantic. Selling focuses on the needs of the seller, marketing on the needs of the buyer. Selling is preoccupied with the seller's need to convert his product into cash; marketing with the idea of satisfying the needs of the customer by means of the product and the whole cluster of things associated with creating, delivering, and finally consuming it.

In some industries the enticements of full mass production have been so powerful that for many years top management in effect has told the sales departments, "You get rid of it; we'll worry about profits." By contrast, a truly marketing-minded firm tries to create value-satisfying goods and services that consumers will want to buy. What it offers for sale includes not only the generic product or service, but also how it is made available to the customer, in what form, when, under what conditions, and at what terms of trade. Most important, what it offers for sale is determined not by the seller but by the

---

[4] *The Affluent Society* (Boston: Houghton Mifflin Company, 1958), pp. 152–60.

buyer. The seller takes his cues from the buyer in such a way that the product becomes a consequence of the marketing effort, not vice versa.

Lag in Detroit

This may sound like an elementary rule of business, but that does not keep it from being violated wholesale. It is certainly more violated than honored. Take the automobile industry:

Here mass production is most famous, most honored, and has the greatest impact on the entire society. The industry has hitched its fortune to the relentless requirements of the annual model change, a policy that makes customer orientation an especially urgent necessity. Consequently the auto companies annually spend millions of dollars on consumer reasearch. But the fact that the new compact cars are selling so well in their first year indicates that Detroit's vast researches have for a long time failed to reveal what the customer really wanted. Detroit was not persuaded that he wanted anything different from what he had been getting until it lost millions of customers to other small car manufacturers.

How could this unbelievable lag behind consumer wants have been perpetuated so long? Why did not research reveal consumer preferences before consumers' buying decisions themselves revealed the facts? Is that not what consumer research is for—to find out before the fact what is going to happen? The answer is that Detroit never really researched the customer's wants. It only researched his preferences between the kinds of things which it had already decided to offer him. For Detroit is mainly product-oriented, not customer-oriented. To the extent that the customer is recognized as having needs that the manufacturer should try to satisfy, Detroit usually acts as if the job can be done entirely by product changes. Occasionally attention gets paid to financing, too, but that is done more in order to sell than to enable the customer to buy.

As for taking care of other customer needs, there is not enough being done to write about. The areas of the greatest unsatisfied needs are ignored, or at best get stepchild attention. These are at the point of sale and on the matter of automotive repair and maintenance. Detroit views these problem areas as being of secondary importance. That is underscored by the fact that the retailing and servicing ends of this industry are neither owned and operated nor controlled by the manufacturers. Once the car is produced, things are pretty much in the dealer's inadequate hands. Illustrative of Detroit's arm's-length attitude is the fact that, while servicing holds enormous sales-stimulating, profit-building opportunities, only 57 of Chevrolet's 7,000 dealers provide night maintenance service.

Motorists repeatedly express their dissatisfaction with servicing and their apprehensions about buying cars under the present selling setup. The anxieties and problems they encounter during the auto buying and maintenance processes are probably more intense and widespread today than 30 years ago. Yet the automobile companies do not *seem* to listen to or take their cues from the anguished consumer. If they do listen, it must be through the filter of their own preoccupation with production. The marketing effort is still viewed as a necessary consequence of the product, not vice versa, as it should be. That is the legacy of mass production, with its parochial view that profit resides essentially in low-cost full production.

* * * * *

Product provincialism

The tantalizing profit possibilities of low unit production costs may be the most seriously self-deceiving attitude that can afflict a company, particularly a "growth" company where an apparently assured expansion of demand already tends to undermine a proper concern for the importance of marketing and the customer.

The usual result of this narrow preoccupation with so-called concrete matters is that instead of growing, the industry declines. It usually means that the product fails to adapt to the constantly changing patterns of consumer needs and tastes, to new and modified marketing institutions and practices, or to product developments in competing or complementary industries. The industry has its eyes so firmly on its own specific product that it does not see how it is being made obsolete.

The classical example of this is the buggy whip industry. No amount of product improvement could stave off its death sentence. But had the industry defined itself as being in the transportation business rather than the buggy whip business, it might have survived. It would have done what survival always entails, that is, changing. Even if it had only defined its business as providing a stimulant or catalyst to an energy source, it might have survived by becoming a manufacturer of, say, fanbelts or air cleaners.

What may some day be a still more classical example is, again, the oil industry. Having let others steal marvelous opportunities from it (e.g., natural gas, as already mentioned, missile fuels, and jet engine lubricants), one would expect it to have taken steps never to let that happen again. But this is not the case. We are now getting extraordinary new developments in fuel systems specifically designed to power automobiles. Not only are these developments concentrated in firms outside the petroleum industry, but petroleum is almost systematically ignoring them, securely content in its wedded bliss to oil. It is the story of the kerosene lamp versus the incandescent lamp all over again. Oil is trying to improve hydrocarbon fuels rather than to develop *any* fuels best suited to the needs of their users, whether or not made in different ways and with different raw materials from oil.

* * * * *

Management might be more likely to do what is needed for its own preservation if it thought of itself as being in the energy business. But even that would not be enough if it persists in imprisoning itself in the narrow grip of its tight product orientation. It has to think of itself as taking care of customer needs, not finding, refining, or even selling oil. Once it genuinely thinks of its business as taking care of people's transportation needs, nothing can stop it from creating its own extravagantly profitable growth.

* * * * *

DANGERS OF R&D

Another big danger to a firm's continued growth arises when top management is wholly transfixed by the profit possibilities of technical research and development. To illustrate I shall turn first to a new industry—electronics—and then return once more to the oil companies. By comparing a fresh example with a familiar one, I hope to emphasize the prevalence and insidiousness of a hazardous way of thinking.

Marketing shortchanged

In the case of electronics, the greatest danger which faces the glamorous new companies in this field is not that they do not pay enough attention to research and development, but that they pay *too much* attention to it. And the fact that the fastest growing electronics firms owe their eminence to their heavy emphasis on technical research is completely beside the point. They have vaulted to affluence on a sudden crest of unusually strong general receptiveness to new technical ideas. Also, their success has been shaped in the virtually guaranteed market of military subsidies and by military orders that in many cases actually preceded the existence of facilities to make the products. Their expansion has, in other words, been almost totally devoid of marketing effort.

Thus, they are growing up under conditions that come dangerously close to creating the illusion that a superior product will sell itself. Having created a successful company by making a superior product, it is not surprising that management continues to be oriented toward the product rather than the people who consume it. It develops the philosophy that continued growth is a matter of continued product innovation and improvement.

A number of other factors tend to strengthen and sustain this belief:

1. Because electronic products are highly complex and sophisticated, managements become top-heavy with engineers and scientists. This creates a selective bias in favor of research and production at the expense of marketing. The organization tends to view itself as making things rather than satisfying customer needs. Marketing gets treated as a residual activity, "something else" that must be done once the vital job of product creation and production is completed.

2. To this bias in favor of product research, development, and production is added the bias in favor of dealing with controllable variables. Engineers

and scientists are at home in the world of concrete things like machines, test tubes, production lines, and even balance sheets. The abstractions to which they feel kindly are those which are testable or manipulatable in the laboratory, or, if not testable, then functional, such as Euclid's axioms. In short, the managements of the new glamour-growth companies tend to favor those business activities which lend themselves to careful study, experimentation, and control—the hard, practical, realities of the lab, the shop, the books.

What gets shortchanged are the realities of the *market*. Consumers are unpredictable, varied, fickle, stupid, shortsighted, stubborn, and generally bothersome. This is not what the engineer-managers say, but deep down in their consciousness it is what they believe. And this accounts for their concentrating on what they know and what they can control, namely, product research, engineering, and production. The emphasis on production becomes particularly attractive when the product can be made at declining unit costs. There is no more inviting way of making money than by running the plant full blast.

Today the top-heavy science-engineering-production orientation of so many electronics companies works reasonably well because they are pushing into new frontiers in which the armed services have pioneered virtually assured markets. The companies are in the felicitous position of having to fill, not find markets; of not having to discover what the customer needs and wants, but of having the customer voluntarily come forward with specific new product demands. If a team of consultants had been assigned specifically to design a business situation calculated to prevent the emergence and development of a customer-oriented marketing viewpoint, it could not have produced anything better than the conditions just described.

*   *   *   *   *

Beginning and end

The view that an industry is a customer-satisfying process, not a goods-producing process, is vital for all businessmen to understand. An industry begins with the customer and his needs, not with a patent, a raw material, or a selling skill. Given the customer's needs, the industry develops backwards, first concerning itself with the physical *delivery* of customer satisfactions. Then it moves back further to *creating* the things by which these satisfactions are in part achieved. How these materials are created is a matter of indifference to the customer, hence the particular form of manufacturing, processing, or what-have-you cannot be considered as a vital aspect of the industry. Finally, the industry moves back still further to *finding* the raw materials necessary for making its products.

The irony of some industries oriented toward technical research and development is that the scientists who occupy the high executive positions are totally unscientific when it comes to defining their companies' overall needs and purposes. They violate the first two rules of the scientific method—being aware of and defining their companies' problems, and then developing testable hypotheses about solving them. They are scientific only about the convenient things, such as laboratory and product experiments. The reason that the customer (and the satisfaction of his deepest needs) is not considered as being "the problem" is not because there is any certain belief that no such problem exists, but because an organizational lifetime has conditioned management to look in the opposite direction. Marketing is a stepchild.

I do not mean that selling is ignored. Far from it. But selling, again, is not marketing. As already pointed out, selling concerns itself with the tricks and techniques of getting people to exchange their cash for your product. It is not concerned with the values that the exchange is all about. And it does not, as marketing invariably does, view the entire business process as consisting of a tightly integrated effort to discover, create, arouse, and satisfy customer needs. The customer is somebody "out there" who, with proper cunning, can be separated from his loose change.

Actually, not even selling gets much attention in some technologically minded firms. Because there is a virtually guaranteed market for the abundant flow of their new products, they do not actually know what a real market is. It is as if they lived in a planned economy, moving their products routinely from factory to retail outlet. Their successful concentration on products tends to convince them of the soundness of what they have been doing, and they fail to see the gathering clouds over the market.

CONCLUSION

Less than 75 years ago American railroads enjoyed a fierce loyalty among astute Wall Streeters. European monarchs invested in them heavily. Eternal wealth was thought to be the benediction for anybody who could scrape a few thousand dollars together to put into rail stocks. No other form of transportation could compete with the railroads in speed, flexibility, durability, economy, and growth potentials. As Jacques Barzun put it, "By the turn of the century it was an institution, an image of man, a tradition, a code of honor, a source of poetry, a nursery of boyhood desires, a sublimest of toys, and the most solemn machine—next to the funeral hearse—that marks the epochs in man's life."[5]

Even after the advent of automobiles, trucks, and airplanes, the railroad tycoons remained imperturbably self-confident. If you had told them 60 years ago that in 30 years they would be flat on their backs, broke, and pleading for government subsidies, they would have thought you totally demented. Such a future was simply not considered possible. It was not even a discussable subject, or an askable question, or a matter which any sane person would consider worth speculating about. The very thought was insane. Yet a lot of

---

[5] Barzun, "Trains and Mind of Man," p. 20.

insane notions now have matter-of-fact acceptance—for example, the idea of
100-ton tubes of metal moving smoothly through the air 20,000 feet above
the earth, loaded with 100 sane and solid citizens casually drinking
martinis—and they have dealt cruel blows to the railroads.

What specifically must other companies do to avoid this fate? What does
customer orientation involve? These questions have in part been answered
by the preceding examples and analysis. It would take another article to show
in detail what is required for specific industries. In any case, it should be
obvious that building an effective customer-oriented company involves
more than good intentions or promotional tricks; it involves profound
matters of human organization and leadership. For the present, let me merely
suggest what appear to be some general requirements.

Visceral feel of greatness

Obviously the company has to do what survival demands. It has to adapt
to the requirements of the market, and it has to do it sooner rather than later.
But mere survival is a so-so aspiration. Anybody can survive in some way or
other, even the skid-row bum. The trick is to survive gallantly, to feel the
surging impulse of commercial mastery; not just to experience the sweet smell
of success, but to have the visceral feel of entrepreneurial greatness.

No organization can achieve greatness without a vigorous leader who is
driven onward by his own pulsating *will to succeed*. He has to have a vision of
grandeur, a vision that can produce eager followers in vast numbers. In
business, the followers are the customers. To produce these customers, the
entire corporation must be viewed as a customer-creating and customer-
satisfying organism. Management must think of itself not as producing products but as providing customer-creating value satisfactions. It must push this
idea (and everything it means and requires) into every nook and cranny of
the organization. It has to do this continuously and with the kind of flair that
excites and stimulates the people in it. Otherwise, the company will be merely
a series of pigeonholed parts, with no consolidating sense of purpose or
direction.

In short, the organization must learn to think of itself not as producing
goods or services but as *buying customers*, as doing the things that will make
people *want* to do business with it. And the chief executive himself has the
inescapable responsibility for creating this environment, this viewpoint, this
attitude, this aspiration. He himself must set the company's style, its direction,
and its goals. This means he has to know precisely where he himself wants to
go, and to make sure the whole organization is enthusiastically aware of
where that is. This is a first requisite of leadership, for *unless he knows where
he is going, any road will take him there.*

If any road is okay, the chief executive might as well pack his attaché case
and go fishing. If an organization does not know or care where it is going, it

does not need to advertise that fact with a ceremonial figurehead. Everybody will notice it soon enough.

QUESTIONS

1. What, exactly, does Levitt feel business leaders are myopic about? How could you avoid falling into this "trap"?
2. What does Levitt mean about having a "visceral feel of greatness"? Who should have this feel? What relevance would it have for someone just looking for a permanent job?
3. In the examples cited by Levitt, which industries failed because of social change and which failed because of technological improvements? Cite two more examples of firms that failed because of one or the other of these types of changes. Explain.
4. Select a current social, economic, or technological change such as declining birth rates, rising energy costs, or computer-controlled machinery. What industries are apt to suffer because of this change? Are there industries that will benefit from, or perhaps be created by, this change?
*5. Would Levitt consider Kotler and Levy (Reading 3) "myopic"? That is, have they lost sight of what marketing is about? Explain.

---

* Question relates concepts in this and other readings.

5
Competition for differential advantage

Wroe Alderson

Target marketers seek a differential advantage over their competitors as they attempt to satisfy their objectives. Alderson helped popularize this term among marketing people, showing that it had relevance not only for business planning but also for public policy. This article describes the theoretical basis for the behavior of businesses as they attempt to survive and prosper.

THE ECONOMICS OF DIFFERENTIAL ADVANTAGE

The functionalist or ecological approach to competition begins with the assumption that every firm must seek and find a function in order to maintain itself in the market place. Every business firm occupies a position which is in some respects unique. Its location, the products it sells, its operating methods, or the customers it serves tend to set it off in some degree from every other firm. Each firm competes by making the most of its individuality and its special character. It is constantly seeking to establish some competitive advantage. Absolute advantage in the sense of an advanced method of operation is not enough if all competitors live up to the same high standards. What is important in competition is differential advantage, which can give a firm an edge over what others in the field are offering.

Differential advantage and dynamic competition

It is the unending search for differential advantage which keeps competition dynamic. A firm which has been bested by competitors according to certain dimensions of value in products or services always has before it the possibility of turning the tables by developing something new in other directions. The company which has the lead is vulnerable to attack at numerous points. Therein is a strong incentive for technical innovation and other forms of economic progress, both for the leader who is trying to stay out in front and for others who are trying to seize the initiative.

Departures from previous product designs or patterns of practice will not

---

Source: Reprinted (with deletions) with permission of the publisher from Wroe Alderson, *Marketing Behavior and Executive Action* (Homewood, Ill.: Richard D. Irwin, Inc., 1957), pp. 101–9. At the time of writing, Wroe Alderson was a professor of marketing at the Wharton School of the University of Pennsylvania and a consultant to many corporations.

be successful unless they appeal to needs or attitudes of the buyer. Differentiation by the seller is an adaptation to differences in taste and requirements among consumers. Demand is radically heterogeneous or diversified and quite independent of the actions of the seller. Supply also breaks down into heterogeneous segments according to differences in location, raw materials, plant equipment, and the skills of management and labor. The process of exchange in the market place is directed toward matching up segments of supply and demand to provide the best fit.

This conception of an economics of differential advantage has important consequences for the analysis of monopoly and competition and for the choice of criteria to determine the degree of competitiveness in a given industry. New firms enter a field because of an expectation of enjoying differential advantage. Their chance for survival depends on whether their expectations were realistic in the first place and whether the original advantage is maintained or wrested from them by others. The profit incentive provides the drive for vigorous competition, but this drive is directed toward differential advantage because of the fundamentally heterogenous character of markets. The enterpriser accepts the risks of innovation in his search for differential advantage. Success may be rewarded by profits until other enterprises overtake him. Later sections will develop further implications of this view for both market structure and market behavior.

The term "differential advantage" is currently being used by J. M. Clark, who developed the concept of workable competition. It is adopted here as the term which best characterizes the dynamics of competitive advantage. Much of the underlying analysis was developed by E. H. Chamberlin, who inaugurated a new era in the theory of the firm something over twenty years ago.

Differential advantage and monopolistic competition

In his formulation of the theory of monopolistic competition, Chamberlin was applying to a wider field and developing with a greater elegance methods of analysis which, in their essentials, are already to be found in earlier economists such as Walras and Marshall. The roots of the economics of differential advantage go back still further, to the treatment of the division of labor and regional specialization by Adam Smith and Ricardo. J. M. Clark makes a fresh start by dealing directly with the struggle for differential advantage as the essence of competition. Chamberlin reaches a similar position in his later discussions of monopolistic competition by beginning with the traditional concepts of monopoly and pure competition and showing how they are usually blended in concrete situations.

Not a few economists join with Chamberlin in the advancement of a theory blending monopoly and competition. Arthur R. Burns in 1936 wrote: "The elements of monopoly . . . can no longer be regarded as occasional and relatively unimportant aberrations from competition. They are such an organic part of the industrial system that it is useless to hope they can be removed by law." W. A. Joehr points out that bilateral monopolies and oligopolies form a part of the competitive system. "Thus even if the existing structure of the present market economy could be called a 'world of monopolies,' its system of coordination could nevertheless be termed a competitive mechanism." It is the opinion of another contemporary, Kurt Rothschild, that the more realistic models of competition advanced by Chamberlin and Joan Robinson seemed to destroy the last nimbus which the idea of competition had managed to save through all the years of skepticism and criticism, by showing that so many adverse features were not occasional blemishes but were part and parcel of the way competition works in our world.

Such terms as "pure competition" and "pure monopoly" have little relevance except for tracing the transition from an atomistic model to what is essentially an ecological view of the competition among business firms. If Chamberlin had been the first major student of the subject, he might have moved more directly toward the creation of an appropriate theory. That would have meant starting with a recognition that markets are radically heterogeneous on both the supply side and the demand side. Under this approach, pure competition is nothing more than a limiting case in which there is a tendency to approach homogeneity. It is only an analytical reference point; and the true norm is effective competition, or that state of affairs which will facilitate the flow of goods in heterogeneous markets.

The fact that Chamberlin started from the traditional view led him to apply the slightly invidious term of "monopolistic competition" to what he recognized as the normal situation.

Preoccupied as they were with the problem of resource allocation, economists of the classical school devised an ingenious framework for the solution of the allocative problem. In the classical system, market structures were classified under either of two mutually exclusive categories, pure monopoly or perfect competition. In capsule form, a perfectly competitive market situation is one in which large numbers of atomistic buyers and sellers exchange an identical product. Since by assumption the quantities purchased or offered by any one buyer or seller do not represent a significant portion of the total amount being exchanged, no individual has an appreciable influence on the selling price. And since in any market the product is homogeneous, buyers are indifferent as to the source of their supply. It is assumed, moreover, that all productive resources are completely mobile and will move promptly to industrial sectors where money rewards are highest. Finally, in a perfectly competitive market all buyers and sellers and productive services are fully informed of available alternatives.

The functionalist approach

Within these assumptions (and taking the distribution of income as given), the allocation of resources will be "ideal." Consumer want-satisfaction will be maximized. All productive services will be compensated according to their contribution to the national income. Business firms will be compelled to produce at lowest costs per unit of output in the short run and to adopt the most efficient size of plant in the long run. Should an innovation create economic rents (excess profits), additional resources will flow into the industry until the rents are dissipated. In brief, under static conditions, changes in demand or costs will set in motion adjustments which will bring about a new position of equilibrium.

BUSINESS EXPECTATIONS IN HETEROGENEOUS MARKETS

Chamberlin formulated the principle that the market for every competitor is in some degree unique, thus initiating a drastic revision in competitive theory. This "market uniqueness" he believed to be due mainly to the phenomenon known as "product differentiation," a concept involving both monopoly and competition. Grether and his associates, pursuing this lead from a marketing viewpoint, have suggested the equally helpful concept of enterprise differentiation which is implicit in the present treatment. Chamberlin writes that ". . . a general class of product is differentiated if any significant basis exists for distinguishing the goods (or services) of one seller from those of another." The basis may be real or fancied, so long as it is of any importance to buyers and leads to a preference for one variety of the product over another. The market for each seller is unique, for ". . . where such differentiation exists, even though it be slight, buyers will be paired with sellers, not by chance and at random as under pure competition, but according to their preferences."

Product differentiation

Product differentiation takes various forms. It may be based upon certain characteristics of the product itself: patented features; trademarks; trade names; peculiarities of the package or container; singularity in quality, design, color, or style. Product differentiation may also exist with respect to the conditions surrounding its sale. Examples of this are convenience of the seller's location, reputation and good will of the seller, services provided by the seller, and various other links which attach the customers to the seller. Product differentiation, broadly interpreted, represents a control over supply in the sense that only one seller offers a product of that exact name and identity. The seller offering a product different from others actually does occupy a monopoly position in that limited sense. A seller in a particular location is a monopolist in more ways than merely the obvious sense that two physical bodies cannot occupy the same space, for his geographical location ties certain customers to him. This is often called "spatial monopoly." The customer's approach and attitude are essential, for it is noteworthy that buyers take the product differences into account when purchasing.

Behind the acceptance of differentiation are differences in tastes, desires, incomes, locations of buyers, and the uses for the commodities. It may safely be generalized that such differences among buyers have always existed, and it follows that products have differed. Of course, the merchandising tools of advertising and promotion, plus technological advances, have emphasized and widened the scope of product differentiation. This differentiation, which is a reality in the economy, leads Chamberlin and others to point out the necessity of substituting for the concept of a "competitive ideal" an ideal involving both monopoly and competition. In the economist's role, and in the immediate situation of public policy, it would be advantageous to measure and evaluate activities in the economy against an ideal which represents something more readily approaching reality. Pure monopoly, on the one hand, is impossible because of substitutability. Pure competition is not possible because of the presence of heterogeneous products and markets.

Differentiation and monopoly

With heterogeneous products each seller has a "complete monopoly" of his own product. This type of monopolist, however, is not free from outside competition but only partially insulated from it. The monopolist's demand curve is vitally affected by competing substitutes. Control over total supply of all related products is impossible. Recognition and acceptance of Chamberlin's concept that the real world evidences a complex of monopoly and competition, based on product diversity—a natural consequence of the system of demands—leads to several useful analytical concepts. These include market segmentation, local oligopoly, and multilevel competition.

The economics of differential advantage, building on the foundations laid by Chamberlin, holds that no one enters business except in the expectation of some degree of differential advantage in serving his customers, and that competition consists of the constant struggle to develop, maintain, or increase such advantages. In large part, these efforts in any industry or area, of course, offset each other and cancel out; and to the extent that they do, a kind of "equilibrium" results, consisting of the offsetting of various differential advantages. It is possible under certain restricted assumptions to define with precision an equilibrium situation where a general and complete "balance" of such efforts would be achieved. But in real life, conditions are constantly changing, so that at any particular time some firms will be gaining and others falling back. Any concept of competition which does not include its dynamic aspects would have little relevance to reality.

This summary of the economics of differential advantage suggests several aspects of the theory which require further explanation. It is necessary to examine the following areas: (1) bases on which a differential advantage may be obtained; (2) risk and uncertainty involved in the expectation and exploitation of a differential advantage; (3) entry and exit of firms; (4) industry structure, "balance," and equilibrium; and (5) problem solving by firms and by public administration.

Differential advantage and the "product"

From the broad definition of "product" it is possible to determine these general bases for differential advantage. Differential advantage today rests on technological as well as on legal or geographical grounds. The legal and geographical grounds account for differential advantages due to trademarks, patents, and to location (spatial monopoly). The technological basis for obtaining a differential advantage receives increased emphasis in the American economy, in which there has been a shift in relative importance away from geographical advantage to technological advantage. The various aspects of technological advantage are in general related to use requirements, production processes, and marketing methods. An advantage may be obtained by styling a product to meet a particular consumer taste or desire, such as the production of golf clubs for left-handed players. Advantages based on production processes may be exploited by use of unique assembly-line methods, new equipment, or application of results from a time and motion study. Marketing methods offer an ever-widening basis for exploiting an advantage. A differential advantage may be obtained by a new and different distribution system, or by a revised warehousing or inventory control system.

In this kind of competitive process the innovator may enjoy monopolistic profits for a time. When he introduces his new product or his new method of production or marketing, he is a monopolist at least in the formal sense that he is the only seller of the product or process.

Business expectation as to differential advantage is subject to uncertainty. In attempting to exploit any anticipated advantage, the firm risks resources and effort on the possibility that its expectations may be justified. Even if successful, the duration of an advantage is highly uncertain with the present pace of technological change. The chances are good that some other firm will soon find a way of competing away any excess profits by introducing another innovation along the same or some other dimension of differential advantage. It is not necessary for dozens of firms just like the innovating firm to enter the field in order to deprive it of excess profits. There are several dimensions of differential advantage, actual or potential, in any field. All are vulnerable to immediate attack with the exception of those backed up by the power of the state—as, for example, patents. Geographic advantage may, it is true, place an effective barrier around a trade territory for some commodities. But over a period of time it is constantly shifting and being transformed through improved transportation and communication, through technological developments, and through changes in the distribution of natural resources and of markets. In brief, the existence of opportunity creates an almost irresistible attraction to profit-seeking resources.

Differential advantage and competition

Competition among problem solvers is inherently dynamic. If seller is at a competitive disadvantage under present conditions, he is likely to direct much of his organization's skill and resources to redressing the balance. He is in no way compelled to play the competitive game as it stands but is constantly exploring new dimensions of advantage. Sellers' competition is not merely a matter of tactics as in the case of two military forces in fixed positions gradually wearing each other down. Competition is a war of movement in which each of the participants is searching for strategies which will improve his relative position.

Further insights into the concept of differential advantage have been provided in a recent essay by Professor J. M. Clark. Clark points out that active competition consists of a combination of (1) initiatory actions by a business unit and (2) a complex of responses by those with whom it deals and by its rivals. The more aggressive firm will give the buyers more inducement (lower prices, better quality, a differentiated product to suit the buyers' tastes, greater selling efforts). The resulting advantage to the initiator consists of increased sales, wholly or partly at the expense of rivals. A rival's response seeks to neutralize or offset the initiator's advantage by offering the buyers something more effective, establishing a positive sales-increasing advantage for himself. In poker-playing terms, he may "see" the initial move or "raise" it.

Differentiation and the neutralizing process

Inasmuch as the initiator's and rival's inducements are confined to price, the neutralizing process—the meeting of price reductions—is conceived as being complete and instantaneous. But with respect to quality (or other variables of "product"), formal theory had previously emphasized the initiating action (establishing of a quality differential) and minimized the neutralizing process, treating the initiating process as establishing a limited monopoly. The outcome of initiating and responding actions hinges on the relative speeds, or expected speeds, of the initiator's gain and of the neutralizing process whereby rivals destroy or offset his differential advantage, the initiator's actions becoming standard practice.

The initiation and neutralization generally take a substantial time in the case of new productive methods or products (technological advantage along the dimension of consumer uses, production processes). Incentive to innovate or differentiate would vanish if the initiator expected neutralization to be complete before he had recovered the costs of innovation. Thus the elements of risk and uncertainty enter. Fortunately, the pessimistic viewpoint of immediate neutralization is not common. Most innovators expect some enduring residue of advantage. If neutralization were permanently blocked with no further exploitation of a differential advantage possible or permitted, the initiator would have a limited monopoly, in the sense of a permanent differential advantage. To the extent that patent rights, secret processes, or strictly locational advantages exist, such a condition may be approximated.

Instantaneous neutralization occurs only in the case of price reductions on homogeneous or very closely competitive products, with few sellers. But even here, the initiator can shade list prices, vary his discount policies, make forward contracts, or benefit from other market "imperfections," so that competitive action seldom stalls completely unless marketing processes are strongly standardized. As the opportunity to differentiate marketing practices is widely available and attractive, even this qualification nearly disappears.

Clark maintains that the desirable case "lies somewhere between too prompt and too slow neutralization." He does not call this an "optimum" for the reason that the term suggests a precision that no actual system could obtain. "Neutralization needs to take time enough to leave the innovator incentive that is adequate, but not more, and then diffuse the gains as promptly as is consistent with there being ample gains to diffuse." Such neutralization in our terms is the offsetting or destroying of rivals' differential advantages. It may take away the sales gains the innovator has made, or it may merely stop further gains. It may stop further gains quickly and encroach more gradually on gains already made, so that a residue of these gains may last a fairly long time. "If such a residue is expected, it is the innovator's chief incentive, since small but long-lasting gains outweigh large temporary ones."

QUESTIONS

1. What does the phrase "competition for differential advantage" mean?
2. Alderson talks about "heterogeneous markets." What does he mean, and how are they relevant to public policy?
3. What alternative methods does Alderson suggest are possible to differentiate a market offering?
4. Is seeking differential advantage desirable from a macro view? Explain.
*5. Are Alderson's ideas relevant in the broader context discussed by Kotler and Levy (Reading 3)?

---

* Question relates concepts in this and other readings.

6
Market segmentation as a competitive strategy

Nelson N. Foote

In this article, Foote explains how the concept of developing a differential advantage can be implemented. Although the article was written in 1969, its still timely discussion shows the advantage of target marketing and, in particular, of market segmentation. Foote also illustrates that an innovative strategy will probably be more successful than imitating competitors.

Let us assume we have made the discovery that consumers of ice cream differ significantly in their preferences for chocolate, strawberry, and vanilla. And let us assume that these flavor preferences are not distributed randomly among all kinds of people, but are differentially associated with some other characteristic of customers for ice cream, such as hair color, and that these associations are substantial in degree and practical to ascertain. For example, let us say that brunettes tend strongly to like chocolate, redheads to favor strawberry, and blondes, vanilla. Finally, let us imagine that this pattern is just that simple and orderly—product differences nicely match customer differences.

Then what?

What is the businessman who wants to sell ice cream in this market to do about our findings? Is he to conclude that he should offer all three flavors, the same as the rest of the industry, lest he forgo any important sources of sales? Or should he try to serve only blondes and brunettes, since there are not enough redheads to make serving them profitable? Or should he seek to establish a reputation as the producer of the finest Dutch chocolate ice cream, so that he captures nearly all that segment of the market? Or should he go after the great mass of vanilla fans, by upgrading this lowly flavor with a French accent? Or should he take account of his newness or smallness in the industry and challenge the incumbent giants of the trade by introducing pistachio or frozen custard? Or should he offer the normal product line of his industry, but allow some major chain of retail outlets to apply its store brand to his product? Should he go after the door-to-door trade with a very short line—like Neapolitan only—or open his own chain of soda fountains with 28

Source: Reprinted (with deletions) by permission of the Rand McNally College Publishing Company from Leo Bogart, ed., *Current Controversies in Marketing Research* (Chicago: Markham Publishing Co., 1969), pp. 129–39. At the time of writing, Nelson Foote was with the General Electric Company.

flavors? Or should he be creative and try to think up some utterly new way to exploit his knowledge of differing customer preferences, since all these strategies—and more besides—are already in use today in the ice cream business?

Plainly, even if one knew far more than is known already about patterns of correlation between product and customer differences in any particular market, it takes a lot of thinking and doing before this knowledge can be turned into a calculated competitive strategy. Meanwhile we find examples of marketing managers who have very successfully employed a strategy of market segmentation, quite without the resources of detailed information that as professional marketers we like to think are indispensable to decision-making in matters of such complexity and risk.

It seems important throughout discussion of market segmentation to recognize that the main source of interest in the concept is its potential value as a competitive strategy. There may be quite a number of people whose interest is in promoting the sale or purchase of data regarding the "stratigraphics" of consumer choice. But unless these data can be put to practical use in improving or defending the market position or profits of their user, only the data seller will benefit, and he not for long. So my self-chosen assignment here is to bear down on the task of thinking out the use of such data in actual marketing management. Although I make my living as a marketing researcher, I think that we need more thinking on this matter as much as we need more research.

Immediately, however, the question arises of who is going to discuss competitive strategy in public—especially in the presence of competitors of his own firm—save in empty generalities. A salesman of research data, or representatives of advertising agencies or media, might set forth some hypothetical tactics of market segmentation as a means of soliciting business. But other than personal vanity or the desire to solicit another job, what would induce someone connected with a manufacturer or a retailer to disclose his thinking about competitive strategy? The incentives of professional exchange of technique or the teaching of younger members of the fraternity are not sufficient justification. Many kinds of professional know-how are properly kept proprietary by the firm which paid for their development. If market segmentation is to be analyzed publicly and candidly from the standpoint of an actual competitor in a market, it has to be justified by some benefit that it will bring to this competitor. If it were not my conviction that in fact it is to the benefit of every competing firm that market segmentation be discussed publicly in terms of its implications for competitive strategy, you would not be listening to these words at this moment.

Moreover, we can go one step further and declare that market segmentation as a competitive strategy is also in the interests of customers. If it were not—if it did not offer customers a firmer base for choice among competing offerings and a wider array of genuine choices—it would not work as a competitive strategy. Like any deal, market segmentation is good business only when both parties to the transaction benefit. Market segmentation is thus in effect a logical extension of the basic principles of marketing.

The process of market segmentation, however, when approached as a task of formulating and executing a marketing strategy, involves matching not merely customer characteristics and product characteristics, but a tripartite matching of customers and offerings *and* the array of competitors in the market, as seen from the standpoint of any one competitor within this constellation. If we think of offerings by competitors as expressions of their differing *capabilities,* it will not only be easy to remember the three Cs—*customers, competitors,* and *capabilities*—but the full task of developing a strategy is more clearly pushed into view.

Let me illustrate concretely by referring to one of our most respected competitors in the Chicago area, the Zenith Radio Corporation.* Zenith won a preeminent position in the television receiver market some ten years ago by becoming established in the minds of consumers as the leading exemplar of product reliability. Its policy of manufacturing products of good workmanship goes back many years, but during the middle fifties many consumers became quite concerned to identify the set that would, they hoped, give them the least trouble from breakdown. That was when Zenith's market share soared, until it surpassed the erstwhile industry leader. Servicemen and the radio–TV specialty stores with which they are associated lent vigorous aid. Zenith's management and its advertising agency pressed the opportunity that had widened for them. But Zenith had not adopted product reliability as a self-consciously opportunistic, short-term tactic. As far as known, Zenith's strategy was not derived through marketing research, although marketing research by competitors soon verified its efficacy. After some delay, other competitors raised their quality control standards, but none has been able, coming in later on a me-too basis, to emulate Zenith's success. One could quibble about some details of Zenith's reputation—whether hand-wiring is in fact more or less reliable than printed circuits, whether reliability has not been confused to some extent with repairability, whether Zenith sets any longer enjoy the lowest breakdown rate—but from the marketing standpoint, Zenith remains king of that segment of the set market which emphasizes reliability above other virtues when buying sets. The quality standards of the whole industry were forced up by Zenith's success, an outcome of obvious benefit to the consumer, but of at least equal benefit to all the other competitors in the industry, whose personnel devote their whole lives to their industry and much prefer feeling proud of their occupation to feeling ashamed of it.

The meaning of the Zenith example would be very incomplete, however, if we paid attention only to the success story and failed to note that there are many other virtues in television sets which consumers prize besides reliability. If there were not, it would be hard to explain why the Zenith brand share at its

---

* Editors' note: The television industry has undergone considerable change since this article was written almost a decade ago. Nevertheless, the example Dr. Foote presents is as conceptually accurate today as it was then, and his major points continue to be relevant.

zenith rose barely above a fifth of the market. To be sure, Zenith may have preferred its profitability to the greater volume it may have deliberately foregone by upholding a price premium. On the other hand, maybe not; a price premium is just about the loudest advertisement for quality there is.

Meanwhile Zenith's major rival did not simply decide it had to emulate Zenith, but staunchly pursued its strategy of industry statesmanship through the introduction of color, achieving handsome victory and reward from matching its offering with the rising wants of all those customers who were reaching for color in magazines, movies, photography, and other visual media. Alongside these two industry leaders were certain other manufacturers, one of whom has done well by stressing portability and personalization, another by treating the television set as a major piece of furniture, and so on. What is important here is that several competitors held their own or improved their position, even during the period of greatest success by Zenith and RCA, not by seeking to manufacture some hypothetically optimum television set, but by addressing themselves to some substantial segment of the market which *they saw themselves as peculiarly fitted to serve*. The firms which got shaken out during the past dozen years—among which some were big for a time—or which severely lost position can best be described as undistinguishable in their capabilities and offerings, hence undistinguished by consumers.

Now what has been added to the understanding of market segmentation by the example of television receivers? What has been added that is indispensable is the element of competitive capability—a virtue that one particular competitor preeminently possesses—which matches a substantial or rising consumer want. In colloquial terms, what have I got that the other guy hasn't, and which the customer wants badly enough to walk a mile for it?

A few years back, we looked at some commonplace demographic characteristics of television customers arrayed by the brands they tended to favor. When we looked at these demographic characteristics simultaneously, certain results were far more revealing in combination than singly. Only a limited example—because here we are indeed verging on the disclosure of competitive intelligence: we found that one highly meaningful segment of the market—meaningful in terms of sensitivity of discrimination among brands—consisted of households below the median in years of schooling but above the median in income. For convenient reference we called them merely the new-rich, obviously an inexact term. One particular brand seemed to be designed and advertised and priced—properly overpriced, as it were—specifically for this segment, and in fact it enjoyed at that time an inordinate share of their set-buying. Now that company has not noticeably changed its offerings during recent years; they still seem pointed toward the new-rich segment; but its brand share has dwindled substantially. It appears that people with more money than schooling nonetheless are able to learn from experience and do upgrade their taste, given a little time.

The moral of this example is that market segmentation has to be viewed as a continuous process, and marketing strategy has to keep in step with the changing structure of the market. While this implication is probably obvious, perhaps less obvious is the corollary that, just as consumers learn, it is necessary for competitors to learn to exercise differing capabilities from those which may have won them success in the past. And here we come to a matter which lies beyond not only research but also ordinary logic and in the realm of managerial will. Who is to tell a manufacturer that he is capable of doing something he has not done before, and of doing it better than any of his other competitors? By definition, the ordinary kinds of evidence are lacking because there is no past experience to be projected forward.

In the course of interpersonal relations among individuals, a teacher or a parent may tell a child that he possesses talents he did not previously recognize; the child may then adopt this observation as a conviction about himself which empowers him to demonstrate that it is true. All of us are familiar enough with instances of this outcome not to need to debate whether they occur. The faith of a coach in an athlete, of a critic in a writer, of an employer in an employee, of a wife in a husband, is often the ingredient which brings out a latent capability. Because so little is understood about the process, we cannot make it happen on demand. We are fortunate to recognize it when it does happen, even more so when we spy the opportunity beforehand and do not waste it, for ourselves or for others. Even further beyond present understanding is the possibility of specifying here a reliable formula whereby the management of a company can truly discern those latent talents in its own organization which can be mobilized more effectively by itself than by any of its competitors to satisfy some important emerging customer want.

I do know this, however: recognition of such a talent feeds on itself; it is a cumulative process, a benevolent spiral. I am positive that when the management of Zenith found itself being recognized by consumers for its virtues of good workmanship, it was immensely stimulated to push further in that direction. Thus one of the most valuable functions of marketing research in implementing a strategy of market segmentation is to listen to what is being said about a company by its customers in terms of recognizing its special talents. Developing something that is already there—watering a plant that is already growing, to mix a metaphor—is surely much easier and more likely to succeed than trying to create new capabilities out of whole cloth or, for that matter, borrowing the garments of others, in the sense of imitating or acquiring another company and offering that as an expression of one's own capability.

Part of the growing sophistication of consumers is their increasing interest in the character of the organization they are dealing with. At General Electric we are acutely conscious that certain of our competitors, whose products are no better and sometimes not as good as ours by any measure of product quality, nonetheless enjoy the preference of certain customers. This problem repeatedly confronts the manufacturer who finds himself in competition with retailers who handle only store brands. The whole fascinating issue of what is going to emerge as private branding widens its sway is too vast to open up here. Yet it deserves mention here as constituting market segmentation on an utterly different axis from market segmentation on the axis of product features and brand images.

Segmentation varies in degree as well as in kind. The famous case of the ordinary salt which "rains when it pours" illustrates a valued product feature which has maintained for a particular brand a large and stable market share for many years, while conferring on consumers a valued satisfaction for which they are quite willing to pay a price premium and a rewarding degree of brand loyalty. Many such product features are easily imitated, however, and the reputation for distinctiveness originally achieved may dissolve in the minds of consumers despite advertising. The impermanence of minor product features as a source of competitive distinctiveness and effective market segmentation is a conspicuous failing of the current picture in package goods competition. Like rock-and-roll music, there is too little difference between the new ones and the old ones to make much difference. The proliferation of trivial product differences which appeal to trivial differences among consumers and represent trivial differences among the capabilities of their makers is in effect a mockery of the theory of market segmentation. This proliferation of trivial differences provokes denunciation by producers, retailers, and consumers alike as market fragmentation rather than segmentation and makes an industry vulnerable to the outsider who commences to segment on a different axis. The effective response to the trivialization of market segmentation, however, is not to abandon it as a strategy. To do that would be to abdicate all initiative to competitors. The way out of the expensive waste of trivial segmentation is to engage in serious segmentation, which means segmentation on a larger scale or even on another axis.

Serious, large-scale innovation seems often to come from outside an industry rather than inside. Examples like General Motors in locomotives, Volkswagen in autos, IBM in typewriters, Corning in housewares, Lestoil in detergents, come to mind. Rivalry within a going constellation of competitors seems often to lead to implicit imitation, even when everyone involved is convinced that he is trying to be different from everyone else. How this result occurs is not hard to discern. Close rivals tend very easily to magnify the importance of small differences, whether initiated by themselves or others. If created by another, a close competitor often feels he must come up with a rival innovation but only of corresponding scale.

One detects nothing very distinctive about Silvertone television sets, to mention another respected Chicago competitor. Viewed as manufactured products, they are close to the industry's average line. But where Zenith stresses the reliability built into the product, Sears stresses the services offered by the stores in which Silvertone sets are bought—the promptness of repair service, the easy credit, the ample parking, the special sales well advertised in local newspapers or by direct mail. That is, Sears segments the market on another axis than Zenith. But thus far, Silvertone has encroached far less upon Zenith's clientele than upon the portions of the market occupied by companies whose offerings are less distinctive.

We shall come back to this intriguing question of how far the competition of store brands with manufacturer brands may go before some equilibrium is reached. Some companies as yet have a less urgent private-brand problem anyway, like the auto and gasoline firms and the sellers of services—insurance, banking, air travel, lodging, dry cleaning—which distribute through their own exclusive retail outlets. So for some moments longer, let us stay within the sphere of competition among manufactured products and nationally advertised brands.

Assuming this sphere, we can now state our main hypothesis in further detail: Market segmentation works best as a competitive strategy, i.e., contributes most to the success of competitors and the satisfaction of customers, when product and brand and maker are closely identified in the minds of all concerned.

If we were to assume that one by one more competitors in a market choose to attract particular segments of customers on the basis of correct appraisal of their own special capabilities to satisfy these segments, then the competitors who do not make such deliberate choices will find themselves increasingly confined to the miscellaneous and dwindling residue. As alluded to in our first example, such a development is to some extent a description of what has already happened in some markets, so we may be prophesying simply an intensification of current tendencies rather than anything new under the sun. In other words, self-conscious segmentation may become not only a means of success but the price of survival in a market.

Beyond the ordinary criteria of survival or success as measured in profitability and market share, however, are some other benefits of segmentation to an industry and the various competitors in it. We have mentioned the feeling of pride in their occupation and the quality of its products which most people desire in their life work. Some other benefits of belonging to an industry which steadily adds to the values it offers its customers also deserve explicit recognition. They include the fact that being bested by a competitor whom one respects is easier to accept than being bested by a competitor whom one does not respect. There is a good deal of satisfaction to the producer as well as the consumer in seeing an industry progress over time through advanced applications of science and technology. In an industry plagued with cut-throat price competition instead of value competition, imitation is almost inevitable, because no one can afford the research and development required for innovation. In the vicious downward spiral which obtains in such an industry, jobs are insecure because companies are insecure; and morale and morality seem to decline together. Enough examples spring to mind. An industry trapped in such a spiral, worst of all, has rarely been able to reverse it without outside help, as from major suppliers. DuPont, for example, has struggled quite nobly to raise the plastics molding industry from its swamp. Customers themselves, especially in recent years, have sometimes under these conditions willingly paid substantial premiums for quality and reliability, and this has brought a turnabout, but not before the damage became painful to all concerned.

Both competitors and customers share the benefit of stabilized markets wherein strong degrees of mutual loyalty exist between particular companies and particular segments of customers. Distribution and advertising costs are significantly lower under conditions in which repeat sales make up a high proportion of total sales. The model line of any competitor can be shorter, yet his volume nowadays may be higher, than when he tries to carry everything everyone else in the industry offers. All phases of marketing are much more intelligently, effectively, and efficiently conducted when companies and customers, having chosen each other with care and sophistication, can rely on each other's growing discrimination and sympathetically anticipate the orderly developing and unfolding and matching of their future wants and capabilities. Some marketing researchers even envision a paradise in which companies will spend as much money in listening as in talking and will make more money doing so.

Let us commence to summarize while injecting a few additional elements into this consideration of market segmentation as a competitive strategy. Our first proposition was that any approach to market segmentation which dealt only with matching customer characteristics with product features was seriously incomplete. The very incentive for exploring market segmentation is to gain advantage—to seek some basis for customer preference—against the array of other competitors and their offerings in a particular market. If one plays only with customer characteristics and product features, he may arrive at the notion of some optimum product for an average customer, in effect, a recipe for reducing his product to commodity status, hence the very opposite of market segmentation, which implies product differentiation. But if he goes to the opposite extreme and tries to equal or surpass the total array of differing products offered by all competitors to all segments of his market, he courts the usual fate of me-too-ism, while suffering impossibly mounting marketing costs. Hence he must seek to identify those offerings which most appeal to some desirable segment of the total market and simultaneously express those capabilities in which he is strongest. The problem of choice here is analogous with that of the boy who must seek distinction from a brother who excels him athletically and another who excels him academically: what talent can he develop which, though different, will seem equivalent in the eyes of those whose approval he seeks? To be all things to all people, to excel in every virtue, is impossible; to be average in all means indistinguishability. Achieving only trivial distinctiveness is a barely veiled form of imitation, although it can immensely add to promotional expense in an industry. Hence the evolution of a criterion for selecting which customer segments and matching product distinctions to pursue must come from and be disciplined by correct identification of the real strengths and weaknesses of the company itself, as compared with other competitors in its market.

Companies, like individuals, sometimes involuntarily suffer crises of identity, as when merged with other companies. A company embarking upon market segmentation as a competitive strategy is deliberately precipitating a crisis of identity. In place of identity, however, which seems to apply only to the maker of a product rather than to a triple set of interrelations, I believe the concept of theme is more applicable and explanatory of the common element which has to be discovered or invented to match customer characteristic with product feature with company capability. The so-called total marketing approach in its sophisticated form seems finally to come forth with such recognizable themes. The theme of *ease of use* of essentially highly technical equipment has served Kodak for generations and recurs in numerous notable expressions—from the Brownie to the Instamatic, from the ubiquitous yellow box to the universally recognizable name itself. It illustrates how versatile in its manifestations a theme can be.

But just as product innovation can be trivialized through pointless small variations which make no real contribution to anyone, the concept of theme can be trivialized also, and in fact is, whenever some advertising agency tries to adorn an advertiser with a superficial image that has no real structural relationship to customer segments, competitive constellation, or company capabilities.

The concept of theme is useful in teaching marketing and market segmentation to managers whose experience has been in more exact fields. It helps to avoid the mental blocks that arise when segmentation is grasped as a series of pigeonholes in which various kinds of customers are filed for separate treatment, whereas the manager is eager for all the sales he can get from any source whatever, and finds it hard enough to devise one marketing strategy without having to devise many. To return to our main example, the television receiver market, the theme of reliability can be applied by one manufacturer to all the models in his line and throughout all the functions of marketing in his total marketing program. But the same manufacturer could hardly pursue simultaneously with equal thoroughness and equal success such contrasting themes as modern and traditional cabinetry, portability, technical innovation, and retail convenience, although he may keep pace with the industry average in these respects. Market segmentation does not deal with water-tight compartments, but with emphases sufficiently simple and distinctive to win notice and preference among customers to whom they are important, without alienating customers by being deficient in the other virtues which they more or less take for granted.

In terms of demographic and other statistical dimensions by which customers and products may be differentiated, the possibilities for market segmentation are troublesomely infinite. But when the problem of choosing a theme to emphasize is disciplined by attempting to match customers, competitors, and capabilities, these troubles are usually reduced to very few choices that are actually open to a particular firm—though hopefully at least one. The real difficulties of choice are not statistical but spiritual—the anguish of facing up to the fact that if a company is going to move in one direction, it must forego moving in all the others. Such a decision comes especially hard in diversified companies, yet some diversified companies have achieved real synergy through this discipline.

Once this clarifying commitment has been made, its effect on everyone in the organization is to release spontaneous ingenuity in its implementation. A good theme stimulates numberless applications and suggestions, furnishes a guide in numberless subordinate decisions, and eases numberless chores of communication, both inside and outside.

Not only does a positive theme help to mobilize an organization in pursuit of its marketing objectives and heighten their satisfaction, but it wins respect from competitors, even while strengthening and securing its position against them. Spirit is harder to imitate than matter; hardware is easy to copy, but the spirit of a whole organization is not. the competitor who wishes to emulate the success of a competitor's dominant theme must, instead of echoing it, come up with an equivalent theme that uniquely fits himself to his situation, that matches his own three Cs. . . .

QUESTIONS

1. Discuss why competing for a differential advantage leads to market segmentation.
2. Compare and contrast Foote's main hypothesis with the major points of the marketing concept.
3. Why does Foote place so much emphasis on competitors and even include them in his "three Cs"?
4. What does Foote mean by "theme"? Illustrate.
*5. Does Foote seem to agree with Alderson's treatment of "differential advantage" (Reading 5)?

---

* Question relates concepts in this and other readings.

7
The high cost of government regulation

Murray L. Weidenbaum

This article, with a postscript from The Wall Street Journal, *discusses a possible negative impact of government regulation–increasing the cost of the things we buy. Weidenbaum is not "antiregulation," since he recognizes the need for some regulation of business. Rather, he points out that there is no such thing as a "free lunch," that is, the cost of government regulation to protect consumers, especially the increased cost of doing business so as to meet these regulations, is passed on to the consumer in higher prices.*

As the American public is learning to its dismay, government actions can cause or worsen inflation in many ways. Large budget deficits and excessively easy monetary policy are usually cited as the two major culprits, and quite properly. Yet, there is a third way—less obvious and hence more insidious—in which government can worsen the already severe inflationary pressures affecting the American economy.

That third way is for the government to require actions in the private sector that increase the costs of production and hence raise the prices of the products and services which are sold to the public. For example, the price of the typical new 1974 passenger automobile was about $320 higher than it would have been in the absence of federally mandated safety and environmental requirements.

Attention needs to be focused on this third route to inflation for two reasons: first, the government is constantly embarking on new and expanded programs which raise costs and prices in the private economy, and, second, neither government decision makers nor the public recognize the significance of these inflationary effects. Literally, the federal government is continually mandating more inflation via the regulations it promulgates. These actions, of course, are validated by an accommodating monetary policy.

Source: Reprinted with permission from *Business Horizons,* published by Indiana University, August 1975, pp. 43–51. At the time of writing, Murray Weidenbaum was director of the Center for the Study of American Business, Washington University.

THE PUBLIC PAYS

In theory, the monetary authorities could offset many of the inflationary effects of regulation by attempting to maintain a lower rate of monetary growth. In practice, however, public policy makers, insofar as they see the options clearly, tend to prefer the higher rate of inflation to additional monetary restraint and the resulting decreases in employment and real output.

Obviously, most of these government actions are not designed to increase prices. Nevertheless, that is the result. In part because of efforts to control the growth of government spending, we have turned increasingly to mechanisms designed to achieve a given national objective—better working conditions, for example, or more nutritious foods—without much expenditure of government funds. The approach emphasizes efforts to influence private decision makers to achieve specific ends.

Thus, rather than burden the public treasury with the full cost of cleaning up environmental pollution, we now require private firms to devote additional resources to that purpose. Rather than have the federal government spend large sums to eliminate traffic hazards, we require motorists to purchase vehicles equipped with various safety features that increase the selling price.

Government imposition of socially desirable requirements on business appears to be an inexpensive way of achieving national objectives; it costs the government nothing and therefore is no burden on the taxpayer. But, on reflection, it can be seen that the public does not escape paying the cost. For example, every time the Occupational Safety and Health Administration imposes a more costly, albeit safer, method of production, the cost of the resultant product necessarily tends to rise. Every time the Consumer Product Safety Commission imposes a standard which is more costly to attain, some product costs will tend to rise. The same holds true for the activities of the Environmental Protection Agency, the Food and Drug Administration, and so forth.

The point being made here should not be misunderstood. What is at issue is not the worth of the objectives of these agencies. Rather, it is that the public does not get a "free lunch" by imposing public requirements on private industry. Although the costs of government regulation are not borne by the taxpayer directly, in large measure they show up in higher prices of the goods and services that consumers buy. These higher prices, we need to recognize, represent the "hidden tax" which is shifted from the taxpayer to the consumer. Moreover, to the extent that government-mandated requirements impose similar costs on all price categories of a given product (say, automobiles), this hidden tax will tend to be more regressive than the federal income tax. That is, the costs may be a higher relative burden on lower income groups than on higher income groups.

This article does not address the philosophical question of whether government regulation is good or bad. Government regulation is an accepted fact in a modern society. The point being made here is more modest: that a given regulatory activity generates costs as well as benefits. Hence, consideration of proposals—and they are numerous—to extend the scope of federal regulation should not be limited, as is usually the case, to a recital of the advantages of regulation. Rather, the costs need to be considered also, both those which are tangible and those which may be intangible.

It should be acknowledged that what is taking place in the United States represents not an abrupt departure from an idealized free market economy, but rather the rapid intensification of fairly durable trends of expanding government control over the private sector. In earlier periods, when productivity and living standards were rising rapidly, the nation could more easily afford to applaud the benefits and ignore the costs of regulation. But now the acceleration of federal controls coincides with, and accentuates, a slowdown in productivity growth and in the improvement in real standards of living. Thus, the earlier attitude of tolerance toward controls is no longer economically defensible.

Worthy objectives, such as a cleaner environment and safer products, can be attained without the inflationary impact that overregulation brings, and public policy should be revised to this end. But before we turn to this question, we need to examine more closely the phenomenon of government-mandated price increases. It is likely that this unwanted phenomenon will be with us for some time, at least until consumers and their representatives recognize the problem and urge changes in public policy.

GOVERNMENT-MANDATED COSTS

As government-mandated costs begin to visibly exceed the apparent benefits, it can be hoped that public pressures will mount on governmental regulators to moderate the increasingly stringent rules and regulations that they apply. At present, for example, a mislabeled consumer product that is declared an unacceptable hazard often must be destroyed. In the future, the producer or seller perhaps will only be required to relabel it correctly, a far less costly way of achieving the same objective.

Yet, the recent trend is clear—more frequent and more costly governmental regulation of the private sector. If the trend continues unchecked, the resulting loss in productivity could lead to stagnation in real living standards. Further expansion of government control over private industry is not inevitable, however. Not all controls last forever, and the federal government does not adopt every suggestion for increasing government controls over the private sector.

For example, in January 1974, the government ended the interest equalization tax on American holdings of foreign stocks and bonds and the controls over direct investments abroad by U.S. corporations. Simultaneously, the Federal Reserve System ended its guidelines limiting lending and investments overseas by U.S. banks and other financial institutions. Further, on April 30, 1974, the legislation authorizing wage and price controls was allowed to expire, and the formal wage and price control system was dismantled. Yet it is likely that some vestige of government influence over private price formation will remain.

As would be expected, the ever more complicated safety system and the federally mandated pollution controls are increasing the price of motor vehicles. Table 1 shows, for the typical new 1974 passenger automobile, the

Table 1
Automobile price increases resulting from federal requirements, 1968–1974 (estimated retail cost at time of introduction)

Model year	Required action	Price per car
1968	Seat and shoulder belt installations	$ 11.51
	HEW standards for exhaust emission systems	16.00
1968–69	Windshield defrosting and defogging systems	.70
	Windshield wiping and washing systems	1.25
	Door latches and hinge systems	.55
	Lamps, reflective devices, and associated equipment	6.30
1969	Head restraints	16.65
1970	Lamps, reflective devices, and associated equipment	4.00
	HEW standards for exhaust emission systems	5.50
1968–70	Theft protection (steering, transmission, and ignition locking and buzzing system)	7.85
	Occupant protection in interior impact (glove box door remains closed on impact)	.35
1971	Fuel evaporative systems	19.00
1972	Improved exhaust emissions standards required by Clean Air Act	6.00
	Warranty changes resulting from federal requirement that all exhaust emission systems be warranted for five years or 50,000 miles	1.00
	Voluntarily added safety features in anticipation of future safety requirements	2.00
	Seat belt warning system and locking device on retractors	20.25
1972–73	Exterior protection (standard 215)	69.90
1973	Location, identification, and illumination of controls improvements	.60
	Reduced flammability of interior materials	5.80
1969–73	Improved side door strength	15.30
1974	Interlock system and other changes to meet federal safety requirements	107.60
	Improved exhaust emissions systems to comply with the Federal Clean Air Act	1.40
	Total	$319.51

Source: Computed from data supplied by the U.S. Department of Labor, Bureau of Labor Statistics.

estimated cost of the successive changes required in the 1968–74 period to meet federal standards. According to these data, the federally mandated costs average $320 per car. American motorists purchased nearly 9 million new cars in 1974, thereby paying approximately $3 billion extra for the governmentally imposed requirements.

In addition, the added weight and complexity of the mandated features have increased the operating costs of the vehicles, particularly the fuel costs. The cost of the new catalytic converters that will be required on 1975 automobiles is estimated at over $150 per vehicle.

The $3 billion that American new-car buyers paid out in 1974 for the added features mandated by the federal government had a high "opportunity cost." We as a nation had to forego the opportunity to spend that considerable sum on other ways of reducing road accidents. Just think what a fraction of the $1 billion that is being devoted to the "interlock" system alone could have yielded if applied to these alternatives:

Identification and elimination of the serious hazards created by unclear or badly located road signs and the placing of signs where they are needed but are now absent.

More universal and more intensive driver instruction and testing, including the development of simulators that could be used to make driver training and testing more demanding, perhaps with no increase in cost.

Assessment of the cost and benefits of more thorough vehicle inspections, including the feasibility of combining safety inspections with checkups on pollution control equipment and engine operation. This would help to meet safety, environment, and energy conservation objectives simultaneously.

Every benefit to the customer or the public may have a corresponding cost to the car buyer, who ultimately must pay for product changes. In the case of tougher bumpers, for example, any saving in insurance premiums or reduced car repair costs should be weighed against the additional cost of the bumper and the additional gasoline needed to move the cars made heavier by the new bumpers, supporting frame, and related equipment.

TRAINING COSTS FOR REGULATORS

The recent upsurge in the number, variety, and extent of government programs to regulate business has revealed numerous deficiencies in the very process of regulation. Any reader of the horror stories that abound in the national press may, with good reason, jump to the conclusion that the regulators are undergoing some form of rudimentary on-the-job training at the consumer's expense.

For example, a recent issue of the *New York Times* reported: "U.S. to Study Effects of Antipollution Devices." What was revealing and distressing was to learn that this study was taking place after the U.S. Environmental Protection Agency had ordered automobile manufacturers to incorporate a specific and expensive antipollution device—the catalytic converter. Apparently, both private and governmental researchers have shown that the new antipollution equipment may produce harmful amounts of sulphuric acid mists, which can irritate the lungs.

The catalytic converters also emit platinum which, in the words of John B.

Moran, the director of the EPA's fuel and additive research program, is "really adding a new thing to our environment," according to the *Times*. It appears that there is no significant amount of platinum in our air or water at the present time. Just think of governmental and public outrage that would have resulted if a private organization had taken such action without submitting a detailed environmental impact statement and without subjecting itself to the criticism of the various groups desiring to participate in the review process.

The $6 million that EPA is belatedly devoting to studying the adverse environmental effects of its actions is but the tip of the iceberg. Moran estimates that it would take several billion dollars for the oil companies to remove sulphur from gasoline. Moreover, desulphurization might adversely affect the supply of gasoline.

THE CPSC

The relatively new Consumer Product Safety Commission (CPSC) is an important although often overlooked addition to the already impressive array of governmental agencies that regulate one or more facets of business decision making. It has jurisdiction over more than 10,000 products and possesses the authority to set mandatory safety standards, to ban or recall products from the marketplace without a court hearing, to require warnings by manufacturers, to order rebates to consumers, and even to send offending executives to jail.

The likelihood that the CPSC will use the full extent of its power may be remote. Yet, the judicious, restrained approach that might have been expected from the wielders of such awesome power is not apparent in the public statements of the commission members. As the commission chairman, Richard O. Simpson, blithely puts it, "You name it and CPSC probably has jurisdiction over it."[1]

That this statement is not merely rhetoric can be seen in the commission's current plans to declare the average residence an unsafe product and thus bring the entire home into the agency's jurisdiction. Simpson's attitude on enforcement does little to foster better business-government relations: "If a company violates our statute, we will not concern ourselves with its middle-level executives; we will put the chief executive in jail. Once we do put a top executive behind bars, I am sure that we will get a much higher degree of compliance from other companies."[2]

Another CPSC commissioner, R. David Pittle, provides a more graphic analogy to violence: "Any time consumer safety is threatened, we're going to go for the company's throat." There seems little awareness on the part of the commission's members of the difficulties involved in developing new regulatory approaches, of the degrees and range of product safety, or even of the possibility that they may make mistakes. To quote Pittle again, "When it

---

[1] Robert T. Gray, "Washington's Little Giant," *Nation's Business,* September 1973, p. 21.

[2] Gerald R. Rosen, " 'We're Going for Companies' Throats," *Dun's Review,* January 1973, p. 36.

involves a product that is unsafe, I don't care how much it costs the company to correct the problem."[3]

Unless the Consumer Product Safety Commission reverses its course, its actions are likely to produce major increases in the prices that consumers pay for the products they use—with only questionable benefits. It is consumers who ultimately pay for the changes that are required, although the commission seems oblivious of this fact.

The first suit filed in St. Louis by the Consumer Product Safety Commission in January 1974 may indicate the extent of the "overkill" in the commission's approach to safeguarding consumers from potential hazards. The offending items were 1,494 containers of windshield washer solvent which were without child-proof caps and were not labeled with the required statement, "Cannot be made nonpoisonous."

What remedy did the commission seek? That the caps be changed and the necessary four words of "bureaucratese" be pasted on each of the bottles? Hardly. Instead, it ordered that each and every one of the 1,494 containers of windshield washing material be destroyed, thereby no doubt contributing to the nation's pollution problem. And those of us who use that kind of solvent in our cars (and drink more conventional fluids) of course wind up paying the higher price that results from this federally mandated waste.

But this is only part of the story. The company involved, Ace Hardware, did not contest the CPSC ruling and offered to destroy the material or turn it over to a CPSC representative. It was discovered, however, that no CPSC official was authorized to accept the contraband and that the company was prohibited from destroying it. Months later, after a court order was obtained, a duly authorized officer of the law appeared at the company to confiscate the goods.

DOES CONSUMERISM PROTECT?

Max Brunk of Cornell University gets to the heart of the matter: Consumerism is intended to protect the consumer, but look what the regulations do to the consumer "who pays the cost and loses the benefits that a prohibited product or service could have provided." Not much reflection is required to see that business can adjust to these controls more easily than can the consumer because it can pass on the added costs that result.

Brunk notes that the consumer organization sometimes has as much difficulty in convincing the consumer of his or her need for protection as it does in convincing a regulatory body to provide the protection. Experience under the truth-in-lending law is a good example. Has the compulsory requirement to show true interest costs slowed down the growth of consumer debt or the rise in interest rates?

On the contrary, since the passage of the act, the ratio of consumer debt to consumer income has reached an all-time high, and interest rates, for many reasons, have risen sharply. The average credit purchaser still is more in-

---

[3] Ibid., p. 36.

terested in the full amount of the monthly payment than in the amount (and rate) of interest included. Similarly, despite the justification for unit pricing as a means of helping low-income families to stretch their food dollar by buying more intelligently, Brunk notes that available surveys show that it is the high-income, well-educated customers who are most aware of this information.[4]

The Federal Trade Commission is now attempting to obtain "line of business" data from the nation's 345 largest corporations. The FTC staff estimates that the start-up costs of providing this new information will average $548,000 for each of twenty-five companies that it has studied. As shown in Table 2, the cost may range from a low of $45,000 for a publishing firm to a

Table 2
Estimated start-up costs for FTC
line-of-business reports

Company	Estimated mean start-up costs (in thousands)
American Metal Climax	$ 75
Anaconda	1,000
Combustion Engineering	100
Crown Zellerbach	100
Deere	1,000
Dow Chemical	400
DuPont	500
Ex-cell-o	350
Exxon	1,000
General Instrument	100
Inland Steel	100
Lear Siegler	400
McGraw-Hill	45
Mobil	500
Nabisco	100
Northrop	300
Outboard Marine	100
R. J. Reynolds	1,000
Singer	500
Standard Oil, California	800
Union Carbide	1,100
U.S. Steel	2,000
Varian Associates	63
Westinghouse	2,000
Westvaco	75
Total	$13,708
Mean	$ 548

Source: U.S. Senate, Committee on Government Operations, *Hearings on Corporate Disclosure* (Washington: U.S. Government Printing Office, 1974), p. 922.

---

[4] Max E. Brunk, "Consumerism and Marketing," in George Steiner, ed., *Issues in Business and Society* (New York: Random House, 1972), pp. 462–65.

high of $2 million for a large steel or electrical manufacturer. Applying the average of $548,000 to each of the 345 corporations results in an estimated cost of $190 million just to get ready to fill out this one form. This may be a "modest" sum from the viewpoint of the government, but it is a substantial overhead cost to the companies involved and ultimately will be passed on, in good measure, to the consumer.

THE ANNOUNCEMENT EFFECT

One unmeasurable impact of federal regulation is the "announcement effect." For many years economists have noted its existence in the field of government spending or taxation. Thus, potential government contractors may start preparing to bid on a project before Congress has appropriated the funds, or consumers may increase their expenditures as soon as a tax cut is voted on or even while it is being considered.

Anticipated changes in governmental regulatory programs may stimulate somewhat similar responses. In Illinois, the very rumor that the Occupational Safety and Health Administration might impose more stringent standards for migrant worker housing caused strawberry farmers to reduce their production. The largest grower in the Centralia area was quoted as saying, "We don't know if OSHA is coming or not, but when it was even rumored, it put it [strawberry production] out."

The basis for the concern was the possibility that farmers would have to provide migrant workers with the same amenities as permanent workers— 100 square feet of living space (the present state standard is 60 square feet), flush toilets and showers in each room. Apparently at least some Illinois strawberry farmers concluded that the capital investment required could not be justified for a two-week harvest.

According to James Mills, an official with the Illinois Department of Public Health, a basic problem is the lack of distinction under OSHA regulations between long- and short-term migratory farm worker housing. Centralia farmers, he was quoted as saying, "just can't compete said, if OSHA puts the pressure on them, they'll get out of the migrant business completely and go strictly U-Pick," that is, allow consumers to pick the fruit for their own use for a fee.

THE VARIOUS COSTS OF REGULATION

In this day of rising attention to the costs as well as the benefits of public action, we must recognize the substantial costs that consumers pay for the truly massive expansion in government regulation of the private sector. These costs stem in part from the increased and unproductive overhead expenses that government requirements impose. They may not mean much to the taxpayer, but to the extent that they raise the cost of production, they result in higher prices to consumers. Because the government-mandated costs result in no measurable output, they also are reflected in the lower rate of productivity that has been experienced by the American economy in recent years.

John C. Whitehead of the investment banking firm of Goldman, Sachs and Company has measured the cost of one aspect of government regulation of business, the growing mass of financial information required by the SEC prior to its approval of a new securities issue. He reports that a foreign-based firm, a world-famous public company, concluded that SEC requirements were so cumbersome that the company would raise its money elsewhere until there was at least a 1 percent annual interest differential in favor of issuing in the United States.[5]

Yet, the critical price we pay for government regulation is the attenuation of the risk-bearing and entrepreneurial nature of our private enterprise system, a system which, at least in the past, has contributed so effectively to rapid rates of innovation, productivity, and growth. A hidden cost of governmental restrictions of various kinds is a reduced rate of innovation. The longer it takes for some change to be approved by the federal regulatory agency—a new or improved product, a more efficient production process, and so on—the less likely that the change will be made. In any event, innovation will be delayed.

William Wardell of the University of Rochester's School of Medicine and Dentistry has studied in detail the advantages and disadvantages of Britain's liberal policy toward the introduction of new drugs. He concludes that, on balance, in comparison with the United States, Great Britain gained from its more "permissive" policy toward the marketing of new drugs:

> Britain suffered more toxicity due to new drugs than did the United States, as could have been anticipated from the fact that more new drugs were marketed there. However, considering the size of the total burden of drug toxicity, the portion due to new drugs was extremely small, and would in any case be at least partially offset by the adverse effects of older alternative drugs had the latter been used instead. Conversely, Britain experienced clearly discernible gains by introducing useful new drugs either sooner than the United States or exclusively.[6]

Sam Peltzman of the University of Chicago has estimated some of the costs of the drug lag in the United States. He analyzed the 1962 amendments to the Food and Drug Act, amendments ostensibly designed to keep ineffective drugs off the market by extending the process of authorizing new drugs prior to their being available to the public.

The main impact of the legislation has been to delay the introduction of effective drugs by about four years and to lead to higher prices for drugs. He estimates the resultant loss to the consumer to be in the neighborhood of $200–300 million a year. Peltzman also calculates that if the drugs that combat tuberculosis had been delayed by two years, the average delay now

[5] John C. Whitehead, "SEC Must Drop Role of Industry Adversary," *Money Manager*, July 1, 1974, p. 21.

[6] William M. Wardell, "Therapeutic Implications of the Drug Lag," *Clinical Pharmacology and Therapeutics*, January 1974, p. 73.

imposed by the Food and Drug Administration, the result would have been approximately 45,000 additional deaths.[7]

The adverse effect of regulation on innovation is likely to be felt more strongly by smaller firms than by the large companies. Thus it will have an anticompetitive impact. According to Mitchell Zavon, president of the American Association of Poison Control Centers, in the St. Louis Post-Dispatch: "We've got to the point in regulatory action where it has become so costly and risky to bring out products that only the very largest firms can afford to engage in these risky ventures. To bring out a new pesticide you have to figure a cost of $7,000,000 and seven years of time."

Federal regulation imposes other "costs" on the economy. The impact on the prospects for economic growth and productivity can be seen by examining some recent estimates of the size and composition of investment by manufacturing companies. Lewis Beman has estimated that, in real terms (after eliminating the effects of inflation), total capital spending by American manufacturing companies was no higher in 1973 than it was in 1969—about $26 billion in both years.

However, in 1973 a much larger proportion of capital spending was devoted to pollution and safety outlays than in 1969—$3 billion more. Hence, the effective additions to plant and equipment—the real investment in modernization and new capacity—were lower in 1973. This helps to explain why the American economy, for a substantial part of 1973, appeared to lack needed productive capacity, despite what had been large annual investments in new plant and equipment in recent years.

This is not a general attack on all forms of government regulation of business. A society, acting through government, can and should act to protect consumers against rapacious sellers, individual workers against unscrupulous employers, and future generations against those who would waste the nation's resources. Thus, controls to avoid infant crib deaths can be advocated without supporting a plethora of detailed federal rules and regulations dealing with the color of exit lights and the maintenance of cuspidors.

Society should take a new and hard look at the existing array of government controls over business because of the substantial costs and other adverse side effects they produce. An effort should be made to eliminate those controls that generate excessive costs. Rather than blithely continuing to proliferate government controls over business, alternative means of achieving important national objectives should be explored and developed, solutions that expand rather than reduce the role of the market.

A good beginning might be based on the environmental regulations. In general, society is supposed to examine the impact on the environment of the various actions that it takes. Would it not also be appropriate to require each environmental agency to assess the impact of its action on society as a whole

---

[7] Sam Pletzman, "An Evaluation of Consumer Protection Legislation: The 1962 Drug Amendments," Journal of Political Economy, September–October 1973, p. 1090.

and particularly on the economy? Surely a cleaner environment is an important national objective. But it is not the only national objective, and certainly society has no stake in selecting the most expensive and most disruptive ways of achieving its environmental goals.

Unpopular as it may be, the same balanced attitude may be appropriate for the other new regulatory programs, including product safety, job health, equal employment, and energy. As in most things in life, the sensible questions are not matters of either/or, but rather of more or less and how. In this way, business can help to attain the nation's social goals while it achieves the basic economic function of more efficient production and distribution of goods and services. Government regulation would be carried to the point where the incremental benefits equal or exceed the incremental costs; over-regulation (which can be defined as situations were the costs to society exceed the benefits) thus would be avoided.

A postscript: Appliance firms expect industry turmoil if Congress tightens energy-saving rules

David M. Elsner

This article from The Wall Street Journal *illustrates Weidenbaum's concern about government regulation— here, as it applies to the appliance industry. The article also suggests that the increasing costs of government regulation may be a continuing problem.*

Manufacturers of major home appliances feel that they're about to go through a wringer.

The companies are facing another government-mandated reduction in the energy consumed by their products. As a result, they foresee huge outlays to meet the proposed energy standards, sharply higher retail prices for appliances and thus possible damage to the industry's recent sales recovery. They also fear that some companies will be forced to cut back on the number

---

Source: Reprinted with permission from *The Wall Street Journal,* June 29, 1977, p. 30. At the time of writing David Elsner was a staff reporter for *The Wall Street Journal.*

of models they make and that others will be pushed out of business altogether. And they believe that this turmoil is being stirred up with little prospect of saving much energy anyway.

The cause of all this apprehension is currently grinding through Congress. A House subcommittee on energy on Monday approved legislation, favored by President Carter, that would require the Federal Energy Administration to set testing procedures and then announce mandatory minimum energy-saving standards for each type of appliance by late 1979. The Senate Energy and Natural Resources Committee is considering similar legislation.

The minimum standards would replace the considerably milder provisions of current law. Under the Federal Energy Act of 1975, manufacturers have to cut energy consumption only on average across their entire lines, and thus they can continue to produce cheaper, low-efficiency models. But the proposed amendments to the 1975 act would eliminate the low-efficiency units from the market.

COSTS "SIGNIFICANT"

"There's no question minimum standards are coming," says John S. Platts, chairman of Whirlpool Corp. "We have the technology to improve our products, but it's going to cost us and the consumer money. We don't know exactly how much until the standards are written, but it will be a significant amount."

Even though the industry recently softened its opposition to the proposed legislation, many executives still are rankled by their belief that little energy will be saved. Appliances account for only about 4.4 percent of all energy used in the U.S. Since the 1975 act was aimed at an overall saving of 20 percent on appliances, that law would reduce the nation's total consumption by less than 1 percent, and even that wouldn't be achieved until all appliances currently in use are worn out and replaced by more efficient models. The proposed legislation doesn't state any goals because the standards would have to be set by the FEA.

Undeterred by the likelihood of small savings, some proponents of the proposed changes talk up the public-relations value. "Appliances are highly visible, everyone uses them, and we've got to get people to start thinking about saving energy," an FEA official explains.

Appliance-industry executives, however, are busy thinking about the costs of meeting the expected FEA standards. They estimate that the companies, which last year recorded sales of about $6.4 billion, would have to spend $500 million to more than $1 billion over the next few years. Whether all appliance makers would be able or willing to bear the extra expense seems doubtful.

"There's bound to be some attrition," says Joseph V. McKee Jr., chairman of National Union Electric Corp. Adds Charles R. Lair, a vice president of Tappan Co.: "Manufacturers in this business are getting fewer and farther between every year. Any new standards won't help companies with specialty lines that have been hanging on year after year." And Edward Williams, chairman of McGraw-Edison Co., observes: "We have only about 3 percent of the air conditioner market nationally. If the regulations cut the size of our market, we probably would decide to phase out."

Just how many smaller manufacturers decide to give up will partly depend, of course, on what the FEA's new standards require. It's widely anticipated that the standards—at least for refrigerators, freezers and air conditioners—will closely resemble those already slated in California.

The California standards, due to take effect in November [1977] and to be followed by more stringent regulations two years later, will bar a sizable portion of current appliance lines from the state. The Association for Home Appliance Manufacturers estimates that 15 percent of all refrigerator models and 40 percent of all room air conditioner models won't meet the November 1977 standards and that few will meet the tougher 1979 rules.

According to the association's figures, for example, only 23 of 70 air conditioner models made by Carrier Air Conditioning Co. now meet California's 1977 standards, and only five made by the Carrier Corp. subsidiary clear the 1979 hurdle. Airtemp Corp., a unit of Fedders Corp., qualifies only 14 of 50 models under the 1977 rules and just seven under 1979's. And Sears, Roebuck & Co., which carries 48 models, will be able to sell only 16 of them in California after November, and only one of these can be considered a lightweight bedroom unit; six current Sears models meet the 1979 standards.

CONSUMERS' REACTION

Another major worry of appliance makers is that consumers will keep their old appliances rather than pay more for high-efficiency units. So far, consumers have generally shunned high-efficiency air conditioners, which retail for $50 to $100 more than low-efficiency models. And the companies also note that Philco-Ford Corp., a discontinued subsidiary of Ford Motor Co., couldn't successfully market a heavily insulated, energy-saving refrigerator. (Ford last year stopped making refrigerators and subsequently sold its equipment and patents to White Consolidated Industries Inc.)

Whirlpool estimates that to cut energy consumption 30 percent in its current 17-cubic-foot refrigerator with a top-mounted freezer will cost about $13 more at the manufacturing level. By the time dealers tack on their markups, the customer will pay from $26 to $39 more for the refrigerator, which now retails for $470.

WELCOMED BY AMANA

Of the major appliance manufacturers, only Amana Refrigeration Co. has welcomed minimum standards. The Raytheon Co. unit, which already makes a number of energy-saving models, expects to benefit from the proposed rules. "We feel we have a two-to-three-year jump on our competition," says Dan R. McConnell, vice president for planning.

Amana recently invested $9.5 million in a new refrigerator assembly line. Last year the company introduced six new, foam-insulated models, which it claims can cut operating costs as much as 57 percent. The energy-saving units cost up to $200 more than lower-efficiency models made by other companies, but Amana says the difference can be recovered quickly in reduced electricity bills.

"Consumers are becoming more conscious of the costs of energy," Mr. McConnell contends. Amana's new refrigerators are selling well, he says, especially in areas where electricity is costly. The company's 14-cubic-foot refrigerator, for example, uses 7 to 45 percent less power than the 18 similarly sized, rival units. In New York, where electricity costs average almost 9.2 cents a kilowatt hour, that reduction could offer a saving of as much as $1,157 over the average 15-year life of a refrigerator.

QUESTIONS

1. There is relatively little discussion of the costs to consumers of particular government regulations, despite the obvious costs of some kinds of legislation and consumer complaints regarding high prices. Why is this?

2. Do you think most consumers are aware of the costs *to them* of *specific* pieces of government legislation? If consumers had the option of paying higher costs for the things they buy with the certainty that they met government standards, or paying lower prices without governmental standards, which do you think they would choose? Should consumers be allowed this option?

3. What standards should be established to help decide if a particular item of legislation should be passed or not?

4. Weidenbaum calls for alternative methods of evaluating the need for and value of proposed legislation. Do you think something like cost/benefit analysis should be applied to proposed legislation? What problems do you see in trying to do cost/benefit analysis in this area? Do you think such analysis is likely to be done? Why or why not?

5. In the postscript Elsner suggests that if more rigorous energy standards were passed the less efficient but cheaper appliances would have to be taken off the market. Who would be hurt by this result? Who would benefit?

8
The law closes in on managers

Breaking the law has never been openly condoned by corporate executives. But until recently top managers rarely risked personal penalties if their employees were found guilty of illegal activities, such as price fixing. New laws and revised interpretations are changing this. Managers, including marketing managers, can no longer hide behind the corporation. They are being held personally liable for the misdoings of their employees and the corporation.

American managers are earning more than ever, but along with their traditional load and responsibilities, they face a new—and more perilous—burden. The shield that protects them from individual accountability for corporate acts of negligence and lawlessness seems far less impregnable than it used to be. Even now, managers at several levels—from chief executive officers to plant managers—are feeling the heat as new regulatory laws go on the books and established regulatory agencies take a harder line toward those who err. There are ominous signs that more prosecutions, accompanied by fines and even jail sentences, may be in the offing.

Directors have already been braced by the Securities and Exchange Commission and by the courts, mostly regarding their obligations to shareholders. Now it is the managers' turn to deal with the problems of ever-widening personal liability.

Executives have never been entirely free of legal liability growing out of their corporate duties: The electrical industry price-fixing case of a decade ago sent men to prison. But their obligations, as spelled out in the antitrust and securities laws, for instance, have become pretty well defined through the years. Now there are new regulations, enforced by such traditional agencies as the Justice Department and the SEC; new agencies, such as the Environmental Protection Agency (EPA), the Consumer Product Safety Commission (CPSC), and the Equal Employment Opportunity Commission (EEOC); and new laws, such as the Employee Retirement Income Security Act (ERISA) and the Occupational Safety and Health Act (OSHA).

It is all the more frightening because the black-and-white prohibitions of the past have suddenly given way to uncertain mandates. The new laws are often vague, the body of legal opinion not yet built up—and the potential penalties for transgression heavy.

For example, the Supreme Court ruled just last year [1975] in a case involving Acme Markets Inc. and its president, John R. Park, that an execu-

Source: Reprinted with permission from *Business Week,* May 10, 1976, pp. 110–16. Copyright © 1976 by McGraw-Hill, Inc.

The risks executives face under federal law

Agency	Year enforcement began	Complaint may name individual	Maximum individual penalty	Maximum corporate penalty	Private suit allowed under applicable statute
Internal Revenue Service	1862	Yes	$5,000, three years, or both	$10,000, 50% assessment, prosecution costs	No
Antitrust Division (Justice Dept.)	1890	Yes	$100,000, three years, or both	$1 million, injunction, divestiture	Yes
Food and Drug Administration	1907	Yes	$1,000, one year, or both for first offense; $10,000, three years, or both thereafter	$1,000 for first offense; $10,000 thereafter; seizure of condemned products	No
Federal Trade Commission	1914	Yes	Restitution, injunction	Restitution, injunction, divestiture, $10,000 per day for violation of rules, orders	No
Securities and Exchange Commission	1934	Yes	$10,000, two years, or both	$10,000, injunction	Yes
Equal Employment Opportunity Commission	1965	No		Injunction, back pay award, reinstatement	Yes
Office of Federal Contract Compliance	1965	No		Suspension, cancellation of contract	Yes
Environmental Protection Agency	1970	Yes	$25,000 per day, one year, or both for first offense; $50,000 per day, two years, or both thereafter	$25,000 per day, first offense; $50,000 per day thereafter; injunction	Yes
Occupational Safety and Health Administration	1970	No*	$10,000, six months, or both	$10,000	No
Consumer Product Safety Commission	1972	Yes	$50,000, one year, or both	$500,000	Yes
Office of Employee Benefits Security (Labor Dept.)	1975	Yes	$10,000, one year, or both; barring from future employment with plan; reimbursement	$100,000, reimbursement	Yes

* Except sole proprietorship.
Data: *Business Week*.

tive's liability for criminal conduct can extend to a business unit far below his direct supervision. In that case the president of the multibillion-dollar food chain was personally fined for failing to ensure that the company keep rats out of a Baltimore warehouse as required by law. And regulatory agencies seem to be preparing to build on that precedent. New FDA regulations that will become effective by yearend will require drug companies to pinpoint individuals responsible for quality control. "Many of the companies," a pharmaceutical industry official notes wryly, "are thinking about hiring a vice-president in charge of going to jail."

The point is serious even if the proposed title is not. Consider that within the past month:

The manager at an H. J. Heinz Co. plant in Tracy, Calif., received a suspended six-month sentence and summary probation after being cited by California state food and drug officials for unsanitary conditions in his plant.

A Minneapolis municipal judge ordered Illinois-based Lloyd A. Fry Roofing Co. to select one of its executives to serve a 30-day jail term after the judge ruled that odors coming from the company's Minneapolis plant violated the city's air pollution standards. Later the judge rescinded his action, but only because of a technicality—the company but not the individual officers had actually been indicted.

The Internal Revenue Service's intelligence division has recommended criminal proceedings against Braniff International Corp. for allegedly filing false income tax returns in 1970 and 1971 involving unlawful political contributions already disclosed. Commissioner Donald C. Alexander of the Internal Revenue Service, although declining comment on Braniff, says that the agency is investigating 30 major corporations for possible serious tax frauds and that criminal prosecutions of top executives may result.

"You shudder at the risk of innocent violation," says Chairman William B. Johnson, of IC Industries Inc. "You have to be very alert and conscientious. We have no interpretation of what the new pension law really means, for example, but we're supposed to be applying it right now."

For many executives, just keeping up with the regulations is becoming a wearisome chore. C. J. Gauthier, chairman and president of Northern Illinois Gas Co., in Aurora, Ill., says that he has been commuting to Washington at least one day out of every two weeks in recent months to deal with Federal Power Commission and Federal Energy Administration regulations. Charles J. Pilliod Jr., chairman and chief executive officer of Goodyear Tire & Rubber Co., of Akron, Ohio, estimates that he spends 25 percent of his time dealing with the increasing number of government regulations and forms.

WHAT NEXT?

But it is a feeling of uncertainty about what is to come that is making executives really nervous. Although few of the new regulatory agencies have moved against an individual manager as yet, several—such as the EPA and the CPSC—clearly have the power to do so. Well-established regulators such as the FDA are already busy prosecuting managers as well as corporations. The FDA took pains, in fact, to notify 175 heads of companies of alleged criminal violations in the last six months of 1975 alone. Couple such warnings with the Supreme Court ruling in the Park case, and it is easy to see why a Washington lawyer says the FDA has succeeded spectacularly at "executive consciousness raising."

Moreover, old Washington watchdogs like the SEC and the Antitrust Division of the Justice Department are, as always, on the prowl today for individual transgressors. And state regulatory bodies often act tougher than federal agencies, while local units try to outdo even the states. Fibreboard Corp., for example, claims that it will cost several million dollars more to comply with San Francisco Bay Area odor emissions standards than to comply with those of the state.

The peril does not end there. Much of the recent legislation setting up new agencies specifically allows companies and individuals to file private suits to collect damages, using the standards set forth in the acts.

Still more punitive legislation may be enacted in the wake of the recent corporate payoff scandal. Pending in the Senate, for example, is bill S.1, a codification of federal criminal laws, which would subject business executives to criminal penalties for a potentially revolutionary new offense called "reckless default." An officer would be personally subject to prosecution for failing to supervise properly employees who violated federal regulations.

"Too often," says Louis B. Schwartz, University of Pennsylvania law school professor and director of the National Commission on Reform of the Federal Criminal Laws, "the top executive officers escape when a company is prosecuted for failing to comply with federal regulations. They say, 'We didn't know anything about it,' and a vice-president will wind up in jail." If S.1 passes with the "reckless default" provision intact, says Schwartz, chief executive officers of companies charged with price-fixing would not be able to escape personal liability with the "I didn't know" excuse, as did chief executives of General Electric, Westinghouse, and Allis-Chalmers during the electrical equipment cases.

Such legislation clearly would go beyond the traditional personal legal liability of managers for fraud against the company or its stockholders or negligence in their stewardship of assets. But the national commission Schwartz headed recommended that S.1 go even further, giving trial judges the option of disqualifying executives from holding high-responsibility jobs in the future. A similar suggestion comes from Christopher D. Stone, professor of law at the University of Southern California and author of *Where the Law*

Ends: The Social Control of Corporate Behavior. Stone says that the law should not rely on the indirect effect of fines, citations, and the like, which he holds are mostly ineffective in making corporations more responsible. Rather, he says, it should "require direct management changes."

In Stone's view, the law should require companies to employ supervisors for "key tasks" in industries where there are potential safety, environmental, or health problems. If a law were broken, the supervisor would be the obvious target for the regulators. Drug companies, of course, already put a supervisor in charge of tests and changes of formulas for each drug under development.

Although such measures are not the solutions most executives would suggest, some managers agree that there is a need for more accountability. "Corporate officers have enjoyed a fair amount of immunity," says Bob S. Bridwell, financial vice-president of Houston-based CRS Design Associates Inc., a publicly held engineering design firm. "As a result, there has been a tendency on the part of a lot of executives to relax—to be less conscious of the responsibilities that should go along with the rewards of a management job."

Bridwell points out that European countries have long emphasized the individual responsibility of businessmen, and, indeed, in recent months British and French executives have been horrified by a rash of indictments in which top executives are being held legally liable—and sometimes are being sent to jail—for on-the-job factory accidents. In fact, legislation is expected to be drafted this fall in France that would specify that top managers bear formal responsibility for worker safety—a burden now borne mostly by low-ranking foremen.

Although U.S. executives almost never go to jail for crimes of their companies, there is increasingly the likelihood that some at least will be indicted, convicted, and fined. Much of the heat is coming from such older federal agencies as the Antitrust Division, the SEC, the IRS, and the FDA. But three newer agencies—the EPA, the CPSC, and the administrators of ERISA—may also begin to make things hot for individual managers.

Just how far regulations can push personal liability has already been demonstrated by the FDA. The basis for such personal liability is contained in the Food, Drug and Cosmetic Act. Similar liabilities are set forth in other federal statutes, including the Hazardous Substances Act. These laws can impose criminal sanctions on corporate officials responsible for overseeing such areas as sanitation if, because of their inadequate supervision, the corporation violates health or safety requirements.

Although the Food and Drug Act has been on the books for decades, executives in large companies never worried much about their potential liability until last June, when the Supreme Court affirmed the conviction of Acme Markets' Park. Park argued that after receiving a warning from the FDA he delegated the job of cleaning out the rats to responsible subordinates and that there was nothing more that he could personally have done. Acme, a

GOVERNMENT WATCHDOGS BARE THEIR TEETH

Aside from the special case of the Food and Drug Administration, the threat of individual liability for corporate decisions comes chiefly from four older federal agencies and three newer ones. Among the areas of exposure:

The Justice Department

This agency has always tried to get jail sentences for company officials actually involved in price-fixing, but now—armed with new laws—it is redoubling its efforts. In 1974 Congress substantially increased the penalties for violating the Sherman Act to a maximum individual fine of $100,000 and a maximum jail term of three years. The maximum sentence had been one year. The change automatically makes the crime a felony rather than a misdemeanor. Although price-fixing almost never draws anything close to the old one-year maximum sentence, the new felony status triggers state penalties that can range from loss of voting rights to expulsion as an officer of a country club that holds a liquor license.

The Antitrust Division is spending more time these days on price-fixing cases, with at least 90 grand juries now hearing testimony on them. "We have every intention of seeking felony indictments and recommending prison sentences for individuals convicted of price-fixing violations," says Thomas E. Kauper, assistant attorney general in charge of the Antitrust Division.

Furthermore, after several years in which employment slots were frozen at 629, the Antitrust Division's job total rose to 712 in fiscal 1975 and 856 this year [1976].

The FTC

Staff growth at the Federal Trade Commission has been much less marked than at the Justice Department but what resources the commission has are being marshaled increasingly for antitrust activities. Both agencies are making more use of in-house economists to determine where in the economy competition is not working and to decide which cases to target in on.

The SEC

The Securities and Exchange Commission always moves against individual officers as well as companies when that is warranted. But the enforcement staff of 780 will grow only slightly this year, and the special enforcement division task force on "management fraud"—which handles the foreign and domestic political payments cases—will still number hardly more than a dozen. That is why, as it has done in other types of cases, the SEC will try to settle most of the corporate bribery cases with consent decrees, requiring among other things that companies submit to special investigation by outside directors.

"We have to have consents, otherwise the thing would not run," says Stanley Sporkin, the SEC's enforcement chief. If the commission had to litigate every case, its force of trial lawyers would dry up fast. Still, contemplating the potential glut of corporate payments cases ahead, Sporkin says one way to cope with it may be "a couple of good strong litigations."

The IRS

There is intensifying scrutiny of corporations and their executives at the Internal Revenue Service, too. Not only is it likely that criminal prosecutions of executives will grow out of the bribery cases now being investigated, but managers may also find themselves increasingly subject to civil suits as a result of a tactic increasingly used by the IRS. And the agency plans to go after both the executives responsible for corporate tax violations and the companies, as well. "It is true you can't put a corporation in jail, but you can assess corporations a 50 percent civil penalty for tax fraud," says IRS Commissioner Donald C. Alexander. "We intend to use that tool." As the IRS presumably begins to collect such penalties, Alexander thinks, there will be an upsurge of stockholder suits against the responsible executives to recover damages in behalf of the corporation.

ERISA, EPA, CPSC

The newer agencies have yet to make much use of their power to haul executives into court, but just the fact that they have the authority to do so is enough to give many executives qualms.

The Employee Retirement Income Security Act (ERISA) of 1974, which is administered jointly by the Labor Department and the IRS, provides for fines of up to $5,000 and jail terms up to a year for "willful" violation of the reporting and disclosure provisions. A key feature of the law is the requirement that those who manage pension fund money do so prudently. The trouble is that no one yet knows what that means—and will not until the courts begin to rule on suits charging managers with imprudence. Although it is the outside managers of pension funds who have been most concerned

about their liability under the legislation, company executives have fiduciary responsibilities under the law, too. The act's complexity and the blizzard of ERISA regulation make this worrisome.

The Environmental Protection Agency (EPA), established in 1970, has managed to settle most of its compliance problems with administrative actions and has rarely gone to court. But the agency is empowered to take managers as well as companies to court. Moreover, the EPA will administer the toxic substances law that is expected to be passed by Congress in some form this year. The government has been trying to empower the agency to remove hazardous chemicals from the market in the same way the Food and Drug Administration can remove food or drugs. EPA officials plan to enforce the new law by seizing illegal chemicals, and they profess no interest in jailing managers. But bills before Congress contain criminal penalties of up to a year in jail as well as fines of up to $25,000 a day.

The Consumer Product Safety Commission (CPSC), established just four years ago, maintains that it can cite individual officers in litigation and has already cited them in cases that did not or have not yet moved past the administrative stage. Two years ago, in a matter involving an attempt to enforce a product code for refrigerators, the CPSC sought an order against Kelvinator Commercial Products Inc. and specifically cited the chairman of the board. Eventually the product issue was dropped, but not before the administrative law judge in the case ruled that naming an individual would be more likely to assure compliance than citing only the corpo-

ration. In a more recent consent ac-   so also named Donald M. Kendall,
tion, still at an internal level, the CPSC   chairman of Wilson's parent com-
tried to force Wilson Sporting Goods   pany, PepsiCo Inc. The company filed
Co. to comply with a standard for   a motion to dismiss Kendall from the
aluminum baseball bats and in doing   motion, but the judge denied it.

Philadelphia-based chain of 874 outlets with nearly $2 billion in annual sales,
then had 15 other warehouses. The Court rejected Park's argument.

INCREASING THE PRESSURE

The Park case has increased pressure on food company officials, and will
affect drug makers next. In March the FDA proposed a set of regulations
governing "good manufacturing practices" (GMPs), which, among other
things, require each drug manufacturer to establish clear lines of authority for
quality control of production lines. Due to take effect by the end of the year,
the regulations require quality control officials to submit detailed written reports of product or manufacturing deficiencies to top management. The FDA
explained that it is "essential for appropriate responsible management personnel to be aware of possible failures of drug products to meet established
specifications." In other words, top management will no longer be able to
claim ignorance of discoveries that subordinates make.

In some cases the FDA would now rather expose a chief executive officer
to personal penalties than enjoin his company from future wrongdoing, as has
been the traditional practice. Since 1972, for example, the FDA has been
considering whether it should seek an injunction against the practices of
Travenol Laboratories Inc. in connection with the production of intravenous
fluids. The FDA decided not to go forward when it received a letter in which
Travenol's chairman, William B. Graham, accepted future responsibility personally for rectifying the problems—in effect, putting himself up as collateral.

In the coming months, the potential for personal liability will spread to
CEOs in other medical areas—specifically in laboratory testing and medical
device manufacturing. Several hundred medical devices currently on the
market would be subject to a "premarket testing" procedure under a bill that
has just emerged from a Congressional conference committee and is awaiting
final passage. The bill would subject CEOs and other responsible managers to
criminal penalties for marketing such devices as cardiac pacemakers and
defibrilators that seriously violate FDA regulations.

The FDA is also speeding up the development of "good laboratory practice" standards as a result of the G. D. Searle & Co. case. FDA inspectors
charged the Skokie (Ill.) drug company with juggling results of tests on a series
of new drugs. Claiming that it has uncovered evidence that unnamed persons
were pressured into falsifying test data to confirm earlier incorrect tests, the

FDA has forced Searle to carry various warning labels on packages of the drugs. Daniel C. Searle, chief executive officer, denies that his company committed any fraud. "No facts were developed supporting any conclusion of fraud. No facts support any conclusion of misrepresentation, but errors of various kinds did in fact exist. Deficiencies in procedural controls were identified," Searle says. A corporate shake-up and new quality control executives were announced early this month.

But the FDA is convinced that the facts are more serious and has asked the Justice Department to convene a grand jury to investigate whether fraud charges should be brought against the Searle managers and lab technicians who signed data sheets that are alleged to have been falsified.

GROWING PAPERWORK

Of course, this ferment in the drug and food industries stems in part from a specific statute (and a broad court interpretation of it) that gives prosecutors sweeping power to go after managers. By its terms, the statute cannot be extended to other fields without Congressional authorization, such as that contained in S.1. But at least one corporate general counsel believes that courts may adapt the principle to similar situations. A company president, he says, who fails to read his chief engineer's report about a product defect may find himself facing personal liability, at least in civil lawsuits.

The new liability posed by regulation—to both their companies and themselves—is forcing managers to take compliance seriously, and it is complicating their lives. The myriad of rules and regulations that appear daily in the densely printed *Federal Register* is consuming more of the scarce time of top officials, and taxing the mental agility of staff specialists, who often have to comply with contradictory requirements.

According to Robert J. Brotje Jr., vice-president and treasurer of Champion Spark Plug Co., in Toledo, the company now files more than 500 reports to some 15 bureaus and agencies of the federal government and 2,500 other reports to local and state agencies across the country. Raymond F. Good, president of Heinz U.S.A., cites the requirement that he sign annually 25 copies of an alcohol control document for the U.S. Agriculture Department, "stating that our vinegar is not used for alcoholic purposes." Kenneth W. Anderson, senior vice-president for finance of Dallas-based Campbell Taggart Inc., an international commercial baking firm, complains that "in the last 10 years the paperwork has more than tripled."

In many companies, legal staffs have doubled to handle compliance problems. Heinz is increasing its legal staff 30 percent this year to handle the additional work generated by agency regulations. "There's more need for me to seek advice from lawyers than ever before," says Good. T. L. Austin Jr., chairman of Texas Utilities Co., says, "We've got more lawyers than we've got kilowatt hours."

But staff growth also includes more specialized compliance offices. At

Deere & Co., the Moline (Ill.) manufacturer of farm equipment, which has $2.5 billion annual sales, the office of Charles W. Toney, director of minority relations, has grown from a staff of two in 1972 to eight now, and it spends more than $1 million annually on EEOC compliance matters. To avoid problems with the Agriculture Department and the FDA, Heinz U.S.A. employs a former marine drill sergeant with thorough knowledge of the applicable regulations to make unannounced inspection tours of all Heinz factories and warehouses.

Gates Rubber Co. tries to anticipate trouble by running its own inspection programs parallel to OSHA's and other agencies. "We follow the same procedures," says H. D. Harris, engineering vice-president. "And we establish a fine for violations, though it's symbolic."

Executives often feel particularly vulnerable because many rules are vague or so complex as to be unreadable. "There's so much detail in ERISA," complains Leonard Savoie, vice-president and controller of Clark Equipment Co. in Buchanan, Mich., "that I really don't have a good grasp on all the requirements that are laid out. I just haven't got the time."

Moreover, even the most conscientious manager can fall into the trap of conflicting rules enforced by different agencies. Good of Heinz U.S.A. cites one instance when the company followed an FPC order to "turn down the lights, you're using too much power," only to be told by OSHA, "Turn up the lights, you are creating a safety hazard."

Companies have generally tried to shield their officers from the direct effects of liability by agreeing to indemnify them against any expenses— including fines, court costs, and attorneys' fees. The Delaware corporation law permits corporations to do so even for criminal matters as long as the officer "acted in good faith and in a manner he reasonably believed to be in or not opposed to the best interests of the corporation." Even if found guilty, the officer's defense costs may be reimbursed if he "had no reasonable cause to believe his conduct was unlawful."

But officers are not automatically shielded. Armco Steel Corp., for example, refuses to help with the legal expenses of any employee involved in price-fixing. That meant Harry H. Gray, retired assistant manager of Armco's Southwestern area sales district, had to pay a $5,000 fine and $15,000 in attorneys' fees out of his own pocket when he pleaded no contest to a 1974 federal price-fixing charge.

SHYING FROM D&O

Most large corporations do buy directors and officers liability (D&O) insurance. Until recently, securing such insurance and obtaining payments under it was relatively routine. Now, however, because of the increasing frequency of suits against corporate officers, insurance companies have become edgy.

Lloyds of London, for example, is defending a suit filed last year by Flintkote Co. to test under what circumstances an insurer need not make payment in a criminal case. Flintkote and two of its officers pleaded no contest to Justice Department criminal price-fixing charges, and the officers sought reimbursement of legal costs amounting to some $870,000. Lloyds balked, claiming that it is contrary to public policy to pay the costs of defendants who have not been acquitted. The suit is still pending, but depending on the outcome, a major part of D&O coverage may become vastly more difficult and costly to obtain.

Meanwhile, managers want more coverage. Guido A. Rothrauff Jr., senior vice president and general counsel for Eastern Gas & Fuel Associates in Boston, says: "Managers do perceive a threat. So even though they are indemnified by this company, we are considering taking out new liability insurance for some 70 or 80 officers and directors."

Businessmen accept that they cannot turn back the clock, but they are pushing for changes in present laws that may at least put a rein on new regulations. One proposal would enable Congress to veto more easily individual regulations of the agencies it has created. Many managers like this idea because they are convinced that Congress never intended the agencies to go nearly as far as they have. Another would, in effect, require Congress to "reestablish" agencies at periodic intervals, perhaps every five years. Presumably that would put the regulators out of business unless they could justify their function.

Meanwhile, businessmen are trying to deal as best they can with what often seem to them increasingly hostile regulators. A decade ago, says a Houston executive, businessmen felt comfortable going to the SEC or the IRS to discuss what was proper and what was improper. "Now the agencies too often seem to presume guilt as they ask questions," he laments.

Many managers sense this antagonism in many of the government officials they deal with, and it worries them. "They are less likely to work with you now," says John E. Watson, vice-president for gas and regulatory affairs at Houston-based Mitchell Energy Corp., a subsidiary of Mitchell Energy & Development Corp. "Their approach seems to be, 'We are the controller, and you are the regulated.' I'm afraid this is an era of suspicion."

QUESTIONS

1. Should the top executives or middle managers, or both, be held criminally liable for violations of laws governing the conduct of business? If you feel that only middle managers should be held liable, how do you reconcile this with the fact that they are likely to lose their jobs if their units' performance is under par?

2. Should the marketing manager go to jail if the products the firm produces fail to meet consumer expectations? (Assume that the marketing manager has responsibility for the total marketing effort of the company.)

3. The reading suggests several ways to make the regulatory agencies more responsible to Congress, including allowing Congress to "veto" specific

regulations of agencies and to force the agencies to reestablish the need for their existence every five years. Do you think such laws would be a good idea? Why or why not?

4. If legislators had to make a choice between regulations establishing civil penalties (such that the injured consumer could obtain payment for his injury) or criminal penalties (such that responsible executives of offending firms would go to prison), what recommendation would you make to these legislators? Why?

Part 2

Selecting target markets

Marketing strategy planning consists of two steps: (1) selection of a target market, and (2) development of an appropriate marketing mix for that target market. The readings in Part 2 are concerned with the first step—selecting a target market. Part 3 focuses on the second step.

Two important aspects in selecting a target market are what techniques should be used to identify possible target markets, and what dimensions should be included when segmenting a market. One aspect deals with methodology and the other with the variables involved.

Most of the readings in this part are concerned with methodology, although several discuss the relevance of various kinds of dimensions. The first article focuses on demographics (in the soft drink industry), while others place emphasis on attitudes, needs, psychographic and life-style variables, and benefits sought. Taken together, these articles should deepen your understanding of market segmentation.

Understanding target markets is vital to marketing strategy planning, so careful evaluation of the different points of view in these articles should help you do a better job of segmenting markets and planning marketing mixes.

9
The graying of the
soft-drink industry

Markets and market segments are not static. They constantly change. This article from Business Week discusses
the changing market for soft drinks. It points out that
changes in the market, in the United States and abroad, are
related to both changing demographics and the behavior
of customers in the market. The article also highlights the
strategies being followed by Coca-Cola to adjust to these
changes.

For at least a generation, the United States has given a special blessing to
producers of soft drinks: a bountiful supply of consumers between the ages of
13 and 24. Today there are nearly 49 million of them, and they are the
lifeblood of the soft-drink industry. On average, each of them consumes 823
cans of soda pop each year, while the average for all age groups is only 547
cans.

But during the next decade that key market will shrink, and by 1985 there
will be some 4 million fewer persons in the 13-to-24 age group. And those 4
million missing persons would have consumed some 3.3 billion cans of soft
drinks annually [see Figure 1].

Soft-drink companies will not be the only business affected. Few industries
in the coming years will escape the impact of this shift in the demographics of
the U.S. population. The baby-food industry has already felt its effects, and its
leaders have hurried to diversify into other food lines; one of them has even
bought an insurance company. Some industries—pharmaceutical producers,
for instance—stand to benefit from an aging population. Others—tobacco
producers, record makers, and fast-food outlets among them—will suffer in
the next few years. Right now it is the turn of the soft-drink producers to learn
how to get by in an aging nation.

The company that could feel the sharpest impact of the population change
is the kingpin of them all: Coca-Cola Co. Coke generates 95 percent of both
its $3 billion in revenues and its $285 million in net income from soft drinks
and other beverages. Soft drinks alone are estimated to account for 75 percent of sales and 85 percent of pretax earnings. The No. 2 producer, PepsiCo
Inc., is less exposed. It has diversified widely in the past decade into sporting
goods, a van line, and snack foods, so that today the beverage business
accounts for only 46 percent of its sales. And although the others in the

Source: Reprinted with permission from Business Week, May 23, 1977, pp. 68–72.
Copyright, © 1977, McGraw-Hill, Inc.

Figure 1
Key problems for the soft-drink producers

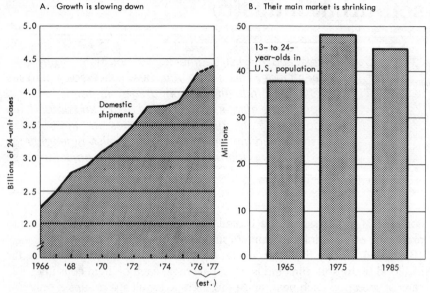

A. Growth is slowing down

B. Their main market is shrinking

Source: Data, Part A, *Beverage World*, National Soft Drink Association, *Business Week* estimate; Part B, U.S. Census Bureau.

industry, Royal Crown, Seven-Up, and Dr Pepper, are more heavily dependent on beverage sales, they are much smaller than the leaders and may be able to hang on by beefing up their still limited distribution networks.

Coca-Cola professes to be unperturbed by the certainty that the key segment of its market will shrink by almost 8 percent in the coming decade, compared with a 27 percent increase in that segment during the decade just passed. "We're not disconcerted or discouraged by the demographic trends," says Albert E. Killeen, Coca-Cola's executive vice president for marketing. "It means that we have to do a better job."

Certainly the company is not about to lose its No. 1 position in the soft-drink business. Its sales and earnings far outrank those of the competition [Table 1], and its years of skillful marketing on a global scale give it a decisive edge. But though Coke chooses publicly to ignore the impact of the population shift, there is solid evidence that it is priming its mammoth marketing operation to compensate for the shrinkage of its core market. Among the strategies taking shape at the company's Atlanta headquarters:

A major push in foreign markets. Overseas business now brings in 44 percent of Coke's revenues and 55 percent of its earnings. But to stay on the growth curve the company figures it must develop foreign markets far more effectively.

Table 1
Ranking the soft-drink producers, 1976

Company	Sales (in millions)	Net income (in millions)	Beverage sales as percent of total
Coca-Cola	$3,032.8	$285.0	95%
PepsiCo	2,727.5	136.0	48
Royal Crown	282.0	17.3	78
Seven-Up	233.3	24.8	93
Dr Pepper..........	151.8	15.5	100

Data: Investors Management Sciences.

More diversification at home. Coca-Cola bought Taylor Wine Co. last year for some $90 million worth of stock. Now the company is talking about acquiring at least one more wine producer to bolster Taylor's product line and markets.

A big expansion of its Houston-based Foods Division. Coke has the avowed objective of boosting the division's revenues from their current estimated $600 million to $1 billion within five years. The Foods Division is already a major producer of beverages such as orange juice, coffee, and tea.

A slow and careful shift in U.S. advertising for Coke itself, the world's top-selling soft drink. With a 26 percent domestic market share, Coke already outsells PepsiCo's entire soft-drink line. The aim is to hold onto more of those current 13- to 24-year-old customers as they grow older.

Underscoring Coke's attempt to boost its overseas soft-drink sales, the company went through a management restructuring late last year. Until then, Coca-Cola Export Corp. handled all the company's overseas operations, while Coca-Cola USA looked after the domestic market. Now Coke has divided its world into three parts, with an executive vice-president in charge of each. Donald R. Keough oversees operations in the U.S. and Central and South America, Claus M. Hale looks after Europe, Africa, Southwest Asia, and the Indian subcontinent, and Ian R. Wilson is in charge of Canada, the Far East, and the Pacific.

"The growth potential out there is unlimited," says Chairman J. Paul Austin. And to take advantage of it, he decided that a different viewpoint was needed. "Instead of there being an offshore business and a domestic business, there is a world market," Austin adds.

WAITING FOR THE MARKETS

In the United States, with 6 percent of the world's population, Coke has 581 bottlers, 10 of them company-owned. In the 134 other countries around the world in which Coke sells, it has about 750 bottlers, 16 of them company-owned. By some estimates, soft-drink consumption outside the United States probably averages no more than about 10 cans per person annually. And the demographics overseas are, of course, radically different.

"If one talks about zero population growth in the United States, we're talking about a population problem in much of the rest of the world," says Wilson. "In the underdeveloped countries you've got 50 percent of your population under 25."

Population in the underdeveloped countries is projected to increase by 72 percent, to 4.9 billion, by the year 2000. It may be a while before many more of those people can acquire the discretionary income that will permit them to purchase soda pop and other nonessentials. But by the time they do, Coca-Cola intends to make sure that they prefer Coke. Efforts are now under way to imprint the brand name on the consciousness of some of those countries even though the product itself is not always available. Last year, for example, Coke launched a program promoting soccer clinics and soccer games for youngsters in Africa and the Middle East. The company will spend about $5 million over the next few years on this promotion even though distribution of Coke itself in many areas is minuscule or nonexistent.

It is certainly nonexistent in much of the Middle East. Coca-Cola was ousted from the Arab countries in 1967 after it awarded a bottling franchise in Israel. Regularly for the past five years, Coke executives have been shuttling back and forth from Atlanta to Cairo, trying to persuade Egypt and other Arab nations to stop boycotting the company.

Three months ago, Austin met with Egyptian President Anwar el-Sadat, and while Austin refuses to say what was discussed at the meeting, the ice does appear to be breaking. Coca-Cola President J. Lucian Smith indicates that the company may be on its way back to Egypt. "Some negotiations are now going on, and they're sort of at a midpoint," he says.

One means by which Coke may get back into the Arab world is through two of its subsidiaries, the Foods Division and Aqua-Chem Inc., a Milwaukee-based manufacturer of water purification equipment, which Coca-Cola bought in 1970. Both these Coca-Cola units possess technology that is of vital interest to Arab countries with plentiful oil revenues to spend: the Food Division's expertise in agriculture (it operates vast citrus groves in Florida) and Aqua-Chem's knowhow in water desalination.

Aqua-Chem is more than just a wedge to open the way to soft-drink sales in the Middle East. Coca-Cola is looking for a contract for its Milwaukee subsidiary. "Saudi Arabia has a plan to spend $5 billion on desalting over the next five years," says John K. Collings Jr., Aqua-Chem's chairman. "All we'd have to get is a small piece of that, and we would be very busy."

The Middle East may be a hard market for Coke to reopen, but the Soviet Union is perhaps Coca-Cola's biggest frustration. The company has seen its main competitor, Pepsi, establish a beachhead in Russia, thanks in part to Pepsi Chairman Donald M. Kendall's close relationship with former President Nixon.

THE BACK DOOR TO RUSSIA

At present, Pepsi operates only one plant in the Soviet Union, on the Black Sea at Novorossisk. "Our problem in the Soviet Union is production," says Victor A. Bonomo, president of Pepsi-Cola Div., PepsiCo's soft-drink marketer. "Our plant is about the size of the one we have serving New Brunswick, N.J., but it supplies the entire Soviet Union." In the next few years, however, Pepsi is scheduled to open plants in Moscow, Leningrad, Yevpatoriya, and Tallinn.

As in the Middle East, Coke is trying a roundabout route to establish itself in the Soviet Union. In 1974 Coke and the Russians agreed to exchange food-processing and water-purification technologies. Since then, Coke executives and Soviet officials have also talked many times about getting soft drinks into that country. "Where we aren't in business, we want people to know how we do business, which we're proud of," says Austin. "And we're perfectly willing to bide our time with the main product." But while Coke negotiates, Pepsi is establishing itself with the Soviet consumer.

Although the Middle East and the Soviet Union still have Coke locked out, the rest of the world is another matter. In the next decade, Coke looks for substantial growth overseas in the areas where the company is already well established. "There's a lot of horizontal expansion still possible," says Halle, executive vice-president for Europe, Africa, Southwest Asia, and the Indian subcontinent. As likely targets, Halle cites Bulgaria, Czechoslovakia, Hungary, Poland, and Yugoslavia. Combined, these countries have only 15 Coke bottling plants, compared with 116 in West Germany alone. Next month, Coke will begin operations in Portugal, culminating an effort that began 20 years ago.

Even the developed nations outside North America show plenty of promise to Halle. Supermarkets have yet to develop in some of these areas—and in the United States, 55 percent of soft drinks are sold in supermarkets. "So all that growth is waiting for us," says Halle.

Keough, executive vice-president in charge of Latin America, sees major potential for growth there, too. Taking Brazil as an example, Keough points out that the country's overall average per-capita consumption of Coca-Cola amounts to only 47 cans annually, while in sophisticated Rio de Janeiro alone, it is 150 to 160 cans. "In that one country," he says, "you have a developed country, a developing country, and an underdeveloped country. The only thing that's going to hold back our growth there for the next several decades is going to be a lack of machinery, trucks, and equipment."

But, as many multinational corporations have found in the past few years, there are perils in heavy reliance on foreign sales when currencies are fluctuating sharply and governments are growing less stable in an increasing number of nations. Coca-Cola, though, believes that it can cope with such problems better than many other companies because of the way it does business. Corey R. Smith, Coke's assistant treasurer, maintains that sharp swings in currency values have had little effect on Coke's results. "We are so diversified geographically in about 135 countries that when you have minuses in one country, you're having pluses in another," he says.

Nationalism can, of course, cost Coke valuable markets, as has happened in the Middle East. But because the company has exported its franchised-bottler concept around the world, limiting its own capital investments, such losses are minimized. Only about 2 percent of its overseas bottling plants are company-owned. Almost all the others are in the hands of nationals of the countries in which they operate. Coke also controls the raw materials (the syrup formula) that goes into making pop. Without it, no product exactly like Coke can be made.

MEANWHILE, BACK HOME

While Coca-Cola is high on overseas growth potential, it is not settling for flat results in the U.S. market. But Coke, along with other soft-drink producers, did see one of its plans for selling to an aging population derailed this year when the Food and Drug Administration proposed a ban on saccharin. Until then, the soft-drink producers felt they had a sure bet in their lines of low-calorie, saccharin-sweetened diet drinks. Sales of these diet sodas have been growing at a pace of 13 percent annually, about double the annual rate for colas and other carbonated beverages laced with sugar. And the bulk of sales were being made to the over-24 age groups.

By July, unless Congress acts or the FDA changes its mind, the industry must come up with a substitute for saccharin or reformulate its diet drinks, using small quantities of sugar. Some industry analysts think that a move to sugar could cut unit sales of diet drinks by half. "There are no other calorie-free sweeteners available, so we intend to market lower-calorie products," says Pepsi's Bonomo. "It remains to be seen how well these will be accepted by the consumer. We think there'll be some level of acceptance, but it's hard to tell how much."

With or without a true diet line, the soft-drink producers are trying to win wider markets among older population groups. Keough, who is in charge of Coke's U.S. market as well as Latin America, maintains that company data bear out the contention that older consumers are gradually increasing their consumption of soft drinks. His claim is backed by a study made by American Can Co. in 1970, which shows that while people over 45 drank less soda than any other age group, their per-capita consumption of 243 cans that year was greater than the 200 cans per capita for all age groups of 10 years earlier.

One reason more older people are drinking colas, Keough says, is that Coke's sales efforts are penetrating the youth market much more deeply than before, so more people are continuing their soft-drink habit as they grow older. For this reason, Coke intends to direct the bulk of its hard-sell advertising (on which it spent $144.2 million last year) toward the youth market.

But there is a change in the pitch of Coca-Cola's ads. Its current campaign stresses the theme "Coke adds life," and adults are appearing increasingly in its commercials. "This particular theme is adaptable to any age segment of our society," says Keough. "Coke can add life to a retired persons' picnic."

A changing lifestyle helps, too, he maintains. "A 50-year-old woman who's out there playing tennis three times a week is totally different from a 50-year-old woman of the 1940s or 1950s," he says. Bonomo of Pepsi believes in the same approach. "The Pepsi generation is anything from 13 to 75," he says. "It's a state of mind rather than a physical age."

FAST DRINKS FROM FAST FOODS

Changes in eating habits among U.S. consumers also give the soft-drink producers a break. The mushrooming growth of the fast-food industry in the past decade has helped boost soda sales. Here Coca-Cola has benefited more than its competitors because it dominates the soda fountain market, primarily through sales to such fast-food chains as McDonald's, Burger King, and Pizza Hut.

There is some danger, though, that the fast-food companies and restaurants, in their constant efforts to improve margins, will integrate backward, producing their own lines of soft drinks. Howard Johnson Co. did that in the 1960s, installing its own HoJo soda fountains and dropping its contracts with the major soft-drink makers. Robert J. Gaudrault, president of Friendly Ice Cream Corp., of North Wilbraham, Mass., which operates 590 fast-food outlets in the Northeast, says the company has been making and selling its own sodas much of the time since it was founded 44 years ago, despite continued efforts by the major producers to find room for their products on Friendly's counters. Just six months ago, says Franklin Feiler, Friendly's director of public relations, Coke tried to make a deal with his company, but after analyzing it, Friendly decided it did not make economic sense. "We have done this before, and it always comes out in favor of our own soft drinks," he says.

While McDonald's says that so far it has no plans to switch to its own line of sodas, the danger is always there. As Keough concedes: "We can't control what our customers or potential customers do."

A further uncontrollable that worries Coca-Cola and other soft-drink makers is the possibility of another wild jump in the price of sugar like the one in 1974 that drove sugar prices from 10 cents to 72 cents a pound. At that time, Coke and the other producers passed the added costs through to the consumer, but consumers resisted so fiercely that industrywide unit sales flattened out. In some markets, such as New York City, a six-pack of Coke cost more than a six-pack of beer. "I've always wondered at what level we would meet price resistance," said one Coke executive at the time. "And now I've found out."

Coke would like the sugar producing and consuming nations to agree on ceiling and floor prices for the commodity so growers could get a consistent fair price and users would not be gouged. John M. Mount, Coke's vice-president and director of purchasing, figures that a range of 10 to 20 cents a pound between ceiling and floor would be proper. "In the middle of that range, the market would operate on its own," he says. But if the price approached the bottom of the range, he says, stockpiles would be built up to push prices up, and those stocks would enter the market if prices approached the top of the range.

As a slight hedge against a further price escalation, Mount says, Coke has made "a small equity investment" along with Mitsui Sugar Co. of Japan and Tate & Lyle of Britain in a sugar mill in Swaziland, in southern Africa. This plant could not supply Coke's needs, of course, but he suggests that Coke might get into the sugar business in a bigger way if prices gyrate wildly again. "It shows we are looking at these types of things for protection," he says.

The soaring cost of sugar had more than just a temporary effect on Coca-Cola's business. When soft-drink prices jumped, many U.S. consumers switched to cheaper alternatives, particularly powdered soft drinks. These had been on the market for years, but until 1974 they were considered a children's summertime beverage.

INTO THE POWDERED-MIX RACE

Since 1974, sales of powdered soft drinks have surged from $200 million annually to $700 million, though their annual growth rate has now slowed to a more modest 13 to 15 percent. Most of the money being spent on the powdered mixes formerly went for canned and bottled soft drinks.

The surge in demand for powdered soft drinks swelled the number of companies in the field. Initially the market was the private domain of General Foods Corp.'s Kool Aid and Borden Inc.'s Wyler's. One of the relative newcomers is RJR Foods Inc., the R. J. Reynolds Industries subsidiary.

RJR introduced Hawaiian Punch mix in five flavors, and in less than a year, after it spent about $10 million for advertising, volume mushroomed to more than $70 million. "We feel many people who abandoned soda pop when prices soared have stayed with the mixes even though soda prices have since settled," says Robert L. Remke, chairman of RJR Foods.

The powdered mixes have been marketed from both price and quality standpoints. "An 8-ounce cola costs 11 cents, while you can mix your own powdered drink for 4.8 cents," says Remke. He also claims that in the past few years, the quality of mixes has greatly improved and that the industry has been able to position mixes from a children's drink to a family beverage.

Seeing its market chipped away, Coca-Cola is now introducing a mix of its own. Its Hi–C will compete not only with its soft-drink line but also with its Hi–C canned beverage. Some in the powdered-drink industry think that Coke is too late. "Coca-Cola's primary mistake was coming along with a me-too product," says one food company president. "General Foods, Borden, and Reynolds already have this market locked up. If Coke had come along with a cola mix, they might have had something. But this one is going to cut into their canned Hi–C."

Coke, however, does not agree that its entry is too late. And the company is now planning to extend the Hi–C line even further. The latest extension is Hi–C noncarbonated, nonfruit beverage that will sell for slightly less than the traditional canned beverage. Coke's Foods Division will begin test-marketing the new version late this month, offering five flavors and positioning the beverage in supermarkets near the soft-drink sections.

Ira C. Herbert, former vice-president of marketing for Coca-Cola USA and now president of the Foods Division, agrees that the new line, to be directed toward the family and not just children, is quite similar in appeal to Coke's Fanta line of flavored drinks. "It might well cannibalize 20 percent of the Fanta line, but if you end up with 180 percent, the total business will be larger than the one you started with," he says.

Such talk of cannibalizing one of the company's own product lines, particularly a soft drink, would have been heresy at Coca-Cola as recently as 10 years ago, when soda pop reigned as absolute king. Today its crown is slightly tilted, and the company is scrambling to market new products to old consumers whose tastes are changing with age.

QUESTIONS

1. Baby foods, record manufacturers, and fast-food outlets were mentioned in the article as other industries that are likely to suffer along with soft drinks as the country feels the impact of a lower birth rate. Can you think of some other industries that are likely to really be hurt by having fewer customers? What industries are likely to benefit as the older segment of the population becomes larger?

2. Are there segmentation opportunities in the soft-drink market? (Note: What competitors are doing might suggest possibilities.)

3. The changing proportions of people in the various age categories is just one demographic measure. Others include geographic distribution of the population, income distribution, and occupational patterns. For example, the fastest growing part of the country is the South, or the "sun belt." What industries do you think will be hurt by the numbers of people moving to the sun belt? Which industries do you think will be helped?

4. Coca-Cola is combating the loss of its major market, in part, by diversifying into a variety of other businesses. From a societal standpoint, should a company that has been as successful as Coke be allowed to expand into other product areas? Isn't such expansion likely to interfere with the opportunities of other firms to be successful, especially if Coke uses marketing capabilities developed in the marketing of Coke?

*5. Is or was Coca-Cola "myopic" about its opportunities, as suggested in Levitt (Reading 4)?

---

* Question relates concepts in this and other readings.

10
Measures of brand attitude can be used to predict buying behavior

John Pavasars and William D. Wells

The nature of attitudes and the effects they have on buying behavior have received a great deal of attention in the marketing literature in the past several years. But there has also been some confusion about the meaning of attitudes and their relation to buying behavior. This article does a good job of clarifying the ways the terms have been used and suggesting how an understanding of attitudes can help in planning marketing strategies.

Can measures of brand attitudes be used to predict buying behavior? That question has been asked so many times and answered so differently by so many investigators that the real answer has got to be "it depends." It depends, mainly upon three things: Exactly what one means by the terms 1. "attitude" and 2. "predict," and 3. what events are allowed to intercede between the measurement of the attitude and the observation of the buying behavior.

1. THE MEANING OF "ATTITUDE"

In its original social-psychology usage, attitude was defined as "an emotionalized predisposition to respond, positively or negatively, to an object or class of objects." "Emotionalized" separates "attitudes" from "opinions," "preferences," and "intentions" concepts that have much less affective bite. "Predisposition" here assumes attitudes are more or less stable inner states that may or may not be manifest in behavior on any particular occasion.

But when "attitude" was appropriated by marketing research, its meaning was stretched. Some investigators used it to indicate a general positive disposition, as measured by the evaluative scales of the semantic differential, for example.

Some used it to mean essentially the same thing as preference ("Please rate each brand on this 10-point scale"). And some used "attitude" to mean "intention."

The stretching of "attitude" to include "intention" made it easier to get

Source: Reprinted with permission from *Marketing News,* published by the American Marketing Association, April 11, 1975, p. 6. At the time of writing both John Pavasars and William Wells were associated with Needham, Harper, and Steers Advertising, Inc., an advertising firm.

from attitude to behavior. As Martin E. Fishbein of the University of Illinois has emphasized, an important logical distinction exists between attitude toward an object and attitude toward a specific behavior with respect to that object. One can have a very positive general evaluation of a Cadillac automobile without having any disposition to buy one.

Or one can have a very negative attitude toward hangovers and still drink too much. Therefore, while the relationship between a general affective disposition and a specific behavior ought by definition to be pretty loose, the relationship between behavior and a specific intention ought to be pretty tight.

But that's not all there is to it. Experience suggests that intentions predict best when they are defined as "the probability of buying a particular brand relative to the probabilities of buying competitive brands on the next purchase." This definition incorporates both intentions toward a particular brand and intentions toward a specific behavior (purchase) with respect to that brand in a competitive environment.

These probabilities can be measured by using a constant sum scale where respondents are asked to allocate a fixed number of points to a set of brands in proportion to their estimated likelihood of buying each brand on the next purchase.* The number of points allocated to each brand, divided by the total number of points, then represents the probability of purchasing that brand for a particular individual.

The fact that intention toward a particular brand is expressed as a probability has several implications. It says first of all that it is not very likely that intention measured in this way will predict exactly what brand a particular individual will buy on the next purchase.

It also says however, that over a series of purchases for that same individual, the proportions of various brands purchased should approximate the probability distribution as initially measured by the constant sum scale.

Therefore, generalized dispositions—"attitudes" in the original meaning of the term—usually won't predict brand purchasing behavior very well. Specific intentions often do, especially when they are viewed as probability distributions manifest over a series of purchases.

2. THE MEANING OF "PREDICT"

When one asks how accurately intentions can predict buying behavior, the answer depends greatly upon whether the prediction is of aggregate behavior or individual behavior. When the prediction is of aggregate behavior, intentions work very well.

---

* Editors' note: A respondent using a constant sum scale might be told, "You have ten points to allocate. Making sure that the total number of points equals ten, how many points represent the likelihood that you will buy brand A and how many that you will buy B?" The consumer might respond by saying: "four of the ten points go to A and six of the ten go to B." The researcher would therefore assume that the probability of the respondent buying A was 4/10, or 40 percent, and the probability of buying B was 6/10, or 60 percent.

Expressions of intentions to view particular movies or particular TV programs almost invariably make important contributions to predictions of the audiences they will attain. And even though election polls sometimes fail to name the winner, properly conducted polls almost always have come within a few percentage points of the actual vote.

On an individual level, the answer to the same question depends upon how the intentions are measured and upon whether the dependent variable is a single purchase or a series of purchases. If the intention measure is "yes-no" intention toward a single purchase of a single brand, prediction is likely to be very weak.

But if the intention measure is probabilistic (as in the point allocation method described above) and if the dependent variable is a series of purchases, prediction can be quite strong. Even under these conditions, however, individual level predictions are not likely to be as accurate as aggregate level predictions.

One final point on individual vs. aggregate prediction: it is always important to ask whether individual prediction or aggregate is more relevant for the marketing problem at hand.

While the answer to that question must depend upon the use to which the research is to be put, it seems obvious that marketers often are interested in aggregate rather than individual behavior. Tweedledum contributes just as much to market share as Tweedledee.

3. WHAT INTERVENES?

Finally, the ability of attitudes to predict behavior must depend upon what happens between the measurement of the attitude and the observation of the behavior.

Many studies show that if nothing happens, if expressions of attitudes and reports of behavior are recorded in the same interview (a form of cheating condoned by many professional journals), the relationship is likely to be quite strong. On the other hand, if external events are allowed to intervene, prediction is liable to be exceedingly weak if not downright wrong.

To some extent this problem can be overcome by identifying important extraneous events and accounting for them so that the net effect of the attitude component can be measured. Some studies have been able to do that better than others, and studies that have done it best, and have thus been relatively "noise free," have generally shown that attitudes (expressed as intentions) predict behavior quite well.

In one important class of situations, one must make a very strong assumption about the relationship between attitude and behavior. When attitudes (or intentions) are used in evaluating the effectiveness of advertising, one must assume not only that intentions predict behavior, but also that changes in intentions predict changes in behavior.

Most specifically, one must assume that in the absence of extraneous events, messages that produce the greatest changes in intentions also will produce the greatest changes in the movement of goods.

Here the evidence is mixed but generally positive. Some studies have reported changes in intentions unaccompanied by changes in sales, and some have reported changes in sales unaccompanied (or at least not preceded) by changes in intentions. In none of these cases, however, can the influence of extraneous events be ruled out.

On the other hand, several researchers working for ad agencies or commercial testing firms have reported strong evidence that commercials which produce attitude or intention change also produce changes in market share.

The most hopeful sign of all is in the reported success of new product models that incorporate and depend upon reactions to introductory advertising. There the effect of ads upon intentions, and the ability of intentions to predict aggregate behavior, can be most clearly seen.

CONCLUSIONS

The extent to which attitude can predict buying behavior depends on a number of "ifs":

If the classical definition of "attitude" is used in attitude measurement, the likelihood of a successful prediction is smaller than if attitude is defined and measured using the "constant sum probability to purchase" approach.

If the prediction is attempted on an individual level the likelihood of success is much smaller than on an aggregate basis.

If intervening events in the "real world" are not successfully isolated, the likelihood of predicting sales is small.

QUESTIONS

1. Why is so much made of the difference between (a) attitude toward an object and (b) attitude toward a behavior about an object? Should marketers be more concerned about attitudes toward their products or attitudes about intention to buy their products?

2. Is it dangerous for marketers and advertisers to learn so much about how people think and how it affects what they buy? Why or why not? If so, should anything be done about it? Why or why not? What could be done?

3. How could the ability to measure attitudes toward a product help a marketer (a) segment a market and (b) make improvements in the marketing mix?

11
Psychology in industrial marketing

Ernest R. Dichter

A common misconception in marketing is the idea that industrial markets are characterized by rational buying behavior, while so-called emotional considerations appear
only in consumer markets. This article argues that the industrial buyer is governed by just as many emotions as the
typical consumer. Understanding this may be of help in
segmenting industrial markets as well as in developing
appropriate marketing strategies. Dichter attempts to put
the role of psychology in industrial marketing in proper
perspective.

A naive consumer may be misguided by his emotions when making buying
decisions even though such an idea is disputed by people who believe in the
rationality of homo sapiens. Notions of this type when talking about the
industrial buyer usually are rejected completely.

How rational is the purchasing agent, engineer, community planner or
product specifier? Our experience has shown that although he studies specifications, prices and quality much more than the consumer, when we dig a
little bit deeper, we find that he is governed by just as many emotions as the
average housewife. He, too, suffers from illusions and is much more embar-
rassed to admit the often irrationality of his behavior.

Let's discuss a few practical examples. A purchasing agent for a company
making food products has a choice between packaging food in glass jars or in
tin cans. He has all the tables and technical data. The glass people tell him the
obvious things—that glass can be recycled and that it has sales appeal because the product can be seen. The can people, on the other hand, tell him
that the product can be preserved much longer, is unbreakable and can be
stored more readily.

In a study it was found that there are some technical people who simply do
not like glass—no matter how many practical and factual reasons were presented to them. They would always invent counter arguments. One way to
really communicate with them, as we finally did, was to develop little glass

Source: Reprinted with permission from *Industrial Marketing,* February 1973, Copyright ©
1973 by Crain Communications, Inc., Chicago, Ill. At the time of writing Ernest Dichter was
chairman of his own consulting firm.

statuaries to leave with them so the material would become familiar. Hopefully the technical buyer would develop a feeling and even a fondness for it.

Contrary to common belief, the technical buyer often has a product that he is dealing with which is much more mysterious and complex than cereal, coffee or a refrigerator. A mistake in design can cost millions of dollars.

Yet, the industrial buyer often selects a design or a special part based on emotion rather than fact. Correctly communicating with his technical mind through advertising, promotion and other marketing strategies means understanding him.

He deals with materials and products of all kinds. Metals and materials of various types have a very special appeal. Steel, for example, is inflexible and strong. Yet, recently I had to develop a new creative concept for a German steel company which wanted to get away from the war-time "blood and iron" association which prevailed there.

By suggesting that factory—or even office buildings—add some frivolous little designs to otherwise cold and forbidding buildings, we helped to establish with the company a changed image for steel.

Wood, in contrast to plastic materials, lives. It has depth while a plastic surface is psychologically impenetrable. Irregularity, rather than complete perfection, is a proof of naturalness. In selling plastic material, therefore, the purchasing agent who likes natural products has to be sold on the idea that it, too, lives, has depth and somehow comes from natural sources, although passing through laboratory changes.

Engineers often have deep-seated prejudices. It is still difficult to sell a huge vat made of aluminum—even from duraluminum, which has almost equal strength when compared to steel or cast iron.

Rather than attempting to convince the technical reader with rational arguments in the ad, the real subsconscious origin of his attitudes could be pointed out to him. Weight is not a modern criterion for strength or durability. Humor often helps: "What is heavier, a pound of steel or a pound of feathers?" could be asked.

Miniaturization represents another interesting psychological barrier. Modern motors and solid state electronic equipment are much smaller than the average engineer (particularly if he is older) is accustomed to believe in. The way to reach him is to explain through modern models, atomic concepts and concentration of power in advertising.

Above all, the real problem we always face with an industrial buyer is to get him to admit that an apparently solid fact suddenly has become outdated by a new development. He hates to admit that he has been "wrong" and simply does not want to give up his well established convictions and apparently scientifically founded beliefs.

For General Electric we carried through a study trying to convince engineers that a d.c. motor is more modern for variable speed in automation than the otherwise modern a.c. motor.

Rather than talking about the qualities of the d.c. motor, we flattered the engineer. "You have a flexible mind; therefore, you have changed your ideas about certain developments many times before. You surely will have no problem accepting this new development." This approach worked very well, according to GE records.

Engineers often deal with special characteristics of their machines— durability, resilience, absorption, fatigue. Some of these qualities are almost of a human intricacy. Why should steel get fatigued? Advertisers dealing with such factors should reach for human and easily understandable parallels. Amfac talking about slicing a potato 19 different ways in its advertising is on the right track.

In a study for a maker of big industrial kettles, we found that it was much easier for the technician to explain the size of his vats by a comparison with two private homes that could be put into it. This was much more dramatic than the cubic feet content.

In many ways a technical buyer is closer to an infantile mind than he likes to admit. We analyzed for a big utility company how best to tell the story of the installation of a new utility company. After talking to several engineers we found they did not react to the gleaming picture of the grand new generators but, rather, to the "fertile moment," the moment when the switch was being pulled and all the generators started humming. This moment of truth represented for the plant engineer the real experience of now having extra power. This was the illustration which was then used in the ads.

Another important factor we discovered was that in international technical advertising, the manufacturer has to be very careful not to antagonize national pride by stressing the fact of the superiority of German engineering, for example, in ads appearing in Mexico. He can do the same thing with much less danger in countries which have a highly developed economy of their own, such as Australia or South Africa or the United States.

Engineers, like other people, are very subtle, complex and, above all, very sensitive. A pharmaceutical company stressing its laboratories and superior research is likely to offend the physician who—rightly or wrongly—is convinced that it is he who made all the research possible by his diligent application and day-to-day observations in medical practice. He is the GI on the front who feels all the credit is given to the generals.

In a study on surgical instruments we also found that often the language spoken by a surgeon is much less technical than the language of the manufacturer. He, the engineer, talks about gauges and sharpness. The surgeon looks upon his needles and sutures as tools of his art and, therefore, uses terms like smooth, beautiful and elegant.

This applies to many other technical areas; not unlike a mathematician who can refer to an equation as beautiful, an engineer, too, can fall in love with the humming of a motor or the smooth click of a transmission.

Once we admit that engineers are more than the sum total of statistics, that they exist in a dynamic rather than a static sense—changing, modifying their attitudes and being modified by their surroundings—then it becomes impossible to see them in any way except as developing organisms.

It is in this area that the social sciences, seeking to understand human behavior, have effectively proven the necessity for probing beneath superficial and often rationalized answers to the emotional factors which determine our actions and attitudes.

Engineers, like other people, are inconsistent and contradictory. These facts make it all the more difficult to establish the significant consistencies and variations in a technical employe or in an entire population such as an industrial plant.

How does motivational research find out what makes technical people tick? What influences their living patterns, their social ideas, their industrial buying habits? This quote may throw some light on these questions: "Like all other humans, we like a pat on the back when we do something good," an engineer confessed to a motivational researcher studying an industrial problem. In the course of the same study another engineer talked about a mistake he had made. "It could have happened to anyone," he said. "There's team work in our plant, so not too much was made of it."

On the basis of information from spontaneous remarks like these, motivational psychologists told one company why it was having trouble with its technical employes. They advised the company to build up the technical man's self-esteem. It could do this by giving engineers more credit for the company's progress and success. The company also should speak of the facilities used by its technical employees as constantly developing tools in the progress of science, for these men like to think of themselves as adventurous and progressive.

In order to arrive at such a practical solution we analyzed approximately 150 "depth interviews" conducted with engineers, consultants, technicians, executive and management personnel, dealers, salesmen and technical editors. A depth interview is totally different from a standard questionnaire used by conventional market researchers. Instead of seeking yes and no answers to a list of questions, it depends on spontaneous remarks made in the course of a lengthy, rambling conversation with a skilled interviewer who probes for attitudes and feelings, as well as for simple choice or preference.

In the study under discussion, we found that engineers and technical experts tend to have an exalted image of the kind of people they ought to be. When they are unable to live up to this goal—which is almost always the case because the goal itself is unrealistically high—they dislike being reminded of their shortcomings. They set up various defenses so they will not have to reproach themselves for failing to be perfect.

First the engineer reassures himself that he is "only human." Then, seeking safety in numbers, he tells himself that he is "just part of a team." The team becomes a scapegoat for his mistakes. At the same time, he identifies with the team and regards it as having special status—he wants the team to be appreciated and respected.

Another tool of motivational research is the projective test, both written and representational, which allows the respondent to project his real feelings about a subject. For example, in a study for an oil company, we showed architects a rough drawing indicating the shadowy outlines of "the dream gasoline station" under construction. We asked them to tell us what the attributes of this ideal station would be. In this type of test, motorists and architects have a chance to sit back and dream about what they really would like to have in terms of supplies, services and even aesthetic appeals in future gas stations.

A good ad we found which illustrates this kind of thinking is one put out by Hitachi stressing the fact that engineers, too, are human beings and have the same problems as everybody else.

On the other hand, an ad for BART lacks any kind of human involvement and just shows a slick modern train; interesting, but without indicating what it can do for me, the purchasing agent, and eventually for me as a commuter.

We too often forget that the technical person is only too frequently a consumer at the same time. Modern school texts often can be helpful in explaining, even to a well-trained person, "how things work." The attempt to explain in a crystal clear fashion a complex piece of machinery requires a lot of imagination, which is often lacking in industrial advertising. The explanation of the principle of a new product or technical development must be done in such a way that the reader can say, "Aha, I've got it."

One of the persistent fallacies of our times is the belief that when a man undertakes a technical job, or is solving a technical problem, he can separate himself from his ordinary human emotions and act coldly and logically, functioning as an intelligent calculating machine. Many advertisers, agencies and even industrial executives believe this implicitly. However, the factors which move the industrial buyer to a purchasing decision, once the initial "illusion of rationality" is created, are frequently the same irrational and emotional ones—often subconscious—which move the average consumer to make his buying decisions.

This all means that the industrial purchaser has a specific self-image. He sees himself as different from the consumer, as more sophisticated and knowledgeable in his capacity as a buyer. Because he may actually be responding to some irrational appeal, he also seeks to be provided with a rationalization to support his preference.

A key problem of industrial advertising is to reach the actual decision-making level. A recent quantitative marketing study bears out one of the conclusions arrived at in our own psychological studies—that the purchasing agent is circumscribed in his actual power to make a choice of products.

Often, on the basis of decisions made at higher levels, he is limited in his choice to two or three products. The emotional factors which move the decision-maker, the strategic purchaser, become all-important to the advertiser. Similarly, it requires a new sales approach, teaching salesmen to help the purchasing agent by equipping him with the arguments and reasoning with which the purchasing agent can convince his own superiors.

This way you become not only a firm which understands the problems of the decision-maker in making purchasing decisions, but you also become the helpful ally of the purchasing agent in dealing with his own problems.

Although you as a manufacturer and advertiser consider the impact of your merchandising program on the industrial buyer as your major promotional problem, the fact is that the industrial consumer sees your program as part of a field. Your problem is to make your advertising, as one phase of your promotion, sufficiently distinct and believable so that it stands out from the field.

The tendency to advertise gimmicks or new product developments alone frequently has a negative effect. Initially, your competitors will counter by their own product changes, or by their own new product.

The industrial consumer sees this advertising and merchandising as a pattern of sameness, virtually indistinguishable behind that "grey curtain." There is a solution to this. Forget the gimmick. Use product development to enforce a picture of a consistent, believable company personality.

The development and use of a gestalt—overall—approach to presenting your company and its products will achieve a real differential over the years. Company personality cannot be copied. It cannot be dissipated by the competition's new products, and it gives the buyer a reason for knowing and remembering your company.

QUESTIONS

1. Is it any surprise to read that industrial buyers are affected by their feelings and emotions and that these, in turn, affect their decisions? Explain.

2. The article points out that industrial buyers are subjected to a variety of influences from others in the firm and that, as a result, the range of the buyer's alternatives may be very limited. Does this concept have a parallel in consumer goods marketing? Explain.

3. If, as Dichter suggests, many variations exist in the way purchasing agents make decisions, in the extent to which they are influenced by others, and in the nature of the emotional factors that affect them, then how could a firm trying to sell goods to industrial buyers develop effective marketing strategies?

12
Psychographics: A critical review

William D. Wells

In this edited version of Wells's review of psychographics, his critical discussion of major research methodology questions and his 148-item bibliography of relevant literature have been deleted. The interested student is encouraged to go to the original source for these parts of the article. (If some of the remaining technical [statistical] terminology is unfamiliar, the reader should skip over these words. They describe data manipulation techniques; the essence of the material can be understood without mastering these terms.) The sections that have been retained present five case examples illustrating the variety of uses of psychographics and the contributions they have made to marketing management and to an understanding of consumer behavior.

Among the standard fixtures in marketing research, the demographic profile is probably the most familiar. Age, income, education, and other indications of position in life space have so much influence on so many kinds of consumer behavior that users of a product or a brand, viewers of a TV program, or readers of a magazine are virtually certain to differ from the rest of the population on one or more of the common demographic dimensions. Marketing researchers collect demographics as a matter of routine, and marketers feel comfortable using them.

But demographic profiles, essential though they may be, have not been deemed sufficient. Especially since the end of World War II researchers have engaged in a continuous search for new, more comprehensive, and more exciting descriptions. It is as though demographics provided only a nodding acquaintance, and marketers wanted to know their customers much better.

Until recently this search has followed two somewhat different directions. Starting with the classic study by Koponen, investigators have repeatedly tried to correlate consumer behavior with scores obtained from standardized personality inventories. And, starting with Dichter's innovative studies of consumers' motivations, students of the consumer's mind have tried to apply the concepts and methods of clinical psychology to virtually every aspect of marketing.

Source: Reprinted (with deletions) with permission from the *Journal of Marketing Research,* published by the American Marketing Association, vol. 12 (May 1975), pp. 196–213. At the time of writing William Wells was an associate of Needham, Harper, and Steers Advertising, Inc.

From Koponen's study on, the work with personality inventories has been judged "equivocal." The correlations have almost invariably been low, and the relationships uncovered have often been so abstract that they could not be used with confidence in making real-world marketing decisions.

Motivation research has fared much better. In spite of severe criticisms on both ethical and methodological grounds, motivation research enjoyed a tremendous vogue; in its current form—the small scale "qualitative study"—it still has many busy practitioners. It is somewhat ironic that the more rigorous of these two approaches has proved relatively sterile, while the sloppier methodology continues to produce results that intelligent people judge to be of great value.

Sometime during the 1960s a blend of these two traditions began to take shape. Variously called "life style," "psychographic," or "activity and attitude" research, this blend combines the objectivity of the personality inventory with the rich, consumer-oriented, descriptive detail of the qualitative motivation research investigation. This new blend has attracted considerable attention, both among "academics" and among "real-world" marketers. It has also attracted its share of criticism, and its share of skeptical questions as to its true usefulness and value.

This review attempts to take stock of the present status and future prospects of psychographic research, including consumer-oriented research with standardized personality inventories. It begins with a definition of the field. It continues with examples of five somewhat different approaches to psychographic analysis. And it concludes with a critical discussion of the reliability, validity, and usefulness of psychographic measurements.

DEFINITIONS

Although the need for a common definition of psychographics is obvious, no single definition has met with general approval. Twenty-four articles on psychographics contain no less than 32 definitions, all somewhat different, and each new publication seems to produce still another version of what psychographic research is or is not. Within this diversity, however, certain common elements are clearly visible.

Something more than demographics

All psychographic researchers have attempted to move beyond demographics into areas that are relatively untried and unfamiliar. Depending upon the investigator's objectives and to some extent upon his taste, the added dimensions have run from one or two to several hundred and have embraced a wide range of content, including activities, interests, opinions, needs, values, attitudes, and personality traits. In some cases the variables have been "homemade," and in others they have been borrowed from standardized attitude scales or personality inventories. In all cases, however, the common theme has been that demographic attributes alone are not enough.

Quantitative, not qualitative

Second, most psychographic researchers have employed precoded, objective questionnaires that can be self-administered or administered by ordinary survey interviewers. Precoding makes the data amenable to complex multivariate statistical analysis; ease of administration encourages—or at least permits—use of large, representative samples. Both practices distinguish psychographic studies from studies in the qualitative motivation research tradition.

Operationally, then, psychographic research can be defined as quantitative research intended to place consumers on psychological—as distinguished from demographic—dimensions. Because it goes beyond the standard and the accepted, it offers the possibility of new insights and unusual conclusions. Because it is quantitative rather than discursive, it opens the way to large, representative samples of respondents, and to multivariate statistical analysis of findings.

FIVE EXAMPLES

A psychographic profile based on general "life-style" dimensions

The need for good descriptions of consumers is well expressed in the following comment by an advertising copywriter:

. . . Imagine that I've got to write an ad on a Sunday afternoon, and I want to feel sure I'm on the right track. I want to double check myself that people will understand it/react to it/remember it, plus a few subtleties like will they like it, dislike it, etc.

So, I trudge all the way around the block, talking to the neighbors, and forty houses later I have a slight idea of what will happen to my ad when it reaches the world. That's what I understand Research does, only a lot more intelligently and a lot more thoroughly and in a lot more neighborhoods.

A writer writes out of his personal collection of life experiences and his knowledge of people, and he imagines and projects them and he tries to translate them into his viewer's or his reader's terms. But he's feeding off himself. He's just one person. He can't afford to trust just his own experience. Research extends the writer. Information is his life blood. He can't write out of thin air. Anything that adds to his storehouse of information is necessary and vital.

Similar needs are felt by all others who must create products, services, or messages for customers they cannot meet in person. Just as the writer knows that he cannot feed only off himself, so also the product designer and the marketing manager know that they run grave risks when they rely solely on their own assumptions. Almost all of marketing is communication; marketers are most effective when they know their audiences.

As an example of the descriptive value of psychographic dimensions, consider the somewhat esoteric problem of communicating with consumers who are heavy users of shotgun ammunition. Persons of this sort would be of special interest to anyone who manufactures, markets, or advertises shotguns, ammunition, or associated hunting paraphenalia; to operators of hunting lodges and private hunting areas; to publishers of hunting magazines; and to government officials who promote or regulate this form of recreation.

A demographic profile of the heavy user of shotgun ammunition appears in Table 1. The man who spends at least $11 per year on shotgun shells differs from the nonbuyer in that he tends to be younger, lower in income and education, and more concentrated in blue-collar occupations. He is also more apt to be living in rural areas, especially in the South.

Table 1
Demographic profile of the heavy user of shotgun ammunition

	Percent who spend $11 + per year on shotgun ammunition (141)	Percent who don't buy (395)
Age		
Under 25	9	5
25–34	33	15
35–44	27	22
45–54	18	22
55+	13	36
Occupation		
Professional	6	15
Managerial	23	23
Clerical-sales	9	17
Craftsmen	50	35
Income		
Under $6,000	26	19
$6,000–$10,000	39	36
$10,000–$15,000	24	27
$15,000+	11	18
Population density		
Rural	34	12
2,500–50,000	11	11
50,000–500,000	16	15
500,000–2 million	21	27
2 million+	13	19
Geographic division		
New England–Mid-Atlantic	21	33
Central (North, West)	22	30
South Atlantic	23	12
East South Central	10	3
West South Central	10	5
Mountain	6	3
Pacific	9	15

Now reflect upon the implications of this pattern. Hunting is a risky sport. Is the hunter a risk taker? Is he likely to follow rules on his own, or does he require external control? Hunting is a violent sport. Is the hunter attracted by violence in general? What other products would make good tie-in sales with hunting equipment? Is the hunter also a fisherman or a camper? Is he especially interested in food? Is he a regular newspaper reader? Is he a regular patron of discount stores? From the demographic profile alone, a marketer with a thorough knowledge of young, blue-collar, nonurban life-styles might be able to guess the answers to at least some of these questions, but few would guess them all.

The data in Table 2 show how psychographic information can put flesh on demographic bones. These data came from a general life-style study that

Table 2
Psychographic profile of the heavy user of shotgun ammunition

	Percent who spend $11 + per year on shotgun ammunition (141)	Percent who don't buy (395)
Base		
I like hunting	88	7
I like fishing	68	26
I like to go camping	57	21
I love the out-of-doors	90	65
A cabin by a quiet lake is a great place to spend the summer	49	34
I like to work outdoors	67	40
I am good at fixing mechanical things	47	27
I often do a lot of repair work on my own car	36	12
I like war stories	50	32
I would do better than average in a fist fight	38	16
I would like to be a professional football player	28	18
I would like to be a policeman	22	8
There is too much violence on television	35	45
There should be a gun in every home	56	10
I like danger	19	8
I would like to own my own airplane	35	13
I like to play poker	50	26
I smoke too much	39	24
I love to eat	49	34
I spend money on myself that I should spend on the family	44	26
If given a chance, most men would cheat on their wives	33	14
I read the newspaper every day	51	72

happened to contain a question about shotgun ammunition along with questions about approximately 100 other products and services. The questionnaire also contained questions about a wide range of activities, interests, and opinions; about reading of major magazines; and about viewing of a large number of television programs. The study was not designed around shotgun users, or around the users of any other single product.

In spite of this lack of focus, the data in Table 2 show some interesting patterns. First, it is obvious that hunting is not an isolated phenomenon but rather is associated with other rugged outdoor endeavors. Shotgun shell buyers not only like to hunt, they also like to fish and to go camping. They even like to work outdoors. These relationships are interesting and useful because they suggest activities and settings, other than hunting scenes, that might be appropriate for shotgun ammunition advertising. They suggest products that might be especially appropriate for joint promotions or other cooperative marketing ventures, such as displaying shotgun ammunition near camping or fishing equipment in retail outlets. Table 2 also shows that ammunition buyers are apt to be do-it-yourselfers, which suggests that hunters are apt to be buyers of hardware and tools.

Items in the third group in Table 2 suggest some hypotheses about the psychological makeup of the shotgun ammunition buyers. Compared with the nonbuyer he is definitely more attracted by violence, suggesting that detective, war, and violent Western TV programs ought to draw audiences with disproportionate numbers of shotgun users, and that action and adventure magazines ought to be considered when placing advertising associated with hunting. Relationships between product use and media exposure are always best documented by direct cross-tabulation, but when these data are not available (and they often are not) relationships suggested by life-style patterns can provide helpful direction.

The relatively high levels of agreement with the fourth section of Table 2 suggest that the hunter is generally less risk-averse than is his nonhunting counterpart. To policy makers charged with keeping hunters from shooting themselves and each other, this willingness to accept risk would suggest that sober warnings about the dangers of firearms may well be ineffective. Lest this conclusion seem hopelessly naive, let it be noted that sober warnings about the dangers of firearms are exactly what some policy makers have attempted.

The relatively high levels of agreement with the fifth section suggest a combination of self-indulgence and lack of internal control that seems congruent with the attitude toward risk just noted. If the hunter is in fact self-indulgent and relatively conscienceless, it would seem unwise to rely on appeals to fair play and conservation to regulate his activities. Again, such appeals have been tried with less success than expected.

The level of agreement with "I love to eat" and the hunter's professed willingness to spend money on himself suggest markets for premium foods designed to be taken along on hunting expeditions. These two findings also suggest the suitability of game-preparation recipes for hunting magazines, and they indicate that quantity and quality of food should get particular attention from proprietors of hunting lodges. Hunters don't mind roughing it, but they want it to be a well-fed roughness.

Finally, the relatively low level of agreement with "I read the newspaper every day" should serve as a warning to shotgun ammunition advertisers. This is not to assert that media decisions, positive or negative, should ever be based on responses to a single survey item. Rather, it suggests that any shotgun ammunition advertiser who is spending his budget in newspapers should think twice about alternatives.

This brief example shows how a psychographic profile obtained almost incidentally in the context of a large, general life-style survey can provide suggestions and hypotheses that bear on a wide range of marketing and policy decisions. A demographic profile alone would perhaps have provided some of these inferences, but surely not all of them.

This example also shows how a psychographic profile can help the marketer avoid some traps a demographic profile would have set for him. Knowing that heavy users of shotgun ammunition tend to be younger, more in blue-collar occupations, and less urban than nonusers might suggest that they would be heavier users of beer, more interested in television, more interested in spectator sports, more prone to use credit, and more apt to shop at discount stores. Yet buyers of shotgun ammunition do not differ significantly from nonbuyers on any of these dimensions.

Other psychographic life-style profiles that have appeared in the literature include carryout foods; eye makeup, shortening, oranges, and lemons; beer; mouthwash; heavy-duty hand soap; bank charge cards; department stores; and air travel. They also include profiles of the readers of magazines and of viewers of various television programs. In all these cases the psychographic data have provided rich, descriptive detail that could not have been inferred from demographics. . . .

A product-specific psychographic profile

In the previous example, the psychographic profile was drawn from a large set of general life-style items. Because the item list was large and diverse, some of the items happened to be related to consumption of shotgun ammunition. When a psychographic study is devoted to a single product category, it is not necessary to depend on item diversity to get useful relationships. Rather, the investigator can focus upon a limited set of relevant, product-related dimensions.

An excellent example of this use of psychographics is provided in a report by Young on the "positioning" of the Ford Pinto. According to Young, the introductory Pinto advertising portrayed the car as "carefree, small (and) romantic." The strategy was "to sell to small car prospects; to compete against imported small cars; to say that the car was carefree, trouble free, beautifully styled, and economical."

As the introduction of the Pinto proceeded, psychographic research disclosed that potential Pinto buyers had a less romantic orientation toward cars and driving. They endorsed statements like "I wish I could depend on my car more," "I am more practical in car selection," "A car offers me a chance to tinker with machinery," "I like to feel how powerful my car is," and "The only function for a car is transportation." They rejected statements like "The kind of car you have is important as to how people see you" and "Taking care of a car is too much trouble."

As a result of this research, the Pinto was repositioned (in advertising, by its new agency) as "The epitomy of function, exemplifying basic economical transportation, trading on Ford's heritage of the Model A." Consequently, "Today Pinto is the largst selling subcompact, outselling Volkswagen by a sizeable margin."

Now it is admittedly farfetched to assume that all (or maybe even most) of Pinto's success was due to this change in position. But it does seem reasonable to believe that emphasis on economy and practicality appealed to the salient needs of potential subcompact buyers, and that the revised message communicated ideas that potential customers would find most persuasive.

Personality traits as descriptors

A report on "Ecologically Concerned Consumers: Who Are They?" provides a third example of psychographic analysis. In this report the dependent variable was an "index of ecological concern" that included both attitudes toward ecological issues and conservationist behavior. The independent variables were 7 demographic characteristics, 12 personality traits taken from standardized personality inventories, and a variable called "perceived consumer effectiveness." This attribute was measured by degree of disagreement with "It is futile for the individual consumer to try to do anything about pollution."

The 20 independent variables were first screened by analysis of variance to determine which of them discriminated between respondents who were high and respondents who were low in ecological concern. The 10 variables that survived the screening were then input to Multiple Classification Analysis to "predict" the degree of ecological concern expressed by each respondent. To avoid confusion it should be noted that in this study, as in most psychographic studies, the term "predict" cannot be taken literally. Since the data were all collected at the same point in time, "prediction" really means correlation.

The MCA coefficients for the "factors that were found to be most significant" in "predicting" ecological concern are shown in Table 3. The coefficients show how much the members of each category differ in ecological concern from the total sample. Thus, respondents who were low in perceived consumer effectiveness were 2.49 points below average in ecological concern, respondents who were medium were 4.04 points below average, and so on.

This study differs from the ammunition study and the Pinto study in two important ways. First, in the ammunition and Pinto studies the descriptions of

Table 3
MCA profile of the ecologically concerned consumer

Factor	Level	Regression coefficient
Perceived consumer effectiveness	Very low	—
	Low	−2.49
	Medium	−4.04
	High	−1.04
	Very high	2.54
Tolerance	Very low	0.15
	Low	−0.79
	Medium	−0.39
	High	−0.04
	Very high	1.00
Understanding	Very low	−0.92
	Low	−0.81
	Medium	0.22
	High	0.27
	Very high	1.25
Harm avoidance	Very low	−0.59
	Low	0.13
	Medium	0.27
	High	0.73
	Very high	−1.22
Annual family income	Under $5,000	−0.39
	$5,000 to $6,999	−0.24
	$7,000 to $9,999	0.10
	$10,000 to $14,999	−0.15
	$15,000 and over	0.74

Mean = 11.31.
$R^2 = 0.28$.

the target groups were developed by considering *all* the psychographic items that discriminated between the target group and the remainder of the population. In this study, on the other hand, the answers that respondents gave to the personality scale questions were summed to produce higher level, more abstract scores on "tolerance," "understanding," and "harm avoidance." This procedure had the effect of eliminating much of the rich descriptive detail that might have been provided by the individual questions. We do not know what answers produced high scores or low scores on the personality dimensions.

Second, in the ammunition and Pinto studies the profiles were developed by cross-tabulating *all* of the psychographic items with the dependent variable. In this study, the independent variables were linked to the dependent variable by a type of multiple regression. Like all other forms of multiple regression, MCA suppresses variables that are closely related to variables that are allowed to enter the equation. As a result, variables closely related to each other could not all have entered the description of the ecologically concerned consumer, even though they might have discriminated sharply in a cross-tabulation.

Many other examples of this general approach are to be found in the literature. In one of the earliest psychographic studies, Koponen regressed Edwards Personal Preference Schedule scores on consumption of cigarettes and readership of several magazines. A group of investigators from the Advertising Research Foundation regressed the same set of independent variables against consumption of toilet paper, with predictable and poetically just results. Frank, Massy, and Lodahl did the same for coffee, tea, and beer. Wilson factor analyzed an activity, interest, and opinion inventory and regressed various AIO factors against consumption of a list of products that included soft drinks, lipstick, and stomach remedies. And Darden and Reynolds used scales representing fashion interest, fashion venturesomeness, cognitive style, information seeking, relative popularity and relative self-confidence to "predict" fashion opinion leadership.

In all these cases a large set of descriptive items was reduced to a smaller number of more abstract scores, and this reduced set of independent variables was then linked to the dependent variable by means of some form of multiple regression. The descriptions thus provided were therefore more abstract and less redundant than the descriptions that would have been provided by simple cross-tabulation of the uncondensed raw data.

A general life-style segmentation study

A report of a major study by the Newspaper Advertising Bureau provides an example of still another approach to psychographics. In this study a national sample of approximately 4,000 respondents completed questionnaires containing 300 psychographic questions, several dozen questions about product use, and questions about exposure to various media. The psychographic questions were reduced to a smaller set of scales by R-type factor analysis, and the resulting factor scores were input to Q-type factor analysis to place the respondents into relatively homogeneous groups. Condensed descriptions of the eight male groups are given in Figure 1.

Figure 1
Eight male psychographic segments

Group 1.   "The Quiet Family Man" (8% of total males)

He is a self-sufficient man who wants to be left alone and is basically shy. Tries to be as little involved with community life as possible. His life revolves around the family, simple work and television viewing. Has a marked fantasy life. As a shopper he is practical, less drawn to consumer goods and pleasures than other men.

Low education and low economic status; he tends to be older than average.

Group II.   "The Traditionalist" (16% of total males)

A man who feels secure, has self-esteem, follows conventional rules. He is proper

Figure 1 *(continued)*

and respectable, regards himself as altruistic and interested in the welfare of others. As a shopper he is conservative, likes popular brands and well-known manufacturers.

Low education and low or middle socio-economic status, the oldest age group.

Group III.   "The Discontented Man" (13% of total males)

He is a man who is likely to be dissatisfied with his work. He feels bypassed by life, dreams of better jobs, more money and more security. He tends to be distrustful and socially aloof. As a buyer, he is quite price conscious.

Lowest education and lowest socio-economic group, mostly older than average.

Group IV.   "The Ethical Highbrow" (14% of total males)

This is a very concerned man, sensitive to people's needs. Basically a puritan, content with family life, friends, and work. Interested in culture, religion, and social reform. As a consumer he is interested in quality, which may at times justify greater expenditure.

Well educated, middle or upper socio-economic status, mainly middle-aged or older.

Group V.   "The Pleasure Oriented Man" (9% of total males)

He tends to emphasize his masculinity and rejects whatever appears to be soft or feminine. He views himself a leader among men. Self-centered, dislikes his work or job. Seeks immediate gratification for his needs. He is an impulsive buyer, likely to buy products with a masculine image.

Low education, lower socio-economic class, middle-aged or younger.

Group VI.   "The Achiever" (11% of total males)

This is likely to be a hardworking man, dedicated to success and all that it implies: social prestige, power, and money. Is in favor of diversity, is adventurous about leisure-time pursuits. Is stylish, likes good food, music, etc. As a consumer he is status conscious, a thoughtful and discriminating buyer.

Good education, high socio-economic status, young.

Group VII.   "The He-Man" (19% of total males)

He is gregarious, likes action, seeks an exciting and dramatic life. Thinks of himself as capable and dominant. Tends to be more of a bachelor than a family man, even after marriage. Products he buys and brands preferred are likely to have "self-expressive value," especially a "Man of Action" dimension.

Well educated, mainly middle socio-economic status, the youngest of the male groups.

Group VIII.   "The Sophisticated Man" (10% of total males)

He is likely to be an intellectual, concerned about social issues, admires men with artistic and intellectual achievements. Socially cosmopolitan, broad interests. Wants to be dominant and a leader. As a consumer he is attracted to the unique and fashionable.

Best educated and highest economic status of all groups, younger than average.

This study differs from the first three in that it did not assume that members of any target group are all very similar. Instead of attempting to discover what hunters, Pinto buyers, or ecologically concerned consumers have in common, this study admitted the possibility that users of a product might fall into several quite different segments.

The wisdom of this approach is illustrated in Table 4. There it can be seen that the heavy users of several products and several brands, the readers of some magazines and the viewers of some TV programs tend to be concentrated in two or more segments that differ quite significantly from each other. When that is the case, any attempt to discover the characteristics of an undifferentiated target group—e.g., "the heavy beer drinker," "the user of Brand X deodorant," "the *Playboy* reader," or "the TV news viewer"—whether by simple cross-tabulation or by multiple regression will be sure to underestimate the importance of the attributes upon which the segments differ. In extreme cases, when one segment of the target group is above average on a particular attribute and another segment is below average, merging the two segments into one target group can make the target group appear to be not different from the remainder of the population. . . .

A product-specified segmentation

In the preceding example, the segmentation was based on general—as opposed to product-related—psychographic items. When the investigation is devoted to one product, the investigator can focus upon product-related material. An example of the latter approach is given in a report by Pernica of a stomach remedy segmentation. Pernica developed a list of 80 items that included symptom frequency, end benefits provided by different brands, attitudes toward treatment, and beliefs about ailments. Items tapping general personality traits were recast so as to be product specific. For instance, "I worry too much" was translated into "I seem to get stomach problems if I worry too much."

The 80 product-specific items were reduced to 13 factors by R factor analysis, and scores on the 13 factors were input into Q factor analysis to assign the respondents to homogeneous groups. The segments were described both in terms of the variables that went into the segmentation and in terms of personality traits, life-style attributes, and demographic characteristics (Figure 2). The ability of this procedure to discriminate among the brands in this product category is shown in Table 5.

Note that the discrimination produced by the product-specific approach is somewhat sharper than the discrimination produced by the more general segmentation. This outcome is common. When the segmentation is based upon the dimensions upon which brands differ, it is almost certain to discriminate more sharply among brands than when it is based upon more general considerations. . . .

This case history and the four that precede it provide five different examples of psychographic analysis. Collectively they show how psychographics

Table 4
Product and media use by psychographic group

	Psychographic group* percentages							
	I	II	III	IV	V	VI	VII	VIII
Drink beer	45	56	57	51	75	59	80	72
Smoke cigarettes	32	40	40	29	54	42	51	38
Air travel outside U.S.	4	4	6	7	5	8	12	19
Air travel, domestic	14	15	14	26	19	32	20	42
Use brand X deodorant	7	7	6	8	14	10	9	12
Used headache remedy in past four weeks	53	60	66	61	61	64	65	67
Read current issue of:								
Playboy	8	11	8	13	25	27	36	30
National Geographic	21	13	11	30	13	28	16	27
Time	17	8	7	16	9	26	17	29
Newsweek	17	14	8	20	11	18	13	22
Field and Stream	10	12	14	8	12	9	13	3
Popular Mechanics	11	6	9	9	9	9	8	6
Viewed in past week:								
Sanford and Son	32	35	29	19	26	25	27	23
Sonny and Cher	17	24	22	19	14	24	30	22
Marcus Welby	26	25	26	23	20	16	20	18
Rowen and Martin	21	23	17	15	22	20	23	21
New Dick Van Dyke	19	15	16	13	11	8	10	12

* Described in Figure 1.

Figure 2
Segmentation of stomach remedy users

The Severe Sufferers

The Severe Sufferers are the extreme group on the potency side of the market. They tend to be young, have children, and be well educated. They are irritable and anxious people and believe that they suffer more severely than others. They take the ailment seriously, fuss about it, pamper themselves, and keep trying new and different products in search of greater potency. A most advanced product with new ingredients best satisfies their need for potency and fast relief and ties in which their psychosomatic beliefs.

The Active Medicators

The Active Medicators are on the same side of the motivational spectrum. They are typically modern suburbanites with average income and education. They are emotionally well adjusted to the demands of their active lives. They have learned to cope by adopting the contemporary beliefs of seeking help for every ill, and they use remedies to relieve even minor signs of ailments and every ache and pain. In a modern product, they seek restoration of their condition and energy, mental recovery, and a lift for their active lives. They are influenced by a brand's reputation and by how well it is advertised. They tend to develop strong brand loyalties.

The Hypochondriacs

The Hypochondriacs are on the opposite side of the motivational spectrum. They tend to be older, not as well educated, and women. They have conservative attitudes toward medication and a deep concern over health. They see possible dangers in frequent use of remedies, are concerned over side effects, and are afraid of remedies with new ingredients and extra potency. To cope with these concerns, they are strongly oriented toward medical authority, seeking guidance in treatment and what products they should use. They hold rigid beliefs about the ailment and are disciplined in the products they use, and how frequently. They want a simple, single-purpose remedy which is safe and free from side effects, and backed by doctors or a reputable company.

The Practicalists

The Practicalists are in the extreme position on this side of the motivational spectrum. They tend to be older, well educated, emotionally the most stable, and least concerned over their ailment or the dangers of remedies. They accept the ailment and its discomforts as a part of life, without fuss and pampering. They use a remedy as a last resort, and just to relieve the particular symptom. They seek simple products whose efficacy is well proven, and they are skeptical of complicated modern remedies with new ingredients and multiple functions.

Table 5
Brand use of stomach remedy segments (percent of segment using brand most often)

Brand	Severe sufferers	Active medicators	Hypochondriacs	Practicalists
A	6	3	1	1
B	32	23	10	8
C	16	17	12	5
D	16	19	24	8
E	5	29	37	51

can supplement demographics in interesting and useful ways. Individually they show the range of capabilities of these techniques, and they provide previews of some problems and ambiguities.

* * * * *

APPLICATIONS TO MARKETING PROBLEMS

The last two sections of this review bear upon usefulness—first in the context of real-world marketing problems, then in the context of present and potential contributions to a more general understanding of consumer behavior. The real-world discussion will argue that reliability and validity are neither necessary nor sufficient to insure that psychographic data can be used. The remainder of the discussion will argue that psychographic methods have already made significant contributions to the understanding of consumer behavior, and these contributions are likely to become more important as time goes on.

How to get valid, useless results

The results of psychographic research can be reliable and valid, and still not useful, when relationships that should not have been expected fail to appear. This may seem like a perfectly obvious observation, yet—as Kassarjian and Jacoby have already indicated—the literature is full of attempts to predict consumer behavior from personality test scores in the absence of any good reason to believe that the two should be related. Perhaps the classic example of this shot-in-the-dark approach is an early psychographic effort in which scales from The Edwards Personal Preference Schedule—scales intended to measure such needs as autonomy, dominance, order, and endurance—were correlated with purchases of single- and double-ply toilet tissue. Even if it were true that all of the measurements in this study were perfectly reliable and perfectly valid, the failure to find a significant correlation between need for dominance, for example, and purchase of toilet paper, could hardly come as much of a surprise. The same general comment applies to Evans' finding that the Edwards scales cannot separate Ford owners from

Chevrolet owners; to Robertson and Myers's finding that California Psychological Inventory scores do not account for much of the variance in innovativeness or opinion leadership; to Kollat and Willett's finding that a set of general personality traits, including optimism, belief in fate, and belief in multiple causation of events, did not predict impulse purchasing; and to many other negative findings that have not been published. The general proposition is: when one has no reason to believe that the psychographic constructs should be related to the consumer behavior in question, a negative finding— even though all the measurements may be highly reliable and highly valid—is not worth much.

Another way to circumvent usefulness is to be too abstract. A grand example of abstraction carried to extremes is provided in a study by Sparks and Tucker. This study found that a latent canonical root with heavy positive loadings on sociability and emotional stability, and a heavy negative loading on responsibility, accounted for much of the variance of a dimension that represents heavy consumption of alcoholic beverages, cigarettes, and shampoo. The study also found that a second latent dimension represented by a heavy positive loading on emotional stability and a heavy negative loading on cautiousness accounted for much of the variance of a dimension that represents heavy consumption of after-shave lotion, light consumption of headache remedies, light consumption of mouthwash and coffee, and disinclination to adopt new fashions. Assuming for the moment that this finding is both reliable and valid, just what does one do with it?

Third, psychographic measurements may be reliable and valid but so close to the behavior being studied that the relationship is essentially redundant. In Table 2, the best predictor of shotgun ammunition use is "I like to hunt." In Table 3, the best predictor of low ecological concern is agreement with "It is futile for the individual consumer to try to do anything about pollution." In Darden and Reynolds's study of men's fashions, the best predictors of fashion opinion leadership were two scales measuring "fashion interest" and "fashion venturesomeness." Findings of this sort are useful in the very restricted sense that they point to the construct validity of the psychographic items, but they are hardly likely to be greeted by marketing managers as world-shaking revelations.

To be useful in making real-world marketing decisions, psychographic data must be in some middle range between being almost totally redundant and being entirely unrelated to the behavior being studied. They must contain just the right amount of surprise. When that is the case, they can be very useful indeed, even when correlations are not high and even when questions about reliability and validity cannot be completely answered. This principle applies to profiles and to segmentations, for the same basic reason.

Why psychographic profiles are useful

To see why psychographic profiles are useful even in the absence of assured reliability and validity, it is necessary to consider the alternatives.

Consider, for example, the copywriter quoted toward the beginning of this review. Confronted with a deadline for creating an advertisement, he could sit in his office and imagine his audience. But he might be wrong. As he said, he can't afford to trust just his own experience. He might do his own informal psychographic study—trudge all the way around the block talking to the neighbors. But to the degree that his neighbors are different from his customers, this informal research might easily be misleading.

The copywriter might depend upon a qualitative motivation study. If he did, he would be looking at findings from a small unrepresentative sample, and he would be depending upon the subjective judgment of the motivation research analyst. He might examine a demographic profile obtained from a large-scale quantitative market survey. But, as the shotgun study illustrates, he would almost surely miss some valid relationships, and he would almost surely make some false inferences. Given these alternatives, it is easy to see why psychographic profiles have seen wide use in spite of legitimate questions as to reliability and validity. The copywriter cannot wait for convergent and discriminant validation. He must produce an advertisement, and to do that, he must use whatever information he can get.

The same basic problem confronts product designers, package designers, product managers, and media analysts. What product features will fit the life-style of the potential customer? To what sort of person should the package be designed to appeal? Is the customer for this product or service unusually price conscious? Fashion conscious? Concerned about pollution? Concerned about his health? What are consumers' attitudes and opinions about what appears in magazines, newspapers, radio, and TV? All of these questions are regularly answered by some combination of intuition and quantitative and qualitative research. In many cases psychographic profiles add information that would not otherwise be available.

Why psychographic segmentations are useful

General segmentations like the Newspaper Advertising Bureau study offer the opportunity to tailor new products and services to the needs of different groups within the consumer population. It is easy to see that the "Quiet Family Man," the "Traditionalist," the "Ethical Highbrow," and the "Pleasure Oriented Man" (Figure 1) ought to have quite different requirements in automobiles, entertainment, vacations, insurance policies, food, and clothing. The life-style descriptions show those need patterns in considerable detail, and the media data normally collected in such studies show how to reach each group.

Product-specific segmentations like the stomach remedy study offer the opportunity to position and reposition existing brands. They show what needs the product meets within each group, and which brands are best at meeting them. With this information the marketer can appeal directly and efficiently to those groups most apt to find his brand appealing, and he can create new brands to fit need patterns his brand cannot satisfy. Parallel values accrue to marketers of services.

But the question remains—are the descriptions of the segments reliable and valid? Do real groups of real consumers fitting these descriptions actually exist? If the answer is yes, the user of a psychographic segmentation has at his disposal a new and superior way of understanding his customers. If the answer is no, the marketer who takes a segmentation study seriously is marketing to a family of fictions.

In view of the reservations already expressed as to the reliability and validity of segmentation procedures it might seem that the wisest course would be to ignore psychographics until the procedures have been thoroughly validated. But again, one must consider the alternatives. Marketers know that the customers for a product or a service are frequently not much alike. They know that empirical segmentation procedures hold out the possibility of new insights into how consumers may be divided into groups. And they know that the reliability and validity of segmentation procedures have not been established beyond all doubt. Given that dilemma, many marketers have elected to conduct and to use segmentation studies even when fully aware of the art's imperfections.

UNDERSTANDING CONSUMER BEHAVIOR

Finally, psychographic methods have contributed to more general knowledge of consumer behavior in at least three ways. Psychographic profiles have shed new light on some of the familiar and recurring topics in consumer research. Trend data now becoming available have shown how consumers are changing and how they are not. And general segmentations of the consumer population have created new typologies within which consumer behavior might be more efficiently described and better understood. This review concludes with brief descriptions of studies in each of these fields.

Profiles

Psychographic profiles have already contributed to our understanding of opinion leadership, innovativeness, retail out-shopping, private brand buying, social class, consumerist activism, catalog buying behavior, store loyalty, differences between Canada and the United States, differences between French-speaking and English-speaking Canadians, and concern for the environment. In all these cases the value added by the psychographic profile was much the same as the value added to the description of the shotgun ammunition buyer. Sometimes psychographics confirmed the existence of attributes that might have been inferred from demographic profiles. Sometimes they revealed the existence of attributes that a demographic profile did show. And sometimes they disconfirmed inferences that would have been incorrect. It seems certain that the trend toward psychographic descriptions of interesting groups of consumers will continue, and that such descriptions will become accepted as necessary components of studies of this kind.

Trend data

As studies are repeated, it becomes possible to accumulate trend data that show how consumers are changing and how they are not changing. Such data are particularly valuable in an era when every other observer is prepared to describe "the changing consumer" and to make predictions about the effects of these changes upon markets for goods and services. In monitoring trends, the task of empirical psychographic analysis is to separate the changes that are actually happening from the changes that are not.

New typologies

The third application of psychographics to the study of consumer behavior is just now beginning to take shape. General segmentations, like the Newspaper Advertising Bureau study and the series of life-style studies conducted by the Leo Burnett Company, have begun to produce the outlines of a new consumer typology. As groupings like those shown in Figure 1 are identified and confirmed by independent sets of investigators, it is at least possible that marketers will begin to think routinely in terms of segments marked off by common sets of activities, interests, needs, and values, and to develop products, services, and media schedules specifically to meet them.

At present, agreement among general segmentation studies is pretty far from complete. Differences in item content, sampling procedure, and analytic technique have produced different sets of findings, each claiming to be real. Yet, even though the segments produced by various general segmentation studies differ in a number of ways, there is enough similarity among them to suggest that eventual consensus is not a vain hope. If consensus eventually is reached, there will be a new way of thinking about consumers as life-style groups.

Summary of uses

To the marketing practitioner, psychographic methods have offered a way of describing consumers that has many advantages over alternative methods, even though much work on reliability and validity remains to be done. To researchers with more general interests, psychographic methods have offered new ways of looking at old problems, new dimensions for charting trends, and a new vocabulary in which consumer typologies may be described.

From the speed with which psychographics have diffused through the marketing community, it seems obvious that they are perceived as meeting a keenly felt need. The problem now is not so much one of pioneering as it is one of sorting out the techniques that work best. As that process proceeds, it seems extremely likely that psychographic methods will gradually become more familiar and less controversial, and eventually will merge into the mainstream of marketing research.

QUESTIONS

1. How, in your own words, does psychographics (or life-style analysis) differ from demographic analysis? Do you think psychographics will replace demographic analysis for marketers? Is it possible that the two could be used together to help marketers segment target markets?

2. Describe, in your own words, the approaches used in the five examples discussed by Wells. Then explain which you would try if you could use only one and were responsible for marketing a new kind of high-performance bicycle.

3. What do you feel are the prospects of marketers developing a commonly accepted set of market segments, like those described in Figure 1?

4. Write a set of 15 general psychographic statements such as those in Table 2 to be used with college males (or females). Then create two segment descriptions such as those in Figure 1. As a final step, describe (record) whether people in each of your segments would agree or disagree with each of your statements.

*5. In Reading 10 Wells, with Pavasars, discussed the use of attitudes in predicting purchase behavior. Do you think attitudes and psychographics are complementary concepts? Should they be considered as substitutes for one another? Or are they unrelated? How might a marketer use both of them?

---

* Question relates concepts in this and other readings.

13
Benefit segmentation: A decision-oriented research tool

Russell I. Haley

There are different ways to segment a market. While most of the approaches can be valuable, few get at the basic reason a person spends money to buy a product or service—that is, the benefits a person expects to receive from the purchase. In this article Haley discusses an approach called benefit segmentation which focuses specifically on this factor.

Market segmentation has been steadily moving toward center stage as a topic of discussion in marketing and research circles. Hardly a conference passes without at least one session devoted to it. Moreover, in March [1968] the American Management Association held a three-day conference entirely concerned with various aspects of the segmentation problem.

According to Wendell Smith, "Segmentation is based upon developments on the demand side of the market and represents a rational and more precise adjustment of product and marketing effort to consumer or user requirements."[1] The idea that all markets can be profitably segmented has now received almost as widespread acceptance as the marketing concept itself. However, problems remain. In the extreme, a marketer can divide up his market in as many ways as he can describe his prospects. If he wishes, he can define a left-handed segment, or a blue-eyed segment, or a German-speaking segment. Consequently, current discussion revolves largely around which of the virtually limitless alternatives is likely to be most productive.

SEGMENTATION METHODS

Several varieties of market segmentation have been popular in the recent past. At least three kinds have achieved some degree of prominence. Historically, perhaps the first type to exist was geographic segmentation. Small manufacturers who wished to limit their investments, or whose distribution channels were not large enough to cover the entire country, segmented the U.S. market, in effect, by selling their products only in certain areas.

Source: Reprinted with permission from the *Journal of Marketing*, published by the American Marketing Association, vol. 32 (July 1968), pp. 30–35. At the time of writing, Russell Haley was vice president and corporate research director of D'Arcy Advertising in New York City.

[1] Wendell R. Smith, "Product Differentiation and Market Segmentation as Alternative Product Strategies," *Journal of Marketing*, vol. 21 (July 1956), pp. 3–8.

However, as more and more brands became national, the second major system of segmentation—demographic segmentation—became popular. Under this philosophy targets were defined as younger people, men, or families with children. Unfortunately, a number of recent studies have shown that demographic variables such as age, sex, income, occupation and race are, in general, poor predictors of behavior and, consequently, less than optimum bases for segmentation strategies.[2]

More recently, a third type of segmentation has come into increasing favor—volume segmentation. The so-called "heavy half" theory, popularized by Dik Twedt of the Oscar Mayer Company,[3] points out that in most product categories one-half of the consumers account for around 80 percent of the consumption. If this is true, the argument goes, shouldn't knowledgeable marketers concentrate their efforts on these high-volume consumers? Certainly they are the most *valuable* consumers.

The trouble with this line of reasoning is that not all heavy consumers are usually available to the same brand—because they are not all seeking the same kinds of benefits from a product. For example, heavy coffee drinkers consist of two types of consumers—those who drink chain store brands and those who drink premium brands. The chain store customers feel that all coffees are basically alike and, because they drink so much coffee, they feel it is sensible to buy a relatively inexpensive brand. The premium brand buyers, on the other hand, feel that the few added pennies which coffees like Yuban, Martinson's, Chock Full O'Nuts, and Savarin cost are more than justified by their fuller taste. Obviously, these two groups of people, although they are both members of the "heavy half" segment, are not equally good prospects for any one brand, nor can they be expected to respond to the same advertising claims.

These three systems of segmentation have been used because they provide helpful guidance in the use of certain marketing tools. For example, geographic segmentation, because it describes the market in a discrete way, provides definite direction in media purchases. Spot TV, spot radio, and newspapers can be bought for the geographical segment selected for concentrated effort. Similarly, demographic segmentation allows media to be bought more efficiently since demographic data on readers, viewers, and listeners are readily available for most media vehicles. Also, in some product categories demographic variables are extremely helpful in differentiating users from non-users, although they are typically less helpful in distinguishing between

---

[2] Ronald E. Frank, "Correlates of Buying Behavior for Grocery Products," *Journal of Marketing*, vol. 31 (October 1967), pp. 48–53; Ronald E. Frank, William Massy, and Harper W. Boyd, Jr., "Correlates of Grocery Product Consumption Rates," *Journal of Marketing Research*, vol. 4 (May 1967), pp. 184–90; and Clark Wilson, "Homemaker Living Patterns and Marketplace Behavior—A Psychometric Approach," in John S. Wright and Jac L. Goldstucker, eds., *New Ideas for Successful Marketing: Proceedings 1966 World Congress* (Chicago: American Marketing Association, June 1966), pp. 305–31.

[3] Dik Warren Twedt, "Some Practical Applications of the 'Heavy Half' Theory," Advertising Research Foundation 10th Annual Conference, New York City, October 6, 1964.

the users of various brands. The heavy-half philosophy is especially effective in directing dollars toward the most important parts of the market.

However, each of these three systems of segmentation is handicapped by an underlying disadvantage inherent in its nature. All are based on an ex post facto analysis of the kinds of people who make up various segments of a market. They rely on *descriptive* factors rather than *casual* factors. For this reason they are not efficient predictors of future buying behavior, and it is future buying behavior that is of central interest to marketers.

BENEFIT SEGMENTATION

An approach to market segmentation whereby it is possible to identify market segments by causal factors rather than descriptive factors might be called "benefit segmentation." The belief underlying this segmentation strategy is that the benefits which people are seeking in consuming a given product are the basic reasons for the existence of true market segments. Experience with this approach has shown that benefits sought by consumers determine their behavior much more accurately than do demographic characteristics or volume of consumption.

This does not mean that the kinds of data gathered in more traditional types of segmentation are not useful. Once people have been classified into segments in accordance with the benefits they are seeking, each segment is contrasted with all of the other segments in terms of its demography, its volume of consumption, its brand perceptions, its media habits, its personality and life-style, and so forth. In this way, a reasonably deep understanding of the people who make up each segment can be obtained. And by capitalizing on this understanding, it is possible to reach them, to talk to them in their own terms, and to present a product in the most favorable light possible.

The benefit segmentation approach is not new. It has been employed by a number of America's largest corporations since it was introduced in 1961.[4] However, case histories have been notably absent from the literature because most studies have been contracted for privately, and have been treated confidentially.

The benefit segmentation approach is based upon being able to measure consumer value systems in detail, together with what the consumer thinks about various brands in the product category of interest. While this concept seems simple enough, operationally it is very complex. There is no simple straightforward way of handling the volumes of data that have to be generated. Computers and sophisticated multivariate attitude measurement techniques are a necessity.

Several alternative statistical approaches can be employed, among them the so-called "Q" technique of factor analysis, multi-dimensional scaling, and

---

[4] Russell I. Haley, "Experimental Research on Attitudes toward Shampoos," unpublished paper, February 1961.

other distance measures.[5] All of these methods relate the ratings of each respondent to those of every other respondent and then seek clusters of individuals with similar rating patterns. If the items rated are potential consumer benefits, the clusters that emerge will be groups of people who attach similar degrees of importance to the various benefits. Whatever the statistical approach selected, the end result of the analysis is likely to be between three and seven consumer segments, each representing a potentially productive focal point for marketing efforts.

Each segment is identified by the benefits it is seeking. However, it is the *total configuration* of the benefits sought which differentiates one segment from another, rather than the fact that one segment is seeking one particular benefit and another a quite different benefit. Individual benefits are likely to have appeal for several segments. In fact, the research that has been done thus far suggests that most people would like as many benefits as possible. However, the *relative* importance they attach to individual benefits can differ importantly and, accordingly, can be used as an effective lever in segmenting markets.

Of course, it is possible to determine benefit segments intuitively as well as with computers and sophisticated research methods. The kinds of brilliant insights which produced the Mustang and the first 100-millimeter cigarette have a good chance of succeeding whenever marketers are able to tap an existing benefit segment.

However, intuition can be very expensive when it is mistaken. Marketing history is replete with examples of products which someone felt could not miss. Over the longer term, systematic benefit segmentation research is likely to have a higher proportion of successes.

But is benefit segmentation practical? And is it truly operational? The answer to both of these questions is "yes." In effect, the crux of the problem of choosing the best segmentation system is to determine which has the greatest number of practical marketing implications. An example should show that benefit segmentation has a much wider range of implications than alternative forms of segmentation.

An example of benefit segmentation

While the material presented here is purely illustrative to protect the competitive edge of companies who have invested in studies of this kind, it is based on actual segmentation studies. Consequently, it is quite typical of the kinds of things which are normally learned in the course of a benefit segmentation study.

The toothpaste market has been chosen as an example because it is one with which everyone is familiar. Let us assume that a benefit segmentation study has been done and four major segments have been identified—one

---

[5] Ronald E. Frank and Paul E. Green, "Numerical Taxonomy in Marketing Analysis: A Review Article," *Journal of Marketing Research,* vol. 5 (February 1968), pp. 83–98.

particularly concerned with decay prevention, one with brightness of teeth, one with the flavor and appearance of the product, and one with price. A relatively large amount of supplementary information has also been gathered (Table 1) about the people in each of these segments.

Table 1
Toothpaste market segment description

Segment name	The Sensory Segment	The Sociables	The Worriers	The Independent Segment
Principal benefit sought	Flavor, product appearance	Brightness of teeth	Decay prevention	Price
Demographic strengths	Children	Teens, young people	Large families	Men
Special behavioral characteristics	Users of spearmint flavored tooth-paste	Smokers	Heavy users	Heavy users
Brands dispropor-tionately favored	Colgate, Stripe	Macleans, Plus White, Ultra Brite	Crest	Brands on sale
Personality characteristics	High self-involvement	High sociability	High hypo-chondriasis	High autonomy
Life-style characteristics	Hedonistic	Active	Conservative	Value-oriented

The decay prevention segment, it has been found, contains a disproportionately large number of families with children. They are seriously concerned about the possibility of cavities and show a definite preference for fluoride toothpaste. This is reinforced by their personalities. They tend to be a little hypochondriacal and, in their life-styles, they are less socially oriented than some of the other groups. This segment has been named The Worriers.

The second segment, comprised of people who show concern for the brightness of their teeth, is quite different. It includes a relatively large group of young marrieds. They smoke more than average. This is where the swingers are. They are strongly social, and their life-style patterns are very active. This is probably the group to which toothpastes such as Macleans or Plus White or Ultra Brite would appeal. This segment has been named The Sociables.

In the third segment, the one which is particularly concerned with the flavor and appearance of the product, a large portion of the brand deciders are children. Their use of spearmint toothpaste is well above average. Stripe has done relatively well in this segment. They are more egocentered than other segments, and their life-style is outgoing but not to the extent of the swingers. They will be called The Sensory Segment.

The fourth segment, the price-oriented segment, shows a predominance of men. It tends to be above average in terms of toothpaste usage. People in this segment see very few meaningful differences between brands. They switch more frequently than people in other segments and tend to buy a brand on sale. In terms of personality, they are cognitive and they are independent. They like to think for themselves and make brand choices on the basis of their judgment. They will be called The Independent Segment.

MARKETING IMPLICATIONS OF BENEFIT SEGMENTATION STUDIES

Both copy directions and media choices will show sharp differences depending upon which of these segments is chosen as the target—The Worriers, The Sociables, The Sensory Segment, or The Independent Segment. For example, the tonality of the copy will be light if The Sociable Segment of The Sensory Segment is to be addressed. It will be more serious if the copy is aimed at The Worriers. And if The Independent Segment is selected, it will probably be desirable to use rational, two-sided arguments. Of course, to talk to this group at all it will be necessary to have either a price edge or some kind of demonstrable product superiority.

The depth-of-sell reflected by the copy will also vary, depending upon the segment which is of interest. It will be fairly intensive for The Worrier Segment and for The Independent Segment, but much more superficial and mood-oriented for The Sociable and Sensory Segments.

Likewise, the setting will vary. It will focus on the product for The Sensory Group, on socially oriented situations for The Sociable Group, and perhaps on demonstration or on competitive comparisons for The Independent Group.

Media environments will also be tailored to the segments chosen as targets. Those with serious environments will be used for The Worrier and Independent Segments, and those with youthful modern, and active environments of The Sociable and The Sensory Groups. For example, it might be logical to use a larger proportion of television for The Sociable and Sensory Groups, while The Worriers and Independents might have heavier print schedules.

The depth-of-sell needed will also be reflected in the media choices. For The Worrier and Rational Segments longer commercials—perhaps 60-second commercials—would be indicated, while for the other two groups shorter commercials and higher frequency would be desirable.

Of course, in media selection the facts that have been gathered about the demographic characteristics of the segment chosen as the target would also be taken into consideration.

The information in Table 1 also has packaging implications. For example, it might be appropriate to have colorful packages for The Sensory Segment, perhaps aqua (to indicate fluoride) for The Worrier Group, and gleaming white for The Sociable Segment because of their interest in bright white teeth.

It should be readily apparent that the kinds of information normally obtained in the course of a benefit segmentation study have a wide range of marketing implications. Sometimes they are useful in suggesting physical changes in a product. For example, one manufacturer discovered that his product was well suited to the needs of his chosen target with a single exception in the area of flavor. He was able to make a relatively inexpensive modification in his product and thereby strengthen his market position.

The new product implications of benefit segmentation studies are equally apparent. Once a marketer understands the kinds of segments that exist in his market, he is often able to see new product opportunities or particularly effective ways of positioning the products emerging from his research and development operation.

Similarly, benefit segmentation information has been found helpful in providing direction in the choice of compatible point-of-purchase materials and in the selection of the kinds of sales promotions which are most likely to be effective for any given market target.

GENERALIZATIONS FROM BENEFIT SEGMENTATION STUDIES

A number of generalizations are possible on the basis of the major benefit segmentation studies which have been conducted thus far. For example, the following general rules of thumb have become apparent:

It is easier to take advantage of market segments that already exist than to attempt to create new ones. Some time ago the strategy of product differentiation was heavily emphasized in marketing textbooks. Under this philosophy it was believed that a manufacturer was more or less able to create new market segments at will by making his product somewhat different from those of his competitors. Now it is generally recognized that fewer costly errors will be made if money is first invested in consumer research aimed at determining the present contours of the market. Once this knowledge is available, it is usually most efficient to tailor marketing strategies to existing consumer-need patterns.

No brand can expect to appeal to all consumers. The very act of attracting one segment may automatically alienate others. A corollary to this principle is that any marketer who wishes to cover a market fully must offer consumers more than a single brand. The flood of new brands which have recently appeared on the market is concrete recognition of this principle.

A company's brands can sometimes cannibalize each other but need not necessarily do so. It depends on whether or not they are positioned against the same segment of the market. Ivory Snow sharply reduced Ivory Flakes' share of market, and the Ford Falcon cut deeply into the sales of the standard-size Ford because, in each case, the products were competing in the same segments. Later on, for the same companies, the Mustang was success-fully introduced with comparatively little damage to Ford; and the success of Crest did not have a disproportionately adverse effect on Gleem's market position because, in these cases, the segments to which the products ap-pealed were different.

New and old products alike should be designed to fit *exactly* the needs of some segment of the market. In other words, they should be aimed at people seeking a specific combination of benefits. It is a marketing truism that you sell people one at a time—that you have to get *someone* to buy your product before you get *anyone* to buy it. A substantial group of people must be interested in your specific set of benefits before you can make progress in a market. Yet, many products attempt to aim at two or more segments simulta-neously. As a result, they are not able to maximize their appeal to any segment of the market, and they run the risk of ending up with a dangerously fuzzy brand image.

Marketers who adopt a benefit segmentation strategy have a distinct competitive edge. If a benefit segment can be located which is seeking exactly the kinds of satisfactions that one marketer's brand can offer better than any other brand, the marketer can almost certainly dominate the pur-chases of that segment. Furthermore, if his competitors are looking at the market in terms of traditional types of segments, they may not even be aware of the existence of the benefit segment which he has chosen as his market target. If they are ignorant in this sense, they will be at a loss to explain the success of his brand. And it naturally follows that if they do not understand the reasons for his success, the kinds of people buying his brand, and the benefits they are obtaining from it, his competitors will find it very difficult to successfully attack the marketer's position.

An understanding of the benefit segments which exist within a market can be used to advantage when competitors introduce new products. Once the way in which consumers are positioning the new product has been deter-mined, the likelihood that it will make major inroads into segments of interest can be assessed, and a decision can be made on whether or not counterac-tions of any kind are required. If the new product appears to be assuming an ambiguous position, no money need be invested in defensive measures. However, if it appears that the new product is ideally suited to the needs of an important segment of the market, the manufacturer in question can introduce a new competitive product of his own, modify the physical properties of existing brands, change his advertising strategy, or take whatever steps ap-pear appropriate.

Types of segments uncovered through benefit segmentation studies

It is difficult to generalize about the types of segments which are apt to be discovered in the course of a benefit segmentation study. To a large extent, the segments which have been found have been unique to the product categories being analyzed. However, a few types of segments have appeared in two or more private studies. Among them are the following:

The Status Seeker.   A group which is very much concerned with the prestige of the brands purchased.

The Swinger.   A group which tries to be modern and up to date in all of its activities. Brand choices reflect this orientation.

The Conservative.   A group which prefers to stick to large successful companies and popular brands.

The Rational Man.   A group which looks for benefits such as economy, value, durability, etc.

The Inner-Directed Man.   A group which is especially concerned with self-concept. Members consider themselves to have a sense of humor, to be independent and/or honest.

The Hedonist.   A group which is concerned primarily with sensory benefits.

Some of these segments appear among the customers of almost all products and services. However, there is no guarantee that a majority of them or, for that matter, any of them exist in any given product category. Finding out whether they do and, if so, what should be done about them is the purpose of benefit segmentation research.

CONCLUSION

The benefit segmentation approach is of particular interest because it never fails to provide fresh insight into markets. As was indicated in the toothpaste example cited earlier, the marketing implications of this analytical research tool are limited only by the imagination of the person using the information a segmentation study provides. In effect, when segmentation studies are conducted, a number of smaller markets emerge instead of one large one. Moreover, each of these smaller markets can be subjected to the same kinds of thorough analyses to which total markets have been subjected in the past. The only difference—a crucial one—is that the total market was a heterogeneous conglomeration of sub-groups. The so-called average consumer existed only in the minds of some marketing people. When benefit segmentation is used, a number of relatively homogeneous segments are uncovered. And, because they are homogeneous, descriptions of them in terms of averages are much more appropriate and meaningful as marketing guides.

QUESTIONS

1. What is the difference between a descriptive dimension and a causal dimension? Which should prove a better tie to future purchases? If so, should we ever use the other type for segmenting markets?

2. Take a particular consumer goods market—the ice cream market, for example—and develop a table like Table 1 for this market. (Use your own judgment—do not conduct a survey, etc.).
3. For each of the segments you listed in your answer to Question 2, suggest what a good marketing mix might look like.
*4. Does benefit segmentation have any relevance for Kotler and Levy's nonbusiness organizations (Reading 3)? If so, illustrate. If not, explain why.
*5. How might benefit segmentation be used in conjunction with psychographics (Reading 12) to improve the definition of market segments?

---

* Question relates concepts in this and other readings.

14
Market segmentation: A strategic management tool

Richard M. Johnson

This article shows how market analysis techniques can contribute to the development of strategic alternatives. Johnson shows that markets can be thought of as spaces into which specific products can be placed, depending on the dimensions used and consumers' perceptions of the products. Not only existing products but "ideal products" can be positioned in these spaces. By analyzing the relationships among products in the spaces, managers can define market segments. And this can help them conceive of alternative marketing strategies.

Like motivation research in the late 1950s, market segmentation is receiving much attention in research circles. Although this term evokes the idea of cutting up a market into little pieces, the real role of such research is more basic and potentially more valuable. In this discussion *market segmentation analysis* refers to examination of the structure of a market as perceived by consumers, preferably using a geometric spatial model, and to forecasting the intensity of demand for a potential product positioned anywhere in the space.

Source: Reprinted with permission from the *Journal of Marketing Research,* published by the American Marketing Association, vol. 8 (February 1971), pp. 13–18. At the time of writing, Richard Johnson was vice president of Market Facts, Inc.

The purpose of such a study, as seen by a marketing manager, might be:

1. To learn how the brands or products in a class are perceived with respect to strengths, weaknesses, similarities, etc.
2. To learn about consumers' desires, and how these are satisfied or unsatisfied by the current market.
3. To integrate these findings strategically, determining the greatest opportunities for new brands or products and how a product or its image should be modified to produce the greatest sales gain.

From the position of a marketing research technician, each of these three goals translates into a separate technical problem:

1. To construct a product space, a geometric representation of consumers' perceptions of products or brands in a category.
2. To obtain a density distribution by positioning consumers' ideal points in the same space.
3. To construct a model which predicts preferences of groups of consumers toward new or modified products.

This discussion will focus on each of these three problems in turn, suggesting solutions now available. Solutions to the first two problems can be illustrated with actual data, although currently solutions for the third problem are more tentative. This will not be an exhaustive catalog of techniques, nor is this the only way of structuring the general problem of forecasting consumer demand for new or modified products.

CONSTRUCTING THE PRODUCT SPACE

A spatial representation or map of a product category provides the foundation on which other aspects of the solution are built. Many equally useful techniques are available for constructing product spaces which require different assumptions and possess different properties. The following is a list of useful properties of product spaces which may be used to evaluate alternative techniques:

1. *Metric.* Distances between products in space should relate to perceived similarity between them.
2. *Identification.* Directions in the space should correspond to identified product attributes.
3. *Uniqueness/reliability.* Similar procedures applied to similar data should yield similar answers.
4. *Robustness/foolproofness.* Procedures should work every time. It should not be necessary to switch techniques or make basic changes in order to cope with each new set of data.
5. *Freedom from improper assumptions.* Other things being equal, a procedure that requires fewer assumptions is preferred.

One basic distinction has to do with the kinds of data to be analyzed. Three kinds of data are frequently used.

Similarity/dissimilarity data

Here a respondent is not concerned in any obvious way with dimensions or attributes which describe the products judged. He makes global judgments of relative similarity among products, with the theoretical advantage that there is no burden on the researcher to determine in advance the important attributes or dimensions within a product category. Examples of such data might be: (1) to present triples of products and ask which two are most or least similar, (2) to present pairs of products and ask which pair is most similar, or (3) to rank order $k - 1$ products in terms of similarity with the kth.

Preference data

Preference data can be used to construct a product space, given assumptions relating preference to distances. For instance, a frequent assumption is that an individual has ideal points in the same space and that product preference is related in some systematic way to distances from his ideal points to his perception of products' locations. As with similarity/dissimilarity data, preference data place no burden on the researcher to determine salient product attributes in advance. Examples of preference data which might lead to a product space are: (1) paired comparison data, (2) rank orders of preference, or (3) generalized overall ratings (as on a 1 to 9 scale).

Attribute data

If the researcher knows in advance important product attributes by which consumers discriminate among products, or with which they form preferences, then he may ask respondents to describe products on scales relating to each attribute. For instance, they may use rating scales describing brands of beer with respect to price vs. quality, heaviness vs. lightness, or smoothness vs. bitterness.

In addition to these three kinds of data, *procedures* can be *metric* or *nonmetric*. Metric procedures make assumptions about the properties of data, as when in computing a mean one assumes that the difference between ratings of values one and two is the same as that between two and three, etc. Nonmetric procedures make fewer assumptions about the nature of the data; these are usually techniques in which the only operations on data are comparisons such as "greater than" or "less than." Nonmetric procedures are typically used with data from rank order or paired comparison methods.

Another issue is whether or not a *single product space* will adequately represent all respondents' perceptions. At the extreme, each respondent might require a unique product space to account for aspects of his perceptions. However, one of the main reasons for product spaces' utility is that they summarize a large amount of information in unusually tangible and compact form. Allowing a totally different product space for each respondent would certainly destroy much of the illustrative value of the result. A compromise would be to recognize that respondents might fall naturally into a relatively small number of subgroups with different product perceptions. In this case, a separate product space could be constructed for each subgroup.

Frequently a single product space is assumed to be adequate to account for important aspects of all respondents' *perceptions.* Differences in *preference* are then taken into account by considering each respondent's ideal product to have a unique location in the common product space, and by recognizing that different respondents may weight dimensions uniquely. This was the approach taken in the examples to follow.

Techniques which have received a great deal of use in constructing product spaces include nonmetric multidimensional scaling [3, 7, 8, 12], factor analysis [11], and multiple discriminant analysis [4]. Factor analysis has been available for this purpose for many years, and multidimensional scaling was discussed as early as 1938 [13]. *Nonmetric* multidimensional scaling, a comparatively recent development, has achieved great popularity because of the invention of ingenious computing methods requiring only the most minimal assumptions regarding the nature of the data. Discriminant analysis requires assumptions about the metric properties of data, but it appears to be particularly robust and foolproof in application.

These techniques produce similar results in most practical applications. The technique of multiple discriminant analysis will be illustrated here.

EXAMPLES OF PRODUCT SPACES

Imagine settling on a number of attributes which together account for all of the important ways in which products in a set are seen to differ from each other. Suppose that each product has been rated on each attribute by several people, although each person has not necessarily described more than one product.

Given such data, multiple discriminant analysis is a powerful technique for constructing a spatial model of the product category. First, it finds the weighted combination of attributes which discriminates most among products, maximizing an F-ratio of between-product to within-product variance. Then second and subsequent weighted combinations are found which discriminate maximally among products, within the constraint that they all be uncorrelated with one another. Having determined as many discriminating dimensions as possible, average scores can be used to plot products on each dimension. Distances between pairs of products in this space reflect the amount of discrimination between them.[1]

---

[1] McKeon [10] has shown that multiple discriminant analysis produces the same results as classic (metric) multidimensional scaling of Mahalanobis' distances based on the same data.

Figure 1
The Chicago beer market

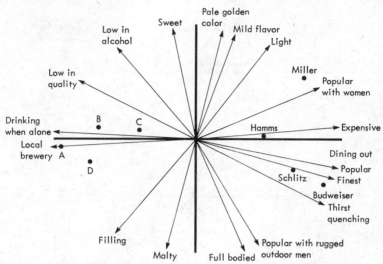

Figure 1 shows such a space for the Chicago beer market as perceived by members of Market Facts' Consumer Mail Panels in a pilot study, September 1968. Approximately 500 male beer drinkers described 8 brands of beer on each of 35 attributes. The data indicated that a third sizable dimension also existed, but the two dimensions pictured here account for approximately 90 percent of discrimination among images of these 8 products.

The location of each brand is indicated on these two major dimensions. The horizontal dimension contrasts premium quality on the right with popular price on the left. The vertical dimension reflects relative lightness. In addition, the mean rating of each product on each of the attributes is shown by relative position on each attribute vector. For instance, Miller is perceived as being most popular with women, followed by Budweiser, Schlitz, Hamms, and four unnamed, popularly priced beers.

As a second example, the same technique was applied to political data. During the weeks immediately preceding the 1968 presidential election, a questionnaire was sent to 1,000 Consumer Mail Panels households. Respondents were asked to agree or disagree with each of 35 political statements on a four-point scale. Topics were Vietnam, law and order, welfare, and other issues felt to be germane to current politics. Respondents also described two preselected political figures, according to their perceptions of each figure's stand on each issue. Discriminant analysis indicated two major dimensions accounting for 86 percent of the discrimination among 14 political figures.

The liberal vs. conservative dimension is apparent in the data, as shown in Figure 2. The remaining dimension apparently reflects perceived favorability of attitude toward government involvement in domestic and international

Figure 2
The political space, 1968

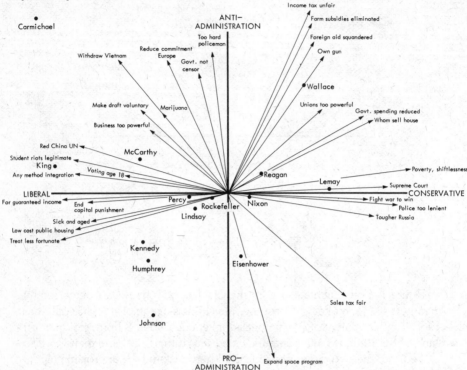

matters. As in the beer space, it is only necessary to erect perpendiculars to each vector to observe each political figure's relative position on each of the 35 issues. Additional details are in [5].

Multiple discriminant analysis is a major competitor of nonmetric multidimensional scaling in constructing product spaces. The principal assumptions which the former requires are that: (1) perceptions be homogeneous across respondents, (2) attribute data be scaled at the interval level (equal intervals on rating scales), (3) attributes be linearly related to one another, and (4) amount of disagreement (error covariance matrix) be the same for each product.

Only the first of these assumptions is required by most nonmetric methods, and some even relax that assumption. However, the space provided by multiple discriminant analysis has the following useful properties:

1. Given customary assumptions of multivariate normality, there is a test of significance for distance (dissimilarity) between any two products.
2. Unlike nonmetric procedures, distances estimated among a collection of products do not depend upon whether or not additional products are

included in the analysis. Any of the brands of beer or political figures could have been deleted from the examples and the remaining object locations would have had the same relationships to one another and to the attribute vectors.

3. The technique is reliable and well known, and solutions are unique, since the technique cannot be misled by any local optimum.

OBTAINING THE DISTRIBUTION OF CONSUMERS' IDEAL POINTS

After constructing a product space, the next concern is estimating consumer demand for a product located at any particular point. The demand function over such a space is desired and can be approximated by one of several general approaches.

The first is to locate each person's ideal point in the region of the space implied by his rank ordered preferences. His ideal point would be closest to the product he likes best, second closest to the product he likes second best, etc. There are several procedures which show promise using this approach [2, 3, 7, 8, 12], although difficulties remain in practical execution. This approach has trouble dealing with individuals who behave in a manner contrary to the basic assumptions of the model, as when one chooses products first on the far left side of the space, second on the far right side, and third in the center. Most individuals giving rank orders of preference do display such nonmonotonicity to some extent, understandably producing problems for the application of these techniques.

The second approach involves deducing the number of ideal points at each region in space by using data on whether a product has too much or too little of each attribute. This procedure has not yet been fully explored, but at present seems to be appropriate to the multidimensional case only when strong assumptions about the shape of the ideal point distribution are given.

The third approach is to have each person describe his ideal product, with the same attributes and rating scales as for existing products. If multiple discriminant analysis has been used to obtain a product space, each person's ideal product can then be inserted in the same space.

There are considerable differences between an ideal point location inferred from a rank order of preference and one obtained directly from an attribute rating. To clarify matters, consider a single dimension, heaviness vs. lightness in beer. If a previous mapping has shown that Brands A, B, C, and D are equally spaced on this one dimension, and if a respondent ranks his preferences as B, C, A, and D, then his ideal must lie closer to B than to A or C and closer to C than to A. This narrows the feasible region for his ideal point down to the area indicated in Figure 3. Had he stated a preference for A, with D second, there would be no logically corresponding position for his ideal point in the space.

Figure 3
A one-dimensional product space

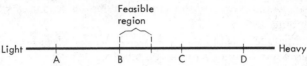

However, suppose these products have already been given the following scale positions on a heavy/light dimension: A = 1.0, B = 2.0, C = 3.0, and D = 4.0. If a respondent unambiguously specifies his ideal on this scale at 2.25, his ideal can be put directly on the scale, with no complexities. Of course, it does not follow *necessarily* that his stated rank order of preference will be predictable from the location of his ideal point.

There is no logical reason why individuals must be clustered into market segments. Mathematically, one can cope with the case where hundreds or thousands of individual ideal points are each located in the space. However, it is much easier to approximate such distributions by clustering respondents into groups. Cluster analysis [6] has been used with the present data to put individuals into a few groups with relatively similar product desires (beer) or points of view (politics).

Figure 4 shows an approximation to the density distribution of consumers' ideal points in the Chicago beer market, a "poor man's contour map." Ideal points tended somewhat to group themselves (circles) into clusters. It is not implied that all ideal points lie within the circles, since they are really distributed to some extent throughout the entire space. Circle sizes indicate the relative sizes of clusters, and the center of each is located at the center of its circle.

A representation such as this contains much potentially useful marketing information. For instance, if people can be assumed to prefer products closer to their ideal points, there may be a ready market for a new brand on the lower or "heavy" side of the space, approximately neutral in price/quality. Likewise, there may be opportunities for new brands in the upper middle region, decidedly light and neutral in price/quality. Perhaps popularly priced Brand A will have marketing problems, since this brand is closest to no cluster.

Figure 5 shows a similar representation for the political space, where circles represent concentrations of voters' points. These are not ideal points, but rather personally held positions on political issues. Clusters on the left side of the space intended to vote mostly for Humphrey and those on the right for Nixon in the 1968 election. Throughout the space, the percentage voting Republican increases generally from left to right.

It may be surprising that the center of the ideal points lies considerably to the right of that of the political figures. One possible explanation is that this study dealt solely with positions on *issues*, so matters of style or personality did not enter the definition of the space. It is entirely possible that members of

Figure 4
Distribution of ideal points in product space

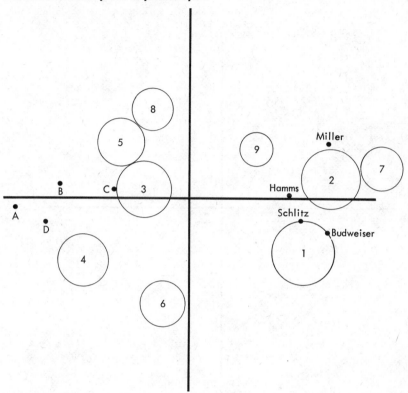

clusters one and eight, the most liberal, found Nixon's position on issues approximately as attractive as Humphrey's, but they voted for Humphrey on the basis of preference for style, personality, or political party. Likewise, members of cluster two might have voted strongly for Wallace, given his position, but he received only 14 percent of this cluster's vote. He may have been rejected on the basis of other qualities. The clusters are described in more detail in [5].

A small experiment was undertaken to test the validity of this model. Responses from a class of sociology students in a western state university showed them to be more liberal and more for decreasing government involvement internationally than any of the eight voter clusters. Their position is close to McCarthy's, indicated by an "S."

STRATEGIC INTEGRATION OF FINDINGS

Having determined the position of products in a space and seen where consumer ideal points are located, how can such findings be integrated to determine appropriate product strategy? A product's market share should be

Figure 5
Voter segment positions relative to political figures

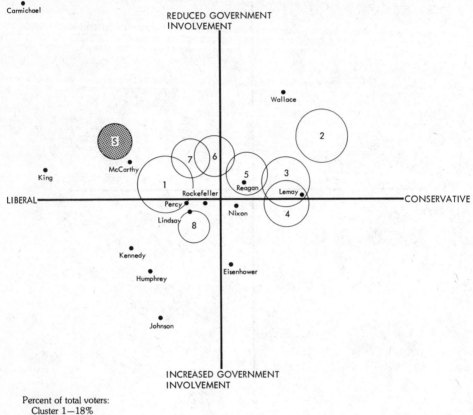

Percent of total voters:
  Cluster 1—18%
  Cluster 2—14%.
  Cluster 3—14%.
  Cluster 4—13%.
  Cluster 5—12%.
  Cluster 6—11%.
  Cluster 7—10%.
  Cluster 8—8%.
  Cluster S—College students, est. 5%.

increased by repositioning: (1) closer to ideal points of sizable segments of the market, (2) farther from other products with which it must compete, and (3) on dimensions weighted heavily in consumers' preferences. Even these broad guidelines provide some basis for marketing strategy. For instance, in Figure 4, Brand A is clearly farthest from all clusters and should be repositioned.

In Figure 5, Humphrey, Kennedy, and Johnson could have increased their acceptance with this respondent sample by moving upwards and to the right, modifying their perceived position. Presumably, endorsement of any issue in the upper right quadrant or a negative position on any issue in the lower left quadrant of Figure 2 would have helped move Humphrey closer to the concentration of voters' ideal points.

Although the broad outlines of marketing strategy are suggested by spaces such as these, it would be desirable to make more precise quantitative forecasts of the effect of modifying a product's position. Unfortunately, the problem of constructing a model to explain product choice behavior based on locations of ideal points and products in a multidimensional space has not yet been completely solved, although some useful approaches are currently available.

As the first step, it is useful to concentrate on the behavior of clusters of respondents rather than that of individuals, especially if clusters are truly homogeneous. Data predicting behavior of groups are much smoother and results for a few groups are far more communicable to marketing management than findings stated in terms of large numbers of individual respondents.

If preference data are available for a collection of products, one can analyze the extent to which respondents' preferences are related to distances in the space. Using regression analysis, one can estimate a set of importance weights for each cluster or, if desired, for each respondent, to be applied to the dimensions of the product space. Weights would be chosen providing the best explanation of cluster or individual respondent preferences in terms of weighted distances between ideal points and each product's perceived location. If clusters, rather than individuals, are used, it may be desirable to first calculate preference scale values or utilities for each cluster [1, 9]. Importance weights can then be obtained using multiple regression to predict these values from distances. If explanations of product preference can be made for *existing products,* which depend only on locations in space, then the same approach should permit *predictions* of preference levels for new or modified products to be positioned at specific locations in the space.

Models of choice behavior clearly deserve more attention. Although the problem of constructing the product space has received much attention, we are denied the full potential of these powerful solutions unless we are able to quantify relationships between distances in such a space and consumer choice behavior.

SUMMARY

Market segmentation studies can produce results which indicate desirable marketing action. Techniques which are presently available can: (1) construct a product space, (2) discover the shape of the distribution of consumers' ideal points throughout such a space, and (3) identify likely opportunities for new or modified products.

In the past, marketing research has often been restricted to *tactical* questions such as package design or pricing levels. However, with the advent of new techniques, marketing research can contribute directly to the development of *strategic* alternatives to current product marketing plans. There remains a need for improved technology, particularly in the development of models for explaining and predicting preferential choice behavior. The general problem has great practical significance, and provides a wealth of opportunity for development of new techniques and models.

REFERENCES

1. Bradley, M. E., and R. A. Terry. "Rank Analysis of Incomplete Block Designs: The Method of Paired Comparisons," *Biometrika,* 39 (1952), 324–45.
2. Carroll, J. D. "Individual Differences and Multidimensional Scaling." Murray Hill, N.J.: Bell Telephone Laboratories, 1969.
3. Guttman, Louis. "A General Nonmetric Technique for Finding the Smallest Space for a Configuration of Points," *Psychometrika,* 33 (December 1968), 469–506.
4. Johnson, Richard M. "Multiple Discriminant Analysis," unpublished paper, Workshop on Multivariate Methods in Marketing, University of Chicago, 1970.
5. ———. "Political Segmentation," paper presented at Spring Conference on Research Methodology, American Marketing Association, New York, 1969.
6. Johnson, Stephen C. "Hierarchial Clustering Schemes," *Psychometrika,* 32 (September 1967), 241–54.
7. Kruskal, Joseph B. "Multidimensional Scaling by Optimizing Goodness of Fit to a Nonmetric Hypothesis," *Psychometrika,* 29 (March 1964), 1–27.
8. ———. "Nonmetric Multidimensional Scaling: A Numerical Method," *Psychometrika,* 29 (June 1964), 115–29.
9. Luce, R. D. "A Choice Theory Analysis of Similarity Judgments," *Psychometrika,* 26 (September 1961), 325–32.
10. McKeon, James J. "Canonical Analysis," *Psychometric Monographs,* 13.
11. Tucker, Ledyard. "Dimensions of Preference," Research Memorandum RM-60-7. Princeton, N.J.: Educational Testing Service, 1960.
12. Young, F. W. "TORSCA, An IBM Program for Nonmetric Multidimensional Scaling," *Journal of Marketing Research,* 5 (August 1968), 319–21.
13. Young, G. and A. S. Householder. "Discussion of a Set of Points in Terms of Their Mutual Distances," *Psychometrika,* 3 (March 1938), 19–22.

QUESTIONS

1. Explain, in your own words, what the concept of a product space means. Does the concept deal only with the physical attributes of the product?
2. Discuss how a marketing manager might make use of the information in a product space which shows the relative positions of the firm's product, its competitors' products, and various ideal points. Would such information help more in identifying a target market or in developing a marketing mix?
*3. Could the concept of market segmentation and product space be used by not-for-profit enterprises, as suggested by Kotler and Levy (Reading 3)?
*4. Discuss how a marketer could combine the concepts in Haley's article on benefit segmentation (Reading 13) with the product space approach to market segmentation illustrated by Johnson.

---
* Question relates concepts in this and other readings.

Part 3

Development of the marketing mix

The second step in marketing strategy planning is the development of an appropriate marketing mix for each target market. A marketing mix is a combination of the variables which are under the control of the marketing manager. They include (1) product, (2) place, (3) promotion, and (4) price—the four Ps. Because each market segment can be different from others in the same general market area, it is usually necessary to develop a separate marketing mix for each target market.

Most of the 12 readings in Part 3 are concerned with (or are examples of) making decisions about the four Ps so as to gain a differential advantage in one or more market segments. While a few of the readings are concerned with constraints on marketing mix planning, such as shortages, inflation, and actual or potential legislation, the primary focus is still on the four Ps.

There are several articles on each of the Ps, but it is important to keep in perspective that, eventually, all four Ps must be blended into one marketing mix. Most of the authors in this part would agree with this, but their own special interest or experience may cause them to focus on only one P. Although they may seem to be considering only one, sometimes they are actually "thinking" all four. But sometimes authors discuss their special P as the dominant or all-important one. Watch out for this kind of "myopia."

15
New products: How they differ; why they fail; how to help them do better

Fred L. Lemont

New products are the lifeblood of a firm. It is through new products that firms are able to protect themselves against the erosion of their sales by other firms' advances and against sales losses resulting from changing consumer tastes. Yet the successful development and introduction of a new product is a difficult task which results in many more failures than successes. In the following discussion, Lemont identifies several categories of new products and suggests strategies for improving the ratio of successes to failures in new-product intoductions.

This comes to you from waist deep in the "Big Muddy" of package goods marketing—new-product development.

And here, as in the original Big Muddy, victory is elusive, power and wealth are no guarantees of success, the enemies are many (and frequently hard to identify), and one yearns nostalgically for the "good wars" of the recent past.

Five or ten years ago, new products were the "good wars" of package goods marketing—a sound, reasonably financed new-product effort usually brought a profitable return on investment. Occasionally enough, the return was outstanding, and the company, and sometimes the key new-products people, rode their creations to new levels of profit and glory.

Then it seemed reasonable that every package goods company could share in the new-products action. All sorts of companies—big, little, amateur, professional—seemed able to find some new need, and fill it.

Today, however, only a very few companies—General Foods, Clairol, Carnation, Estee Lauder, S. C. Johnson—seem able to come up consistently with genuinely new and genuinely successful products. (And every so often, P&G brings out another blockbuster like Pampers.)

Source: Reprinted (with deletions) from *Advertising Age,* April 5, 1971, pp. 43–45. Copyright 1971/1973 by Crain Communications, Inc. At the time of writing, Fred Lemont was partner in The Project Group, Inc., New York.

MOST LOSE MONEY ON NEW PRODUCTS

Are there really fewer successful new package goods products today than there were ten years ago, or are we simply too media-battered, information-dazed, polarized and segmented to notice them?

To start with, no one's counting. The vague feeling is that there may be fewer, there may be the same number, but certainly not more. But there is a very strong, very unvague judgment that even if there are the same number, the new products of today are the result of a dollar and time investment three, four or five times that of ten years ago. Only a minority of package goods companies seem to be getting back their new-product investment, let alone earning a good return on it.

The total new-product investment is staggering, and the companies which think they are spending x dollars on new products are probably, in fact, spending $2x$ or $3x$ when the true dollar, time and opportunity costs are totaled.

Yet investment in new-product development is a management article of faith [. . . ,] and companies plow doggedly on, looking for that better mousetrap, because the conventional management wisdom—taught us by business schools, management seminars, consultants, *Fortune* and published declarations to stockholders or competitors ("This company is committed to new-product development . . . 50 percent of our volume is in products which did not exist five years ago . . .")—is that a company must have new products or die. And, of course, that is true.

But what is also true is that some companies have died in the new-product quest, and many others have grievously injured themselves. For many, the new-product search has been as injurious as the new-product lack.

Why are so many companies failing today in the new-product search? Again, the conventional wisdom: "Somewhere in the past decade we came to the end of the post—World War II marketing revolution based on speed, ease, convenience and new technology, where products could be successful as soon as consumer income rose sufficiently to afford them. All the obvious needs which can be easily and profitably filled have been identified."

Again, much of this may be true, but it is not particularly helpful to a company . . . in desperate need of new products. It is also probably true, as we are told constantly, that the successful new products of the 1970s [and 1980s] must be based as much on changing life-styles and social attitudes as on rising buying power and technology.

Again true, and again not particularly helpful. And terribly seductive, as company after company attacks two of the most obvious symbols of the new life-style—breakfast and youth. How many instant breakfasts spelled backwards and Pop-Tarts spelled sideways, and how many singing, swinging, youth versions of middle-aged cosmetics products can the battered consumer . . . stand? (Orphan Annie in a see-through blouse is still a 43-year-old kid, unattractive in several aspects.)

At least National Student Marketing had the good grace to leave town.

FIVE KINDS OF NEW-PRODUCT SUCCESS

Of course, there have been a number of new-product successes in the [recent] past. Let's look at some different kinds of successful new products of the latter 1960s (admitting in advance that the borders between them are quite blurry):

1. *A genuine product breakthrough:* Arrid Extra Dry, Shell No-Pest, instant breakfast, electric toothbrushes, Water Pik.
2. *A major product improvement or differentiation:* Slender, Pampers, Heublein's Club cocktails, Love cosmetics.
3. *Unique products that meet real (if sometimes subtle) needs:* Clairol's heated curlers and lighted mirror, Lauder's Clinique and Aramis, Shake 'n Bake, Cool Whip, Binaca, Formula 409, Baggies, S. C. Johnson's Edge, Breck Basic, Party Tyme powder cocktail mixes, plastic garbage bags.
4. *We've got a major share of the product category, and we've got to keep coming out with new versions:* A new General Mills or Kellogg's cereal, a new P&G detergent, a new Reynolds cigaret, a new Clairol hair coloring, Ocean Spray line extensions.
5. *Noninnovative, well-executed positionings with lots of marketing muscle:* Scope, Ultra Brite, Clairol's Great Body, Gillette's Soft & Dri.

It's in this last *seductive* area, the noninnovative, marketing positioning marketing muscle approach, that the great mass of failures occur—fail nationally, fail in test market, fail before they get to any market. The area is seductive because all men believe they are great lovers, great drivers and have tough beards—and all marketing men also believe they are great marketing positioners. (It would be better for the stockholders and the consumers if all marketing men stopped believing in marketing positioning, period.)

These four products that succeeded in this area—Scope, Ultra Brite, Great Body, Soft & Dri—were marketed by four of the most skillful package goods operations in the world, in areas of unique competence of each.

In three of these four cases (excluding P&G's Scope), these companies were forced to bring out these noninnovative products to respond to competitors' innovations. Not only is that the best reason for doing what they did, it might be the only reason, unless you are P&G.

Even these companies, as good as they are, have trouble with noninnovative products. If it's tough for them, how can the average package goods company believe it has a chance with a noninnovative product, a "fake new product?" They believe it all right, like lemmings running to the sea, they believe it.

Unfortunately for these companies, the consumer seems to be highly skilled at sorting out fake new products from real ones. They have developed consumer deafness to the constant claims of newness for noninnovative products. Consumer deafness is like husband deafness.

Husband Deafness:
   Wife to husband: I found the most stylish, most flattering midi today, It's
the most delicate shade of mauve, and just hits my calf . . .
   Husband (to himself): She bought another dress.

Consumer Deafness:
   Television set to consumer (who is washing dishes): In this wonder day of
wonder drugs! Incredibly advanced toothpaste! Toughens teeth beyond
belief! Molars grow before your eyes!
   Consumer to television set (spoken into sinkful of dishes): It's like Crest.

FEWER MARKET SEGMENTS THAN YOU THINK

   The more candid statement by the manufacturer would be: "It's almost
like Crest, we think it's a little better, and Lord knows we need the money
more than P&G does" (that, incidentally, is the way it filters through "trade
deafness").
   Let's define a fake new product as a noninnovative product which seeks to
achieve its newness through minor but differentiating formula changes (taste,
color, packaging) and the mystic "marketing/advertising" positioning appealing to a vulnerable consumer segment.
   It is true that there are undiscovered market segments out there waiting for
a 10 percent different product, but the problem is, first, there are far fewer
than that fellow trying to sell you a segmentation study believes there are; and
second, the companies which are really in a good position to take advantage
of that segment opportunity are the owners of the brands on either side of it.
(Just think how easy it would be for them to do what it would be so hard for
you to do.)
   A classic fake new-product route is the premise that the way to beat the
market leader—Crest, say—is better copy. "We've got to out-write them!"
(Does anyone really believe the Crest brand group is saying: "Relax fellows,
we don't need great copy. Just make it fair. We're 'way ahead.") Of course,
what good agency man is going to deny the possibility Crest can be out-
written?
   The failure of the fake new-product device is simply one of the many basic
differences in new and going products. On a going product, a restaging as a
fake new product can frequently be quite effective. Keep it in the going
products area—you may not always look busy, but you won't look stupid,
either.
   Another facet of new-product failure is the "gold rush syndrome," or
"Everyone else is going to get rich in new products; we've got to get ours!"
Scott Fitzgerald said, "All gold rushes are essentially negative in character" (in
that the gold rushers are fleeing something rather than seeking something),
and in this case what marketers are fleeing is hard, unglamorous work on
going products. And today, there are clearly cases of companies caught up in

the new-product gold rush losing as much or more volume and profit on going products than they have made on new products. Companies should rush to new products only after they have maximized their going business.

COPYING DOESN'T REALLY PAY

There is, too, the fear of pioneering or innovating—the obsession with a somewhat better mousetrap, when the consumer is up to her neck in new, improved lemon-flavored mousetraps. Perhaps at one point in the postwar period it was not smart to innovate. (That is hard to believe when one looks at Sara Lee, Clairol, Tropicana, and a dozen other marketing empires founded on unique ideas.) Be that as it may, today it is crystal clear that copying does not pay. New products *must* be innovative. The hundreds of millions of dollars that package goods have wasted in marketing fake new-product failures in the last decade is eloquent proof of that. If love died in the '60s, so did knock-off products.

Another sure route to new-products failure is the 1950s approach, or, "What made this company great was two or three guys with ideas and guts!" Many companies are still attacking new products with new-product management methods 20 years old. This is marketing's version of fundamental football (three yards and a cloud of dust), and consists of two or three marketing men with an armload of Nielsen books, someone from consumer research (itching to do a landmark segmentation study) and an R&D man (scared to death of marketing people). Shazam! A new-products committee, a venture group, or a task force!

Six months, or three years, or four hours, of intense effort usually brings out the same result: Let's go after Alka-Seltzer or Sara Lee or Crest (it's much better to make this kind of decision in four hours, because you avoid the cost of the segmentation study).

WHY NEW PRODUCTS FAIL

There are even rational, orderly reasons for new-product failures:

1. *The inability to audit new-product progress.*   Marketing management is awash in daily, weekly and monthly measurement of the progress of going products. Audits, sales, warehouse withdrawals, attitude studies, penetration, copy test scores all measure facets of an established product, and do it pretty well. The methods used to measure new-product progress—committees, reviews, reports, timetables, Pert, Critical Path—are not very good at measuring hopes and dreams. They are only good once you are past the hoping and dreaming stage—and getting past that stage with something good is the whole trick.

2. *The lack of new-product interest by agencies.*   New-product work is hated in many agencies—for good and bad reasons. The valid reasons are that most of the new products that clients assign are fake (and always come in

with an exhortation to out-write the competition), the work is frequently done free, and an agency can very quickly run up a sizable investment in a new product, only to see it killed by corporate whim.

The bad reasons are the antagonism of many of the contemporary creative people to new products (it doesn't fit their objective of getting work on film fast), and the simple lack of skill and interest in the entire new-product area. (New-product copy tends to be best if it's a little flatfooted, and not only is this very hard to write, but there are not many awards passed out for new-product concepts ads.) Also, new-product creative work is terribly time-consuming and subject to a lot of slow research, highly antagonistic to fast ideas.

3. *The failure of consumer research in the new-product area.* New products in too many cases continue to be measured by the same methods used for measurement of established products. These methods simply are not sensitive enough, and the result is too many go to the marketplace to fail in the marketplace. And, of course, so much product planning is based on mammoth and intriguing segmentation research studies, theoretically the key to new products in a given market. Their success is modest in the new-product development area (unless you consider the new-product development needs of the research supplier. One major segmentation study can certainly solve his new-products needs for a year).

4. *The lack of formal analysis of new-product failures by top management.* An objective analysis of failures is vital to improve a new-product development operation, yet the number of well-run companies which do not do this is stunning. It can be bloody, embarrassing work, but it must be done if a company is to develop and polish the unique set of skills it must have to develop new products in its own unique atmosphere, to meet its own unique needs. If you don't know what you did wrong, you keep doing it.

5. *Lack of discipline, objectives and concentration on what you really have a chance at.* In "Marketing Myopia" [Reading 4] Ted Levitt quoted: "If you don't know where you're going, all roads lead there." The route to fake new products is "all roads," because if a company is not very clear on where it's going, it follows the same set of roads that all other similar thinking (or unthinking) companies are following.

6. *Over-managed R&D and under-managed R&D.* The research and development function in package goods companies is highly analogous to an agency creative department: The same evils—over-management, over-direction management in detail, fragmentation of effort by too many small projects—destroy creativity in both places. But just as sales effectiveness is the ultimate creative discipline in advertising, so it is in product development. And in both copy and R&D, the objectives must be clear and realistic, and management must insist they are met. Great entertainment that doesn't make the sales point and technological achievements meaningless to the consumer have a great deal in common—they are expensive indulgences, and they are management's fault.

7. *Increased government regulation and consumerism.* If you had a new cyclamate product or "fun" cereal or sleep remedy ready for market a year ago, these factors have cost you real money. On the other hand, the subsequent cries of "foul" and "creeping socialism" have cost manufacturers much more. Consumerism-oriented new products are going to succeed, and new proprietaries are going to move through the Food and Drug Administration, and are going to be marketed by companies which understand the consumer and regulatory revolutions and move with them.

HOW TO THINK ABOUT DOING IT

It's not "how to do it," but "how to think about doing it." How to do it is much harder than how not to do it (or as Carl Reiner put it: "I may not know from good, but I know from terrible").

1. Think of the unthinkable—maybe you shouldn't be interested in new products this year. Maybe you should have very narrow new-product interests or maybe you should only be interested in true innovation, in one or more narrow areas. What are you really good at? What can you be better at than anybody else? Where are your odds best? How much is a new-products effort going to hurt your going business? Maybe your game plan is to maximize your going brands, and concentrate on acquisitions. (You can be better at acquisitions than the giants, simply because the government isn't as antagonistic toward your making them. That's an advantage you can exploit.)

2. Where can you innovate? In the laboratory? In the marketplace? Do you know where innovations are needed? Will you know that innovation when you see it? Can you measure what is meaningful innovation—something that really does the job *enough* better for a woman to change her purchase/usage patterns, and perhaps even more important, pay the added pennies your innovation will cost? Is your innovation going to be an innovation to the consumer, or simply another wishful fake new product?

3. Swear off fake new products unless they are absolutely necessary to defend your basic business. Beyond defensive necessity, only believe in the opportunity of marketing/advertising positioning for a new noninnovative product, if you have immense marketing power, if you have extremely strong evidence that the specific positioning is powerful, if it is a difficult one for established competition to adopt quickly, and if your career can stand a real setback.

4. Concentrate your effort. Probably every new-product effort in the country would benefit if on a random basis half of each effort's projects were dropped. Pick those products where you really can bring the consumer something unique and needed and profitable.

5. The new-product effort should have the judgment, intuition, the feel of top management. In the typical marketing company, it is a truism that the president is the brand manager of the biggest brand. If that company has a

major new-product effort, the sound course is probably for him to devote that attention to his new-product effort. New-product efforts are led, not managed. There are no Nielsens on a new-product development effort.

6. Pick your new-products people very carefully. Your own definition of your new-product effort will define the kind of people you need. The best administrator in the world can't turn nothing into something. The new-product manager must lead an effort to develop and measure ideas, and he must turn the best of those ideas into products. The brand man in your company with all the ideas might be very bad at new products, simply because if he is going to succeed for you he is going to have to be receptive to ideas from many sources. One person's new-product ideas are hardly ever enough. And finally, don't be afraid to change the new-products team pretty rapidly if you don't see the results you want. (You would be surprised at how many people are quite happy to leave new-products work under virtually any circumstances.)

7. Be very clear on what product attributes are meaningful to a consumer before you set your R&D operation to work.

8. Find a consumer research person who is bright about new-product research, and who has done a lot of it. Remember that new-products research is rapidly becoming a highly specialized area of research. If you can't afford a full-time new-products researcher, find a consultant who is one, and who can work directly with your new-product marketing group.

9. Only be interested in protectable new products. Only develop and market products that you can protect—with patents, lead time or sufficient marketing power—from imitative competition. There are too many cases of small companies innovating and in fact running a test market for a larger company with both the technical and marketing power to exploit the concept once its basic appeal is proven. Don't develop products for highly competitive markets unless you are sure you will feel comfortable spending the kind of marketing dollars required to enter and stay in these markets. (This sounds a lot more negative than it is. If you stay out of the soapers' way, of the GFs and GMs in their basic areas—detergents, coffee, cereals—the record shows that a moderate-size company [$50–$100 million sales, $5–$10 million profits], *if it has a good product,* can protect itself very well, indeed.)

10. Recognize that new-product development always is going to be a conflict area between the idea people and the money people (or, "Here you stand with reluctant feet where creativity and big business meet"). And in the heat of the conflict, creative people are going to ask in inflammatory tones: Are you trying to discipline creativity? Are you trying to put a dollar tag on an idea? Are you trying to play it safe? Depend more on research than on creative judgment? The appropriate answer to all these questions is yes. You are going to lose some creative people, but surprisingly, keep most of those who are good at new products. And you are not going to lose your shirt on a fake new product.

BE STRATEGIC, CREATIVE, DISCIPLINED

Recognize, believe—best yet, *know* in the pit of your stomach—that your company can develop a systematic approach to new products that has a very, very good chance of getting results, if the company really wants it.

That system must be *strategic,* in that it must reflect your own company's abilities, goals and people; it must be *creative,* in that it uses many different sources to develop new-product concepts; it must be *disciplined,* in that the creative must be very specifically directed and channeled; it must be *research-oriented* (recognizing full well that research will kill off an occasional good idea, but will also kill off most of the bad ones); it must be *tough-minded*—have plenty of proof from its consumers that they will buy your concept before you spend a lot of R&D money developing it; and it must be *philosophical,* in that most of your concepts are going to be judged unsuccessful, and most of your work will be on losers, yet the effort must continue.

And finally, if new-products work has one cardinal principle, it is this: Make sure the consumer needs and wants the product, and you can sell the product, *before* you make the product.

QUESTIONS

1. Lemont lists five categories of new products classified by the degree of innovativeness. In which category do you think it is the hardest to introduce a new product? Why? Which category or categories of new products do you think critics of marketing are most critical of?

2. Lemont makes the point that consumers are not as naive (or fooled as often) as marketing managers and, certainly, critics of marketing seem to think they are. Do you think his point is correct? What does this suggest about the relative power of advertising?

3. Lemont suggests that there are fewer market segments than people think, yet others suggest that in the final analysis every individual is different and could be considered a separate segment. Are these two points of view really different? (Is Lemont thinking about profitability as well as differences?)

16
Exploit the product life cycle

Theodore Levitt

As a product progresses from its introduction through maturity to decline, different strategies are required. In this article, Levitt discusses the several life cycle stages and suggests that most firms should lengthen the maturity stage. He offers four possible extension strategies.

Most alert and thoughtful senior marketing executives are by now familiar with the concept of the product life cycle. Even a handful of uniquely cosmopolitan and up-to-date corporate presidents have familiarized themselves with this tantalizing concept. Yet a recent survey I took of such executives found none who used the concept in any strategic way whatever and pitifully few who used it in any kind of tactical way. It has remained—as have so many fascinating theories in economics, physics, and sex—a remarkably durable but almost totally unemployed and seemingly unemployable piece of professional baggage whose presence in the rhetoric of professional discussions adds a much coveted but apparently unattainable legitimacy to the idea that marketing management is somehow a profession. There is, furthermore, a persistent feeling that the life cycle concept adds luster and believability to the insistent claim in certain circles that marketing is close to being some sort of science.[1]

The concept of the product life cycle is today at about the stage that the Copernican view of the universe was 300 years ago: a lot of people knew about it, but hardly anybody seemed to use it in any effective or productive way.

Now that so many people know and in some fashion understand the product life cycle, it seems time to put it to work. The object of this article is to suggest some ways of using the concept effectively and of turning the knowledge of its existence into a managerial instrument of competitive power.

Since the concept has been presented somewhat differently by different authors and for different audiences, it is useful to review it briefly here so that

Source: Reprinted (with deletions) with permission from the *Harvard Business Review*, vol. 43 (November–December 1965), pp. 81–94. Copyright © 1965 by the President and Fellows of Harvard College; all rights reserved. At the time of writing, Theodore Levitt was on the faculty of the Graduate School of Business Administration of Harvard University.

[1] For discussions of the scientific claims or potentials of marketing, see George Schwartz, *Development of Marketing Theory* (Cincinnati, Ohio: South-Western Publishing Co., 1963); and Reavis Cox, Wroe Alderson, and Stanley J. Shapiro, eds., *Theory in Marketing: Second Series* (Homewood, Ill.: Richard D. Irwin, Inc., 1964).

every reader has the same background for the discussion which follows later in this article.

HISTORICAL PATTERN

The life story of most successful products is a history of their passing through certain recognizable stages. These are shown in Exhibit 1 and occur in the following order:

Exhibit 1
Product life cycle—entire industry

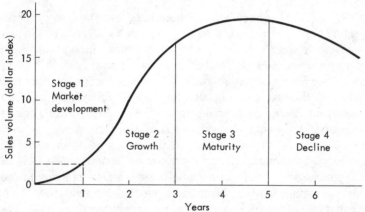

Stage 1: Market development. This is when a new product is first brought to market, before there is a proved demand for it, and often before it has been fully proved out technically in all respects. Sales are low and creep along slowly.

Stage 2: Market growth. Demand begins to accelerate and the size of the total market expands rapidly. It might also be called the "Takeoff Stage."

Stage 3: Market maturity. Demand levels off and grows, for the most part, only at the replacement and new family—formation rate.

Stage 4: Market decline. The product begins to lose consumer appeal and sales drift downward, such as when buggy ships lost out with the advent of automobiles and when silk lost out to nylon.

Three operating questions will quickly occur to the alert executive:

Given a proposed new product or service, how and to what extent can the shape and duration of each stage be predicted?

Given an existing product, how can one determine what stage it is in?

Given all this knowledge, how can it be effectively used?

A brief further elaboration of each stage will be useful before dealing with these questions in detail.

DEVELOPMENT STAGE

Bringing a new product to market is fraught with unknowns, uncertainties, and frequently unknowable risks. Generally, demand has to be "created" during the product's initial *market development stage*. How long this takes depends on the product's complexity, its degree of newness, its fit into consumer needs, and the presence of competitive substitutes of one form or another. A proved cancer cure would require virtually no market development; it would get immediate massive support. An alleged superior substitute for the lost-wax process of sculpture casting would take lots longer.

While it has been demonstrated time after time that properly customer-oriented new product development is one of the primary conditions of sales and profit growth, what have been demonstrated even more conclusively are the ravaging costs and frequent fatalities associated with launching new products. Nothing seems to take more time, cost more money, involve more pitfalls, cause more anguish, or break more careers than do sincere and well-conceived new product programs. The fact is, most new products don't have any sort of classical life cycle curve at all. They have instead from the very outset an infinitely descending curve. The product not only doesn't get off the ground; it goes quickly under ground—six feet under.

It is little wonder, therefore, that some disillusioned and badly burned companies have recently adopted a more conservative policy—what I call the "used apple policy." Instead of aspiring to be the first company to see and seize an opportunity, they systematically avoid being first. They let others take the first bite of the supposedly juicy apple that tantalizes them. They let others do the pioneering. If the idea works, they quickly follow suit. They say, in effect, "The trouble with being a pioneer is that the pioneers get killed by the Indians." Hence, they say (thoroughly mixing their metaphors), "We don't have to get the first bite of the apple. The second one is good enough." They are willing to eat off a used apple, but they try to be alert enough to make sure it is only slightly used—that they at least get the second big bite, not the tenth skimpy one.

GROWTH STAGE

The usual characteristic of a successful new product is a gradual rise in its sales curve during the market development stage. At some point in this rise a marked increase in consumer demand occurs and sales take off. The boom is on. This is the beginning of Stage 2—the *market growth stage*. At this point potential competitors who have been watching developments during Stage 1 jump into the fray. The first ones to get in are generally those with an exceptionally effective "used apple policy." Some enter the market with carbon copies of the originator's product. Others make functional and design improvements. And at this point product and brand differentiation begin to develop.

The ensuing fight for the consumer's patronage poses to the originating producer an entirely new set of problems. Instead of seeking ways of getting consumers to *try the product,* the originator now faces the more compelling problem of getting them to *prefer his brand.* This generally requires important changes in marketing strategies and methods. But the policies and tactics now adopted will be neither freely the sole choice of the originating producer nor as experimental as they might have been during Stage 1. The presence of competitors both dictates and limits what can easily be tried—such as, for example, testing what is the best price level or the best channel of distribution.

As the rate of consumer acceptance accelerates, it generally becomes increasingly easy to open new distribution channels and retail outlets. The consequent filling of distribution pipelines generally causes the entire industry's factory sales to rise more rapidly than store sales. This creates an exaggerated impression of profit opportunity which, in turn, attracts more competitors. Some of these will begin to charge lower prices because of later advances in technology, production shortcuts, the need to take lower margins in order to get distribution, and the like. All this in time inescapably moves the industry to the threshold of a new stage of competition.

MATURITY STAGE

This new stage is the *market maturity stage.* The first sign of its advent is evidence of market saturation. This means that most consumer companies or households that are sales prospects will be owning or using the product. Sales now grow about on a par with population. No more distribution pipelines need be filled. Price competition now becomes intense. Competitive attempts to achieve and hold brand preference now involve making finer and finer differentiations in the product, in customer services, and in the promotional practices and claims made for the product.

Typically, the market maturity stage forces the producer to concentrate on holding his distribution outlets, retaining his shelf space, and, in the end, trying to secure even more intensive distribution. Whereas during the market development stage the originator depended heavily on the positive efforts of his retailers and distributors to help sell his product, retailers and distributors will now frequently have been reduced largely to being merchandise-displayers and order-takers. In the case of branded products in particular, the originator must now, more than ever, communicate directly with the consumer.

The market maturity stage typically calls for a new kind of emphasis on competing more effectively. The originator is increasingly forced to appeal to the consumer on the basis of price, marginal product differences, or both. Depending on the product, services and deals offered in connection with it are often the clearest and most effecitve forms of differentiation. Beyond these, there will be attempts to create and promote fine product distinctions through packaging and advertising, and to appeal to special market segments.

The market maturity stage can be passed through rapidly, as in the case of most women's fashion fads, or it can persist for generations with per capita consumption neither rising nor falling, as in the case of such staples as men's shoes and industrial fasteners. Or maturity can persist, but in a state of gradual but steady per capita decline, as in the case of beer and steel.

DECLINE STAGE

When market maturity tapers off and consequently comes to an end, the product enters Stage 4—*market decline*. In all cases of maturity and decline the industry is transformed. Few companies are able to weather the competitive storm. As demand declines, the overcapacity that was already apparent during the period of maturity now becomes endemic. Some producers see the handwriting implacably on the wall but feel that with proper management and cunning they will be one of the survivors after the industry-wide deluge they so clearly foresee. To hasten their competitors' eclipse directly, or to frighten them into early voluntary withdrawal from the industry, they initiate a variety of aggressively depressive tactics, propose mergers or buy-outs, and generally engage in activities that make life thanklessly burdensome for all firms, and make death the inevitable consequence for most of them. A few companies do indeed weather the storm, sustaining life through the constant descent that now clearly characterizes the industry. Production gets concentrated into fewer hands. Prices and margins get depressed. Consumers get bored. The only cases where there is any relief from this boredom and gradual euthanasis are where styling and fashion play some constantly revivifying role.

PREPLANNING IMPORTANCE

Knowing that the lives of successful products and services are generally characterized by something like the pattern illustrated in Exhibit 1 can become the basis for important life-giving policies and practices. One of the greatest values of the life cycle concept is for managers about to launch a new product. The first step for them is to try to foresee the profile of the proposed product's cycle.

As with so many things in business, and perhaps uniquely in marketing, it is almost impossible to make universally useful suggestions regarding how to manage one's affairs. It is certainly particularly difficult to provide widely useful advice on how to foresee or predict the slope and duration of a product's life. Indeed, it is precisely because so little specific day-to-day guidance is possible in anything, and because no checklist has ever by itself been very useful to anybody for very long, that business management will probably never be a science—always an art—and will pay exceptional rewards to managers with rare talent, enormous energy, iron nerve, great capacity for assuming responsibility and bearing accountability.

But this does not mean that useful efforts cannot or should not be made to try to foresee the slope and duration of a new product's life. Time spent in attempting this kind of foresight not only helps assure that a more rational approach is brought to product planning and merchandising; also, as will be shown later, it can help create valuable lead time for important strategic and tactical moves after the product is brought to market. Specifically, it can be a great help in developing an orderly series of competitive moves, in expanding or stretching out the life of a product, in maintaining a clean product line, and in purposely phasing out dying and costly old products.[2]

* * * * *

STAGE RECOGNITION

The various characteristics of the stages described above will help one to recognize the stage a particular product occupies at any given time. But hindsight will always be more accurate than current sight. Perhaps the best way of seeing one's current stage is to try to foresee the next stage and work backwards. This approach has several virtues:

It forces one to look ahead, constantly to try to reforesee his future and competitive environment. This will have its own rewards. As Charles F. Kettering, perhaps the last of Detroit's primitive inventors and probably the greatest of all its inventors, was fond of saying, "We should all be concerned about the future because that's where we'll have to spend the rest of our lives." By looking at the future one can better assess the state of the present.

Looking ahead gives more perspective to the present than looking at the present alone. Most people know more about the present than is good for them. It is neither healthy nor helpful to know the present too well, for our perception of the present is too often too heavily distorted by the urgent pressures of day-to-day events. To know where the present is in the continuum of competitive time and events, it often makes more sense to try to know what the future will bring, and when it will bring it, than to try to know what the present itself actually contains.

Finally, the value of knowing what stage a product occupies at any given time resides only in the way that fact is used. But its use is always in the future. Hence a prediction of the future environment in which the information will be used is often more functional for the effective capitalization on knowledge about the present than knowledge about the present itself.

SEQUENTIAL ACTIONS

The life cycle concept can be effectively employed in the strategy of both existing and new products. For purposes of continuity and clarity, the remainder of this article will describe some of the uses of the concept from the early stages of new product planning through the later stages of keeping the

---

[2] See Philip Kotler, "Phasing Out Weak Products," *Harvard Business Review*, March–April 1965, p. 107.

product profitably alive. The chief discussion will focus on what I call a policy of "life extension" or "market stretching."[3]

When a company develops a new product or service, it should try to plan at the very outset a series of actions to be employed at various subsequent stages in the product's existence so that its sales and profit curves are constantly sustained rather than following their usual declining slope.

In other words, advance planning should be directed at extending, or stretching out, the life of the product. It is this idea of *planning in advance* of the actual launching of a new product to take specific actions later in its life cycle—actions designed to sustain its growth and profitability—which appears to have great potential as an instrument of long-term product strategy.

NYLON'S LIFE

How this might work for a product can be illustrated by looking at the history of nylon. The way in which nylon's booming sales life has been repeatedly and systematically extended and stretched can serve as a model for other products. What has happened in nylon may not have been purposely planned that way at the outset, but the results are quite as if they had been planned.

The first nylon end-uses were primarily military—parachutes, thread, rope. This was followed by nylon's entry into the circular knit market and its consequent domination of the women's hosiery business. Here it developed the kind of steadily rising growth and profit curves that every executive dreams about. After some years these curves began to flatten out. But before they flattened very noticeably, Du Pont had already developed measures designed to revitalize sales and profits. It did several things, each of which is demonstrated graphically in Exhibit 2. This exhibit and the explanation which follows

Exhibit 2
Hypothetical life cycle—nylon
Subsequent extensions of life cycle

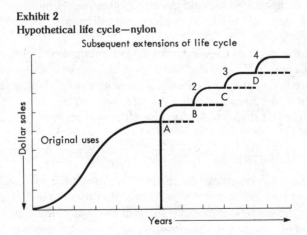

---

[3] For related ideas on discerning opportunities for product revivification, see Lee Adler, "A New Orientation for Plotting a Marketing Strategy," *Business Horizons,* Winter 1964, p. 37.

take some liberties with the actual facts of the nylon situation in order to highlight the points I wish to make. But they take no liberties with the essential requisites of product strategy.

Point A of Exhibit 2 shows the hypothetical point at which the nylon curve (dominated at this point by hosiery) flattened out. If nothing further had been done, the sales curve would have continued along the flattened pace indicated by the dotted line at Point A. This is also the hypothetical point at which the first systematic effort was made to extend the product's life. Du Pont, in effect, took certain "actions" which pushed hosiery sales upward rather than continuing the path implied by the dotted-line extension of the curve at Point A. At Point A action 1 pushed an otherwise flat curve upward.

At points B, C, and D still other new sales and profit expansion "actions" (2, 3, 4, and so forth) were taken. What were these actions? Or, more usefully, what was their strategic content? What did they try to do? They involved strategies that tried to expand sales via four different routes:

1. Promoting more frequent usage of the product among current users.
2. Developing more varied usage of the product among current users.
3. Creating new users for the product by expanding the market.
4. Finding new uses for the basic material.

* * * * *

Exhibit 3
Innovation of new products postpones the time of total maturity—nylon industry

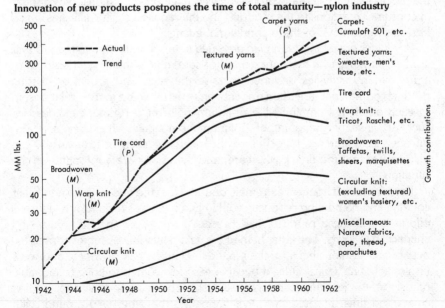

Key:
M = Material influences
P = Product influences
Source: *Modern Textile Magazine,* February 1964, p. 33. Copyright © 1962 by Jordan P. Yale.

Had it not been for the addition of new uses for the same basic material—such as warp knits in 1945, tire cord in 1948, textured yarns in 1955, carpet yarns in 1959, and so forth—nylon would not have had the spectacularly rising consumption curve it has so clearly had. At various stages it would have exhausted its existing markets or been forced into decline by competing materials. The systematic search for new uses for the basic (and improved) material extended and stretched the product's life. [See Exhibit 3.]

*　*　*　*　*

EXTENSION STRATEGIES

The existence of the kinds of product life cycles illustrated in Exhibits 2 and 3 suggests that there may be considerable value for people involved in new product work to begin planning for the extension of the lives of their products even before these products are formally launched. To plan for new life-extending infusions of effort (as in Exhibit 2) at this pre-introduction stage can be extremely useful in three profoundly important ways.

1. *It generates an active rather than a reactive product policy.* It systematically structures a company's long-term marketing and product development efforts in advance, rather than each effort or activity being merely a stop-gap response to the urgent pressures of repeated competitive thrusts and declining profits. The life-extension view of product policy enforces thinking and planning ahead—thinking in some systematic way about the moves likely to be made by potential competitors, about possible changes in consumer reactions to the product, and the required selling activities which best take advantage of these conditional events.

2. *It lays out a long-term plan designed to infuse new life into the product at the right time, with the right degree of care, and with the right amount of effort.* Many activities designed to raise the sales and profits of existing products or materials are often undertaken without regard to their relationship to each other or to timing—the optimum point of consumer readiness for such activities or the point of optimum competitive effectiveness. Careful advance planning, long before the need for such activity arises, can help assure that the timing, the care, and the efforts are appropriate to the situation.

For example, it appears extremely doubtful that the boom in women's hair coloring and hair tinting products would have been as spectacular if vigorous efforts to sell these products had preceded the boom in hair sprays and chemical hair fixers. The latter helped create a powerful consumer consciousness of hair fashions because they made it relatively easy to create and wear fashionable hair styles. Once it became easy for women to have fashionable hair styles, the resulting fashion consciousness helped open the door for hair colors and tints. It could not have happened the other way around, with colors and tints first creating fashion consciousness and thus raising the sales of sprays and fixers. Because understanding the reason for this precise order of events is essential for appreciating the importance of early pre-introduction life-extension planning, it is useful to go into a bit of detail. Consider:

For women, setting their hair has been a perennial problem for centuries. First, the length and treatment of their hair is one of the most obvious ways in which they distinguish themselves from men. Hence to be attractive in that distinction becomes crucial. Second, hair frames and highlights the face, much like an attractive wooden border frames and highlights a beautiful painting. Thus hair styling is an important element in accentuating the appearance of a woman's facial features. Third, since the hair is long and soft, it is hard to hold in an attractive arrangement. It gets mussed in sleep, wind, damp weather, sporting activities, and so forth.

Therefore, the effective *arrangement* of a woman's hair is understandably her first priority in hair care. An unkempt brunette would gain nothing from making herself into a blond. Indeed, in a country where blonds are in the minority, the switch from being an unkempt brunette to being an unkempt blond would simply draw attention to her sloppiness. But once the problem of arrangement became easily "solved" by sprays and fixers, colors and tints could become big business, especially among women whose hair was beginning to turn gray.

The same order of priorities applies in industrial products. For example, it seems quite inconceivable that many manufacturing plants would easily have accepted the replacement of the old single-spindle, constantly man-tended screw machine by a computerized tape-tended, multiple-spindle machine. The mechanical tending of the multiple-spindle machine was a necessary intermediate step, if for no other reason than that it required a lesser work-flow change, and certainly a lesser conceptual leap for the companies and the machine-tending workers involved.

For Jell-O, it is unlikely that vegetable flavors would have been very successful before the idea of gelatin as a salad base had been pretty well accepted. Similarly, the promotion of colored and patterned Scotch tape as a gift and decorative seal might not have been as successful if department stores had not, as the result of their drive to compete more effectively with mass merchandisers by offering more customer services, previously demonstrated to the consumer what could be done to wrap and decorate gifts.

3. *Perhaps the most important benefit of engaging in advance, pre-introduction planning for sales-extending, market-stretching activities later in the product's life is that this practice forces a company to adopt a wider view of the nature of the product it is dealing with.* Indeed, it may even force the adoption of a wider view of the company's business. Take the case of Jell-O. What is its product? Over the years Jell-O has become the brand umbrella for a wide range of dessert products, including cornstarch-base puddings, pie fillings, and the new "Whip'n Chill," a light dessert product similar to a Bavarian Creme or French Mousse. On the basis of these products, it might be said that the Jell-O Division of General Foods is in the "dessert technology" business.

In the case of tape, perhaps 3M has gone even further in this technological approach to its business. It has a particular expertise (technology) on which it has built a constantly expanding business. This expertise can be said to be that of bonding things (adhesives in the case of Scotch tape) to other things, particularly to thin materials. Hence we see 3M developing scores of profitable items, including electronic recording tape (bonding electron-sensitive materials to tape) and "Thermo-Fax" duplicating equipment and supplies (bonding heat-reactive materials to paper).

CONCLUSION

For companies interested in continued growth and profits, successful new product strategy should be viewed as a planned totality that looks ahead over some years. For its own good, new product strategy should try to predict in some measure the likelihood, character, and timing of competitive and market events. While prediction is always hazardous and seldom very accurate, it is undoubtedly far better than not trying to predict at all. In fact, every product strategy and every business decision inescapably involves making a prediction about the future, about the market, and about competitors. To be more systematically aware of the predictions one is making so that one acts on them in an offensive rather than a defensive or reactive fashion—this is the real virtue of preplanning for market stretching and product life extension. The result will be a product strategy that includes some sort of *plan for a timed sequence of conditional moves.*

Even before entering the market development stage, the originator should make a judgment regarding the probable length of the product's normal life, taking into account the possibilities of expanding its uses and users. This judgment will also help determine many things—for example, whether to price the product on a skimming or a penetration basis, or what kind of relationship the company should develop with its resellers.

These considerations are important because at each stage in a product's life cycle each management decision must consider the competitive requirements of the next stage. Thus a decision to establish a strong branding policy during the market growth stage might help to insulate the brand against strong price competition later; a decision to establish a policy of "protected" dealers in the market development stage might facilitate point-of-sale promotions during the market growth stage, and so on. In short, having a clear idea of future product development possibilities and market development opportunities should reduce the likelihood of becoming locked into forms of merchandising that might possibly prove undesirable.

This kind of advance thinking about new product strategy helps management avoid other pitfalls. For instance, advertising campaigns that look successful from a short-term view may hurt in the next stage of the life cycle. Thus at the outset Metrecal advertising used a strong medical theme. Sales boomed until imitative competitors successfully emphasized fashionable slimness. Metrecal had projected itself as the dietary for the overweight consumer, an image that proved far less appealing than that of being the dietary for people who were fashion-smart. But Metrecal's original appeal had been so strong and so well made that it was a formidable task later on to change people's impressions about the product. Obviously, with more careful long-range planning at the outset, a product's image can be more carefully positioned and advertising can have more clearly defined objectives.

Recognizing the importance of an orderly series of steps in the introduction of sales-building "actions" for new products should be a central ingredient of long-term product planning. A carefully preplanned program for market expansion, even before a new product is introduced, can have powerful virtues. The establishment of a rational plan for the future can also help to guide the direction and pace of the ongoing technical research in support of the product. Although departures from such a plan will surely have to be made to accommodate unexpected events and revised judgments, the plan puts the company in a better position to *make* things happen rather than constantly having to react to things that *are* happening.

It is important that the originator does *not* delay this long-term planning until after the product's introduction. How the product should be introduced and the many uses for which it might be promoted at the outset should be a function of a careful consideration of the optimum sequence of suggested product appeals and product uses. Consideration must focus not just on optimum things to do, but as importantly on their optimum *sequence*—for instance, what the order of use of various appeals should be and what the order of suggested product uses should be. If Jell-O's first suggested use had been as a diet food, its chances of later making a big and easy impact in the gelatin dessert market undoubtedly would have been greatly diminished. Similarly, if nylon hosiery had been promoted at the outset as a functional daytime-wear hosiery, its ability to replace silk as the acceptable high-fashion hosiery would have been greatly diminished.

To illustrate the virtue of pre-introduction planning for a product's later life, suppose a company has developed a nonpatentable new product—say, an ordinary kitchen salt shaker. Suppose that nobody now has any kind of shaker. One might say, before launching it, that (1) it has a potential market of x million household, institutional, and commercial consumers, (2) in two years market maturity will set in, and (3) in one year profit margins will fall because of the entry of competition. Hence one might lay out the following plan:

I. *End of First Year: Expand Market among Current Users*
   Ideas—new designs, such as sterling shaker for formal use, "masculine" shaker for barbecue use, antique shaker for "Early American" households, miniature shaker for each table place setting, moisture-proof design for beach picnics.
II. *End of Second Year: Expand Market to New Users*
   Ideas—designs for children, quaffer design for beer drinkers in bars, design for sadists to rub salt into open wounds.

III. *End of Third Year: Find New Uses*

Ideas—make identical product for use as a pepper shaker, as decorative garlic salt shaker, shaker for household scouring powder, shaker to sprinkle silicon dust on parts being machined in machine shops, and so forth.

This effort to prethink methods of reactivating a flattening sales curve far in advance of its becoming flat enables product planners to assign priorities to each task, and to plan future production expansion and capital and marketing requirements in a systematic fashion. It prevents one's trying to do too many things at once, results in priorities being determined rationally instead of as accidental consequences of the timing of new ideas, and disciplines both the product development effort that is launched in support of a product's growth and the marketing effort that is required for its continued success.

QUESTIONS

1. How does a product's stage in the life cycle affect marketing mix planning? Illustrate with a specific product, say a new dessert concept.

2. Illustrate what could be done for a specific industrial product, say a new hand-held wood cutting tool, to move it through Levitt's four approaches for extending the product life cycle.

3. Is Levitt really talking about extending product life cycles or starting new ones?

*4. What are the similarities in Levitt's thinking in this article and his article on marketing myopia (Reading 4)?

*5. Would Levitt's ideas be relevant for Kotler and Levy's nonbusiness organizations (Reading 3)? Explain, with an illustration.

---

* Question relates concepts in this and other readings.

17
The changing role of the product manager in consumer goods companies

Victor P. Buell

The product manager or brand manager approach to the management of consumer goods firms has been popular and successful. But, like all good things, it must undergo change to adapt to changing needs and constraints. This article reports on a recent survey designed to gather information on the changes the product manager approach is undergoing.

What the proper role of the product or brand manager should be remains a troublesome question for the managements of consumer goods companies. It is particularly a problem for packaged goods producers, who are the most frequent users of this organizational device.

The role of the product manager has undergone several changes since the product management system was first introduced. That these changes have not produced entirely satisfactory results is evident in the continuing public debate on this topic. Titles of selected articles and papers illustrate the situation:

The Product Manager System Is in Trouble[1]

Has the Product Manager Failed? Or, the Folly of Imitation[2]

Product Management—Vision Unfulfilled[3]

Brand Manager vs. Creative Man: The Clash of Two Cultures[4]

Brand Manager vs. Advertising Director—Must One of Them Go?[5]

Product Managers and Advertising—A Study of Conflict, Inexperience and Opportunity.[6]

Source: Reprinted with permission from the *Journal of Marketing,* published by the American Marketing Association, vol. 39 (July 1975), pp. 3–11. At the time of writing Victor Buell was an associate professor of marketing at the University of Massachusetts, Amherst.

[1] Stephens W. Dietz, *Advertising Age,* June 2, 1969, pp. 43–44.

[2] *Sales Management,* January 1, 1967, pp. 27–29.

[3] David J. Luck and Theodore Nowak, *Harvard Business Review,* vol. 43 (May–June 1965), p. 143.

[4] Ralph Leezenbaum, *Marketing Communications,* April 1970, pp. 40–43.

[5] *Advertising Age,* January 27, 1969, p. 53.

[6] James F. Pomeroy, paper presented to the Association of National Advertisers, Workshop on Development and Approval of Creative Advertising, New York, April 2, 1969.

The purpose of this article is to review the changes that have occurred in the product management form of organization since its introduction, to explore the reasons behind the continuing controversy, and to examine current changes in management thinking and their implications for the future. To this end, the author uses material from his recent study of several leading consumer goods manufacturers and major advertising agencies.

THE STUDY: BACKGROUND AND APPROACH

Much of the controversy has centered on the degree of control the product manager exercises over advertising. Under a grant from the Association of National Advertisers (ANA), the author studied the advertising decision-making process in companies with major advertising expenditures.[7] Although its overall purpose was broader, the study provided the opportunity to explore management attitudes toward product management and to gather information on the restructuring this system currently is undergoing.

In-depth interviews were held during the summer and fall of 1972 with 63 executives in 20 leading companies which represented ten consumer industry classifications plus one miscellaneous category. Extensive interviews were also held with 23 executives in ten major advertising agencies.

Sixteen of the companies produced packaged goods primarily and four produced consumer durables primarily. Product management was the predominant form of marketing organization in 15 of the companies; a functional form predominated in 5. Some of the companies used one organizational form in some divisions and the other form in other divisions.

Survey sample

The combined domestic sales of the 20 companies surveyed exceeded $60 billion, and their combined advertising expenditures were over $1.5 billion. Seventeen were among the 50 largest advertisers and 10 ranked among the top 20. The primary industry classifications of the consumer packaged goods companies included food; drugs and cosmetics; soaps, cleansers, and allied products; soft drinks; tobacco; paper; liquor; and one miscellaneous category. The consumer durable goods companies fell under the industry classifications of electric appliances, automobiles, and building products.

Participant companies were selected with the assistance of the Management Policy Committee of the Association of National Advertisers. Selection criteria included: (1) company commitment to a large advertising budget, (2) recognized leadership position in the company's industry, (3) management willingness to participate, and (4) multiple industry representation. Preference was given to companies that had extensive experience with product man-

---

[7] Victor P. Buell, *Changing Practices in Advertising Decision-making and Control* (New York: Association of National Advertisers, 1973).

agers. Advertising agencies were selected from among leading agencies that served one or more of the 20 manufacturing companies. To encourage participation and frank discussion, participants were assured that neither companies nor individuals would be identified in the report.

Thirty-one corporate executives were interviewed, including chairmen, presidents, executive and group vice-presidents, and staff vice-presidents. Positions occupied by the 32 divisional executives interviewed included presidents, marketing vice-presidents, directors of marketing or advertising, directors of brand management, and group product managers.

The 10 advertising agencies in the study were among the nation's 20 largest and had combined U.S. billings in excess of $2 billion. Agency executives interviewed included chairmen, presidents, executive and senior vice-presidents, and vice-presidents.

Data collection method

All interviews were conducted by the author. Interviews were open-ended and ranged in length from one to three hours. Policies, procedures, and files were made freely available. Interviews with agency executives provided cross-checks on information developed with their clients.

The purpose of the study was to gain understanding of the reasons behind advertising and marketing management practices rather than duplicate the quantitative data developed by the more commonly used mail questionnaire. Because of the qualitative nature of the study, findings are reported primarily as the author's interpretations of prevailing management practices, attitudes, and intentions rather than in the form of statistical summaries. The findings have been reported to the participating executives and have been discussed in depth with several of them.

While the study provides the principal data source for this article, conclusions are based also on interviews with executives during other research projects by the author, reviews of product management literature, and recent reports of mail surveys.

Because of the selective sample, the findings are not representative of all companies. The findings are important in that they represent managerial viewpoints in consumer goods companies with leadership positions, most of whom employ large numbers of product managers.

HISTORICAL DEVELOPMENTS

The product management system, although introduced nearly 50 years ago, did not come into general use until the 1950s. The Association of National Advertisers, in a recent study among its members, found that the following percentages of participating companies used product managers: packaged goods, 85 percent (93 percent of those with annual advertising expenditures exceeding $10 million); other consumer goods, 34 percent, industrial goods, 55 percent.[8]

Product management is a response to the organizational problem of providing sufficient management attention to individual products and brands when there are too many for any one executive to coordinate effectively all of the aspects of the marketing mix. Companies, or divisions of companies, with a limited line of products normally follow a functional plan of organization wherein departments such as sales, advertising and sales promotion, marketing research, product planning, and customer service report to a common marketing executive. When shifting from this purely functional organization, product managers are added to assist the chief marketing executive by assuming the planning and coordination for individual products or product lines.

Although the product manager has made possible greater management concentration by product, the position also has created new problems. Responsibility often has been assigned to the product manager for achievement of goals such as sales volume, share of market, and even profit in some cases; yet the product manager has no line authority over the functional departments that execute his plans.

Shift of advertising responsibility to the product manager

A key change in the original concept was made when companies shifted the management of advertising from the advertising manager to the product manager. In leading packaged goods companies that currently use product managers, one rarely finds an advertising department on the organization chart. If one is there, it is usually at the group or corporate level, where it provides services common to several divisions, such as media planning and coordinating media purchases.

The reasons for phasing out the separate advertising function were: (1) to reduce costs, which rose as the advertising department expanded to manage the advertising for increasing numbers of products and brands; and (2) to give the product manager more control over execution of a major marketing function. Such a move was possible because the advertising agency was available to develop and place advertising.

Figures 1 and 2 provide examples of typical functional and product management organizations. While details may vary from company to company, these charts reflect the main differences that exist between the two organizational forms in the companies studied by the author.

Companies assume the planning function

Concurrent with the growth of the product management function, companies began to assume the marketing planning and service functions—with

<hr>

[8] *Current Advertising Practices: Opinions as to Future Trends* (New York: Association of National Advertisers, 1974)

Figure 1
Functional marketing organization

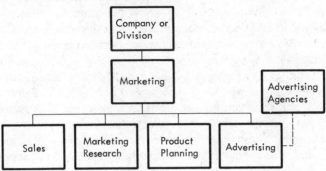

the exception of creative and media—that had been performed for them by their advertising agencies.

As marketing grew in sophistication during the 1950s, much of the know-how was centered in the agencies. Gradually, however, companies expanded their own supporting service functions, and the responsibility for initiating marketing plans became a key function of the product manager. This change has been made with little criticism. Agencies have accepted the idea that marketing planning should originate within the company, and they are aware of the growing effectiveness of the product manager as a planner.

Increases in intervening management levels

As companies grow, the product manager becomes further removed from the real decision-making levels of management. When products were fewer in number product managers reported directly to higher-level executives, who

Figure 2
Product management organization

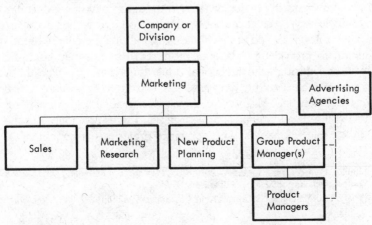

had the authority to make broad decisions and implement programs. As product lines proliferated, and the numbers of product managers grew correspondingly, intervening levels of supervision became necessary. In large companies today, product managers may be anywhere from two to four levels below the executive who has the real decision-making authority and the clout to see that plans are carried out.

Due to rapid growth, companies also have shifted to filling product manager positions with younger, less experienced people. This relative inexperience, plus separation from the key decision maker, has increased management concern over the degree of authority that should be delegated to the product manager. These concerns are particularly strong with respect to advertising because of the magnitude of advertising costs and the importance of advertising to product success.

Continued use of functional organization

The ANA study of its members found that 34 percent of the participating larger consumer durable goods companies used product managers, as compared with 85 percent of the packaged goods companies. Why do some companies stay with the functional form?

Pearson and Wilson believe there may be good reasons why a company should prefer the functional organization.[9] In fact, they think some companies have made a mistake in switching to product management before it was really necessary. They maintain that companies with a line of similar products, with one dominant product line, or with several large product lines (sufficient to support divisionalization) might be better off avoiding product management. It was not long after Pearson left McKinsey & Co. to become president of PepsiCo that the Pepsi-Cola division did away with product managers.[10] This division sells a related line of soft drinks with one dominant product—Pepsi-Cola.

Three of the consumer durable goods companies interviewed by the author had functional marketing setups. The major appliance group of an electrical company and the major division of an automotive manufacturer each had relatively few products although they accounted for large dollar sales. Both companies preferred to use advertising to build the overall brand name in addition to promoting individual products; they felt they could achieve better control through the functional advertising manager. The third company, a manufacturer of building products, organized its product divisions by markets and channels. Historically, the corporate advertising department has supervised the development of advertising and sales promotion for the various market sales managers, who appear to prefer this arrangement.

[9] Andrall E. Pearson and Thomas W. Wilson, Jr., *Making Your Marketing Organization Work* (New York: Association of National Advertisers, 1967).

[10] "The Brand Manager: No Longer King," *Business Week,* June 9, 1973, pp. 58–66.

While there are good reasons why many companies do not use product management, there appears to be no significant defection by current users, as was implied in the article that featured the PepsiCo story.[11] Of the 211 companies surveyed by the ANA, 5 percent had adopted product management during the preceding three years, as compared with 1 percent who had abandoned it.[12] Clewett and Stasch, in a survey of 160 product managers and other marketing executives, found less than 1 percent who felt that product management was likely to be discontinued in their divisions.[13] In the author's study, none of the 15 companies that used product management planned to change.

No doubt some companies will shift from product management from time to time for sound organizational reasons or out of sheer frustration. But there is no evidence of a trend in this direction. If a trend exists it would appear to be in the direction of continued adoption of product management.

CURRENT MANAGEMENT ATTITUDES

Executives interviewed by the author were concerned about the product management system but were committed to making it work better. Their attitudes appeared to be changing with respect to the question of the product manager's responsibility and authority and his role in advertising. They also expressed concern over the scarcity of advertising specialists within their companies.

Disaffection with the "little president" concept

Almost all of the executives interviewed recognized that the earlier concept of the product manager as a "little president" or "little general manager," with profit responsibility, was unrealistic. As the manager of a paper products company said: "We've gotten away from the concept of the guy who runs his own little company. We want our product managers to be profit conscious, but what we're really talking about is sales volume."

Remnants of the concept persist, however, as illustrated by excerpts from two recruiting brochures. The brochure of a household products company states: "The Product Manager has responsibility for his brand. He is not only responsible for its management, he is accountable for its overall performance. . . . The Product Manager is not just a marketing manager, but in many respects a general manager of a good-size business." When this statement was pointed out to an executive of this company the author was told that it no

---

[11] Same reference as footnote 10.

[12] Same reference as footnote 8.

[13] Richard M. Clewett and Stanley F. Stasch, "Product Managers in Consumer Packaged Goods Companies," Working paper, Northwestern University Graduate School of Management, March 1974.

longer represents management opinion; that, in fact, the company's product managers have no decision-making authority.

The brochure of a food company, after explaining the product manager's role in developing objectives and strategies, says: "The Product Manager is responsible for the execution and performance of the brands entrusted to him."

In describing the position, the marketing director of another food company probably came closest to prevailing management attitudes when he avoided mentioning responsibility for execution or performance: "Our product manager's job is planning—objectives and strategy—monitoring progress, coordinating budget development and control, and working with other departments—Home Economics and Manufacturing, for example—on product cost and quality."

Clarifying the advertising role

Packaged goods executives pretty much agree that the typical product manager has insufficient training, experience, or skill to be entrusted with important creative decisions. They tend to share the view of the agency vice-president who told the author: "Advertising is too important a decision to be left in the hands of a product manager. His role should be planning and coordination—not advertising approval."

Agency critics complain that because of his inexperience the product manager is too cautious and too meticulous in judging creative work; he delays the development process and causes dilution of creative copy by requiring repeated rework; and, to compensate for his insecurity, he relies too heavily on copy testing, which normally produces inconclusive data. Company executives agree. All want the product manager involved in advertising decision making, but they are developing procedures that get agency recommendations up the line to the final decision maker as quickly as possible. Agencies, it should be noted, are reassigning responsibility for client contact to higher management levels to correspond with the client management levels making advertising decisions.

Current top management attitudes are reflected in the following comments. The president of a personal products company said: "I want the best people in a profit center working on, and approving, marketing decisions. We try to set the atmosphere and tone so that our brand manager feels important, yet knows that advertising is too important to be decided at the bottom level." The executive vice-president of a drug products company explained his company's position this way: "We give much authority to the product manager other than the copy side—sales promotion, for example. But we let him know he is not to be the final authority on advertising. We say the person who knows the most about advertising should make the ultimate decision."

Companies, however, do make a distinction between *major* and *minor* advertising decisions. Figure 3 indicates the differences in executive levels that

Figure 3
Where advertising companies say creative decisions are made

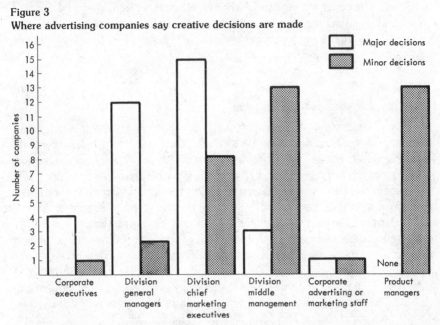

Note: The figures represented by the bars total more than the number of companies because decisions may be made jointly by two or more executives, decisions may be made by one executive in the absence of another, or the decision level may vary by degree of importance within the major or minor categories.

Source: Adapted from Victor P. Buell, *Changing Practices in Advertising Decision-Making and Control* (New York: Association of National Advertisers, 1973), p. 49.

deal with decisions of varying importance. Major decisions may include almost anything to do with an important product or, for less important products, they may involve only significant matters, such as a change in strategy. The author's research showed that advertising decisions considered to be major were made most frequently at the division manager or division marketing manager levels, with some going to the corporate level. None of the companies believed *major* creative-type advertising decisions were made by the product manager. Decisions considered minor, on the other hand, most frequently were made at the product manager and division middle management (group product manager) levels. Understanding this distinction may help to clarify the sometimes confusing results of those mail surveys that indicate that the product manager makes advertising decisions: he does make some decisions, but usually not the major ones.

Considering the past sharp criticisms by agency executives it is worth noting that these complaints have been directed primarily at the product manager's role in the advertising approval process. In contrast, they agree with his role as the authoritative source of information and as marketing planner. An agency vice-president who works with both functional and product management organizations volunteered this comment: "I would rather work with a product manager than with an advertising manager. The product manager has all the information, although he may be unaware of the broader strategies. But in the vertical organization, each person has only a part of the information we require."

Need for the advertising specialist

After several years of operating without advertising departments, many company executives now wonder whether they have any real advertising expertise left in-house. The normal promotion route provides added experience in judging advertising, and one learns from his mistakes and successes. But experience does not necessarily develop the kind of expertise in judging creative work that comes from long and intensive involvement in the development of advertising by talented people. Some marketing executives seem to have better creative judgment than others, but promotion up the line from product manager does not automatically guarantee success in this area.

To replace the skills that were lost with the demise of the advertising department, three companies have created a new position, staff advertising director, to provide creative counsel to product managers and others concerned with advertising decisions. Whereas the former advertising manager made the advertising decision, the new advertising director provides counsel to those charged with the decision-making responsibility.

Where this position has been introduced, it has usually been placed within the division marketing management organization. Executives report that product and other managers exhibit reluctance to avail themselves of staff counsel when it is located in corporate headquarters.

How much authority?

The persistent, unresolved question puzzling management is how much and what kind of authority the product manager needs. Luck, in discussing the many functional areas with which the product manager must interact, states: "Product managers are seriously hampered by ambiguity of authority in the execution of their plans and decisions. . . ."[14]

A common management attitude was expressed by the group vice-president of a liquor company, who said: "The brand manager's authority is the authority of his influence and knowledge." While true as far as it goes, this conclusion seems oversimplified. Several studies bear on the issue.

Lucas, in a mail survey of 60 product managers, found that four in five believed their degree of control over the decision areas of advertising, marketing research, and market testing was "adequate for their assigned respon-

[14] David J. Luck, "Interfaces of a Product Manager," *Journal of Marketing,* vol. 33 (October 1969), pp. 32–36.

sibilities."[15] Smaller proportions reported that they had adequate control over the personal selling, production, and distribution functions and in the areas of legal affairs, advertising expenditures, and pricing. That these product managers did not consider their responsibilities insignificant is evident in the fact that two-thirds felt that they had major, or even 100%, responsibility for product profit.

The mail survey of 160 executives, primarily product managers and group product managers, conducted by Clewett and Stasch found product managers to be "less than major participants" in the decision areas of advertising, product, packaging, pricing, and personal selling.[16] They were reported to be "major participants" in marketing research and promotion. When tasks, as opposed to decision making, were considered this study reported that product managers had a "major role" in planning, budgeting, scheduling, communicating plans and maintaining enthusiasm for them, monitoring progress, revising plans, and reporting performance. The two studies appear to disagree only in the area of advertising decision authority.

Gemmill and Wileman report that in the absence of direct authority, product managers influence action by using reward power, coercive power, expert power, and referent (i.e., personal relationships) power.[17] They found that product managers who primarily employed expert/referent power were the most effective.

Dietz has identified at least two types of product managers the *brand coordinator,* who has no entrepreneurial responsibility; and the *brand champion,* who has responsibility for making entrepreneurial recommendations.[18] Common to both types, he says, are the responsibilities for planning, securing approval of plans, coordinating the execution of plans by functional departments, and evaluating the results of the actions taken. Dietz suggests that the brand coordinator needs little authority to fulfill his responsibility but that the more aggressive brand champion reaches out for authority in frustration over the slowness with which higher levels of management arrive at decisions.

As mentioned earlier, the author's findings indicate that the product manager's authority varies with the relative importance of the decision and that his influence varies with his experience and competence. As a division president in a food products company said: "The product manager system works well for us, but we don't have a set way of working with every product manager. Some are more experienced and some are more aggressive than others."

Consensus appears to exist with respect to the product manager's responsibility for planning, coordinating, and evaluating. Differences continue with

[15] Darrell B. Lucas, "Point of View: Product Managers in Advertising," *Journal of Advertising Research,* vol. 12 (June 1972), pp. 41–44.

[16] Same reference as footnote 13.

[17] Gary R. Gemmill and David L. Wileman, "The Product Manager as an Influence Agent," *Journal of Marketing,* vol. 36 (January 1972), pp. 26–30.

[18] Stephens Dietz, "Get More Out of Your Brand Management," *Harvard Business Review,* vol. 51 (July–August 1973), p. 127.

respect to the questions of authority over execution and the authority to make decisions. The present answer for the last two would seem to be "it all depends."

As a result of these changing management attitudes, all companies interviewed indicated that they had made, or were making, changes in their product manager setups with respect to functions, authority, management decision-making levels, staffing, or length of time in the job. Eight indicated that they were acting in all of these areas.

Management accepts the system but believes it needs improvement. The president of a food company expressed the viewpoint of many when he commented: "There is nothing fundamentally wrong with the product manager system, but I don't think we operate it as well as we should."

Emphasizing position strengths—Deemphasizing weaknesses

In redefining the job, management is emphasizing the functions that product managers can perform well and deemphasizing those aspects of the position with inherent weaknesses. Emphasis is being placed on the role of the product manager as the gatherer and synthesizer of all information about the product and its markets, as the developer of plans, as the communicator of approved plans, and as the monitor of performance. Management expects the product manager to have a deep personal commitment to the success of his product, while they recognize that he alone cannot be held responsible for achievement of sales and profits. Ultimate responsibility, they believe, must rest with the executive in a position to control all marketing activities.

The role of the product manager as decision maker is being deemphasized. The current trend is for decision-making authority to be given in accordance with the importance of the decision area and to vary with the experience and competence of the individual product manager. The product manager will remain involved with the decision-making process, but he will be encouraged to bring key decisions to his manager's attention. As one marketing director said, "The brand manager's job is to get good decisions made irrespective of who makes them.

Controlling resource allocation at higher levels

Management not only wants decisions made where the most competence exists, but it also recognizes the need to control resource allocations among products. The president of a liquor company put it this way: "Our brand managers make many decisions but they don't make the key ones. Someone at a higher level must look at the broad allocation of expenditures."

Obviously, the product manager is not in a position to see the overall picture. The more effective an individual product manager is, the better job he may do in obtaining a disproportionate share of functional resources. It is higher management's job to see that money and other resources are allocated on the basis of profit potential.

The idea that decision making should be moved up the line rather than down the line does not sit well with long-term advocates of decentralized management. However, most executives interviewed seemed to have come to terms with this issue. They recognized that on matters that have a major impact on profit, decisions should be made where all the necessary information is available and where competence exists to make the best judgment. This means that different decisions will be made at different levels, but it does not preclude participation by the product manager, who should have the most information about his product and market. Exceptions to this philosophy were found at the corporate level in three companies. Checks at the division levels in these companies indicate, however, that major advertising decisions were, in fact, being made at the marketing vice-president or division president levels.

Staffing with marketing experience

During the 1960s and early 1970s, a number of companies sought out the recent MBA graduate to fill the assistant product manager position. The graduate schools provided a selective recruiting source of people with broad management training. Though not unhappy with the quality of these recruits, managements have found that their limited training in marketing (particularly in advertising) and the usual absence of marketing experience are drawbacks for product management. They complain, also, that higher competitive compensation levels for the MBA tend to upset established wage patterns.

With the exception of two major packaged goods producers, the companies interviewed had reduced their reliance on the graduate business school as a primary recruiting source for product management. Five had eliminated this source entirely. They were recruiting instead from advertising agencies and other companies and were making internal transfers from sales, marketing research, and the like, in order to obtain people with marketing experience. Some of these people may already have their MBA degree, which is considered a plus, but the emphasis is being placed on marketing experience.

Slowing job turnover

Simultaneously, eight of the companies were upgrading the position and attempting to hold incumbents in the job for longer periods. This has not been easy, since the job attracts high-potential, well-motivated individuals who consider product management a stepping stone to higher management. To attract and hold good people, companies in the past have advanced them from assistant to associate to product manager to group product manager fairly rapidly. Switching to different product groups often occurred along the way.

This "churning" is felt to be undesirable. Incumbents do not stay with a product long enough to develop the desired product and market expertise. Furthermore, short-term assignments do not encourage the long-range planning that can enhance market position. Through different hiring practices and by providing incentives to remain with a product longer, the eight companies hope to increase product manager effectiveness. Other managements that would like to increase longevity in the job explain that they have been unable to do so because of rapid company growth.

FUTURE IMPLICATIONS

In summary, over the years the product manager system has undergone a number of changes and it is still in the process of change. Because the position corresponds to none of the classic line, staff, or functional positions it has never fit neatly into traditional organizational structure. Yet for companies with many products it affords a better means of product-by-product management concentration than does functional organization. For this reason—and despite its acknowledged problems—most companies that are using the product management system plan to stay with it.

It is too early to tell whether the current trend to emphasize planning and coordination, and deemphasize decision making, will resolve the major problems. The same can be said for attempts to improve staffing and to lengthen incumbent tenure.

In some ways the product manager system appears to be in tune with current organizational behavior theory, with its emphasis on group cooperation and participative decision making and its deemphasis of hierarchical authority patterns. The author found, for example, that those organizations with the longest product management experience appeared to be most happy with it, apparently because people throughout these organizations better understand the system. People seem to recognize the reasons for cooperating with the product manager in the absence of any formal authority on his part. The corporate advertising vice-president of one long-time user of product management emphasized this point: "What makes our system tick is not organization or who makes the decision, but something more intangible—our people are trained in the company system and everyone knows how it works."

No doubt we have not heard the last of the product manager problem nor the last of change. Until a better idea comes along, however, we are likely to see continued use of the system and continued efforts to improve it. Product management has been, and will continue to be, an intriguing subject for organizational theorists and practicing managers alike.

QUESTIONS

1. Taking into account the historical development of the brand manager approach, discuss why some consumer goods firms went to a brand manager type of organizational structure. Would this be an appropriate organization for an industrial goods firm? Why or why not?

2. Why are some firms moving away from, or at least modifying, the job and responsibility of the product manager? Based on the article, do you think that the product manager position will disappear?

*3. Why has the primary role of some brand managers been to make advertising decisions? Is this really practicing the marketing concept, or is some kind of "marketing myopia" (Reading 4) involved?

---

* Question relates concepts in this and other readings.

18
Distributors bring back the Crosley appliance

The competition for control of channels of distribution is sometimes intense. In this reprint from Business Week, *the development of a distributor-owned brand of appliances is discussed. The article shows how the brand was obtained and identifies advantages to the distributors of selling their own branded products.*

White-goods shoppers in 3,000 appliance stores across the nation this spring may be surprised to encounter refrigerators, freezers, ranges, and air conditioners bearing the Crosley brand—a brand that vanished from the marketplace in the mid-1950s. A group of independent distributors has revived the Crosley name in an effort to regain industry position, which has been eroding for years as more and more manufacturers have abandoned the appliance business and those remaining have begun selling direct to dealers.

Bringing the Crosley brand back is the handiwork of two distributors who found themselves without a refrigerator line when Aeronutronics Ford Corp. (the former Philco-Ford Corp.) bowed out of the business last August. In five months Carl E. Dixson Sr., a North Carolina distributor, and Robert J. Van

---

Source: Reprinted with permission from *Business Week*, January 31, 1977, pp. 92–93. Copyright © 1977, McGraw-Hill, Inc.

De Velde of Sterling, Ill., contacted each Philco distributor in the country and sought to persuade him to join a cooperative that would pool buying power and manufacture a private brand.

COMPETITION

Dixson says that the need for a private label completely controlled by the distributors was essential if they were to compete with the mass merchandisers and big chains such as Sears, Roebuck & Co. and J. C. Penney Co., which have taken much of the market for white goods.

"The appliance business has been going the way of the automotive business," says Dixson, president of Brown-Rogers-Dixson Co. in Winston-Salem. "Many of the majors have lost their tails and gotten out." Major corporations that have sold off or closed down all or most of their appliance divisions in recent years include Westinghouse, RCA, and Philco-Ford. Today, General Electric Corp. and the Frigidaire Division of General Motors Corp. are the only two major manufacturers that offer a full line of appliances under their own label.

One result of the withdrawals is that most appliances are now produced under independent brand names such as Speed Queen, Waste King, and Kitchen-Aid, whose specialized lines are limited to one or two products, or by companies such as Rockwell International, Revco Inc., White Consolidated Industries, and McGraw-Edison, which produce private-label merchandise for chains and discount stores.

The Philco Div. of Ford Motor Co. sold its laundry and freezer lines in 1968 but held on to its refrigerator business. In 1973 Philco came out with its Cold Guard line of refrigerators, which it claimed would use 10 to 35 percent less energy than competing lines. "We showed that the consumer could recoup the premium price of the Cold Guard through energy savings over the first two years of operation," says Sales Manager James T. McMurphy, "but the consumer wasn't willing to pay the difference." As a result, Aeronutronics Ford quit the business.

To continue to offer a full line of appliances to their dealers, the distributors needed a new refrigerator brand. Adding Frigidaire or GE refrigerators, however, was out of the question. Both manufacturers bypass distributors by selling directly to retailers. Several Philco distributors tried negotiating individually with independent manufacturers to acquire their refrigerator lines but found that they were in a weak position to bargain for price and promotional support. "The independents were used to dealing with a Penney's or a Montgomery Ward's," says Van De Velde, president of Hardware Products Co. of Sterling. "They thought we were a two-headed calf. We had no power individually. But if we looked at the group of affected Philco distributors as a whole, there was real strength." Dixson, whose company was also a major Philco distributor, says, "The obvious answer was for us to band together into a buying cooperative and create our own brand, which could be put on any number of appliances."

A FIND

Several of the independents owned brand names that they were willing to franchise to the distributors, but during the negotiations Van De Velde and Dixson discovered that the ownership of the Crosley brand—which many of the Philco distributors had handled before Avco Corp. sold the brand to Philco in 1956—had been allowed to lapse. "Buddy [Dixson] found an old Crosley refrigerator in his warehouse," says Van De Velde, "and we shipped it in interstate commerce, which allowed us to register the name as our own."

By November, 35 of Philco's 40 former distributors had formed the Crosley group, with Dixson and Van De Velde as co-chairmen. The original 35 distributors, plus eight non-Philco distributors who have since joined them, cover virtually all the United States and have combined annual sales of some $500 million. The group licensed Rockwell International to manufacture refrigerators, Revco to produce freezers, Hardwick Stove Co. to make gas and electric ranges, and McGraw-Edison to turn out air conditioners—all under the Crosley brand. The design of each of the Crosley lines differs from the manufacturers' existing lines. "We're spanning all price ranges so a dealer can go high-end, low-end, or mid-range, depending on what models he decides to order," says Van De Velde.

At this point, the group's initial orders for these four products average $3 million per month. "The refrigerators, freezers, and ranges began arriving in January," Dixson says, "and the air conditioners will be in dealer showrooms in time for the spring selling season."

Dealer response to the idea has been enthusiastic. Of 120 Midwestern dealers who heard the distributors' pitch in Chicago in early January and a similar number of Southeastern dealers who were briefed at a meeting in Atlanta, virtually all have agreed to go along. Dixson anticipates that by the time all the dealers who buy from the group's members have been exposed to the idea, at least 3,000 will sign up.

With that potential dealer base, the group has considerable economic muscle. "We're projecting a retail volume in these four products of $50 million for 1977," says Dixson. "That's very, very conservative and far less than the current business in these products for the distributors who have already joined. But if we said we would do $100 million, no one would believe us." Simply by switching a large number of its more than 400 dealers in North and South Carolina to the Crosley brand, Dixson's company alone can account for about $10 million in sales of the brand this year.

"We won't require any distributor or dealer to take the entire line," Dixson says. "They can pick and choose only those products and models they want. Eventually, though, if the Crosley brand is successful, it will just make sense for them to gradually add the whole line, and that would mean they would drop some of the lines they are now carrying."

PRICING

Dixson stops short of saying that Crosley dealers will be able to compete on price with such giants as Sears, Penney, and Montgomery Ward. But he does say that Crosley dealers will be able to compete with such lines as GE, Frigidaire, and White Westinghouse.

"Those companies have to add a corporate gross profit of around 25 percent to their manufacturing costs, then add their distribution costs on top of that before they set a price to the dealer," Dixson says. "We don't have to add anything for corporate profit. Our group is nonprofit, and our overhead will be practically nil. Even after we're running full steam, there will be no need for more than three people to operate the group's central office. The only thing our group will add is a 1 percent markup, all of which will be used to cover overhead and national advertising, first to the dealers, then to consumers." The opening promotional shot in the Crosley campaign will be double-page spreads in the white goods' trade press in February. The theme of the announcement: "Crosley is back."

QUESTIONS

1. Who really is responsible for the revival of the Crosley brand of appliances? Is it the distributors, the major retail chains, other appliance manufacturers, consumers or something else?

2. What do you think are the chances of success for the Crosley brand? Why do the distributors think they may be able to succeed when many major producers such as Westinghouse, Philco-Ford, and RCA have had to drop some or all of their appliance lines?

*3. Is the revival of the Crosley brand an example of competition for differential advantage (Reading 5)?

---

* Question relates concepts in this and other readings.

19
Bran X: A small cereal-maker has tough struggle in big guys' world

David M. Elsner

Can a small-town cereal manufacturer survive in the world of the giants? The following story from The Wall Street Journal *shows that, despite competitive pressure, a small consumer goods firm with limited resources for advertising can enjoy a degree of success, even when competing against the giants of its industry.*

In 1926, Skinner Macaroni Co. came out with the country's first raisin bran. The breakfast cereal proved popular, and 16 years later both Kellogg and Post began imitating it.

Skinner's head start didn't mean much. Today, Kellogg Co. and General Foods Corp.'s Post brand account for virtually all the sales in the $140 million raisin-bran market while Skinner's struggles to get on grocers' shelves. That is true even though the Omaha cereal—which food experts contend is every bit as good as its competition—generally sells for about 10 cents a box less.

Skinner's, of course, isn't likely ever to challenge for industry leadership. It doesn't even want to. "All we need to be successful is a tiny part of the market," says John McGowan, president of U.S. Mills Inc., the Omaha company that now manufactures Skinner's. "But even that's tough to get."

One of the biggest hurdles for any small manufacturer of a consumer item is to get his product on display where people can see and buy it. In the cereal industry, the staff of the Federal Trade Commission has charged, the four largest manufacturers—Kellogg, General Foods, General Mills and Quaker Oats—tacitly agreed on a plan to divide available supermarket shelf space. The big cereal companies say that the stores allocate the space and that they themselves merely make suggestions. In either case, the result seems to be the same: Largely unknown products like Skinner's are left out in the cold.

NEW MARKETS, MORE SALES

Despite this shelf-space squeeze, Skinner's has managed to break into new markets and increase its sales. A look at its experience is instructive for what it

Source: Reprinted with permission from *The Wall Street Journal,* April 26, 1977, pp. 1, 17. Copyright © 1977 by Dow-Jones, Inc. At the time of writing David Elsner was a staff reporter for *The Wall Street Journal.*

says about the ability of a manufacturer with only limited resources to survive in a highly competitive field.

Skinner Macaroni Co. sold its raisin-bran label to U.S. Mills in 1963. U.S. Mills had been packaging the raisin bran for Skinner and was making another bran cereal, Uncle Sam's laxative cereal, for itself. It saw the Skinner acquisition as a chance to expand its business. It wasn't until 1974, however, that U.S. Mills began trying to sell the Skinner brand outside its traditional Southwestern marketing area.

Skinner's is now sold in about two-thirds of the country's major metropolitan areas and has about 3 percent of the national raisin-bran business, according to Mr. McGowan, a portly, genial man whose grandfather founded U.S. Mills nearly 70 years ago. Sales have increased about fivefold in the last four years, he says—the privately held firm doesn't disclose dollar amounts—and the company soon will install equipment that will double its 60-box-a-minute output.

"THEY DON'T BLISTER"

"As far as quality goes, we can compete with anyone," Mr. McGowan asserts. "We cook our flakes much slower than Kellogg or Post. That means they don't blister and get soggy in milk so quick."

Quality isn't enough. Both the position and the amount of shelf space in supermarkets are important. Each cereal company wants a visible location to attract shoppers' attention, and each wants enough space to make sure that all its products are always on the shelf.

Since the early 1960s, manufacturers have introduced a spate of new cereals, aimed chiefly at children. Available shelf space has grown little in that time. The cereal makers themselves refer to the situation as "the battle for the shelves."

To bring about some order, shelf space today is largely allocated according to turnover. The fastest-selling brands get the most space, and a fair share for all is supposedly assured.

But that doesn't help get shelf space in the first place. "It's a vicious circle," Mr. McGowan complains. "We can't get shelf space unless we show sales movement, and we can't get movement unless we're on the shelves."

STRATEGY INCLUDES FEW ADS

Large food manufacturers, with successful track records and huge advertising budgets, usually don't have much trouble persuading grocers to give their new products a chance. Small companies like U.S. Mills, on the other hand, must either spend heavily on advertising in hopes of creating consumer demand or offer grocers some other inducements.

U.S. Mills has chosen to forsake advertising for the most part. Last year it spent less than $100,000 on it, mostly on newspaper ads and for radio spots on station WOR in New York. (WOR has an older audience, which is more likely to need a laxative cereal like raisin bran, the company feels.) In contrast, Kellogg and Post last year spent an estimated $8 million on raisin-bran advertising alone.

"Advertising is just too expensive," Mr. McGowan explains. "To do any good it would cost us too much. Besides, Kellogg and Post advertise so much that they've made the whole country raisin-bran conscious. That's helped us a bit."

The money that U.S. Mills doesn't spend on advertising goes to subsidize lower prices to supermarkets. A 12-box case of Skinner's usually costs about $1 less at wholesale than either Kellogg's or Post's raisin bran. This, plus various allowances to the stores, enables Skinner's to be sold at retail for about 10 cents a box less, without loss of profit to the grocer. Mr. McGowan says that this alone is often enough to get supermarkets to try it.

Many times it isn't. Then, U.S. Mills offers supermarkets additional cash discounts of up to 50 cents a case and a certain number of free cases, all of which adds up to an even higher profit for retailers.

Frequently, though, stores don't pass along their lower costs to their customers. Edward Shtafman, a food broker for metropolitan New York who handles Skinner's, says most chains make only a few cents a box on either Kellogg's or Post's raisin bran because they use it to attract customers into the store. To make up for their lower margins there, they mark up lesser-known products like Skinner's much more, he says. The result is that Skinner's often sells for the same price as its well-known competitors, or even higher. "Without the price differential, there isn't much reason for people to try us over them," Mr. Shtafman says.

Even where the price differential is maintained, U.S. Mills still has problems. "We're usually put in the worst shelf position"—a top end slot known as "the hole" because it's easy for shoppers to pass by as they swing their carts into an aisle—Mr. McGowan says. "We get lost out there."

Moreover, competitors aren't always happy to see Skinner's on the shelves. "The Post and Kellogg reps work in cahoots up to a point," charges Paul Day, a Los Angeles food broker who handles Skinner's. "They'll go into stores and squeeze the number of our facings (rows) down. Sometimes they shut us out completely. They take the little aluminum strips off the shelves that show the stock boys where our product is supposed to go. The clerks have a million other things to worry about and usually don't notice. So when it's time to restock the shelves, they forget us. Then the buyer will look at his figures at the end of the month and drop us because we're not selling. That's happened to us dozens of times and it takes four or five years generally to get the stores to take you back."

A CASE OF RETALIATION

Mr. McGowan says that Skinner boxes once were slashed with razor blades in a Midwest supermarket. "We knew who did it and slashed theirs right back," he says. "We haven't had that kind of trouble since."

Kellogg denies that its salesmen do such things. Post says it doesn't want to comment because of continuing hearings by the Federal Trade Commission into alleged oligopolistic practices in the cereal industry.

Still, there is no question that Kellogg has designed shelf-space allocation programs for supermarkets. According to estimates by grocers testifying at the FTC hearings, as many as 80 percent of the nation's supermarkets have used such programs to some extent. The giant cereal maker (which last year accounted for about 41 percent of the industry's sales, more than double the combined percentage of runners-up General Mills and General Foods) sought to organize the shelves because it believed it was being given less space than its sales justified.

As the number of cereal brands proliferated, more stores began using Kellogg's sophisticated computers and programs to allocate their shelf space according to turnover. "We couldn't afford all that computer equipment," notes the vice president of a medium-sized Midwest food chain. "We were glad to let them help us. It saved a lot of time and trouble." Other supermarket executives say they let Kellogg salesmen restock and reposition cereal boxes because it frees store personnel to do other things.

But, according to FTC testimony by a Kellogg executive, Kellogg quickly used its computer programs to the disadvantage of its competitors. For instance, it hesitated to recommend taking its own cereals off the shelves. Robert C. Bland, Kellogg's director of marketing research, testified that the standard used by Kellogg for eliminating slower-selling brands was arbitrarily changed from store to store to keep Kellogg products from being discontinued.

Kellogg would recommend removal of one of its items only if five competitive items could be discontinued at the same time, Mr. Bland said. It would suggest that a competitor be given more space only if the basis for the suggestion would result in more space for Kellogg, too.

SUCCESS DISPUTED

The overall success of Kellogg's shelf space program is a matter of some dispute. "If it had been as restrictive as the FTC says, I don't think our market share could have risen five points between 1960 and 1970," says Luther C. McKinney, a senior vice president at Quaker Oats Co., one of the concerns that the FTC staff has charged with oligopolistic practices.

U.S. Mills tries to avoid getting buried on the shelves by getting its boxes off of them. It offers supermarkets various cash and case allowances to set up aisle displays that "shoppers almost can't help but trip over," Mr. McGowan says.

"We've had a lot of success with the offshelf displays," he added. "We try it about two or three times a year and we always get real good movement off of them. Sometimes it encourages the supermarkets to give us a little more space on the shelves."

U.S. Mills uses another stratagem: It makes its boxes a quarter of an inch wider than its competitors' in the hope that they'll be a little more noticeable on the shelves.

A number of supermarkets still are reluctant to try Skinner's. "Retailers don't want 'me-too' products," Walter S. Rubow, vice president for perishable foods at Jewel Food Stores of Chicago, testified recently at the FTC hearings. "If another corn flakes came out, our question would be: What type of support is going to be put behind that item to dissuade the customer from buying the existing corn flakes that is out there? How is it going to increase the market rather than just fractionate it?"

QUESTIONS

1. What are the basic reasons that Skinner's raisin bran product has been able to survive and grow in sales for over 50 years, despite competition from industry giants?

2. Do you think the big three cereal manufacturers could eliminate Skinner (U.S. Mills) from the cereal market if they wanted to? Would there be any advantage to the large firms from doing so? Why might they not want to eliminate this small producer?

*3. Discuss the legal issues (Reading 8) large competitors must consider when competing with U.S. Mills.

---

* Question relates concepts in this and other readings.

20
Retail strategy and the classification of consumer goods

Louis P. Bucklin

The classical consumer goods classification system (convenience, shopping, specialty goods) can be of great value in planning marketing strategy. Bucklin reviews several classification systems and then extends these concepts to retail store types. These ideas are relevant to both retailers and channel members who must select retailers. The article gives a good example of how a small retailer could improve its strategic planning with these store-goods classes.

When Melvin T. Copeland published his famous discussion of the classification of consumer goods—shopping, convenience, and specialty goods—his intent was clearly to create a guide for the development of marketing strategies by manufacturers.[1] Although his discussion involved retailers and retailing, his purpose was to show how consumer buying habits affected the type of channel of distribution and promotional strategy that a manufacturer should adopt. Despite the controversy which still surrounds his classification, his success in creating such a guide may be judged by the fact that through the years few marketing texts have failed to make use of his ideas.

The purpose of this article is to attempt to clarify some of the issues that exist with respect to the classification, and to extend the concept to include the retailer and the study of retail strategy.

CONTROVERSY OVER THE CLASSIFICATION SYSTEM

The starting point for the discussion lies with the definitions adopted by the American Marketing Association's Committee on Definitions for the classification system in 1948.[2] These are:

Convenience goods. Those consumers' goods which the customer purchases frequently, immediately and with the minimum of effort.

Source: Reprinted with permission from the *Journal of Marketing,* published by the American Marketing Association, vol. 27 (January 1963), pp. 51–56. At the time of writing, Louis Bucklin was an assistant professor of marketing at the University of California in Berkeley.

[1] Melvin T. Copeland, "Relation of Consumers' Buying Habits to Marketing Methods," *Harvard Business Review,* vol. 1 (April 1923), pp. 282–89.

[2] Definitions Committee, American Marketing Association, "Report of the Definitions Committee," *Journal of Marketing,* vol. 13 (October 1948) pp. 202–17, at p. 206, p. 215.

Shopping goods. Those consumers' goods which the customer in the process of selection and purchase characteristically compares on such bases as suitability, quality, price and style.

Specialty goods. Those consumers' goods on which a significant group of buyers are habitually willing to make a special purchasing effort.

This set of definitions was retained in virtually the same form by the Committee on Definitions in its latest publication.[3]

Opposing these accepted definitions stands a critique by Richard H. Holton.[4] Finding the Committee's definitions too imprecise to be able to measure consumer buying behavior, he suggested that the following definitions not only would represent the essence of Copeland's original idea, but be operationally more useful as well.

Convenience goods. Those goods for which the consumer regards the probable gain from making price and quality comparisons as small compared to the cost of making such comparisons.

Shopping goods. Those goods for which the consumer regards the probable gain from making price and quality comparisons as large relative to the cost of making such comparisons.

Specialty goods. Those convenience or shopping goods which have such a limited market as to require the consumer to make a special effort to purchase them.

Holton's definitions have particular merit because they make explicit the underlying conditions that control the extent of a consumer's shopping activities. They show that a consumer's buying behavior will be determined not only by the strength of his desire to secure some goods, but by his perception of the cost of shopping to obtain it. In other words, the consumer continues to shop *for all goods* so long as he feels that the additional satisfactions from further comparisons are at least equal to the cost of making the additional effort. The distinction between shopping and convenience goods lies principally in the degree of satisfaction to be secured from further comparisons.

The specialty goods issue

While Holton's conceptualization makes an important contribution, he has sacrificed some of the richness of Copeland's original ideas. This is essentially David J. Luck's complaint in a criticism of Holton's proposal.[5] Luck objected to the abandonment of the *willingness* of consumers to make a special effort

---

[3] Definitions Committee, American Marketing Association, *Marketing Definitions* (Chicago: American Marketing Association, 1960) pp. 11, 21, 22.

[4] Richard H. Holton, "The Distinction between Convenience Goods, Shopping Goods, and Specialty Goods," *Journal of Marketing*, vol. 23 (July 1958), pp. 53–56.

[5] David J. Luck, "On the Nature of Specialty Goods," *Journal of Marketing*, vol. 24 (July 1959), pp. 61–64.

to buy as the rationale for the concept of specialty goods. He regarded this type of consumer behavior as based upon unique consumer attitudes toward certain goods and not the density of distribution of those goods. Holton, in a reply, rejected Luck's point; he remained convinced that the real meaning of specialty goods could be derived from his convenience goods, shopping goods continuum, and market conditions.[6]

The root of the matter appears to be that insufficient attention has been paid to the fact that the consumer, once embarked upon some buying expedition, may have only one of two possible objectives in mind. A discussion of this aspect of consumer behavior will make possible a closer synthesis of Holton's contribution with the more traditional point of view.

A forgotten idea

The basis for this discussion is afforded by certain statements, which the marketing profession has largely ignored over the years, in Copeland's original presentation of his ideas. These have regard to the extent of the consumer's awareness of the precise nature of the item he wishes to buy, *before* he starts his shopping trip. Copeland stated that the consumer, in both the case of convenience goods and specialty goods, has full knowledge of the particular good, or its acceptable substitutes, that he will buy before he commences his buying trip. The consumer, however, lacks this knowledge in the case of a shopping good.[7] This means that the buying trip must not only serve the objective of purchasing the good, but must enable the consumer to discover which item he wants to buy.

The behavior of the consumer during any shopping expedition may, as a result, be regarded as heavily dependent upon the state of his decision as to what he wants to buy. If the consumer knows precisely what he wants, he needs only to undertake communication activities sufficient to take title to the desired product. He may also undertake ancillary physical activities involving the handling of the product and delivery. If the consumer is uncertain as to what he wants to buy, then an additional activity will have to be performed. This involves the work of making comparisons between possible alternative purchases, or simply search.

There would be little point, with respect to the problem of classifying consumer goods, in distinguishing between the activity of search and that of making a commitment to buy, if a consumer always performed both before purchasing a good. The crucial point is that he does not. While most of the items that a consumer buys have probably been subjected to comparison at some point in his life, he does not make a search before each purchase. Instead, a past solution to the need is frequently remembered and, if satisfac-

---

[6] Richard H. Holton, "What Is Really Meant by 'Specialty' Goods?" *Journal of Marketing,* vol. 24 (July 1959), pp. 64–67.

[7] Copeland, same references as footnote 1, pp. 283–84.

tory, is implemented.[8] Use of these past decisions for many products quickly moves the consumer past any perceived necessity of undertaking new comparisons and leaves only the task of exchange to be discharged.

REDEFINITION OF THE SYSTEM

Use of this concept of problem solving permits one to classify consumer buying efforts into two broad categories, which may be called shopping and nonshopping goods.

Shopping goods

Shopping goods are those for which the consumer *regularly* formulates a new solution to his need each time it is aroused. They are goods whose suitability is determined through search before the consumer commits himself to each purchase.

The motivation behind this behavior stems from circumstances which tend to perpetuate a lack of complete consumer knowledge about the nature of the product that he would like to buy.[9] Frequent changes in price, style, or product technology cause consumer information to become obsolete. The greater the time lapse between purchases, the more obsolete will his information be. The consumer's needs are also subject to change, or he may seek variety in his purchases as an actual goal. These forces will tend to make past information inappropriate. New search, due to forces internal and external to the consumer, is continuously required for products with purchase determinants which the consumer regards as both important and subject to change.[10]

The number of comparisons that the consumer will make in purchasing a shopping good may be determined by use of Holton's hypothesis on effort. The consumer, in other words, will undertake search for a product until the perceived value to be secured through additional comparisons is less than the estimated cost of making those comparisons. Thus, shopping effort will vary according to the intensity of the desire of the consumer to find the right product, the type of product, and the availability of retail facilities. Whether the consumer searches diligently, superficially, or even buys at the first opportunity, however, does not alter the shopping nature of the product.

Nonshopping goods

Turning now to nonshopping goods, one may define these as products for which the consumer is both willing and able to use stored solutions to the

---

[8] George Katona, *Psychological Analysis of Economic Behavior* (New York: McGraw-Hill Book Co., Inc., 1951), p. 47.

[9] Same reference, pp. 67–68.

[10] George Katona and Eva Muller, "A Study of Purchase Decisions in Consumer Behavior," Lincoln Clark, editor, *Consumer Behavior* (New York: University Press, 1954), pp. 30–87.

problem of finding a product to answer a need. From the remarks on shopping goods it may be generalized that nonshopping goods have purchase determinants which do not change, or which are perceived as changing inconsequentially, between purchases.[11] The consumer, for example, may assume that price for some product never changes or that price is unimportant. It may be unimportant because either the price is low, or the consumer is very wealthy.

Nonshopping goods may be divided into convenience and specialty goods by means of the concept of a preference map. Bayton introduces this concept as the means to show how the consumer stores information about products.[12] It is a rough ranking of the relative desirability of the different kinds of products that the consumer sees as possible satisfiers for his needs. For present purposes, two basic types of preference maps may be envisaged. One type ranks all known product alternatives equally in terms of desirability. The other ranks one particular product as so superior to all others that the consumer, in effect, believes this product is the only answer to his need.

Distinguishing the specialty good

This distinction in preference maps creates the basis for discriminating between a convenience good and a specialty good. Clearly, where the consumer is indifferent to the precise item among a number of substitutes which he could buy, he will purchase the most accessible one and look no further. This is a convenience good. On the other hand, where the consumer recognizes only one brand of a product as capable of satisfying his needs, he will be willing to bypass more readily accessible substitutes in order to secure the wanted item. This is a specialty good.

However, most nonshopping goods will probably fall in between these two polar extremes. Preference maps will exist where the difference between the relative desirability of substitutes may range from the slim to the well marked. In order to distinguish between convenience goods and specialty goods in these cases, Holton's hypothesis regarding consumer effort may be employed again. A convenience good, in these terms, becomes one for which the consumer has such little preference among his perceived choices that he buys the item which is most readily available. A specialty good is one for which consumer preference is so strong that he bypasses, or would be willing to bypass, the purchase of more accessible substitutes in order to secure his most wanted item.

It should be noted that this decision on the part of the consumer as to how much effort he should expend takes place under somewhat different conditions than the one for shopping goods. In the nonshopping good instance the consumer has a reasonably good estimate of the additional value to be

---

[11] Katona, same reference as footnote 8, p. 68.

[12] James A. Bayton, "Motivation, Cognition, Learning—Basic Factors in Consumer Behavior," *Journal of Marketing*, vol. 22 (January 1958), pp. 282–89, at p. 287.

achieved by purchasing his preferred item. The estimate of the additional cost required to make this purchase may also be made fairly accurately. Consequently, the consumer has a reasonably good estimate of the additional value to be achieved by purchasing his preferred item. The estimate of the additional cost required to make this purchase may also be made fairly accurately. Consequently, the consumer will be in a much better position to justify the expenditure of additional effort here than in the case of shopping goods where much uncertainty must exist with regard to both of these factors.

The new classification

The classification of consumer goods that results from the analysis is as follows:

Convenience goods.   Those goods for which the consumer, before his need arises, possesses a preference map that indicates a willingness to purchase any of a number of known substitutes rather than to make the additional effort required to buy a particular item.

Shopping goods.   Those goods for which the consumer has not developed a complete preference map before the need arises, requiring him to undertake search to construct such a map before purchase.

Specialty goods.   Those goods for which the consumer, before his need arises, possesses a preference map that indicates a willingness to expend the additional effort required to purchase the most preferred item rather than to buy a more readily accessible substitute.

EXTENSION TO RETAILING

The classification of the goods concept developed above may now be extended to retailing. As the concept now stands, it is derived from consumer attitudes or motives toward a *product*. These attitudes, or product motives, are based upon the consumer's interpretation of a product's styling, special features, quality, and social status of its brand name, if any. Occasionally the price may also be closely associated with the product by the consumer.

Classification of patronage motives

The extension of the concept to retailing may be made through the notion of patronage motives, a term long used in marketing. Patronage motives are derived from consumer attitudes concerning the retail establishment. They are related to factors which the consumer is likely to regard as controlled by the retailer. These will include assortment, credit, service, guarantee, shopping ease and enjoyment, and usually price. Patronage motives, however, have never been systematically categorized. It is proposed that the procedure developed above to discriminate among product motives be used to classify consumer buying motives with respect to retail stores as well.

This will provide the basis for the consideration of retail marketing strategy and will aid in clearing up certain ambiguities that would otherwise exist if consumer buying motives were solely classified by product factors. These ambiguities appear, for example, when the consumer has a strong affinity for some particular brand of a product, but little interest in where he buys it. The manufacturer of the product, as a result, would be correct in defining the product as a specialty item if the consumer's preferences were so strong as to cause him to eschew more readily available substitutes. The retailer may regard it as a convenience good, however, since the consumer will make no special effort to purchase the good from any particular store. This problem is clearly avoided by separately classifying product and patronage motives.

The categorization of patronage motives by the above procedure results in the following three definitions. These are:

Convenience stores.   Those stores for which the consumer, before his need for some product arises, possesses a preference map that indicates a willingness to buy from the most accessible store.

Shopping stores.   Those stores for which the consumer has not developed a complete preference map relative to the product he wishes to buy, requiring him to undertake a search to construct such a map before purchase.

Specialty stores.   Those stores for which the consumer, before his need for some product arises, possesses a preference map that indicates a willingness to buy the item from a particular establishment even though it may not be the most accessible.

The product-patronage matrix

Although this basis will now afford the retailer a means to consider alternative strategies, a finer classification system may be obtained by relating consumer product motives to consumer patronage motives. By cross-classifying each product motive with each patronage motive, one creates a three by three matrix, representing nine possible types of consumer buying behavior. Each of the nine cells in the matrix may be described as follows:

1. Convenience store—Convenience good.   The consumer represented by this category prefers to buy the most readily available brand of product at the most accessible store.
2. Convenience store—Shopping good.   The consumer selects his purchase from among the assortment carried by the most accessible store.
3. Convenience Store—Specialty good.   The consumer purchases his favored brand from the most accessible store which has the item in stock.

4. *Shopping store—Convenience good.* The consumer is indifferent to the brand of product he buys, but shops among different stores in order to secure better retail service and/or lower retail price.
5. *Shopping store—Shopping good.* The consumer makes comparisons among both retail controlled factors and factors associated with the product (brand).
6. *Shopping store—Specialty good.* The consumer has a strong preference with respect to the brand of the product, but shops among a number of stores in order to secure the best retail service and/or price for this brand.
7. *Specialty store—Convenience good.* The consumer prefers to trade at a specific store, but is indifferent to the brand of product purchased.
8. *Specialty store—Shopping good.* The consumer prefers to trade at a certain store, but is uncertain as to which product he wishes to buy and examines the store's assortment for the best purchase.
9. *Specialty store—Specialty good.* The consumer has both a preference for a particular store and a specific brand.

Conceivably, each of these nine types of behavior might characterize the buying patterns of some consumers for a given product. It seems more likely, however, that the behavior of consumers toward a product could be represented by only three or four of the categories. The remaining cells would be empty, indicating that no consumers bought the product by these methods. Different cells, of course, would be empty for different products.

THE FORMATION OF RETAIL STRATEGY

The extended classification system developed above clearly provides additional information important to the manufacturer in the planning of his marketing strategy. Of principal interest here, however, is the means by which the retailer might use the classification system in planning his marketing strategy.

Three basic steps

The procedure involves three steps. The first is the classification of the retailer's potential customers for some product by market segment, using the nine categories in the consumer buying habit matrix to define the principal segments. The second requires the retailer to determine the nature of the marketing strategies necessary to appeal to each market segment. The final step is the retailer's selection of the market segment, and the strategy associated with it, to which he will sell. A simplified, hypothetical example may help to clarify this process.

A former buyer of dresses for a department store decided to open her own dress shop. She rented a small store in the downtown area of a city of 50,000, ten miles distant from a metropolitan center of several hundred thousand population. In contemplating her marketing strategy, she was certain that the different incomes, educational backgrounds, and tastes of the potential customers in her city meant that various groups of these women were using sharply different buying methods for dresses. Her initial problem was to determine, by use of the consumer buying habit matrix, what proportion of her potential market bought dresses in what manner.

By drawing on her own experience, discussions with other retailers in the area, census and other market data, the former buyer estimated that her potential market was divided, according to the matrix, in the proportions [shown in Table 1].

Table 1
Proportion of potential dress market in each matrix cell

Buying habit	Percent of market
Convenience store—Convenience good	0
Convenience store—Shopping good	3
Convenience store—Specialty good	20
Shopping store—Convenience good	0
Shopping store—Shopping good	35
Shopping store—Specialty good	2
Specialty store—Convenience good	0
Specialty store—Shopping good	25
Specialty store—Specialty good	15
	100

This analysis revealed four market segments that she believed were worth further consideration. (In an actual situation, each of these four should be further divided into submarket segments according to other possible factors such as age, incomes, dress size required, location of residence, etc.) Her next task was to determine the type of marketing mix which would most effectively appeal to each of these segments. The information for these decisions was derived from the characteristics of consumer behavior associated with each of the defined segments. The following is a brief description of her assessment of how elements of the marketing mix ought to be weighted in order to formulate a strategy for each segment.

A strategy for each segment

To appeal to the convenience store—specialty good segment she felt that the two most important elements in the mix should be a highly accessible location and a selection of widely accepted brand merchandise. Of somewhat lesser importance, she found, were depth of assortment, personal selling, and price. Minimal emphasis should be given to store promotion and facilities.

She reasoned that the shopping store–shopping good requires a good central location, emphasis on price, and a broad assortment. She ranked store promotion, accepted brand names, and personal selling as secondary. Store facilities would, once again, receive minor emphasis.

The specialty store–shopping good market would, she believed, have to be catered to with an exceptionally strong assortment, a high level of personal selling, and more elaborate store facilities. Less emphasis would be needed upon prominent brand names, store promotions, and price. Location was of minor importance.

The specialty store–specialty good category, she thought, would require a marketing mix heavily emphasizing personal selling and highly elaborate store facilities and services. She also felt that prominent brand names would be required, but that these would probably have to include the top names in fashion, including labels from Paris. Depth of assortment would be secondary, while least emphasis would be placed upon store promotion, price, and location.

Evaluation of alternatives

The final step in the analysis required the former dress buyer to assess her abilities to implement any one of these strategies, given the degree of competition existing in each segment. Her considerations were as follows. With regard to the specialty store–specialty good market, she was unprepared to make the investment in store facilities and services that she felt would be necessary. She also thought, since a considerable period of time would probably be required for her to build up the necessary reputation, that this strategy involved substantial risk. Lastly, she believed that her experience in buying high fashion was somewhat limited and that trips to European fashion centers would prove burdensome.

She also doubted her ability to cater to the specialty store–shopping good market, principally because she knew that her store would not be large enough to carry the necessary assortment depth. She felt that this same factor would limit her in attempting to sell to the shopping store–shopping good market as well. Despite the presence of the large market in this segment, she believed that she would not be able to create sufficient volume in her proposed quarters to enable her to compete effectively with the local department store and several large department stores in the neighboring city.

The former buyer believed her best opportunity was in selling to the convenience store–specialty good segment. While there were already two other stores in her city which were serving this segment, she believed that a number of important brands were still not represented. Her past contacts with resources led her to believe that she would stand an excellent chance of securing a number of these lines. By stocking these brands, she thought that she could capture a considerable number of local customers who currently were purchasing them in the large city. In this way, she believed, she would avoid the full force of local competition.

Decision

The conclusion of the former buyer to use her store to appeal to the convenience store–specialty good segment represents the culmination to the process of analysis suggested here. It shows how the use of the three-by-three matrix of consumer buying habits may aid the retailer in developing his marketing strategy. It is a device which can isolate the important market segments. It provides further help in enabling the retailer to associate the various types of consumer behavior with those elements of the marketing mix to which they are sensitive. Finally, the analysis forces the retailer to assess the probability of his success in attempting to use the necessary strategy in order to sell each possible market.

QUESTIONS

1. Relate the job of selecting a target market to the store-goods classification matrix discussed by Bucklin.
2. Draw a three-by-three matrix as Bucklin suggests and insert the name of a local retailer in each box of the matrix. If in doubt about how the "market" would classify a particular store, use your own personal view, but in either case explain why you classify each one the way you do.
*3. Relate Bucklin's store-goods classification system to the concepts of benefit segmentation developed by Haley (Reading 13). In particular, discuss whether, or the extent to which, the various categories in Bucklin's system express benefits desired by consumers.

---

* Question relates concepts in this and other readings.

21
The retail life cycle

*William R. Davidson, Albert D. Bates,
and Stephen J. Bass*

Marketers are familiar with the concepts of a wheel of retailing, the marketing mix, and the product life cycle. This article introduces the concept of an institutional life cycle in retailing—a predictable series of stages through which every major form of retailing is destined to go. The authors present the theory of a retail life cycle and discuss some of its implications, including the types of strategies needed at each of the four stages of the retail life cycle.

For many years executives in manufacturing and retailing have sought to explain patterns of evolution among retail organizations and to forecast future retail innovations. Several meaningful efforts have been made to explain retail development, the most important being the "wheel of retailing" concept, originally advanced by Malcolm P. McNair.[1] In McNair's view new retailing concepts are oriented toward low costs and prices at first. Over time, the retail institution gradually trades up in terms of store decor, services offered, and merchandise stocked. Eventually the institution becomes vulnerable to a newer form of retailing operating with lower costs and prices.

Much of the progress in understanding institutional change can be attributed directly to the spark of controversy ignited by McNair's hypothesis. Efforts to expand, modify, or disprove the wheel of retailing concept have led to the development of numerous explanations of institutional development.[2] Some of the most widely discussed explanations are:

Demographic trends. As the standard of living increases, retailers are naturally attracted by market segments with higher levels of income. This leads to increases in merchandise quality, prices, and the array of services.

Source: Reprinted with permission from the *Harvard Business Review*, November–December 1976, pp. 89–96. Copyright © 1976 by the President and Fellows of Harvard College. At the time of writing, William Davidson was president and co-founder of Management Horizons, Albert Bates was assistant professor of marketing at The Ohio State University, and Stephen Bass was a senior consulting associate with Management Horizons.

[1] Malcolm P. McNair, "Significant Trends and Developments in the Postwar Period," *Competitive Distribution in a Free High-Level Economy and its Implications for the University,* edited by Albert D. Smith (Pittsburgh: University of Pittsburgh Press, 1958).

[2] For a more detailed discussion of these different hypotheses see Stanley C. Hollander, "The Wheel of Retailing," *Journal of Marketing,* July 1960, p. 37.

Imperfect competition. In efforts to avoid direct price competition, retailers place increasing emphasis on additional services, which can only be supported with higher margins.

Scrambled merchandising. As retailers diversify their merchandise assortments, they tend to add higher-margin items that create the illusion of an evolutionary trading-up process.

Managerial evolution. As company founders are replaced by second generation management, cost consciousness gives way to concerns over store appearance and image, thereby creating upward pressures on costs and prices.

Each of these approaches has merit as a basis for understanding the evolution of retail institutions. However, none of them seems entirely sufficient for explaining contemporary retail developments, which are of a decidedly different character from earlier retailing innovations. For instance, the wheel of retailing concept suffers from two important limitations.

1. It focuses almost exclusively on changing cost and gross margin relationships as the key to understanding evolutionary retail behavior. It assumes that breakthrough retailing institutions begin as low-cost concepts that gradually mature into higher-cost distribution mechanisms. This cost focus tends to make the concept somewhat limited in explaining the evolutionary behavior of newer, less price-oriented retail innovations, such as the convenience food store and the home improvement center.

2. It was never really intended to determine the pace with which retail innovations rise and fall. Given the somewhat frenetic rate at which new retailing concepts appear today, it is important to have a basis for appraising future developments.

The changing character of retail innovation and the apparent acceleration of innovative retail activity suggest that another expansion of the wheel of retailing concept is needed. We believe that the life cycle concept has considerable utility as a method for explaining and predicting institutional actions. In fact, detailed analyses using life cycle concepts can help management to project the direction and magnitude of future evolutionary processes.

FOUR STAGES OF THE LIFE CYCLE

The product life cycle has a long and rich history in marketing and serves as a basis for many product line decisions, particularly in the consumer packaged goods field.[3] Much less well understood is the concept of the institutional

---

[3] See, for example, Joel Dean, "Pricing Policies for New Products," *Harvard Business Review,* November–December 1950, p. 44 (repeated as HBR Classic in this issue [November–December 1976], p. 141); Theodore Levitt, "Exploit the Product Life Cycle," *Harvard Business Review,* November–December 1965, p. 81; and Eberhard E. Schering, *New Product Management* (Hillside, Ill.: The Snyder Press, 1974). For a contrary view of the traditional approach, see Nariman K. Dhalla and Sonia Yuspeh, "Forget the Product Life Cycle Concept!" *Harvard Business Review,* January–February 1976, p. 102.

life cycle. This theory argues that retailing institutions, like the products they distribute, pass through an identifiable life cycle.[4]

As Exhibit 1 shows, the retail life cycle, as we see it, is divided into four distinct stages. While the stages are similar to those for the product life cycle, they have their own unique characteristics. We shall examine each stage in turn.

Exhibit 1
The institutional life cycle in retailing

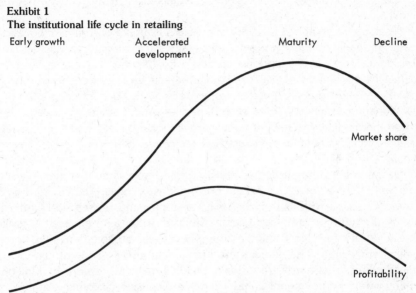

Note: The duration of the stages (horizontal scale) is variable, depending on many circumstances. The four stages are portrayed equally on the time scale for schematic purposes only.

1. Innovation

The first and most exciting stage of retail development is characterized by the emergence of a new, usually entrepreneurial, retail institution. The new concept typically represents a sharp departure from existing retailing approaches and as a result tends to enjoy a significant advantage. The advantage may arise from a tightly controlled cost structure that results in a favorable price position, but not always. The advantage may derive from a unique feature offered, such as a distinctive product assortment, ease of shopping, locational advantages, or even different advertising and promotional methods.

During the innovation period the new advantage produces a level of customer acceptance that causes sales to rise sharply. Profits, on the other hand, may lag as the new institution struggles with the operating problems associ-

---

[4] See William R. Davidson, Alton F. Doody, and Daniel J. Sweeney, *Retailing Management* (New York: The Ronald Press Co., 1975), p. 71; William R. Davidson, "Changes in Distributive Institutions," *Journal of Marketing,* January 1970, p. 9; and Bert C. McCammon, Jr. and Albert D. Bates, "Emerging Patterns of Distribution," *Strictly Wholesaling,* Spring 1972, p. 33.

ated with new ventures. Profits may also suffer because the company lacks the sales to produce significant economies of scale, or because it incurs relatively large levels of start-up cost, many of which cannot be capitalized. Toward the end of the innovation period sales volume begins to increase even more rapidly, and profits also grow as the initial operating problems are overcome.

Let us look briefly at two examples with which many readers may be familiar.

The supermarket of the 1930s is a classic example of a retail innovation based primarily on a cost and price advantage. By eliminating services such as credit, delivery, and telephone ordering, by utilizing self-service, and by achieving economies of scale, the supermarkets were able to operate on a gross margin of only 12 percent, compared with 20 percent for more conventional food outlets. At the same time, the supermarkets produced a net profit margin fully 50 percent above conventional outlets, and some generated as much sales volume in two weeks as conventional food stores did in a year.

In contrast to the supermarket, the home improvement center focused primarily on the "offer" of better combinations of related merchandise and services. Specializing in the sale of home repair and related do-it-yourself items, the home improvement center brings together at one place the tools, the application products, and the information necessary to do an entire home improvement job. The center's product variety and assortment cannot be matched by either hardware stores or building materials dealers. In addition, many home improvement centers provide extensive customer counseling, sponsor in-store seminars on home improvements, and often provide contractor assistance to do-it-yourselfers. Price in this total offer is a factor, but a relatively minor one.

As a result of its marketing efforts the home improvement center has been almost as spectacular a success as the supermarket. From a handful of outlets in the mid–1960s, such stores now account for more than 20 percent of total home improvement product sales, and they can be expected to increase that percentage steadily in future years.

2. Accelerated development

In the second stage of retail evolution, both sales volume and profits experience rapid rates of growth. During this period companies already established in the business are usually actively engaged in geographic expansion. Also, companies that were not innovators typically enter the new field. For example, once the discount department store was firmly established as a dynamic new form of retailing, mature corporations such as Kresge, Woolworth, Federated, and Dayton-Hudson made major commitments to their own discount operations.

As interest in the new concept surges, the market share of the innovating stores increases steadily and conventional outlets get hurt. As a result, companies that earlier had ignored the innovation begin to develop retailiatory programs. In most instances, though, the retailiatory programs are not completely thought through and are often ineffective.

In the accelerated development phase of the discount department store [for example], conventional department store outlets frequently attempted programs of retaliation on the theme of "we will not knowingly be undersold." This often proved ineffective because it focused on only one dimension of discount department store competition and did not give proper recognition to the discounter's nonprice advantages, including a suburban location, the convenience of night and Sunday operating hours, and the availability of open merchandising under a self-service formula.

During the early part of the accelerated development period there is normally a favorable impact on profits. Additional sales volume results in high levels of fixed expense leveraging, and substantial economies of scale are produced. However, toward the end of the period these favorable factors tend to be counterbalanced by cost pressures that arise from the need for a larger staff, more complex internal systems, increased management controls, and other requirements of operating large, multi-unit organizations. Consequently, near the end of the accelerated development period both market share and profitability tend to approach their maximum level.

3. Maturity

The third and most significant stage of development witnesses a dissipation of the earlier vitality of retailers. Market share levels off. As a result, a number of factors come together to create important operating problems.

First, entrepreneurial managers begin to face difficulties in controlling their large and complex organizations. Although they were excellent at maintaining the vitality and excitement of their organizations in the first two stages, they often lack the management skills necessary to direct large organizations in stable markets. Consequently, the quality of operations begins to slip.

Second, too much capacity becomes a problem. Retailers expand beyond the levels justified by the size of the total market, and in doing so they increase the level of total square footage to unprofitable levels. This situation persists until a major shakeout occurs, such as happened in the fast-food field in the late 1960s and among discount department stores in the early 1970s.

Finally, management finds itself facing direct frontal assaults from new forms of distribution. The upstart challengers run off with needed sales, creating profit problems which magnify other difficulties.

The result of such difficulties is a severe reduction in profitability. The discount department store industry offers a case in point.

This concept was pioneered by companies such as Masters, E. J. Korvette, and Two Guys from Harrison in the early 1950s. From this small base the industry grew quite rapidly, led for the most part by dynamic, highly creative, but not technically sophisticated managers. By 1960, the earliest year for which detailed trade data are available, the discount industry had more than

1,300 stores producing a total sales volume of approximately $2 billion. This volume put the industry well into the accelerated development stage of growth.

Sales and profits continued to advance during the early 1960s, spurred on by growth-oriented managements. Sales per store, sales per square foot, and market share rose continually, although not at the dramatic rates characteristic of previous years. At the same time, however, profitability started to fall as expenses outraced sales volume. In other words, the first signs of impending maturity were becoming apparent.

Despite this warning, entrepreneurs in the industry continued to open stores at an uninterrupted pace. "Overstoring" became an economic reality. Between 1965 and 1972, for example, the number of square feet of discount store space per household almost doubled, rising from 3.6 square feet to 6.5 square feet. As a result, sales per square foot fell precipitously throughout the 1960s and 1970s, as did profitability, despite the fact that market share continued to show increases through 1970.

Corporate executives did not start to correct these problems until about 1973, following a significant shakeout of weaker stores. As discount department stores continue to adapt to maturity as a way of life, profitability results can be expected to stabilize at economically sufficient levels. However, they are not likely ever to return to the exciting levels associated with the early stages of the life cycle.

Decline

The last era in the life cycle process is often avoided or greatly postponed by repositioning. By modifying its marketing concepts, management prolongs maturity and avoids decline. However, not all retail species are so lucky. Years ago, central city variety stores went into a downhill stage in most regions. In addition, some of the accustomed industry leaders may contract in size and importance. For example, the announcement in 1975 by A&P that it was closing approximately 1,250 stores was a concession that many of its units were economically obsolete in today's marketplace.

When decline occurs, the consequences are traumatic. Major losses of market share occur, profits are marginal at best, and a fatal inability to compete in the market becomes apparent to investors and competitors.

IS THE LIFE CYCLE GROWING SHORTER?

As the preceding discussion suggests, the institutional retail life cycle is a natural evolutionary process that is impossible to stop. Given the inevitability of the life cycle, management's responsibility in any one company is to anticipate changes in the stages and to adapt the organization to them as effectively as possible. Exhibit 2 highlights some of the activities that become important in different stages.

Exhibit 2
Management activities in the life cycle

Area or subject of concern	Stage of life cycle development			
	1. Innovation	*2. Accelerated development*	*3. Maturity*	*4. Decline*
Market characteristics				
Number of competitors	Very few	Moderate	Many direct competitors Moderate indirect competition	Moderate direct competition Many indirect competitors
Rate of sales growth	Very rapid	Rapid	Moderate to slow	Slow or negative
Level of profitability	Low to moderate	High	Moderate	Very low
Duration of new innovations	3 to 5 years	5 to 6 years	Indefinite	Indefinite
Appropriate retailer actions				
Investment/growth/risk decisions	Investment minimization—high risks accepted	High levels of investment to sustain growth	Tightly controlled growth in untapped markets	Minimal capital expenditures and only when essential
Central management concerns	Concept refinement through adjustment and experimentation	Establishing a preemptive market position	Excess capacity and "overstoring" Prolonging maturity and revising the retail concept	Engaging in a "run-out" strategy
Use of management control techniques	Minimal	Moderate	Extensive	Moderate
Most successful management style	Entrepreneurial	Centralized	"Professional"	Caretaker
Appropriate supplier actions				
Channel strategy	Develop a preemptive market position	Hold market position	Maintain profitable sales	Avoid excessive costs
Channel problems	Possible antagonism of other accounts	Possible antagonism of other accounts	Dealing with more scientific retailers	Servicing accounts at a profit
Channel research	Identification of key innovations	Identification of other retailers adopting the innovation	Initial screening of new innovation opportunities	Active search for new innovation opportunities
Trade incentives	Direct financial support	Price concessions	New price incentives	None

By utilizing different strategies at different stages of life cycle development, and by anticipating shifts from one stage to the next, both retailers and suppliers can maintain adequate profit levels. Difficulties arise in anticipating future developments, though, as the life cycle is far from being a stagnant concept.

Furthermore, innovative retail companies are typically small and relatively difficult to identify. Consequently, they are seldom given widespread notice until they reach the accelerated development stage. However, two widely discussed retail concepts are still at the innovation stage in the United States; both of them are in the food field. The first is the food warehouse, as exemplified by the Grocery Warehouse operation run by Allied Supermarkets in Detroit or the Magnamart division of Lucky Stores in San Antonio. The second is the hypermarket—very large-scale combination food and general merchandise stores—such as Jewel Grand Bazaar in Chicago or the newer units of Meijers Thrifty Acres in Michigan.

What is more, there is ample evidence to suggest that the length of the life cycle is contracting. The time between the introduction of a retail concept and the point at which it reaches maturity is growing progressively shorter.

At maturity, retailers tend to develop sophisticated inventory control procedures, develop five-year plans, and employ other modern management concepts. For suppliers, the main challenge is to hold on to the existing network while beginning to actively search for the next round of innovative companies that may eventually make existing relationships obsolete.

It is difficult to pinpoint the exact year in which a particular retail institution was established, since most innovations have important historical antecedents that can be traced back to the very beginnings of commerce. It is even more difficult to determine when a particular institution reached maturity. Market data are usually not sufficiently precise to indicate maturity, different geographic areas reach maturity at different points in time, and many individual firms run counter to prevailing trends.

Despite these limitations, it is possible to draw on trade data and historical studies to make realistic estimates of the approximate time of innovation and maturity for major retailing institutions.[5] Exhibit 3 documents the life cycle patterns for the downtown department store, the variety store, the supermarket, the discount department store, and the home improvement center.

As can be seen, the downtown department store enjoyed approximately 80 years of uninterrupted development from the time of its introduction to the time of achieving its maximum market share. But [as] the pace of economic activity accelerated, the innovation and accelerated development stages contracted to 45 years for variety stores, 35 years for supermarkets, and 20 years for discount department stores.

---

[5] For example, data on the sales and market share of retail institutions in the latter part of the 19th-century and the first half of the 20th century are found in Harold Barger, *Distribution's Place in the American Economy Since 1869* (New York: National Bureau of Economic Research, 1955).

Exhibit 3
Life cycle characteristics of five retail institutions

Institution	Approximate date of innovation	Approximate date of maximum market share	Approximate no. of years required to reach maturity	Estimated maximum market share	Estimated 1975 market share
Downtown department store	1860	1940	80	8.5%	1.1%
				of total retail sales	
Variety store	1910	1955	45	16.5%	9.5%
				of general merchandise sales	
Supermarket	1930	1965	35	70.0%	64.5%
				of grocery store sales	
Discount department store	1950	1970	20	6.5%	5.7%
				of total retail sales	
Home improvement center	1965	1980 (estimate)	15	35.0%	25.3%
				of hardware and building material sales	

Sources: National Bureau of Economic Research, U.S. Department of Commerce, *Progressive Grocer, Discount Merchandiser,* National Retail Hardware Association, and Management Horizons, Inc.

Present patterns of change lead to the conclusion that the home improvement center probably will achieve its maximum market share by about 1980 only 15 or so years after the time of introduction. For future innovations, the period of market share growth could contract to as little as 10 years.

The institutional life cycle is not the only facet of economic activity that is accelerating. Futurists such as Alvin Toffler, Herman Kahn, and others have documented the accelerating pace of change in American society.[6] In addition, the product life cycle seems to be contracting. As an illustration consider the following observation made by the chief executive of General Electric Company:

The honeymoon cycle of the new product is becoming shorter and shorter. We introduced the GE automatic toothbrush just two years ago. There are now 32 competitors. Our slicing knife, a product that we introduced approximately one year ago, now competes with 7 others, and at least that many more manufacturers are preparing to enter the marketplace.[7]

A sophisticated management group can slow the pace of its company's evolution, and it can hold profitability at adequate levels for an extended period of time. However, a return to exceptional levels of profitability can be

---

[6] See Alvin Toffler, *Future Shock* (New York: Random House, 1970), and Herman Kahn and Anthony J. Wiener, *The Year 2000: A Framework for Speculation on the Next 33 Years* (New York: Macmillan, 1967).

[7] Speech by Fred J. Borch quoted in Philip Kotler, *Marketing Management* (Englewood Cliffs, N.J.: Prentice-Hall, 1972), p. 466.

achieved only by converting to new forms of distribution or by entering new lines of trade.

IMPLICATIONS AND OPPORTUNITIES

The institutional life cycle represents more than just another way to conceptualize changes in retailer behavior and profitability patterns. It can be quite useful in projecting retail developments and planning marketing strategy. In particular, an analysis of current life cycle patterns suggests four important areas of management attention during the next decade.

Stay flexible

For retail executives, the shortening life cycle puts a premium on being able to adapt to changing trends and to work with new management ideas. To cope with continual change, retailers must consider the use of different management styles or even different management groups during succeeding stages of development. In large organizations with multiple types of outlets in various stages of development, this need could greatly increase the complexity of management. It also means, though, that a company can never afford to get "locked in" to some particular approach or philosophy.

An excellent example of a company that has employed different management styles in operations at different stages of development is Federated Department Stores. When setting up its Gold Circle discount division, the company established a management task force that was completely autonomous from the existing Federated management group. The task force was free to try new management concepts and operating procedures. With this approach, Federated had an innovative, free-wheeling management style for its discount division and a more conservative, controlled style for its conventional department store operation.

Merchandise suppliers are likely to have similar concerns about not being locked in to one type of retail outlet for a product. As a result of this concern suppliers probably will become more responsive to new retail ventures than they have been in the past. When, as in the past, manufacturers and wholesalers refrain from selling to new types of retailers for fear of disrupting existing channel relationships, they leave the door open for minor suppliers. The latter can proceed to take market share away from the larger companies by selling to the innovative stores.

Analyze risks and profits

In order to lower the potential risks of failure in new ventures, retailers will become more analytical and innovative. To cut their risks, they are likely to utilize a variety of techniques for increasing sales and profits and decreasing investment requirements. For instance, they will:

Look for second-use space—such as abandoned supermarkets—for new retail ventures.

Place more emphasis on self-service in tasks where clerk service has been the mode.

Emphasize more efficient merchandising techniques.

Try to shift a greater portion of the investment burden back up the channel to merchandise suppliers. (This approach is especially important for financing inventory and fixture needs in the future.)

Suppliers face a dilemma in dealing with new retail concepts. While inclined to respond quickly to new forms of distribution which exhibit a strong customer appeal, they will need substantial financial support through the form of extended datings, floor planning of initial inventory, or even direct term loans. At present, few supply organizations have the ability to evaluate the prospects for innovations with any degree of precision. In order to do so, suppliers are going to be forced to become much more knowledgeable about retailing activities and possibly directly involved in the early operation of retail innovations.

Attempt to extend the maturity stage

As noted earlier, the duration of the four stages shown in Exhibit 1 is variable. This fact is especially important for retailers in the third or maturity stage of the life cycle. As recognition of the life cycle grows, therefore, many retail executives can be expected to devote more attention to ways of attracting and appealing to new market segments; also, many managements will work on ways of renewing and recapturing the interest of their existing customers so as to keep their loyalty in the face of new forms of competition.

For an example of what can be done by alert maturity-stage retailers, consider the department store industry. Originally, the department store was a discount-oriented purveyor of a relatively wide range of basic merchandise. Over time the concept evolved into a mechanism for selling a broad variety of apparel, home furnishings, and general merchandise to a broadly defined middle-class customer base.

But today, leading department stores are giving much more time, attention, inventory investment, and floor space to the sale of fashion merchandise—particularly apparel, fashion accessories, and fashion home furnishings. Many of them see their main market as a more mobile, more affluent section of the middle class. While engaged in these changes and transitions, some conventional department stores have been able to maintain quite acceptable rates of profitability and interesting growth rates.

The marketing programs of key suppliers must evolve with the retail concepts they service. In the latter stages of the life cycle this means that suppliers must be able to cope with buying committees, vendor analysis programs, and similar efforts to assess the relative desirability of alternative supplier relationships. In addition, they must be able to function in programmed merchandising arrangements. Finally, they should be able to provide the product variations and other refinements that retailers will be looking for in order to shield conventional customers from innovative competitors. While doing all this, suppliers must also be able to service less mature retail outlets with less precise methods of operation.

In short, manufacturers will work up programs to satisfy multiple channel requirements. Like several of the other changes outlined, this development should result in a marked increase in the complexity of supplier operations.

Emphasize research

Given the risks in developing new retailing concepts, many retailers may prefer to leave the hard task of experimenting with new approaches to smaller, more entrepreneurial companies. The concepts that prove successful can then be copied—at least, if the large retailers discover the innovations soon enough.

Monitoring experimentation and innovation in the manner required calls for a more substantial and more sophisticated commitment to research than most retailers now employ. Such capabilities must be expanded in the future. Suppliers face an almost identical challenge in developing a monitoring system to identify potential new customers and anticipate their impact on the market.

IN SUMMARY

The retail life cycle is a natural evolutionary process, and executives can do very little to counteract it. What they can do is plan more effectively in order to sustain profitability in the different stages. Such planning implies continuous rethinking and revision of operations. This in turn means that retailing will continue to be an area of turbulence and uncertainty for some time to come.

QUESTIONS

*1. In what ways is the retail life cycle similar to the product life cycle (Reading 16)? In what ways is it different?

2. What are some of the implications of the apparent shortening of the retail life cycle? What does this mean to a manufacturer or wholesaler who supplies the goods sold through retail outlets?

3. Identify a retail institution that may be farther along in its cycle than current retailers and investors think (based on their willingness to open new units).

---

* Question relates concepts in this and other readings.

22
Physical distribution: Managing the firm's service level

Richard J. Lewis

In this article, Lewis suggests that the primary purpose of physical distribution (PD) is servicing demand. But he also shows that physical distribution is linked to obtaining demand through the service level, which has strategic implications. Then Lewis describes the many trade-off decisions which must be made when developing a good PD system.

From its beginning in the 1950s the discipline of physical distribution has steadily developed into a major area of business administration. During its early period of conception the late Professor Paul D. Converse described physical distribution as "the other half of the total costs of marketing."[1] Today it wouldn't be difficult to find those who would argue that physical distribution is not a part of marketing, but rather its co-equal within a firm's organizational structure. Our purpose here is not to settle the argument, but to understand the role of physical distribution within a firm and how it relates to the firm's marketing efforts.

THE NATURE OF DISTRIBUTION MANAGEMENT WITHIN THE FIRM

An interesting way to approach an understanding of distribution management within a firm is to ask why a firm spends money on distribution efforts. That is, what is the purpose (or purposes) of spending money on distribution? Must money be spent on distribution efforts and, if so, why?

The answer to these questions lies in the *inherent purposes* of distribution expenditures and, hence, the purposes of distribution within a firm. Distribution efforts within a firm are directed at accomplishing two inherent purposes: to obtain demand for the firm's goods and services, and to service and supply the demand. Hence, all distribution activities and their respective costs can be identified by their purpose—they are either demand-obtaining or demand-servicing activities. Figure 1 outlines the approach described above and

---

Source: An original contribution. At the time of writing, Richard Lewis was a professor of marketing and transportation administration at Michigan State University.

[1] Paul D. Converse "The Other Half of Marketing," 26th Boston Conference on Distribution (Boston: Boston Trade Board, 1954), pp. 22–25.

Figure 1

shows the respective activities related to each purpose. Thus, advertising, personal selling, sales promotion, merchandising, and pricing are all distribution activities directed at the same common purpose of obtaining demand for the firm's goods and services. Warehousing, inventory management, transportation, and order processing and handling are all activities directed at servicing demand for the firm's goods and services.

Where the identification of the purposes to which a firm's distribution effort is directed identifies its *ends,* the identification of the activities used to accomplish the purposes identifies the *means* used. The importance of classifying activities by their purpose is that the activities must be controlled in relationship to the purpose they share in common and that, where appropriate, the interdependent nature of activities is recognized.

In considering Figure 1, there is a natural tendency to want to make it into an organization chart with all the typical types of professional labels and titles. It is precisely because of this tendency that the terms used were the most neutral that could be found that were still appropriate to the discussion. At this point some would wish to label the managerial area "Marketing effort," rather than "Distribution effort." Others would argue that it is the managerial purpose now labeled "Obtain demand" that should be called marketing and that "Service demand" is really the managerial purpose of physical distribution management. However, what is in a name? The understanding we are after is not found in titles, for the titles can be anything so long as there is a clear understanding and classification of the underlying purposes and how the activities relate to these purposes. Professor Donald Bowersox's statement in this connection is appropriate: "It is not the organization, but rather the philosophy of operation, which is of critical importance."[2]

THE NATURE OF PHYSICAL DISTRIBUTION MANAGEMENT

Whether one desires to organizationally place marketing management above physical distribution management or on a level with it, there is no argument with identifying servicing demand as the purpose of physical distri-

[2] Donald J. Bowersox, "Physical Distribution in Semi-maturity," *Air Transportation,* January 1966, p. 8.

bution management. The National Council of Physical Distribution Management defines physical distribution as: "A term employed in manufacturing and commerce to describe the broad range of activities concerned with efficient movement of finished products from the end of the production line to the consumer. . . ."

This focus on the "broad range of activities" concerned with the movement of finished goods distinguishes the physical distribution concept from previous practices and has led to what has been called the "total-cost approach." The total-cost approach views the costs of the various activities of servicing demand as a *system* of costs resulting in a total cost of performing the supply function.

Prior to introduction of the concept of physical distribution management and the total-cost approach, the practice was to consider each supply activity separately. Attempts to minimize the costs of each activity were made independently, with little or no attention being given to the impact this had on the other elements of supply. At least one author suggested that this approach leads to "the popular corporate pastime of relocating rather than reducing costs."[3] An example often used to illustrate the idea is the attempt by the traffic department of a firm to minimize its costs. Such attempts normally lead to larger, infrequent shipments by slower, lower cost modes of transportation. Having purchased the lowest cost mode of transportation that was feasible and having moved only large-size shipments, the traffic department can sit back, survey the reduction in its costs, and point with pride to the savings it has accomplished for the firm. However, the cost savings realized by the traffic department do not reflect the impact of the actions on the costs of other supply activities. While the traffic department succeeded in reducing *its costs,* it is highly probable that the warehouse manager is extremely unhappy with his rising costs of holding more inventory and providing more space for the larger shipments. If the firm charges an interest cost on the money tied up while products are in transit to a distribution center and not available for sale, then this cost will also rise, due to the increased time the goods are in shipment as a result of using a slower mode of transportation.

The interdependent nature of the costs of supply activities is the basis for the total-cost approach and the concept of physical distribution management. It can be viewed as the management of trade-offs. *Efficient* management of cost trade-offs requires that cost increases in some supply activities are traded for greater cost decreases in other supply activities. The total-cost approach requires centralized cost control over the various supply activities, which may result in cost increases in some activities that will be more than offset by cost reductions in other activities. Similarly, centralized cost control would not permit indiscriminant cost reductions in any one supply activity if the net effect were to raise the cost of other supply activities above the cost savings and, hence, to increase the total costs of supply.

---

[3] H. G. Miller, "Accounting for Physical Distribution," *Transportation and Distribution Management,* December 1961, p. 11.

The necessity for centralizing control over cost of servicing demand does not preclude the individual management of the various activities. It does, however, require that the activities be integrated and coordinated and that constraints be placed on the various activities which will allow the firm to minimize its *total costs* of servicing demand.

CONTROL OBJECTIVE AND THE SERVICE LEVEL

The natural division of distribution purposes, activities, and costs into obtaining demand and servicing demand is further justified by the difference in the objectives of controlling costs associated with each purpose. The objective of controlling costs of obtaining demand is to *maximize the effectiveness* per dollar spent on the various activities (i.e., to maximize the demand obtained per dollar spent). In contrast, the objective of cost control over the activities used to service demand is to *minimize the costs,* consistent with constraints imposed by the desired level of customer service and other constraints imposed outside the firm's control by competitors.

The service level is the connecting link between the two purposes of distribution within a firm. In the final analysis these two purposes are not independent of each other, since the service level a firm provides is a demand-obtaining force itself. The selection of a service level is a major decision within a firm, due to two major operational impacts derived from the decision. First, in setting the service level, the firm is either consciously or unconsciously deciding how important a role it wishes to have service play in obtaining demand for its goods and services. One need only reflect on the importance of the service level of suppliers in the construction industry to see how having the right products, in the right quantities, in the right place, at the right time is critical to the contractor in meeting his schedules.

The service elasticity of demand for the firm's products and services must be determined or estimated so that the correct customer service level can be used as a *demand-obtaining force.* Therefore, planning and control of the overall distribution effort require determining the complementary relationship (trade-offs) between the activities of obtaining demand and the service level to be provided by physical distribution management. In Figure 1 the broken line from the service level to "Obtain demand" portrays this relationship. Recognition of this relationship could result in a firm's decreasing its advertising and personal selling budgets and using the money to increase its physical distribution budget, if it felt that an increase in the service level would increase demand more than the decrease realized by lessening advertising and personal selling efforts.

The second major operational impact stems from the fact that, as noted earlier, the operating objective of physical distribution management is to minimize the costs of supply activities while achieving the service level desired by the firm. Therefore, cost minimization is *relative* to a service level that must be achieved. It is not cost minimization per se that is being sought, but cost minimization while achieving the service level desired.

SERVICE LEVEL DIMENSIONS

Determining the desired service level requires that operating objectives be established for each of the dimensions of the service level. These dimensions are: order cycle time; percent of demand to be satisfied; quality control relative to order processing; and ensuring acceptable physical condition of goods upon delivery.

Order cycle time

The order cycle refers to the total time consumed from placing an order to receiving the goods. From the point of view of the firm's customers, the lower the average time of an order cycle and the lower the dispersion around the average time, the better is the service level. From the customer's point of view, the longer the order cycle, the greater the premium on his ability to forecast his demand and the higher the risk of lost sales. For example, assume the supplying firm has an order cycle to a given customer of 45 days. Assume further that the customer experiences an unusually high demand and runs out of stock five days after placing an order. This means that he will stay out of stock and lose sales for 40 days until the order is finally received. Contrasting the previous situation with one in which the order cycle is one day would mean that, at most, the customer would be out of stock for a maximum of one day.

The disperson around the average order cycle time is of equal and sometimes greater importance to a firm's customers. It is not very useful to tell a customer that his average order cycle time will be 5 days if, in reality, his deliveries will actually vary from 1 day to 20 days. While the average may actually be five days, the average is not typical and cannot be counted on by the customer. He can never be sure when he places an order with the firm whether it will be the 1-day or the 20-day cycle he is facing. The predictability of order cycle time which results from little or no disperson around the average is of major importance to a firm's customers.

The resulting problem for physical distribution management is that both lower average order cycle times and small dispersions around the average tend to require higher costs in physical distribution activities. To lower the average order cycle time, the firm must institute faster order processing and physical handling procedures. This requires more personnel and/or higher cost, high-speed order communications equipment. To maintain a lower level of dispersion around the average delivery time requires quality control procedures similar to those found in manufacturing.

Percent of demand to be satisfied

Like its customers, the firm has the problem of forecasting its demand and establishing production and inventory levels to meet that demand. If the firm maintains stock levels sufficient to fill 100 percent of its demand at any time, it increases its inventory costs. If the firm lowers its inventory cost by keeping a stock level to fill only 80 percent of demand at peak periods, it either increases the time period necessary to fill some orders or loses the sales. The greater the substitutability of competitors' products for the firm's, the more sales the firm will lose and, therefore, the greater its motivation to satisfy a higher percentage of its demand. Figure 2 shows the general relationship between the

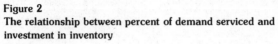

Figure 2
The relationship between percent of demand serviced and investment in inventory

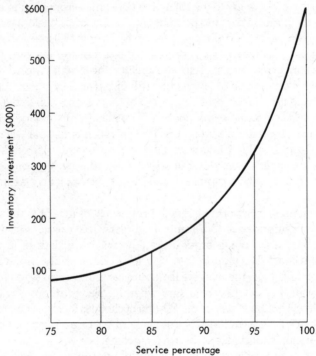

Service percentage

percent of demand able to be serviced and its impact on required investment in inventory. While the absolute amount of investment will vary depending upon the value of the product involved, the relative relationship shown is valid. Note the inventory investment difference needed by the firm to move from an 80 percent to a 90 percent service level as opposed to moving from a 90 percent to a 100 percent service level. It is obvious that the last 10 percent comes at a very high cost in inventory investment.

Order processing quality control

Nothing can be more frustrating to a firm than to have a very fast order cycle with very little dispersion and a high level of service all go down the drain because the wrong goods were shipped. The customer has not been serviced unless the right item, in the right color, size, style, and quantity, has been shipped to the right place. To minimize such mistakes requires several checks and cross-checks to be sure the order and shipment match exactly. Therefore, quality control procedures are also needed for filling orders. While most firms today are very conscientious in designing their systems for the outflow of their goods, few seem to have spent time designing a system to return goods when things go wrong. Perhaps this is the result of giving so much attention to designing and controlling outbound flows that it is hard for the firm to believe things could go wrong. In any case, it is bad enough when a customer receives an incorrect shipment, but the firm can hardly afford to compound the problem by having poorly defined and slow procedures for correcting the situation.

Physical condition upon delivery

Even having the order absolutely correct is not enough if the goods arrive in a damaged, unusable, or unsaleable condition. Concern for the physical condition of goods centers around methods of storage used, transportation methods used, and protective packaging of the goods. A real problem for most physical distribution managers concerns trying to determine when and how damage was done. This is especially true where the firm uses a large number of outside firms in designing its service system, such as multiple private transport carriers, public warehouses, and independent middlemen who take physical possession of the goods. The greater the number of independent businesses involved in the physical flow of the product, the greater the opportunity for things to "fall between the chairs" when goods arrive damaged. The author knows of one consumer goods manufacturer who instituted a "get well check" policy. Upon learning of the arrival of damaged goods, the company immediately makes the financial adjustment to the dealer and assumes the responsibility for determining where the damage occurred and who will ultimately be held responsible for any financial loss.

THE ACTIVITIES OF PHYSICAL DISTRIBUTION

To understand how physical distribution management achieves a given service level requires at least a basic understanding of the various physical distribution activities and how they relate to each other and to the service level. Before discussing each activity, it should be noted that a central policy decision which has a major effect on all the activities is the decision concerning the degree to which the firm pursues a centralized versus a decentralized distribution system. The extreme of a centralized policy would be one distribution center from which all orders would be processed and shipped. The degree of decentralization would be determined by the number of distribution centers the firm establishes. The specific impacts of a centralized versus a decentralized policy will be treated within the discussion of each activity.

Warehousing

Warehousing decisions center around determining the size, number, and location of storage facilities needed to service demand. The centralization versus decentralization issue has a direct bearing on warehousing costs. A decision to centralize all activities into one distribution center would result in the warehousing manager having to provide the minimum space for a given level of demand. This is true because centralization of inventory at one point minimizes the total amount of inventory necessary to meet demand at any specified level. The reason for this will be explained in the inventory discussion. It is also true that there will be some economies of scale on the administrative side resulting in a lower total space requirement for administrative personnel. If a firm decides to decentralize, then the warehouse manager must concern himself with determining the total warehousing cost for various *numbers* of warehouses as well as determining the specific *location* of each. A rather substantial body of knowledge has developed on location theories which concerns determining locations which will minimize ton-miles shipped, cost per ton-miles shipped, and cost-time per ton-miles shipped. A typical example of a warehousing decision would be the determination of whether a firm needs a distribution center in the southwestern part of the United States and, if so, precisely where it should be located.

Inventory management

For a manufacturing firm the ability to forecast demand accurately determines its efficiency in inventory management. If the firm knew exactly when the demand would occur and precisely the number of units, it could schedule production accordingly and hold only a small inventory to guard against production failures. Therefore, for the manufacturing firm, the greater the uncertainty of demand, the more difficult the inventory management problem.

For nonmanufacturing middlemen firms such as wholesalers and retailers, there are two sources of uncertainty which cause difficulty in inventory management. Like manufacturing firms, they are faced with some degree of uncertainty in accurately forecasting their demand. In addition, they must be concerned with the degree of uncertainty caused by the variance in order cycle times when dealing with their various suppliers. As noted in the discussion of order cycle time, the dispersion around the average time is of importance to the customer. As seen from the nonmanufacturing firm's point of view, zero disperson around the average order cycle time would mean the elimination of its second source of uncertainty in managing its inventory.

For the manufacturing firm, a prime consideration is to balance the inventory costs against the manufacturing cost. This dilemma arises due to the conflicting desires to minimize the cost necessary to hold inventories and to maximize the economies of scale realized in large production runs which minimize the per unit production costs. Here again the trade-off concept applies, and the firm must determine how much inventory costs and production costs must increase from their independent ideal positions in order for the firm to minimize its total cost of producing and holding finished goods.

A trade-off also exists for the nonmanufacturing firm. For middlemen firms the nature of the trade-off evolves around minimizing the total of both ordering costs and holding costs. Ordering costs are the expenses incurred in placing a single order times the frequency of orders. Thus, the smaller the quantity ordered, the greater the frequency of orders and the greater the total ordering costs. Holding costs are determined by the average inventory level. The fewer the number of orders, the larger the quantities and the larger the average inventory, which results in higher holding costs. Therefore, when considering the number of orders placed, ordering costs move in the opposite direction of holding costs. A mathematical solution for the trade-off between these two costs has been developed to determine the Economic Order Quantity (EOQ).[4]

The EOQ formula is:

$$EOQ = \sqrt{\frac{2as}{i}},$$

where:

a = Order costs (per order).
s = Annual sales rate (in units).
i = Interest costs per unit per year.

For an example, assume:

a = \$20.
s = 5,200 units.
i = 25 cents per unit.

Therefore:

$$EOQ = \sqrt{\frac{2as}{i}}$$

$$= \sqrt{\frac{2(20)(5200)}{0.25}}$$

$$= \sqrt{\frac{208,000}{0.25}}$$

$$= \sqrt{832,000}$$

$$= 912 \text{ units}$$

This EOQ results in approximately five orders per year.

---

[4] This illustration follows the one in Edward H. Bowman and Robert B. Fetter, *Analysis for Production Management* (Homewood, Ill.: Richard D. Irwin, Inc., 1961); see pp. 272–76 for the mathematical derivation.

While the EOQ formula provides a guide to efficient inventory management, it is not the final answer. The EOQ is used to determine base stock requirements. Base stock consists of the amount of stock needed to meet the *average* level of demand. Since base stocks cover only the average demand, a firm that provides only base stock inventory would tend to be out of inventory 50 percent of the time. In order to minimize this condition, the firm would need to carry *safety* stocks in addition to base stocks to cover demand above average levels. As shown in Figure 2 above, as the firm attempts to position its inventory levels to meet a higher and higher percent of demand at any time, the investment in inventory becomes extremely high due to increases in the cost of safety stocks.

In addition to setting higher percentages of demand to be filled, a firm may also increase its safety stock by decentralizing distribution and using several distribution centers. Multiple distribution centers require multiple safety stocks, one at each distribution center, and increase the total uncertainty in forecasting demand. Typically, it is easier to forecast one aggregate demand than to divide up the aggregate and forecast the uncertainty of many smaller segments. Consequently, a decentralized distribution policy causes higher total levels of safety stocks and, hence, higher total inventory costs.

Transportation

The major objectives in managing the firm's transportation requirements center around choosing methods which will minimize transport costs, time in shipment, and loss and damage resulting from shipment. These trade-offs within the transportation activity are often in conflict. For example, air freight minimizes the transport time, but at a very high cost. Damage in shipment is often a trade-off between special packaging methods and selection of shipment modes which historically have low damage frequencies.

Beyond the trade-offs within the transportation activity are trade-offs between it and other activities. In fact, a major objective of the firm in adopting a decentralized distribution policy stems from its desire to minimize the transportation costs. Using many distribution centers accomplishes this by allowing the firm to ship full carload or truckload shipments at the lower CL and TL rates. It can then reship the small customer orders the short distances from the distribution center to the customer at the higher less-than-carload (LCL) or less-than-truckload (LTL) rates. This minimizes the total transportation costs. Here, however, the firm must concern itself with minimizing the total cost of transporting, warehousing, and inventorying its products. Although the decentralization of warehousing and inventory does lower the total transportation costs, it also, as discussed previously, raises the warehousing and inventory costs. Again we can see the interdependence of the cost of the activities of servicing demand relative to the firm's desire to minimize the total cost of providing a given level of service.

Order processing and handling

The actual order processing and handling deals with the communications necessary to receive, record, and fill an order and with the procedures necessary to physically assemble an order and make it ready for shipment. Management's concern with order processing and handling procedures arises from the amount of time necessary to process and handle an order and the quality control procedures used to ensure that the order is filled and shipped correctly.

It does little good for the firm to pay premium prices for transportation speed if the transportation time is considerably less than the order processing and handling time. Slow order processing and handling procedures increase the total order cycle time just as surely as slow transportation times do.

To increase the speed of order processing, the firm must turn its attention to high-speed data processing techniques to receive, record, process, and check orders. In some cases this is so critical that customers have a direct computer tie-in with their suppliers and are able to know almost instantly what their position is in regard to the number of units on hand of a given product, how many units are on order, how many have been shipped, and when they are expected to arrive.

While procedures used to ensure the correctness of order handling tend to increase the total time for order processing and handling, the firm must again determine the trade-off between increasing the total order cycle time for these quality control procedures and the costs of shipping the wrong goods.

CONCLUSION

This discussion was not meant to provide a definitive technical treatment of physical distribution management. It is meant to provide the student with some insight into what physical distribution is, what it does, and how it relates to the firm's overall distribution effort. Physical distribution management concerns itself with the management of the firm's demand-servicing activities. They must be coordinated in such a way that their interdependent nature is recognized, so that the firm can minimize the total cost of providing its resulting service level.

The service level chosen by the firm can be a demand-obtaining force. Therefore, the firm must consider the cost trade-offs between the traditional demand-obtaining activities such as personal selling and advertising and the service level. In summary, physical distribution management is concerned with the design, implementation, and operation of the firm's demand-servicing system in relationship to how the firm wishes to use the demand-servicing system as a source of obtaining demand for the firm's goods and services.

QUESTIONS

1. Could the concept of service level be used as a means of obtaining a competitive advantage? Explain.

2. How could the concept of elasticity of demand for service aid a manager in selecting and catering to different segments of a market?

3. Many physical distribution managers apparently view their primary task as one of minimizing the total cost of physical distribution. After reading the Lewis article, do you agree or disagree with this view? Why?

*4. Could some kind of change in physical distribution lead to the kind of differential advantage discussed by Alderson (Reading 5)? If so, illustrate. If not, explain why.

_____

* Question relates concepts in this and other readings.

23
The new supersalesman: Wired for success

Today's "supersalesman" is far more than a seller of goods and services. In response to keener competition, better purchasing practices, and a growing recognition that you must satisfy a need rather than simply sell a product, a good salesperson must relate to all the facets of a prospect's business that bear on the product the salesperson is promoting. These might range from equipment amortization and inventory control to distribution. And the salesperson must know the answers to a buyer's questions.*

If you want to rile Herbert D. Eagle, just slide a copy of *Webster's New Collegiate Dictionary* in front of him. "Have you ever read the definition of 'sell'?" fumes Eagle, vice president of marketing for Transamerica Corp. "Things like 'betray' and 'cheat' are capitalized, and there are phrases such as 'to deliver up or give up in violation of duty, trust, or loyalty.' I've been carrying on a running battle with G. & C. Merriam Co. to change that definition."

_____

Source: Reprinted with permission of the publisher from *Business Week,* January 6, 1973. Copyright © 1973, McGraw-Hill, Inc.

* Editors' note: Despite the editors' intent to avoid sexist terminology in this book of readings, it is not always possible to do so because some publications have done less in this respect than others. In this article the word *salesman* is commonly used, as is typical in most business literature. It will probably be many years before the word *salesperson* replaces *salesman* in common usage.

Nevertheless, it is important to recognize that there are many good opportunities for women in personal selling. In fact, sales is an "easy entry" area, and as attitudes have changed about

If anyone can sell Merriam on a new definition, it is 54-year-old Herb Eagle. As marketing vice-president for giant, fast-growing Transamerica Corp. ($1.6 billion in sales last year), Eagle coordinates the marketing and sales strategies for 42 companies that field more than 6,000 internal salesmen and handle everything from insurance and financial services to car rentals. Eagle also doubles as president of Sales and Marketing Executives International, a professional society of 25,000 members scattered through 49 countries. As the official pick of his peers and thus the closest thing to industry's top salesman, Eagle is a drumbeater in the cause of supersalesmanship and the enormous change that is coming over that fine, old American institution: personal selling.

"A few years back," says Eagle, "it was usually the salesman out there alone, pitting his wits against the resistance of a single corporate purchasing agent. Now, more and more companies are selling on many different levels, interlocking their research, engineering, marketing, and upper management with those of their customers. This way, today's salesman becomes a kind of committee chairman within his company. Some manufacturers call them 'account managers.' Either way, his job is to exploit the resources of his company in serving the customer."

As industries consolidate and larger corporations continue to swallow up the small fry, a growing number of companies are also "preselling" their products through massive promotion, advertising, and improved communications between buyer and seller. The result is that the average salesman's prime responsibility is no longer selling, so much as clinching a sale that has already been set in motion even before he makes his first spiel.

MORE SALES PRODUCTIVITY

At the consumer level, this shows up in the cutback of retail sales help and the huge expansion of self-service merchandising. At the industry level, it shows up in a whole new function for the industrial salesman. No longer is he simply a pitchman or prescriber of his company's products. Now he must go beyond that and become a diagnostician.

"If a supplier's job is to service the customer, then the role of the salesman becomes one of problem-identifier first, problem-solver second, and pre-

---

women's work roles, many women have entered the sales area outside of retailing, with great success. Women have tended to move toward consumer goods selling, but there are many more opportunities in industrial selling and selling in the channels. In fact, women are successfully selling computers and other complicated industrial goods.

To modern sales managers, sales are what count, and able women are being sought and being given greater responsibilities in previous male sanctuaries as the innovators demonstrate that they can perform as well as or better than males. It is only fair to note, however, that firms that have hired "token" women as salespersons have fired the ineffective saleswomen just as they do the ineffective salesmen. Ultimately, salespersons must get sales, and opening up sales forces to women is likely to increase the overall level of competitiveness and performance— thereby improving an individual firm's performance and the operation of our macro-marketing system.

scriber third," says Charles S. Goodman, professor of marketing at the University of Pennsylvania's Wharton School. "I don't say this is common today. But as the economy becomes more consumer-oriented"—and thus open to greater challenge on product performance—"it's got to go that way."

An even greater goad is today's spiraling cost of selling, which demands that industry get far more out of its sales dollar. Rex Chainbelt, Inc., for instance, spends $5,000 to $20,000 to train a salesman and $30,000 to $35,000 a year to keep him on the road. That averages out to $52.80 per sales call, double the figure of 10 years ago. What is more, as product lines proliferate and product technology gets more complex, manufacturers and wholesalers have gradually boosted their number of internal salesmen to more than 1 million. And some experts claim that the demand for salesmen will grow by another 250,000 jobs a year over the next few years, not including replacements. "Obviously," as Transamerica's Eagle notes, "something has to give."

To cut costs and raise sales efficiency, more and more companies are reexamining the ways that they recruit, train, pay, equip, and manage their salesmen. Many companies are reorganizing their selling structures. Some are experimenting with new compensation and incentive programs. Nearly all are moving away from the old straight commission system to salary-plus-bonus.

"This is primarily the product of looking upon salesmen as account managers," says William E. Cox, professor of marketing at Case Western Reserve University. "You begin asking him to take on a lot of additional duties other than just simply writing an order. He becomes the company's broader marketing representative."

Industry is also drawing on a whole new battery of selling tools, ranging from audiovisual cassettes and special slide projectors to remote portable terminals that can plug the salesman straight into his home-office computer. The computer itself, of course, has become one of selling's biggest tools of all. It can lay out sales territories, budget the salesman's time by customer and product, and keep track of sales costs, time use, itineraries, payables and receivables, expenses, orders, inquiries, and overall performance.

"Fifteen years ago when I first started selling," says Frederick H. Stephens, Jr., sales vice-president for Gillette Co.'s Safety Razor Division, "we couldn't tell at any point how much volume we did on promotional items, for instance, compared with open stock. Now we have monthly IBM printouts that tell our salesman how much business he's doing with promotions compared to open stock and total business, how much business is being done in his territory, and how much each customer bought of each item. We used to tell a salesman, 'You're up 4.6 percent this year, that's pretty good.' Now we can say, 'You're up 4.6 percent but down 1.6 percent in discount stores and up only 2.1 percent over your territory.' And we have the information to get him back in the ballgame."

IDENTIFYING CUSTOMER NEEDS

Unfortunately, most salesmen are still somewhere between the locker room and the playing field. "Selling is very, very inefficient compared to what it could be," says Edward J. Feeney, vice-president of the Systems Performance Division of Emery Air Freight Corp. "Most salesmen," Feeney claims, "are sitting in lobbies. They're calling on wrong accounts. They're calling on accounts that give them all the business that they can. They're calling on people they think can make the buying decision when, in fact, they do not or cannot make much of it at all. They are efficient in talking about what they do—what their company provides—but not in how it fills the customer's needs, because they haven't probed to find out what those needs are."

Those needs usually go far beyond the purchase of any one supplier's equipment or services. Hugh Hoffman, chairman of Opinion Research Corp., cites the experience of one of his company's clients, a major chemical producer. "Its salesmen told us," he says, "that if they're trying to sell plastic film to a packager who has several million dollars' worth of packaging equipment designed to use some other material, they must now know how to unload the present equipment, purchase new equipment, and work out the intricacies of amortization. Without that background, they cannot persuade the customer to accept delivery of a single carload of plastic film."

This is because today's major competitor is no longer one broom salesman against another. It is alternate uses of money. "And the modern salesman," says John R. Robertson, sales manager for the Business Systems Markets Division of Eastman Kodak Co., "must be able to convince his customer that spending money on the salesman's product is a better investment than spending it elsewhere."

Above all, the supersalesman tries to build more than the old-style buyer-seller relationship. A top marketing executive at International Business Machines Corp., which is one of the companies that has spearheaded the development of superselling, claims that today's salesman must develop a "long-range partnership" with his clients. "The installation of a data-processing system," he emphasizes, "is only the beginning, not the end, of IBM's marketing effort."

To serve their customers better, IBM salesmen not only specialize by product and market. They now specialize by function: installation, equipment protection or maintenance, and upgrading of systems. To sharpen the focus of its salesmen even more, IBM—like most consumer-goods companies—is "segmenting" or targeting its markets. "The costs of developing new accounts by the cold-call approach," says the IBM marketer, "have risen so drastically that we are moving toward far more selective prospecting"— including a special computer experiment for picking only "high-potential prospects."

Among the other special qualities that set off the supersalesman [are the following].

Universality

"Ten years ago when I hired a salesman," says James Schlinkert, Pittsburgh-area branch manager for Olivetti Corp. of America, "I was looking for someone who would make a lot of calls and, through sheer effort and exposure, be reasonably successful. Now I want someone more versed in things unrelated to our business. Today's salesman must be able to talk on any and all current subjects—from the economy to world affairs—because these often affect his business." Not too many years ago, adds the marketing vice-president for a major information-systems company, "you'd hire somebody with personality that you thought would wear well, and you'd point him out the door." Now it takes more. "A top manager's time is very precious," he says, "and we have to give him a meaningful message when we meet with him."

Patience

Because product technology has become more complex and salesmen are interrelating more products and moving deeper into systems selling, the time that it takes to close a sale has stretched out. "There are no quick sales today," says Anthony E. Schiavone, an assistant development manager for Rohm & Haas Co. "It may take a year just to get to know a new customer and his problems." Philip Rosell, Western regional sales manager for Singer's Business Machines Group, claims that he was on the verge of quitting Singer two years ago after he had gone his first full year without writing an order. "You have to gear yourself psychologically for a long haul," he says.

Persistence

With growing cost-consciousness, upper management is increasingly involved in major buying decisions. So the supersalesman often tries to go beyond the first level of decision-making. "This is not usually the best-paid or most creative guy around anyway," says one Boston salesman. "It's when you go beyond this level that you can sell the extras. And it's not true that the top guy never sees salesmen. You can often enlist the aid of your own top people and set up a meeting."

More work, less play

Lavish wining and dining of buyers is out. In fact, Don H. Hartmann, president of Crutcher Resources Corp., calls this "probably the biggest thrust of all—the trend away from the massive entertainment of a few years ago."

One top Eastern salesman adds, of his relations with his customers: "We're no longer a bunch of drinking buddies. I never have lunch with a man I haven't met before, and I never hesitate to talk business at lunch. After all, our relationship is business and not personal."

RESTRUCTURING THE TERRITORIES

Whether he is selling insurance, computers, catalytic crackers, or wholesale cosmetics, today's supersalesman has two big things going for him: improved transportation and communications. This allows him to cover more territory faster and to draw closer to his markets. As the president of a Houston industrial-goods company describes his ideal salesman: "He starts his day flying out nonstop from North Carolina to Chicago, then gets a midafternoon plane to Los Angeles to make two or three calls, and catches a night plane to Dallas. It's a fast-moving situation today. Five years ago, because of aircraft and flight scheduling, we couldn't do this."

Yet how much territory is too much? As far back as 10 years ago, adman and marketing seer E. B. Weiss, a senior vice-president at Doyle Dane Bernbach, was calling for a whole new approach to the organization of sales territories and to the basic corporate selling structure. Then, as now, the problem was to minimize unproductive calls and contacts and to get close to the prospects who had both the need and purchasing authority to buy a given product or service. "The sales organization," Weiss write, "must be reorganized so as to be able to open up its channels of communication to those who make buying decisions, rather than to limit itself primarily to buyers who make merely buying motions. This calls for new sales organizational blueprints."

Those changes are finally beginning to come. Today's three basic levels of selling—manufacturing, wholesaling, and consumer and industrial services—are spawning dozens of highly specialized sub-categories aimed at shortening the lines of communication between buyer and seller. IBM is even experimenting with administrative specialists who help its sales specialists handle order preparation, scheduling, collections, and other paperowk. Along the way, more and more companies are organizing against markets, rather than products. For maximum productivity, a few are even organizing against profits.

"Historically," says Gennaro A. Filice, Jr., vice-president of U.S. marketing for Del Monte Corp., "most food companies have been case-volume-oriented. As long as we could push out a lot of volume, we let the profits take care of themselves. That's no longer true. As products multiply and the competition for shelf space increases, salesmen have to be far more sophisticated in their approach to product management, and the company has to learn to identify those with the most profit potential."

To help pinpoint that potential, Del Monte recently restructured its entire field sales force, expanding from nine regional divisions to 21. "As our emphasis shifted away from case sales," says Filice, "and as the chains got bigger and more dominant, it became more difficult for a salesman to write an order. This restructuring was also designed to get us as close to the customer as possible."

Under Del Monte's new system, the actual selling is handled by an "account representative." He makes the direct calls on retailers and writes up the orders. Then one level below him is the sales representative. He is the junior type who works with store managers on shelf management, restocking, display, and other merchandising chores. Sales representatives are also information-gatherers. Using a new computerized system called "Key Facts," which the company plans to expand nationwide next spring, Del Monte's California salesmen fill out a form during each store visit, listing shelf position, pricing, advertising support, and other basic marketing data. This is fed into the computer and later compared against actual product performance to arrive at maximum profitability.

WOMEN IN THE SALES FORCE

Hunt-Wesson Foods, Gillette, Allied Chemical, and several other companies have found another productivity booster for their field organizations: part-time female workers. Gillette maintains an auxiliary force of 150 middle-aged housewives who operate one rung below the individual store salesmen. The women work 24 hours a week for $3 an hour, plus expenses, and handle retail displays, distribution, and stock replenishment.*

"In 1958, when I started selling," says one sales executive at Gillette, "I spent 30 percent of my time calling on direct customers and 70 percent calling on local stores to work on display and distribution, and writing up turnover orders"—orders passed on to wholesalers to replenish out-of-stock items. "Today, our salesmen spend 85 percent of their time on direct accounts and only about 15 percent of their time at local stores on display and distribution."

Along with tightening the focus of their field forces, more and more companies are also creating broader "account executives," whose job is to crack that tricky, old marketing problem: how to deal with the big chains or a large, diversified company with a variety of product needs. Some suppliers, of course, simply send a battalion of salesmen swarming into such companies at all levels. Now a growing number are creating account executives who oversee all product needs of a single customer, often at the headquarters level. This way, the big customer has one sales contact that can satisfy and interrelate all its needs.

Over the last few years, Dow Chemical Co. has created 14 corporate account managers who operate one notch above the salesman and handle all 1,200 Dow products for a given customer. "There are no firm rules about how big an account must be before a corporate account manager takes

---

* Editors' note: It is important to note that opportunities for women in the sales area are definitely not limited to such "detail" or "merchandising" tasks. Women are now welcomed into all kinds of selling jobs, including industrial goods selling.

over," says M. C. Carpenter, Dow's director of marketing communications. "But they are basically potential multimillion-dollar customers."

At the same time, Dow is trying to crack another problem that comes with the bigness of a customer: the difficulty of getting a territorial fix on where a sale actually occurs. In the past, Dow credited a sale to the office in the territory where the customer was located. Thus, any sale in the Houston area was chalked up to the Houston office, even though the key initiative may have come in New York. Now each sale is credited to the office where the sale originates. "That makes the accounting more complicated and subjective," Carpenter concedes. "But it gives sales managers a better idea of what's really going on in the field. We find out where the key marketing man is."

As sales organizations grow bigger and more complex, the challenge, of course, is to avoid costly duplication of sales effort. Hewlett-Packard Co. ran into this problem. It started out with a highly centralized organization that did most of its selling through outside manufacturers' representatives. By 1963, the company's product line had become so broad and complicated that Hewlett-Packard decided to acquire most of its reps and turn them into a corporate sales staff. "We stayed with reps longer than most companies," says Robert L. Boniface, marketing vice-president. "We felt that it was important to have the sales force represent the customer's viewpoint as much as Hewlett-Packard's. By acquiring them rather than cutting them off, we kept all their experience and momentum."

As Hewlett-Packard moved into medical instruments, calculators, electronic components, and other diverse new markets, the company split its sales staff into eight organizations. "Right away, we developed overlaps," says Alfred P. Oliverio, marketing manager for the Electronic Products Group. "We didn't want two salesmen calling on one customer if the product was not really all that different."

In Hewlett-Packard's most recent shift, the old product-oriented structure gave way to a combined product/market-oriented system. In electronic products, for instance, separate sales groups now concentrate on electrical manufacturing, aerospace, communications, and transportation equipment. Within each group, Hewlett-Packard tries to build a cadre of salesmen, application engineers, and software specialists. "We probably have better than one support person for every salesman," says Oliverio.

SELLING THE "DREAM LIST"

Hans G. Moser, field director for Northwestern Mutual Life Insurance Co. and a chartered life underwriter, sold $4.5 million worth of life insurance last year. That makes him 29th out of the company's 2,900 agents. Moser's distinctive selling approach is typical of how today's supersalesman tackles his customer.

Like a consumer-goods maker who targets his market, Moser ignores "run-of-the-mill types" and zeroes in on prospects who can either afford heavy insurance now or who are obviously on the way up and will be able to in the future. Moser adopted this tactic when he broke into the insurance business in 1960. "Many of my earlier customers," he says, "are now in a position to set up trust accounts, dabble with stocks, and deal with other sophisticated methods of estate planning. And, of course, I am right in there, making a pitch for life insurance and other securities."

Moser keeps two lists of prospects: one made up of day-to-day business that he expects to close within a month, and the other composed of "dream cases"—each ranging anywhere from $100,000 to $500,000 or more of coverage—that may take three months to a year to close. His goal is to add a new dream case every month and maintain a working inventory of at least 10 or 12 such cases. This way, he closes one every four to six weeks. As part of the same goal, Moser keeps a chart of his best January, February, and so on, and uses it as a composite yearly goal.

In pitching the customer, Singer Business Machines' Philip Rosell has come up with such a winning technique for selling electronic point-of-sale systems to retailers that Singer even asked him to write it up in PERT chart fashion. Salesman Rosell's opening strategy is a letter to the prospect's top operating officer, requesting a meeting. Rosell starts at the top because of the big investment involved in buying his equipment. "We seldom get turned down," Rosell says of his request for that first big meeting. Then Rosell teams up with a local salesman and system engineer, and the three go in together and discuss what the system can do for the prospect. "We don't try to sell him any hardware," Rosell says. "That's what he has a purchasing agent for."

THE LESSONS TAUGHT BY FAILURE

If the first meeting is encouraging, Rosell follows it up with store surveys and endless conferences and demonstrations for the store's credit, merchandising, data processing, and financial executives. "We infiltrate the whole company," says Rosell. "In every case where we've made a major sale, the company has felt we were part of its team." Rosell recalls only two occasions when he did not follow his usual selling approach. This was at the insistence of the customer, who wanted a consultant to act as go-between. Both times the sale was lost.

What happens when you do blow the big sale? H. Glen Haney, a marketing director for the Univac Division of Sperry Rand Corp., makes it a point to go back and find out why. "We lost a $4.5 million sale to a large state agency about a year ago," Haney says. "In a four-hour debriefing with the agency head, the state budget bureau people, and all other principals that were involved in the purchase, we found out that the loss of the sale really had nothing to do with the quality of our marketing effort. We lost because we had not clearly enough defined the conversion effort that the customer faced. Though our cost-performance was better than the competition, the agency decided to stay with its current vendor for that reason." Yet the lost sale was not a total loss. "As a result of that session," says Haney, "we have developed a series of conversion tools for our salesmen, aimed at solving that problem."

Owens-Corning Fiberglas Corp. took the same approach when a big customer, a thermoplastic compounder in Detroit, considered switching to an Owens-Corning competitor, which had cut its prices 1½ cents per pound. The competitor had a plant near the compounder, and the compounder decided to pick up its materials there, saving on freight. "It was a legitimate saving," says James MacLean, national sales manager for Owens-Corning's Textile and Industrial Group. "So we put our heads together." The local salesman, along with the group's marketing and packaging experts, finally developed a special package for shipping the material that the compounder could then use to ship his finished product. Savings: 2 cents per pound for the customer and one industrial account for Owens-Corning.

Sam Jackson, an assistant sales manager for U.S. Steel Corp. in Philadelphia, calls it the difference between moving a product for its own sake and fitting the same product to a customer's system. One of Jackson's customers was bemoaning a 10 percent hike in the cost of castings. "I suggested that the part could be converted from a casting to welded steel," says Jackson, "and got together with our metallurgical and research people to test the conversion." The customer finally accepted it, saving the 10 percent boost in cost that he would have paid had he continued to cast the part.

"What makes Jackson stand out is that he knows the different types of metals, the industry that he is selling to, and how to cut costs," says Irwin Rashkover, director of procurement for Gindy Mfg. Corp., a Budd Co. subsidiary. "Jackson knows how to help us save money by working out different tolerances for the steel we buy—for instance, by going to the high side of sheet tolerances. The supersalesman knows this. The ordinary steel salesman doesn't."

DON'T TAKE "NO" FOR AN ANSWER

Robert Hawkins, who sells radio communications systems for Motorola, Inc., has the simplest—and oldest—selling technique of all: He refuses to take "no" for an answer. When Hawkins was pitching the field service organization of a national equipment supply house, he insisted that Motorola's one-way paging system could improve service and cut manpower needs. When a purchasing agent shrugged him off, Hawkins went above him to a vice president and received grudging permission for a one-year study of the company's service coverage and performance in 20 cities. Yet when he completed the study, which showed the need for a paging system, Hawkins still did not receive an order. So he offered to follow that up with an intensive three-month test of the paging system in a single city.

"For the entire three months," says Hawkins, "a day never went by when I didn't spend some time with the prospect." Hawkins even helped the dis-

patcher to design more efficient routes, while soothing the ruffled nerves of its
servicemen. "They were afraid of the dispatcher becoming a Big Brother and
controlling their every move," he says. Finally convinced, the company has
decided to go nationwide with the paging system.

Sometimes, such indecision can go too far. That is when Olivetti's James
Schlinkert calls a halt. "To close a tough sale," he says, "you must establish
yourself—not the buyer—as the authoritative person." Schlinkert describes
just such a sale that he ran up against a few months ago. A small corporation
of five people had a definite need for an accounting system. "We had them all
at our office one evening and presented our solution to their problem," says
Schlinkert. "They were a hard-nosed lot that had evaluated every other
accounting system available. After a couple of hours of haggling over a
$15,000 sale, I finally shut off the machine, put the key in my pocket, and
virtually threatened to throw them out of my office. Immediately, they became very docile and signed a contract. I shocked my salesman when I did
that. But I had to take a calculated risk. The need and solution had been
established."

TRAINING TODAY'S SALESMAN

Developing such instincts takes years. Some salesmen never develop
them, and that puts a heavier burden than ever on today's sales recruiting
and training. "In years past," says Transamerica's Herb Eagle, "you figured
you could take a new salesman and help him develop the qualities that he
needed. With today's higher costs and greater complexity of selling, you have
to look for those qualities first off. And if they aren't there, you don't hire."

Five or 10 years ago, for instance, most large technical or engineering
companies automatically recruited from engineering schools. Now, many of
these same companies are seeking salesmen with a broader outlook and thus
are looking for liberal arts, marketing, and other nonengineering backgrounds. "We have even successfully used English, history, and physical
education majors," marvels Baxter T. Fullerton, sales vice president of
Warner & Swasey Co.'s Cleveland Turning Machine Division. The trick, of
course, is to gain a universal man with broad interests, yet avoid what one
Houston educator calls "the round man who is so round that he just rolls and
develops no depth or substance."

Other companies are looking less for college graduates and more for
seasoned professionals. "We used to steer clear of the retreads," says Peter
Warshaw, a division national products manager for Powers Regulator Co.
"Today when there's a vacancy, we don't contact colleges at all. We contact
employment agencies, professional societies, and use referrals within the industry. We just can't afford to take the guy, make the major investment in him
for two or three years, and then have him sell the training that we gave him to
someone else." The new man, Warshaw stresses, must also be productive

immediately. "The sales quotas are now so large and selling costs so high that we can't afford to have the backup man or bat boy anymore."

At the same time, sales training has broadened out. A growing number of companies offer continuing instruction for all their salesmen—and for good reason. Armour-Dial, Inc., a consumer-goods division of Greyhound Corp., ran a study on salesmen who had attended a recent session at its Aurora (Ill.) sales training center. The result: a boost of 12 percent in the number of calls per day, 25 percent in new-product retail placements, 100 percent in case sales, 62 percent in displays sold, and 250 percent in sales to direct-buying or chain accounts.

The big changes coming in sales recruiting and training—and in the salesman's whole approach to his markets—promise to usher in a broad new relationship between him and his company. Robert W. DeMott, Jr., vice president and general manager of Rex Chainbelt's Industrial Sales Division notes that about 10 years ago, industry's overall marketing effort seemed to eclipse selling in importance. "Now, and more so in the future," he claims, "the trend will be to place selling on a par with marketing."

Wharton's Goodman goes one step further, claiming that the supersalesman of the future will even be ahead of company management when it comes to understanding his markets. "This is going to sound heretical," he admits, "but I see emerging a situation in which the salesman's function within a company is recognized as most important, with management performing a largely supportive role."

While he might get an argument on that, no one can dispute his larger point: the supersalesman is here to stay.

QUESTIONS

1. What does "wired for success" mean in the title of this article? Is it an accurate term to use?

2. The new "supersalesman" seems to be a minicompany or at least a mini-marketing manager. Discuss the implications for corporate organization.

3. What factors have contributed to the evolution of a new type of supersalesperson? Are these new salespeople better than the older type? Why?

*4. Do you think part of the reason for the new salesperson's success could be the application of the concept of benefit segmentation (Reading 13)? Explain how a salesperson might use that concept to do the job better.

*5. Compare the roles of the new "supersalesman" and the product manager (Reading 17). Which might offer more room for creativity and independent decision making?

---

* Question relates concepts in this and other readings.

24
Industrial advertising effects and budgeting practices

Gary L. Lilien, Alvin J. Silk, Jean-Marie Choffray,
and Murlidhar Rao

While industrial organizations still rely heavily on personal selling in their promotion blends, many industrial firms do advertise. This article surveys the research on the effectiveness of industrial advertising and examines industrial advertising budgeting practices. It also makes many points which are applicable to consumer goods marketing, such as use of the task method for budgeting.

The industrial sector has long been regarded as the stepchild of marketing in terms of the amount of research effort devoted to its problems. There are, however, indications that the situation may be changing. Research on industrial/organizational buying behavior is growing, and a considerable body of empirical knowledge about processes surrounding the innovation and diffusion of industrial technologies and products has been developing.[1] This article is concerned with a different set of issues: those surrounding the determination of expenditure levels for industrial advertising. The purpose here is two-fold: (1) to review the available research relating to the effects of industrial advertising, and (2) to examine practices currently used in budgeting industrial advertising in light of what is known about advertising response and costs in this field.

Estimates of total industrial advertising volume are not readily available because of the lack of relevant aggregate data and the vagaries of defining what constitutes "industrial advertising." However, N. W. Ayer estimated that

Source: Reprinted with permission from the *Journal of Marketing,* published by the American Marketing Association, vol. 40 (January 1976), pp. 16–24. At the time of writing Gary Lilien was an assistant professor, Alvin Silk was a professor, and Jean-Marie Choffray and Murlidhar Rao were doctoral students, all at the Alfred P. Sloan School of Management, Massachusetts Institute of Technology.

Note: This paper was prepared with the support of a research grant made to M.I.T. for Project ADVISOR, a study of industrial marketing communications funded by a group of participating companies and coordinated through the Association of National Advertisers. Thanks are due to Donald Gluck and John D. C. Little for stimulating this work.

[1] See, for example, Frederick E. Webster, Jr. and Yoram Wind, *Organizational Buying Behavior* (Englewood Cliffs, N.J.: Prentice-Hall, 1972); and James M. Utterback, "Innovation in Industry and the Diffusion of Technology," *Science,* February 14, 1974, pp. 620–26.

industrial advertising totaled $925 million in 1973;[2] and Marsteller, chairman of one of the major advertising agencies in the industrial marketing field, has indicated that there are 300–500 firms with annual industrial advertising budgets exceeding $1 million.[3] Surveys of industrial advertising budgets show that outlays for research have been running at about 1 percent of expenditures for several years.[4] Considering that the top 100 national advertisers alone spent $5.68 billion in 1973,[5] one can readily appreciate why the cumulative body of studies bearing on industrial advertising effects appears so slight in comparison to that available on consumer advertising.[6]

The advertising budget for the industrial marketer is typically too small to justify or support the kind of research effort required to assess the impact of advertising in a manner that would yield information relevant to expenditure decisions. This condition contributes to the skepticism of many industrial executives toward the effectiveness of advertising. Thus, advertising expenditure policy continues to be a perplexing problem for industrial marketing managers, and it becomes important to ask what is known about the process and effects of industrial advertising and how that knowledge relates to current budgeting practices.

INDUSTRIAL ADVERTISING EFFECTS AND COSTS

At the heart of the problem of budgeting expenditures for advertising is the lack of understanding of the nature of advertising response. This section presents a selective review of published empirical studies that provide information or clues about the effects of industrial advertising. The body of material that meets these criteria is quite small. Release of research undertaken by individual firms is infrequent, with the exception of brief, informal accounts that occasionally appear in the trade press.

Arthur D. Little, Inc. and N. W. Ayer have both recently issued reports surveying the literature in the industrial advertising field.[7] The Arthur D. Little report claimed that 1,100 studies were uncovered, but many of the references listed dealt with consumer advertising research. In fact, only 8 studies were singled out for detailed discussion. The impression gleaned from those re-

---

[2] N. W. Ayer & Sons, Inc., *Industrial Advertising: Past, Present and Future* (Philadelphia, 1974), p. i.

[3] William A. Marsteller, "Field of Industrial Advertising Gets More Competitive," *Advertising Age*, June 17, 1974, p. 23.

[4] See, for example, Sally Strong, "Ad Budgets '74: Trend Is Still to Spend, Spend, Spend," *Industrial Marketing*, vol. 59 (February 1974), p. 57.

[5] Merle Kingman, "Top National Advertisers Hike Ad Total to $5.68 billion," *Advertising Age*, August 26, 1974, p. 1.

[6] Advertising Research Foundation, *Measuring Payout: An Annotated Bibliography on the Dollar Effectiveness of Advertising* (New York, 1973).

[7] Arthur D. Little, Inc., *An Evaluation of 1100 Research Studies on the Effectiveness of Industrial Advertising*, report to American Business Press, Inc. (Cambridge, Mass., 1971); and same reference as footnote 2.

Figure 1
Current state of industrial advertising research

Research design \ Measure of response	Correlational	Experimental
Sales	Occasional	None?
Attitude and other nonsales	Most common	Rare

views, as well as from the present one, is that, from a methodological view-point, the current state of industrial advertising research can be described as indicated in Figure 1.

While only a very limited amount of empirical research is available in this area, some evidence exists that bears on each of the following important phenomena:

1. *Economies of scale.* Is there some relevant range in which additional increments of advertising yield increasing returns?
2. *Threshold effects.* Is there some minimum level of exposure that must be exceeded for advertising to have a discernible effect?
3. *Interaction effects.* Does advertising interact with other elements of the marketing mix (personal selling in particular) to produce effects that are greater than the sum of their separate effects?

This section will examine the current literature in industrial advertising with respect to the effects and costs of such advertising. Particular attention will be paid to the sales and nonsales effects and to specific cost considerations, in an attempt to answer the three questions posed above.

Sales effects

The published literature is almost devoid of either correlational or exper-imental investigations of sales response to industrial advertising. A noteworthy exception is a regression analysis discussed by Weinberg.[8]

Weinberg reported empirical evidence on the marketing effort–sales rela-tionship which implied diminishing returns for that effort. He developed a multiple-equation corporate planning model that was applied to several in-dustrial goods manufacturers. Weinberg reported that a submodel of the

[8] Robert S. Weinberg, "Multiple Factor Break-Even Analysis: The Application of O.R. Tech-niques to a Basic Problem of Management Planning and Control," *Operations Research,* vol. 4 (April 1956), pp. 152–86.

system relating changes in a firm's market share to its "advertising exchange rate" (the firm's advertising expenditures per dollar of sales divided by the corresponding ratio for its competitors) had been successfully used in some of this work. He presented an example in which data consisting of seven observations for an unidentified glass container manufacturer were used to estimate the relationship between annual changes in market share and the exchange rate for advertising expenditures. An excellent fit was obtained ($R^2 = .966$), and the form of the relationship (linear in the logarithms of both variables) implied diminishing returns to advertising effort. Weinberg also demonstrated how the model could be incorporated into a procedure to determine the company's relative advertising effectiveness per dollar expended and, more importantly, to find the advertising level that would maximize profit in the next year given a forecast of competitive activity and economic conditions.[9]

What is perhaps most interesting about the Weinberg study is that it remains a rarity. It showed how quantitative advertising-sales relationships could be *developed* and *used* to help set advertising budgets. Yet there are no reports in the literature of follow-up work.

There are, however, two other areas of sales effects of advertising that have received some attention in the literature: the effect of advertising on competition and advertising's effect on sales call effectiveness. Each of these is examined below.

Effect of advertising on competition. The effect of advertising on competition has long been a subject of considerable interest to economists concerned with industrial organization and economic performance. The debate has centered on whether or not heavy advertising helps raise entry barriers and thereby leads to diminished levels of competition and the earning of monopoly profits. Schmalensee has reviewed a number of "direct tests" of the proposition that advertising adversely affects competition, but interpretation of the available evidence on this question remains controversial for a variety of reasons discussed by him and others.[10] One of these studies, however, deserves mention here because it treated producer and consumer goods separately.

Miller reports a positive correlation between advertising intensity and industry profit rates. He examined the relation of profit rates to advertising intensity (advertising-sales ratios) plus two other variables: concentration (share of industry output produced by the largest firms) and diversity (the extent to which firms specialize in one industry or are diversified into other industries).[11] Multiple linear regressions of profit rates on these three variables

[9] Robert S. Weinberg, *An Analytical Approach to Advertising Expenditure Strategy* (New York: Association of National Advertisers, 1960).

[10] Richard Schmalensee, *The Economics of Advertising* (Amsterdam, Netherlands: North-Holland, 1972), pp. 219–28 and Chap. 7; see also, Julian L. Simon, *Issues in the Economics of Advertising* (Urbana, Ill.: University of Illinois Press, 1970), chap. 9.

[11] Richard A. Miller, "Market Structure and Industrial Performance: Relation of Profit Rates to Concentration, Advertising Intensity, and Diversity," *Journal of Industrial Economics*, vol. 28 (April 1969), pp. 104–18.

were reported for a sample consisting of 71 "Internal Revenue Service minor industries" (roughly the three-digit standard industrial classification level of aggregation) that were manufacturers of producer goods. The regression coefficient for the advertising intensity variable was positive and statistically significant, which implies that those producer goods industries that spent more on advertising tended to be those that realized higher rates of profitability. An unresolved issue here is whether profits determined advertising rather than vice versa.

Effect on sales call effectiveness. Morrill reports results that seem to indicate that advertising increases sales call effectiveness. He has carried out a large body of relevant industrial advertising research sponsored by a dozen major industrial sellers.[12] Some reports have appeared that summarize his results from studies involving 129 brands of 23 products drawn from five industries (utilities, commodities, electrical/electronic, metalworking, and chemical).[13] Over 40,000 telephone interviews at 17,000 buying locations were conducted during the period 1964 to 1969. In each case, an attempt was made to locate one or more "brand-deciders" and to assess purchase behavior, attitudes toward various brands, and magazine reading habits from which advertising exposure could be inferred. Analysis of these data revealed a strong positive association between amount of advertising exposure and various measures of attitudinal and sales response. Figure 2 illustrates some of these relationships using average data for the five industrial classifications.

Morrill also found that dollar sales per salesman's call were much higher for calls made on customers who had been exposed to advertising, as compared to those who had not. Based on estimates of the average costs of an industrial salesman's call ($50.00) and an advertising exposure ($0.16), a subsidiary analysis showed that for the average brand studied, an index of personal selling expense as a percentage of sales declined from a level of 100 with no advertising exposures to a value of 74 for 30 exposures.[14]

Taken at face value, Morrill's results make a strong case for industrial advertising, indicating that advertising pays off by making personal selling efforts more productive. However, certain methodological questions surrounding Morrill's studies deserve mention. Morrill's inferences about the effectiveness of advertising are derived from *ex post facto* comparisons of exposed and unexposed groups. It is well known that this "preexperimental" design is prone to several threats to internal and external validity.[15] Morrill refers to a computer-based method for "matching" the exposed and unexposed

---

[12] John E. Morrill, "Industrial Advertising Pays Off," *Harvard Business Review,* vol. 48 (March–April 1970), pp. 4–14.

[13] McGraw-Hill Book Co., "How Advertising Works in Today's Marketplace" (New York, January 1971); and McGraw-Hill Book Co., "Advertising's Challenge to Management: A Second Report on the Morrill Study" (New York, September 1971).

[14] McGraw-Hill, "Advertising's Challenge," same reference as footnote 13, p. 6.

[15] Donald T. Campbell and Julian C. Stanley, *Experimental and Quasi-Experimental Designs for Research* (Chicago: Rand-McNally, 1963), pp. 12–14.

Figure 2
Levels of response associated with varying amounts of exposure to advertising and salesmen's calls.

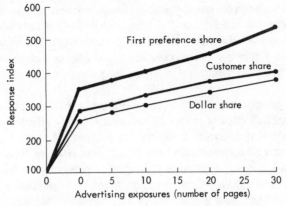

Salesmen's calls: NO   YES ─────────────────────────►

Source: Plotted from data presented in "Advertising's Challenge to Management: A Second Report on the Morrill Study" (New York: McGraw-Hill Book Co., September 1971), p. 8.

groups.[16] Since Morrill's conclusions about advertising's impact depend on the equivalence of such groups (exclusive of advertising exposure), the adequacy of this matching procedure is critical and it is unfortunate that details of the method have not been published. Further, the practice of obtaining response data and self-reports of exposure in the same interview can lead to spuriously high associations between these two types of measures.[17]

Nonetheless, the sheer bulk and consistency of the evidence from Morrill's studies is impressive, and by no means can it be overlooked. The most important finding is that advertising used in conjunction with personal selling can reduce total selling costs. Morrill also refers to evidence of threshold effects in response to advertising. He suggests that less than a certain (small) level of exposure (a frequency of about five advertising pages per year) seems to have no effect.[18]

Attitudinal and nonsales measures of response

Research that focuses on attitudinal and other nonsales measures of response to industrial advertising is, as noted earlier, by far the most common type undertaken. Proprietary studies of this kind are done routinely, and

---

[16] Same reference as footnote 12, p. 6.
[17] Same reference as footnote 15, p. 67.
[18] Same reference as footnote 12, p. 14.

occasionally partial accounts of them are made public.[19] Although these studies are seldom reported in sufficient detail to permit analysis and to provide a basis for generalization, there are some notable exceptions.

Morrill's comprehensive studies provide support for the widely held view that a principal function of industrial advertising is to make buyers more receptive to the advertiser's salesmen by creating a favorable impression of the firm as a supplier.[20] This concept constitutes one of the major rationales for the image-building campaigns frequently undertaken by industrial marketers.[21]

Levitt conducted a controlled laboratory experiment that demonstrated the positive influence of company reputation on the effectiveness of industrial salesmen.[22] Experienced business personnel (113 practicing purchasing agents and 130 engineers and scientists) were used as subjects. Participants were exposed to a ten-minute filmed sales presentation for a fictitious, but plausible, new product. Company reputation was manipulated by varying the name of the firm that the salesman was identified as representing. Immediately after viewing the film, and again five weeks later, subjects responded to a questionnaire that asked if they would recommend that the product be given further consideration by others in their organization and whether they themselves would favor adoption. As anticipated, company reputation was found to influence the favorableness of response on these measures. However, some unexpected differences were detected between the reactions of the purchasing agents and the reactions of the technical personnel. The results suggested that a seller's reputation made a difference in a salesman getting a favorable first hearing for a new product with *both* purchasing and technical personnel. But when it came to making an actual purchasing decision, the advantage of reputation manifested itself with the technical personnel but not with the purchasing agents.

There has been some research on industrial buyers' use of, or preferences for, different information sources in connection with studies of the adoption of new products.[23] The results suggest a pattern of diminishing reliance on impersonal sources such as media advertising and increasing influence of sales-

[19] See, for example, James W. Mason, "The Communication Effect of an Industrial Advertising Campaign," *Journal of Advertising Research,* vol. 9 (March 1969), pp. 35–37; and Harry D. Wolfe, James K. Brown, and G. Clark Thompson, *Measuring Advertising Results* (New York: National Industrial Conference Board, 1962).

[20] Wolfe et al., same reference as footnote 19, p. 7.

[21] See, for example, Wolfe et al., same reference as footnote 19, pp. 40–101.

[22] Theodore Levitt, *Industrial Purchasing Behavior: A Study of Communications Effects* (Boston: Division of Research, Graduate School of Business Administration, Harvard University, 1965).

[23] See, for example, Frederick E. Webster, Jr., "Informal Communication in Industrial Markets," *Journal of Marketing Research,* vol. 7 (May 1970), pp. 186–89; John A. Martilla, "Word-of-Mouth Communication in the Industrial Adoption Process," *Journal of Marketing Research,* vol. 8 (May 1971), pp. 173–78; and Urban B. Ozanne and Gilbert A. Churchill, Jr., "Five Dimensions of the Industrial Adoption Process," *Journal of Marketing Research,* vol. 8 (August 1971), pp. 322–28.

men and other personal sources as buyers move from the initial awareness stage through the evaluation and decision stages of the adoption process. In this regard, Turnbull, in a study of marketing communication policies of ferrous components producers in the United Kingdom, reports "a failure of the companies to understand that buyers may have different communication needs and channel preferences at different stages in the buying process, and in different industries."[24]

Advertising cost studies

The preceding discussion focused on how industrial buyers and markets respond to advertising. This section examines research related to the other key element that enters into advertising expenditure discussions: cost considerations.

The issue of whether or not there are economies of scale in advertising is highly relevant not only to determining advertising expenditure levels, but also to allocating these funds among media and markets and over time. The occurrence of economies of scale in advertising implies that over some range of advertising, an additional unit of advertising input produces a greater marginal return than the previous equal increment yielded.

Schmalensee distinguishes between two sources of varying returns to scale in advertising.[25] The first he terms "technical economies," to refer to differences in the effectiveness of successive exposures. The data from Morrill's studies, plotted in Figure 2, would seem to indicate essentially constant returns to scale and hence reflect the absence of any technical economies. The second variety are "pecuniary economies," which may arise if the cost of advertising exposures changes with the total number of exposures used, such as might occur as a consequence of the media offering quantity discounts.

Economies of scale in advertising are treated to some extent in the economics literature. Increasing returns to scale constitute one mechanism whereby advertising might help raise barriers to entry. The available empirical studies tend to be based on cross-sectional samples consisting either entirely of consumer goods industries or of a combination of consumer and producer goods fields. Only occasionally has the latter distinction been recognized in the analyses reported. Most of these studies are consistent in failing to support the notion of economies of scale in advertising.[26] However, some contrary findings have turned up in cross-sectional studies of marketing costs of individual firms.

---

[24] P. W. Turnbull, "The Allocation of Resources to Marketing Communications in Industrial Markets," *Industrial Marketing Management*, vol. 3 (October 1974), pp. 297–310.

[25] Schmalensee, same reference as footnote 10, pp. 231–32.

[26] George J. Stigler, "The Economies of Scale," *Journal of Law and Economics*, vol. 1 (October 1958), p. 66; and Julian L. Simon and George H. Crain, "The Advertising Ratio and Economies of Scale," *Journal of Advertising Research*, vol. 6 (September 1966), pp. 37–43. For a review, see Schmalensee, same reference as footnote 10, pp. 228–37; and Simon, same reference as footnote 10, chap. 1.

Turnbull obtained information on marketing communications expenditures and sales for a set of firms producing ferrous components whose combined output accounted for 51 percent of the industry total in the United Kingdom.[27] He found a rank order correlation of $-.512$ between firm size (sales) and the ratio of marketing communications expenditures to sales. Although based on only eleven observations, the coefficient approaches significance at the .05 level.

Bailey found evidence of economies of scale in a 1969 study of manufacturers' marketing costs that was conducted by the Conference Board. This study involved data obtained for 828 products, a large proportion of which were industrial goods.[28] Although detailed results were not presented, Bailey states that "the large-volume marketing unit dealing either in consumer or industrial goods generally gives up less of its sales dollar to the cause of marketing than does a small-volume competitor." He goes on to observe that "there is a certain point at which differences in sales volume become critical" and indicates that for industrial products this point is "just below $30 million."[29]

It was noted earlier that Morrill demonstrated a strong interaction effect between personal selling and advertising. Evidence of this phenomenon was also found in a study of industrial firms' marketing costs carried out by McGraw-Hill and reported by Kolliner.[30]

Kolliner reports that the larger the role of advertising in the marketing budget, the lower that budget seems to be as a percentage of sales. In 1961, marketing cost data were obtained via a mail questionnaire from 893 industrial advertisers. The sample contained firms of various sizes from three broad industrial product categories (machinery, materials, and equipment and supplies). Consistent with the view that advertising can increase the efficiency of personal selling, it was found that as the proportion of total sales expense spent on advertising and promotion increased, total sales expense as a percentage of sales tended to decline.

Interpreting this relationship is somewhat hazardous, inasmuch as it was formed by grouping and averaging the original observations on two variables which were ratios whose numerators and denominators contain common elements. It is unfortunate that more disaggregated analyses were not undertaken. Yet some additional results were reported which tend to confirm the basic notion that advertising contributes to marketing efficiency. The relationship between firm size (annual sales volume) and total sales expense as a

---

[27] Same reference as footnote 24.

[28] Earl L. Bailey, "Manufacturers' Marketing Costs," *Conference Board Record,* vol. 8 (October 1971), pp. 58–64.

[29] Same reference as footnote 28, p. 60.

[30] Sim A. Kolliner Jr., "New Evidence of Ad Values," *Industrial Marketing,* Vol. 48 (August 1963), pp. 81–84. See also, McGraw-Hill Laboratory of Advertising Performance, "Advertising and the Cost of Selling" (New York: McGraw-Hill Book Co., July 1964).

percentage of sales was examined separately for firms that had expended "high" (more than 20 percent) and "low" (less than 20 percent) proportions of total sales expense on advertising and promotion. Figure 3 shows these relationships, which are also based on averages of grouped data.

Figure 3
Relative selling costs and company size for high and low advertising–sales promotion allotments

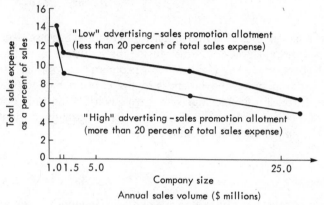

Source: Plotted from data presented in Sim A. Kolliner, "New Evidence of Ad Values," *Industrial Marketing*, vol. 48 (August 1963), p. 82.

For all four size categories, total sales expense (as a percentage of sales) was less with "high" advertising and promotion than with "low." Note that the results indicate economies of scale. The same pattern of results was observed in data from a second, smaller study of 227 firms conducted by McGraw-Hill in 1963.[31] Thus, the results from these cost studies appear to be consistent with the research on advertising response reviewed above in indicating that industrial advertising can serve to enhance the effectiveness of personal selling efforts.

BUDGETING PRACTICES

In light of the dearth of available empirical knowledge about market response to industrial advertising, management in this field must ordinarily depend on some blend of judgment, experience with analogous situations, and simple rules-of-thumb guidance in setting budgets. Heuristics like "X percent of expected sales" and the "objective and task" method are the principal approaches to budgeting that industrial advertisers report using.

Among 557 subscribers to *Industrial Marketing* who responded to a 1968

---

[31] McGraw-Hill, same reference as footnote 30.

mail questionnaire, the following distribution of budgeting practices[32] was found:

Method	Percentage using
Percent of sales	24.8%
Task	35.6
Arbitrary	27.7
Other	11.9
	100.0%

Heavy reliance on rules of thumb and the task method has also been reported in other budgeting studies on firms outside the industrial marketing sector.[33] In recent years, however, measurement programs and models have made some inroads on budgeting practices in the consumer goods field;[34] it is, therefore, surprising to find that Weinberg's work is the only documented account of a comparable analytical method for budgeting industrial advertising that has appeared in the literature.[35]

Heuristics

Percent-of-sales decision rules are a pervasive influence in setting advertising budgets. Schmalensee has analyzed the conditions under which it might be optimal for a monopolist or an oligopolist to maintain a constant advertising-to-sales ratio.[36] However, there have been no empirical investigations to demonstrate that the behavior of industrial advertisers' expenditures indeed are sensitive to key limiting requirements (e.g., the constancy of certain demand elasticities) of such a policy.

The weaknesses of percent-of-sales decision rules are well known,[37] but the most fundamental objection is that they implicitly make advertising a consequence rather than a determinant of sales and profits and can easily give rise to dysfunctional policies. For example, budgeting advertising as a percentage of expected sales would ordinarily lead to reduced expenditures in an economic downturn. Yet the Buchen organization, in a correlational study, indicated that industrial advertisers who maintained their expenditures

---

[32] Murray Harding, "Project Future: More Advertisers Mad than Glad about Budget Policy," *Industrial Marketing*, vol. 53 (August 1968), p. 58.

[33] See, for example, David L. Hurwood, "How Companies Set Advertising Budgets," *Conference Board Record*, vol. 5 (March 1968), pp. 34–41; Albert W. Frey, *How Many Dollars for Advertising* (New York: Ronald Press, 1955); and Walter Taplin, "Advertising Appropriation Policy," *Economica*, vol. 26 (August 1959), pp. 227–39.

[34] Seymour Banks, "Trends Affecting the Implementation of Advertising and Promotion," *Journal of Marketing*, vol. 37 (January 1973), p. 24.

[35] Same reference as footnote 8.

[36] Same reference as footnote 10, chap. 2.

[37] See, for example, Philip Kotler, *Marketing Management*, 2nd ed. (Englewood Cliffs, N.J.: Prentice-Hall, 1972), pp. 669–70.

during recession periods realized better sales performance than those who did not.[38] Nonetheless, some mechanism to control advertising expenditures is required, and in the absence of concrete and current measurements of advertising results, top management frequently establishes some percentage of sales or profit as a budgeting guideline.[39]

DeWolf used the results from the aforementioned McGraw-Hill study of industrial firms' marketing costs to establish a "yardstick that can apply to advertising budgets, present or proposed, to see if they are of the proper magnitude." DeWolf recommended that if a company wanted to take full advantage of the potential of advertising, it should spend more than 20 percent of its marketing budget on advertising. As he put it, "the magic figure seems to be 20 percent—until you get above 20 percent, you are in the lower half of all companies in selling efficiently—and you can safely go up to at least 33 percent."[40]

Much could be learned from a study of the determinants of industrial advertising expenditures. The question of why "advertising intensity" (measured by the ratio of advertising to sales) varies across product categories has attracted some attention from economists.[41] However, this work appears to have been focused exclusively on consumer goods industries with no comparable analyses of data for industrial goods.

Other heuristics, such as "matching" competitive expenditures, also frequently enter into budgeting decisions. All of these methods share some common characteristics in that they serve as a management control device but are difficult to justify. Reliance on simple rules of thumb by industrial marketers appears to have declined over time. A 1939 survey of industrial advertising budgeting practices reported by Borden showed greater use of such methods than was indicated by the 1968 *Industrial Marketing* study mentioned above.[42]

Task method

The task method focuses on communication rather than on sales effects of advertising. A budget is developed by summing estimates of the costs of

---

[38] Buchen Advertising, Inc., *Advertising in Recession Periods: 1949, 1954, 1958, 1961—A New Yardstick Revisited* (Chicago, 1970).

[39] See, for example, George A. Perce, "How Kendall Prepares Its Advertising Budget," in *The Advertising Budget*, Richard J. Kelly, ed. (New York: Association of National Advertisers, 1968), pp. 52–54.

[40] John W. DeWolf, "A New Tool for Setting and Selling Advertising Budgets," paper presented at the Eastern Regional Meeting of the American Association of Advertising Agencies, November 7, 1963, p. 21.

[41] Lester G. Telser, "Some Aspects of the Economies of Advertising," *Journal of Business,* vol. 41 (April 1968), pp. 166–73; and, for a review, see Schmalensee, same reference as footnote 10, pp. 18–20.

[42] Neil H. Borden, *The Economic Effects of Advertising* (Chicago: Richard D. Irwin, 1942), p. 722.

activities and programs required to accomplish the particular functions assigned to advertising. The essential steps involved in applying the method are:

1. Establish specific marketing objectives for the product in terms of factors such as sales volume, market share, and profit contribution, as well as target market segments.
2. Assess the communication functions that must be performed to realize the overall marketing objectives and determine the role of advertising and other elements of the communication mix in performing these functions.
3. Define specific goals for advertising in terms of the levels of measurable communication response required to achieve marketing objectives.
4. Estimate the budget needed to accomplish advertising goals.

Underlying the task method is the notion that the influence of advertising on buyers appears through some type of hierarchy of effects ranging from creating product or company awareness and knowledge through developing favorable supplier or product attitudes and preferences. Implementation of these ideas grew markedly in the early 1960s following the appearance of Colley's oft-cited volume on "DAGMAR."[43] Several examples of applications of this version of the task method and the accompanying use of intermediate measures of communication effectiveness in industrial advertising have been discussed in the literature.[44] *Industrial Marketing*'s 1968 survey found that users of the task method were more likely to be satisfied with their budgeting practices than respondents who relied on other approaches.[45]

The practical difficulty of isolating advertising's impact on sales, plus recognition that advertising's function is to communicate, have motivated adoption of the task method and accompanying measures of intermediate response. The latter provide a basis for some modicum of management control over advertising operations. The great stumbling block in using this approach as a planning tool, however, is that it requires knowledge about how levels of expenditures and various communication response measures are related, and how the latter are linked to the purchase behavior that is relevant to the attainment of marketing goals.[46] The existence and nature of such relation-

---

[43] Russell H. Colley, *Defining Advertising Goals for Measured Advertising Results* (New York: Association of National Advertisers, 1961).

[44] William P. Raines, "Setting Advertising Goals for Industrial Products," in *The Advertising Budget,* Richard J. Kelly, ed. (New York: Association of National Advertisers, 1968), pp. 47–51; Patrick J. Robinson and David J. Luck, *Promotional Decision Making* (New York: McGraw-Hill Book Co., 1964), pp. 168–77; Saul S. Sands, *Setting Advertising Objectives* (New York: National Industrial Conference Board, 1966); and Wolfe et al., same reference as footnote 19.

[45] Same reference as footnote 32, p. 68.

[46] See, for example, the papers on "Advertising Research—DAGMAR Revisited," in *New Directions in Marketing,* Frederick E. Webster, Jr., ed. (Chicago: American Marketing Association, June 1965), pp. 333–58.

ships are highly controversial matters.[47] Progress is being made in understanding and using these relationships for purposes of planning and controlling marketing communications, but these developments appear to have occurred largely in the consumer field.[48]

CONCLUSIONS

A review of the existing literature offers some insight into the existence of economies of scale, threshold effects, and interaction effects in the field of industrial advertising. It also points up the need for additional research in this area.

Evidence exists that supports the notion of economies of scale in industrial advertising, that is, that in some region of advertising expenditure, additional increments of advertising yield increasing returns. However, evidence has also been found that is not supportive of this hypothesis. Definitive information about the existence and location of this region would be of great help to budgeters in determining the level of advertising expenditures.

The existence of threshold effects, a minimum level of exposure needed for advertising to have a measurable effect, is supported by the literature. A manager should not expect to see advertising effects until the level of expenditure is sufficiently high. But *where* that threshold is found has not been established.

Finally, despite methodological problems in many of the studies, the volume of evidence suggests that industrial advertising and personal selling perform complementary and synergistic roles. Most managers might expect that a split of the industrial marketing budget between advertising and personal selling categories would be more efficient than a total allocation to a single category. But there is no indication about either what the overall budget *should* be or what split between advertising and personal selling expenditures would be most efficient.

Thus, the study of the effects of industrial advertising has not yet provided guidance to industrial advertisers faced with specific expenditure decisions, and current budgeting practice reflects the lack of knowledge about response. Simple heuristics and the task method are the most common budgeting approaches used. Both methods provide a control mechanism for spending, but they may lead to inappropriate policies.

This review points to the need for a better understanding of how industrial advertising can be effective. A major field study of advertising response would

---

[47] Kristian S. Palda, "The Hypothesis of a Hierarchy of Effects: A Partial Evaluation," *Journal of Marketing Research,* vol. 3 (February 1966), pp. 13–25; and Michael L. Ray, "Marketing Communications and the Hierarchy of Effects," in *New Models for Communications Research,* Peter Clarke, ed. (Bevery Hills, Calif.: Sage, 1974), pp. 147–76.

[48] Michael L. Ray, "A Decision Sequence Analysis of Developments in Marketing Communications," *Journal of Marketing,* vol. 37 (January 1973), pp. 29–38.

be desirable, but the small size of industrial advertising budgets makes an upsurge of activity in this area appear unlikely. Opportunities do exist, however, for econometric work concerned with developing response functions for individual firms. Another fruitful research direction is to identify and exploit managers' existing knowledge about advertising effectiveness, an approach Bowman and others have shown to be empirically valid in other decision areas.[49] One such study is underway[50] and may help provide a basis for new forms of industrial advertising norms and guidelines.

QUESTIONS

1. Define, in your own words, the three phenomena about industrial advertising referred to early in the article. Why are these considerations important? Are these three considerations equally relevant for consumer goods advertising?

2. Compare and contrast the heuristic approach and the task method for establishing industrial advertising budgets. Which approach do you think is better? (Explain what you mean by "better" as part of your answer.)

3. The authors refer only in passing to research done in the consumer goods field as a source of insights as to what to expect in evaluating industrial advertising. Do you think the results of studies of consumer goods advertising are applicable to industrial advertising? Why or why not? What are the differences between the markets and marketing approaches for consumer goods and industrial products which would make such a transfer difficult?

[49] E. H. Bowman, "Consistency and Optimality in Managerial Decision Making," *Management Science,* vol. 9 (January 1963), pp. 310–21; and Howard Kunreuther, "Extensions of Bowman's Theory of Managerial Decision Making," *Management Science,* vol. 15 (April 1969), pp. B-415–39.

[50] For details of the study, see Gary L. Lilien, "How Many Dollars for Industrial Advertising? Project ADVISOR," Working Paper 735-74, Sloan School of Management, M.I.T., September 1974; and John D. C. Little and Gary L. Lilien, "How Much for Industrial Advertising?" talk before the Advertising Research Foundation Conference, New York, November 18, 1974.

25
Does advertising lower consumer prices?

Robert L. Steiner

*Critics of advertising maintain that advertising raises con-
sumer prices by increasing manufacturers' selling prices
in several ways. Not only must the cost of the promotion be
added to the product's cost, but by limiting entry, advertising leads to concentration and oligopolistic pricing. This
article contends that even if these assertions are valid, advertising lowers consumer prices. It presents a theory of the
relationship between advertising and prices, illustrated by
data from the marketing experience of the toy industry.*

A recent staff report to the Federal Communications Commission entitled
"Advertising and the Public Interest" sums up the conventional notion of the
relationship between advertising and prices with admirable brevity:
". . . the consumer clearly pays for advertising (the cost of which is reflected
in the price he pays)."[1]

While, of course, advertising is a cost, it is generally recognized that the
purpose of advertising is to increase consumption of the advertised product.
When more units are produced, various economies of scale ordinarily ensue
which in some instances exceed the cost of advertising. Whether this is true
for the economy as a whole remains unclear.

A second way in which advertising may increase prices is by reducing
competition among producers. Where advertising succeeds in building a
powerful consumer franchise for a handful of brands in a product category,
entry by other manufacturers can become an extremely difficult proposition.
The result here is a classical case of oligopoly resulting in higher prices than
would obtain with more producers and more perfect competition.

An opposite view is that advertising is a means of entry and of challenge, a
stimulation to new product innovation which, therefore, advances the cause
of competition and reduces prices. Here again one does not know where the
truth lies.

For the purposes of this paper, it is conceded that advertising might result

Source: Reprinted from the *Journal of Marketing,* published by the American Marketing
Association, vol. 37 (October 1973), pp. 19–26. At the time of writing Robert Steiner was retired
from his position as president of the Kenner Products toy company.

[1] John A. Howard and James Hulbert, *Advertising and the Public Interest* (Chicago: Crain
Communications, Inc., February 1973), p. 5.

in higher manufacturers' selling prices. Even so, it is contended that advertising reduces consumer prices. How can that be?

The answer lies in the effects of advertising on the markup between factory and consumer—the distribution margin—which, as students of marketing recognize, usually comprises from 40 to 50 percent of a product's total cost.[2]

The aim of this article is to demonstrate that advertising lowers prices to the ultimate consumer, because the magnitude of its impact on distribution margins is sufficient to overcome any possible tendency of advertising to raise manufacturers' selling prices. The following major arguments will be developed in support of this theory: *first,* advertising results in smaller distribution margins on advertised brands due to (1) the more rapid turnover of advertised products and (2) increased product price comparison through improved product identification; and, *second,* competition from advertised brands brings pressure to reduce prices on unadvertised merchandise of the same type.

PRODUCTIVITY THROUGH MARKETING

A central contention of this paper is that the combination of the marketing forces of mass merchandising and strong advertising is responsible for a major increase in marketing productivity which has brought lower prices to the American consumer.

Of course, there has always been some retail price cutting and some consumer advertising. However, with the emergence of the supermarket, a pervasive marketing revolution occurred in the food and package goods industries during the two decades before World War II. Newspaper, magazine, and radio advertising created consumer demand for specific products. Supermarkets discovered that a handful of such advertised brands were accounting for perhaps 90 percent of their volume in category after category. These recognized brands turned over so rapidly that they could be sold at far below traditional retail markups, and consumers could be lured from traditional stores by a combination of low everyday prices and special sales advertised in the newspaper.

Begining in the mid–1950s, a similar marketing revolution in the general merchandise field resulted from the dynamic growth of discount stores in conjunction with television and other forms of advertising. Like supermarkets, discounters based their profit concept on a return per square foot of store space rather than on percentage markup alone. An item which turned over five times at a markup of 25 percent won the battle for shelf space over one that turned over twice at a 40 percent markup.

Strong advertising created a legion of presold consumers who, in a self-service situation, eagerly plunked the advertised brands into their shopping carts. Supermarkets, discounters, and other mass merchants have become

[2] For various computations of the distribution margin, see Reavis Cox, *Distribution in a High-Level Economy* (Englewood Cliffs, N.J.: Prentice-Hall, 1965), chap. 8.

retail factories geared to purchase, process, and sell demanded merchandise to the public in the most efficient manner at closer markups than offered by traditional retailers, whom they have continually displaced.

ESTABLISHING PRODUCT IDENTITY

This ability of consumer advertising to make products turn over faster on the retail counter is, however, not the only property it has which depresses retail markups. A separate, but seldom understood, quality is identifiableness. Large media budgets build consumer recognition of the advertised item, enabling the public readily to identify and compare its price wherever it is sold. Realizing that, the retailer is reluctant to mark up identifiable products too high for fear that the consumer may readily catch him in the act and conclude that all items in the store are overpriced.

Identifiableness thus creates a de facto price ceiling on widely recognized brands. In addition, the very fact that the product is recognizable and its approximate prevailing price on the market is widely known creates an incentive for the retailer to splash it in the newspaper at a still lower price to engender the impression that his store offers a cornucopia of bargains.

In the case of commodity-type items, consumer comparison is relatively simple—especially when aided by government grading, as in eggs, meats, and so on. Advances in the standard of living, however, require differentiated and complex products, and in this area it is the product recognition value flowing from advertising which enables the consumer readily to make the price comparison in different stores.

Given the high rate of failure among new products, it is true that many heavily advertised consumer goods do not sell especially well. Nevertheless, if our observations are correct, these unsuccessful but strongly promoted brands will move from factory to consumer at very modest markups. Finally, items which are both strongly identifiable and turn over rapidly will have the lowest distribution margins of all, while those which are both "blind" and slow sellers will be marked up the most.

REDUCTION OF MARKUPS AND PRICES FOR NONADVERTISED BRANDS

Some retailers, while admitting that advertising drives down their margins on advertised brands, argue there is no net public benefit since they are then forced to make equivalent price increases on other items to protect their margin structure and stay in business.[3] This has not been historically true and is not presently the case, except where advertised brands must be sold at margins only slightly above (or actually below) variable costs. Even here the

---

[3] James Cooke, Chairman of the Board, Penn Fruit Co., "The President's Report," unpublished address to the Supermarket Institute, May 7, 1973.

retailer is unable to mark up unadvertised items as much as he did before advertising commenced.

In the typical store, all items within a product group are arrayed together for virtually simultaneous inspection by the shopper, setting up a direct and visible competition amongst them for the consumer dollar. Now, suppose the markup on selling price is 50 percent in a nonadvertised category of merchandise into which advertising is then successfully introduced. This causes the markup on the promoted brands to decline to, say, 25 percent. Suddenly the unadvertised items must face two new problems, for their advertised competitors are not only better known to the public but also appear to be better values. The retailer now finds that he must shave his markup on the unadvertised brands to perhaps 40 or 45 percent to erase enough of the competitive value discrepancy to enable the nonadvertised items to turn over with sufficient velocity to earn their counter space.

In the typical product category life cycle, after advertising has been introduced and has expanded the volume in the category, a second generation of nonadvertised competitors—including private labels—now appears. These nonadvertised products gain shelf space because their markups are better than the sharply discounted advertised brands, yet they must be retailed below the promoted brands to compete successfully. The resulting price squeeze virtually mandates that the margins of these new nonadvertised products be below the historic pre-advertising level. Indeed, the markup requirement is often achievable only through a debasement of product quality.

The consumer enjoys the additional purchasing options and the reduced retails. But except perhaps for community-type products, these second generation competitors came into existence as a response to advertising, flourish where advertising remains strong, and tend to disappear if the advertising stops. Therefore, advertising deserves credit for the public benefit!

Private label competition from giant retailers is especially beneficial to the consumer in that it sets up a strong countervailing force against the large manufacturing advertiser, which prevents the latter from overpricing.

THE THEORY OF ADVERTISING AND PRICES SUMMARIZED

This theory of the relationship between advertising and prices can be briefly summarized as follows:

1. There is not enough evidence available to judge whether for the economy as a whole advertising results in a net increase or decrease in manufacturers' selling prices. However, this theory maintains that advertising stimulates product innovation by offering the rewards of very high volume per item.
2. If advertising is found to cause manufacturers' selling prices to increase, the magnitude of the price rise will be more than offset by the power of

advertising to reduce distribution margins. Accordingly, on balance, advertising tends to reduce final consumer prices.

3. Advertising cuts distribution margins on advertised brands for two reasons: *first,* advertising causes goods to turn over rapidly so they can be sold profitably with smaller markups; and, *second,* advertising creates product identity—which, in differentiated products, permits the public to compare prices between stores, thus setting a limit on the retailer's freedom to mark up. Products which are both heavily advertised and are fast sellers will be pulled through the distribution channels with the lowest markups of all.

4. Within an advertised category, various competitive responses force down markups and retail prices on the nonadvertised products, causing them to be better consumer values than in nonadvertised categories.

The above construct presents what is believed to occur in the American economy, especially in areas of differentiated products. Empirical validation is obviously required. The following discussion examines the toy business, where the findings fit the theory—the theory itself being partially built on the insights developed in the course of this research.

HOW THE MARKETING REVOLUTION CHANGED THE TOY BUSINESS

Until the late 1950s, the American toy industry was essentially an unadvertised business. Toy makers made only miniscule efforts to create consumer demand for their playthings. Such advertising and promotional campaigns as there were consisted of a smattering of direct mail, radio advertising, inserts in children's magazines, and department store newspaper ads and Christmas demonstrations.

Toy manufacturers quoted their customers a percentage discount from an even dollar, retail list price. The list price represented the amount the consumer was supposed to pay and almost invariably did pay. The steepest percentage trade discount, which averaged less 50 percent and 5 percent from list price, was offered to wholesalers, who accounted for about two-thirds of toy manufacturers' shipments.[4] Since he shipped the balance to retailers at discounts averaging less 48 percent, the toy maker's total output was sold at about a 51 percent discount from list.

Giving account to estimated markdowns, the occasional off-price sale, and the permissible practice of retailing toys for a few pennies below list price, it can be said with confidence in the period 1947–58 that consumers paid prices which averaged about 4 percent below retail list. That is, they paid 96 cents for the $1 list toy the manufacturer sold for 49 cents.

Hence, the distribution margin (or markup) in the industry as a percentage

---

[4] "Financial and Operating Ratio Report," as compiled from reports submitted to Ernst & Ernst by members of Toy Manufacturers of U.S.A., 1958.

of average retail selling price was 49 percent. The consumer was paying about twice the manufacturer's selling price!

The toy marketing revolution

The first large-scale use of television advertising in the toy industry occurred in 1955 when the Mattel Company of California purchased network time on the Mickey Mouse Club to advertise a toy burp gun that was selling at an indifferent rate but was in large distribution. Results were astonishing! The sudden surge of consumer demand from the television commercials cleared retail shelves well before Christmas.

By the late 1950s, with the growth in the number of television homes and programs directed to children, numerous toy makers had climbed aboard the television bandwagon. Toy television spending boomed until 1970. Since then it has leveled off in the range of $75 million to $80 million annually,[5] where it represents about 3½ percent of toy makers' shipments.[6]

At about the same time that manufacturers were discovering television, widespread discounting of general merchandise began. Discount store sales rose from $2 billion in 1960 to a phenomenal $26.6 billion in 1971.[7] Discounters discovered that toys, especially the heavily televised ones, turned over so rapidly that they could be sold profitably far below the traditional toy retail markup. A discounter might put an everyday price of $3.49 on a $5 list toy. Beyond that, mass merchants found, especially at Christmas time, that a newspaper ad offering the toy at $2.99 drew huge crowds of toy shoppers into their stores.

By 1971, discount stores were the largest single retail outlet for toys and accounted for around 28 percent of retail toy sales. Their toy departments were averaging gross margins of around 26 percent on sales.[8]

To remain competitive, traditional retailers countered by cutting their prices and began to take the initiative on a few hot sellers on which they were determined to become the market price leaders. Merchants also discovered they could not maintain traditional markups on nonadvertised toys in the face of competition from televised items, now often being retailed at close to manufacturers' selling prices. Almost overnight the level of toy prices tumbled, with the television items being slashed the deepest!

This marketing revolution in the toy business was ignited by a combination of three elements: manufacturers' television advertising to children, retail

---

[5] Report from the Television Bureau of Advertising, Inc., based on "B.A.R. Network TV" and "B.A.R. National Spot TV," for the years 1970, 1971, and 1972, prepared annually by Broadcast Advertisers Reports, Inc., New York.

[6] U.S. Department of Commerce, Bureau of the Census, *Annual Survey of Manufacturers,* 1970 and 1971 (Washington, D.C.: U.S. Government Printing Office); and Toy Manufacturers of America, *Toy Industry Statistics* (annual report), 1970, 1971, and 1972.

[7] "The True Look of the Discount Industry, 1971: The Twelfth Annual Marketing Study of the Status of the Discount Industry," *The Discount Merchandiser,* 1972, p. TL–3.

[8] Same reference as footnote 7, p. 48-TL.

newspaper cut-price advertising to parents, and mass merchandising. Under the influence of these three stimuli, distribution margins narrowed; at the same time, research and development budgets rose both absolutely and as a percentage of toy manufacturers' sales[9] under the incentive of the greatly expanded volume per toy which television advertising had produced.

Toy sales boomed. In fact, as Figure 1 depicts, toy manufacturers' shipments per child since the advent of the marketing revolution have far outstripped the growth in consumer goods production per capita.

Figure 1
Percentage increase in constant dollars of toy manufacturers' shipments per child (aged 0–12) and final consumer goods production per capita (total population), 1947–1958 and 1958–1970

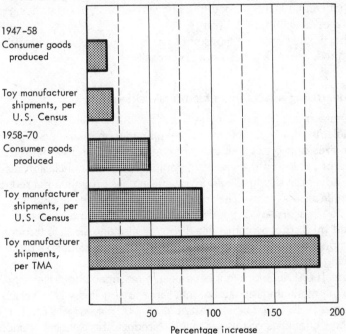

Sources: U.S. Department of Commerce, Bureau of the Census, *Census of Manufactures, Annual Survey of Manufactures,* and *Census of Population* (Washington, D.C.: U.S. Government Printing Office); U.S. Department of Labor, Bureau of Labor Statistics, *Wholesale Price Index of Toys and Sporting Goods* (Washington, D.C.: U.S. Government Printing Office); and Toy Manufacturers of America, *Toy Industry Statistics* (annual report).

HOW LARGE–SCALE ADVERTISING AFFECTS TOY PRICES

In addition to utilizing published data from the *United States Census,* Broadcast Advertisers Reports, the National Retail Merchants Association,

[9] Same reference as footnote 4, 1956 and 1971.

Discount Merchandiser, material printed in the toy trade press, and research studies done for individual manufacturers, the author has sought out and analyzed data from numerous wholesalers and retailers. Much of the latter information was furnished on a confidential basis, since it involves rates of sale and markups; such information cannot, therefore, be referenced.[10] The purpose of these investigations was to provide answers to the following questions in the toy business:

1. Has the great increase in advertising raised manufacturers' selling prices?
2. How has the aggregate distribution margin changed since the introduction of large-scale advertising?
3. What are the correlations between rate of sale, distribution margins, and weight of advertising?
4. What can be learned about the above relationships by studying product categories within the industry?
5. What would happen to consumer prices if toy television advertising were banned, as some groups now propose?

How advertising affects manufacturers' selling prices

Accurate quantification for the industry as a whole is difficult, perhaps impossible, to obtain. One is left to rely primarily on operating experience in the cost area and on overall industry concentration and earnings data as a measure of profit and the extent of competition. The conclusion reached is that the advent of strong television advertising has brought a net reduction in toy manufacturers' costs. The total marketing expenses (including advertising) of toy makers, as a percentage of their shipments, appears to have increased by 3 to 5 percent since 1956.[11] Offsetting savings through large-scale production may be estimated at 7 to 10 percent, creating a probable net cost saving on the order of 5 percent.

Where 100,000 units might have been a reasonable toy sales expectation prior to the marketing revolution, that same toy backed with a strong television budget easily might be forecast at 1,000,000 pieces in 1973. Increases in production quantities of this magnitude produce the classical economies in raw materials and labor per unit of output. Moreover, in the toy business expensive injection molds for the production of plastic parts are typically required. Major savings in piece price are achieved when volume projections are sufficiently great to justify building a high capacity tool.

In the toy business, advertising has not led to a degree of concentration that permits the manufacturer of advertised brands to enjoy the fruits of oligopolistic pricing. Although the number of toy makers has declined since

---

[10] For a more detailed description of data sources and methodology than the present space permits, see Robert L. Steiner, "How Television Advertising Affects Consumer Toy Prices," an address presented at "Children's Television: A Broadcaster's Work Shop," and reprinted in *Toy and Hobby World,* vol. 11 (July 2, 1973), pp. 1, 13–15.

[11] Same reference as footnote 4, 1956 and 1971.

the late 1950s, there are still over 700 of them, with the largest enjoying around 9 percent of the market and the top four about 30 percent.

Competition is so keen that the return on sales and investment is well below that of the average for American manufacturing industry.[12] The risks associated with large-scale television advertising have produced bankruptcies among some of the heaviest television spenders, including Transogram, Remco, and Topper. Mattel, the largest advertiser, lost around $30 million in both 1971 and 1972.

How advertising affects the distribution margin

Based on two separate research projects, the author has concluded that the distribution margin—that is, the difference between the average consumer price and the average manufacturer's selling price as a percentage of the former—has declined by one-third, from 49 percent in the mid-1950s to 33 percent in the early 1970s.

It is important to record that these decisive consumer price savings have occurred only in those nations where all three elements of the marketing revolution were strongly present—specifically in the United States and Canada. In both Australia and England, where there has long been television advertising of toys, distribution margins only now are beginning to tumble with the growth of discounting and newspaper price advertising.

Even more fascinating is the situation in France, where toy television commercials are not yet permitted but over 200 mass merchants carry and discount toys. Unfortunately, the discounting remains confined to the mass merchants themselves. Without the unique mass appeal of television to create demand and recognition for specific items, traditional retailers have been able to ignore the discount competition and maintain their old toy markup practices. Therefore, the impressive growth of mass merchandising has not materially reduced the historic 50 percent distribution margin in France.

The relationship between rate of sale and distribution margins

The theory holds that when consumer goods turn over rapidly, this process permits and encourages such faster sellers to be retailed at lower than average distribution margins. To test this proposition in the toy business, information was obtained on the rate of sale, manufacturers' selling prices, and actual in-store average consumer selling prices on a large list of toy items. Table 1 summarizes the results.

If there is a strong inverse relationship between rate of turnover and distribution margins, it should follow that the very best sellers, especially in large urban areas where discounting is severe, would exhibit even lower margins than the 25.3 percent indicated for the best selling 100 toys. Table 2, which is

---

[12] Same reference as footnote 4, 1956 and 1971.

Table 1
Distribution margins* by rate of sale category,
Christmas season, 1971

Best sellers (representing top 100 toys)	25.3%
Fine sellers (representing next 400 toys)..............	30.7%
Poorer sellers (representing all the rest)	42.1%

* As a percentage of average consumer selling price. Costs are based on manufacturer's lowest selling price.

Table 2
Distribution margins* of fastest selling toys in Chicago

15 fastest sellers, Christmas season, 1971	21.5%
10 fastest sellers, Christmas season, 1971	20.0%
10 fastest sellers, Christmas season, 1972	20.5%

* As a percentage of average consumer selling price. Costs are based on manufacturer's lowest selling price.

based on surveys done in 1971 and 1972 by the leading wholesaler of toys in Chicago, confirms this pattern.

The correlation between advertising and distribution margins

If the theory is correct and advertising can be credited with reducing toy distribution margins, then the faster sellers (which were marked up the least) should be heavily advertised items. That turns out to be the case, since 90 percent of the best sellers in Table 1 and 100 percent of the fastest selling toys in Chicago were televised.

Newspaper price advertising to parents is the other component of the advertising mix. On the basis of information contained in several surveys, including one conducted by the Advertising Checking Bureau,[13] it was discovered that weight of newspaper advertising appears to be even more closely correlated with rate of sale than is television advertising. The explanation is that while both stimulate toy sales, newspaper spending also tends to reflect retail turnover.

The timing of newspaper advertising campaigns is approximately conterminous with the holiday buying season, while television advertising commences back in August and September. This permits discounters, who account for most of the toy lineage, to identify the emerging best sellers from their own sales experience and to insert them into the papers at low prices to build store traffic.

The findings that advertising and rate of sale are closely correlated will hardly come as a surprise. However, it is also claimed that in addition to its

[13] "Newspaper Features Tracking Study. Christmas Season 1971," private manufacturer's report prepared by the Advertising Checking Bureau, 1972.

ability to reduce trade markups by increasing the rate of turnover, advertising has another effect—the creation of product recognition or identity—which also depresses distribution margins. If so, then televised toys as a group, regardless of their popularity (and many of them do not sell well off the counter), should enjoy lower distribution margins than their nonadvertised counterparts.

Two major retailers who had made this kind of comparative markup study and a third who furnished his cost and selling price data were finally located, which permitted the author to make the calculation. Although these firms represented different kinds of retailers—a department store, a variety-discount chain, and a chain of freestanding toy stores—the results were re-markably similar for each and indicated that the margin spread between televised and untelevised toys was close to 25 percentage points. This is a substantially greater margin differential than exists between the best and poorer sellers in Table 1.

In Canada, where toy marketing conditions are quite similar to those in the United States, Elliott Research conducted a survey in 70 representative stores in six cities involving 100 toys carefully selected to be a cross-section of the industry in regard to both price range and product category.[14] When the toys were divided into three groups according to weight of television advertising, the results shown in Table 3 emerged.

Table 3
Toy distribution margins* in Canada,
Christmas season, 1972

Heavily televised toys	20.2%
Medium televised toys	31.4%
Nontelevised toys	46.1%

* As a percentage of average consumer selling price.
Costs are based on manufacturer's lowest selling price.

Elliott also selected a smaller group of toys taken only from the heavily televised and nontelevised groups and asked dealers to rate them by dollar sales volume. (The difference in popularity between the faster and slower sellers selected by this procedure is not as marked as between the best sellers and poorer sellers in Table 1.) In Table 4, the same nineteen toys are arrayed in two groups: first by sales velocity and then by weight of television expenditure.

Again it is confirmed that the margin differential between televised and nontelevised toys is around 25 percentage points and is materially larger than the margin spread based on differences in popularity. From this it can be concluded that in the toy business the power of television to create product

---

[14] "Toy Pricing Study," conducted on behalf of Irwin Toy, Ltd., by Elliott Research Corp., Toronto, December 1972.

Table 4
Distribution margins* on 19 toys in Canada, Christmas, 1972

The 9 faster sellers (includes 6 heavily televised toys)	29.5%
The 10 slower selling toys (includes 4 heavily televised toys)	33.8%
10 heavily televised toys (includes 6 faster sellers)	18.8%
9 nontelevised toys (includes 3 faster sellers).....................	41.6%

* As a percentage of average consumer selling price. Costs are based on manufacturer's lowest selling price.

identity contributes more to lowering distribution margins than its power to create consumer demand.

Insights from studying product categories

Interviews with trade buyers in both Canada and the United States revealed an almost 1:1 inverse relationship between the degree of television advertising and average markup within a category. Games, dolls, toy racing cars, and preschool items get the bulk of television dollars and show the smallest margins. At the other extreme are plush toys, educational and scientific toys, toy musical instruments, arts and crafts, and children's furniture. These segments are characterized by high markup and virtually no television promotion.

Margins in televised categories are lower not simply because the advertised items are marked up less, but because the nonadvertised items in these categories are retailed at a 5 to 10 percent slimmer markup than other nonadvertised toys. A study of markups in a leading Canadian mail order catalog last Christmas illustrates these margin characteristics. Margins in two heavily advertised categories, games and dolls, averaged around 12 percent for the televised toys and 41½ percent for the unadvertised brands. In two nontelevised categories, toy musical instruments and plush animals, margins averaged around 48 percent.

The nonadvertised competition within televised categories is not ordinarily provided by private labels, but by so-called "knock-offs"—lower-priced, higher-markup, and generally lower-quality imitations of the most demanded toys, which are usually produced in the Orient. The speed and ease with which knock-off manufacturers can imitate a successful new product acts to inhibit the domestic maker from overpricing his next year's television entry.

Actually, television has lowered the aggregate industry distribution margin by invading successive categories of previously unadvertised merchandise. For a recent example, until the late 1960s the important preschool category was an unadvertised and high markup segment. Then the two dominant firms, Fisher Price and Playskool, began televising. Severe discounting of the advertised brands ensued. Retailers now complain that they often have to sell the most popular "big ticket" Fisher Price toys below cost.[15] Meanwhile, makers of nonadvertised merchandise agree that dealers have had to trim markups on their items to move them from a gondola of preschool toys which is also loaded with the nationally recognized brands.

What happens if the television stops?

The evidence presented demonstrates that a relatively small expenditure (about 3½ percent of manufacturers' sales) on television advertising has a very large multiplier effect on the level of consumer toy prices. It is also maintained that a severe curtailment or removal of television advertising will lead to an unraveling of the entire toy marketing revolution and the benefits it has brought.

There have been instances where, for various reasons, television advertising has been withdrawn from a category. This affords the fascinating opportunity of running the film in reverse. A spectacular example occurred in the toy gun field.

In 1964, guns represented an important 5 percent of toy sales.[16] All manner of ingenious new toy weapons were introduced yearly. Guns were one of the heaviest televised categories; they received massive newspaper lineage; trade markups were slim. As a consequence of the Vietnam war, out of either conviction or fear of criticism by antiwar-toy groups, toy manufacturers stopped televising guns, and retailers ceased featuring them in ads. Although guns, especially western and other nonmilitary styles, still sell in reasonable quantities, individual gun items no longer appear on best seller lists.

Innovation at the manufacturer's level has almost stopped. Retailers report both that their cost for toy guns has advanced and that their own markups have fattened. The former occurred because there were fewer competitive makers, and guns were produced in smaller quantity. The latter [occurred] because, without television and newspaper advertising, there are virtually no demanded or identifiable items, so the retailer has little to gain from sharp prices and little to fear from inflated ones.

As expressed by a large chain store buyer, "our competition isn't making any noise about toy guns either, so we can keep our prices up."[17] These same results will undoubtedly attend the removal of advertising and promotion from behind any toy category, or toys as a whole.

CONCLUSION

This article has described the process by which advertising lowers consumer prices and has developed a theory to explain why this occurs in

[15] Fred Lifschultz, Prober & Pelta Wholesalers, *Toy and Hobby World,* vol. 11 (January 15, 1973).

[16] A. J. Wood Company, "Toy Buying In The United States," a survey commissioned by the Toy Manufacturers of America.

[17] "Toy Guns Are Still Popping," *Toys Magazine,* vol. 71 (May 1972).

strongly advertised industries whose goods are sold through the general retail trade.

Traditionally, advertising has been analyzed almost exclusively in terms of its effect on manufacturers' selling prices. This effect is believed to be modest compared to advertising's impact on distribution margins. Here, in conjunction with mass merchandising, advertising has slashed markups on advertised brands and reduced them on competing nonadvertised products as well, bringing lower prices to the consumer.

QUESTIONS

1. Explain, in your own words, Steiner's rationale for saying that advertising lowers prices to consumers (even if it raises the manufacturer's selling price).
2. Why do many stores prefer to sell items that turn over fast, even if these items have a lower markup rate? Explain, using some numbers: for markup, 25 percent and 50 percent; for inventory turns, 5 times and 2 times, and for sales volume, $100,000.
3. What might a critic of marketing say about the effectiveness of TV in selling toys, even if it does lower toy prices? Would Steiner's article answer this critic? Explain why or why not.

26
Pricing strategy in an inflation economy

Mild inflation has been with us for many years. But starting in 1973–74 inflation became a serious matter which began to affect management planning. This article discusses and illustrates some of the problems of pricing in an inflationary economy. An electronics industry example shows how prices change over the product life cycle and are dependent on both production costs and competition.

"Lead time on components we buy used to be 30 days. Now it is a year. Because of component shortages, our inventories have doubled in the last year, while sales are up only 30 percent. To price a contract under these conditions, we have to double- and triple-check everything. A year or so ago,

Source: Reprinted (with deletions) with permission from *Business Week*, April 6, 1974, pp. 42–49. Copyright © 1974, McGraw-Hill, Inc. All rights reserved.

we budgeted every six months, made cash projections quarterly, and used the computer only for payroll. Now we budget quarterly, make cash projections weekly, and plug virtually every pricing factor into the computer."

Those are the pricing problems is the minicomputer field, as described by Donald W. Fuller, chairman and president of Microdata Corp. of Irvine, Calif. In varying degree, they are also the problems in steel, food processing, petrochemicals, retailing, paper and pulp, and nearly every other business.

In today's inflationary economy, pricing a product or service is like no other pricing in recent history. While nearly all prices are moving higher over the long haul, short-term pricing patterns may be up, down, or every which way.

In the oil and food industries, where demand is high and costs are skyrocketing, prices are up 10 to 50 percent or more above a year ago. In other industries, notably electronics, cutthroat competition and economies of scale are driving prices through the floor. Three years ago, electronic handheld calculators retailed for $240 each. Now they are down to $19.95. Steel prices verge on the chaotic. After years of tightly competitive, follow-the-leader pricing, shortages and rulings by the Cost of Living Council have all but wrecked the industry's traditional single-tiered pricing structure. This week, for instance, U.S. Steel Corp. is offering hot-rolled carbon bars at anywhere from $178 to $211 per ton, depending upon the area of the country, compared with $188 for Republic, $207 for Armco, and $206 for Youngstown.

As Phase IV controls approach their April 30 [1974] cutoff date, there is scant relief in sight. An almost incendiary rate of inflation—easily the country's biggest and most pressing economic problem—is wiping out any relationship between yesterday's price and today's worth of the dollar. As part of the same spiral, costs are surging at a spectacular rate. Raw material shortages are beginning to cripple whole industries. Then, to complicate an already forbidding equation, antitrusters are stepping up their pricing vigilance. "I can't name a major company that hasn't been challenged by the Justice Department on its prices," says Fred Kniffen, professor of marketing at the University of Connecticut.

More and more, today's pricing environment demands better, faster, and more frequent pricing decisions than ever before. It is also forcing companies to take a whole new look at pricing and its role in an increasingly complex marketing climate. While the central objective of pricing will always remain the same—to bring in more money than is spent—a growing number of companies are changing many of their basic strategies and tactics for achieving that objective.

PROFIT VS. VOLUME

For years, most companies used price simply to attract more customers and build more sales. Where they saw the prospect for greater volume, they were often willing to let prices and profit margins slip. Now, corporate policy increasingly stresses profit growth ahead of volume growth, and many companies that previously boosted profits by simply trying to boost volume are focusing more on maintaining profit margins, holding down costs, and pricing for profit, as well as sales.

As one New York metals executive puts it: "All four basic elements of marketing—product, promotion, distribution, and price—contribute toward volume, but only price directly generates profit. The other three represent costs that, if reduced, can generate profit—but then only if the company holds its price."

Fairchild Camera & Instrument Corp., for instance, recently bowed out of a price war with Texas Instruments, Inc. At stake were two control modules for Polaroid Corp.'s SX–70 camera. "We were sorry to walk away from that business," says Wilfred J. Corrigan, Fairchild's executive vice-president. "Our price at the end was very close to Polaroid's requirements. But it wouldn't have provided an adequate margin." A few years ago, Corrigan concedes, Fairchild would probably have held onto that business.

Along the way, Fairchild and other companies are also getting more formal and structured in their pricing. Some companies have pulled pricing responsibility in from the field and are moving it higher in the corporate organization, sometimes all the way up to the chief executive. Others are bringing more specialists into the pricing act: production, marketing, financial, market research, and so on. Many more are making greater use of the computer to sharpen their price and cost analysis. Says one academic: "Before the computer, pricing used to be part of the budget ritual, since it was almost impossible to keep track of the factors going into price. Any good company now has an information flow system that allows prices to be reviewed at least weekly, if not daily."

One of these is the Jewelry Division of Zale Corp., the big, Dallas-based national retail jewelry chain. Says Marvin Rubin, group vice-president: "We are constantly looking for flags that tell us that costs have gone up and that we had better re-examine our margins." Zale's highest flying flag is daily computer printout that shows the current relationship between cost and margin on all Zale inventory. This is used by division buyers and management for regular review.

CLASSIC PRICING THEORY

The landmark book on U.S. corporate pricing is *Pricing in Big Business,* published in 1958 by the Brookings Institute and written by A. D. H. Kaplan, Joel B. Dirlam, and Robert F. Lanzillotti. It analyzes the pricing policies and strategies of 20 of the country's largest companies, including Goodyear, U.S. Steel, Sears, Gulf Oil, American Can, Union Carbide, General Electric, and General Foods.

The complexities of electronics pricing

Pricing strategies among industries, companies, and even divisions within the same company defy generalization. This is especially true of the $35 billion electronics industry, which runs the gamut from TV tubes that have not changed in price for a decade to small handheld calculators that are selling for less than half the price that prevailed a year ago. Yet, like a tiny silicon "chip" that can duplicate the function of a thousand or more transistors, the electronics industry probably comes closest to being a miniature model for all the factors that shape today's complex pricing environment and dictate some of those strategies.

At one end of the industry product spectrum are the "mature" or established products that are either nearing or have surpassed their peak growth period. Among these products, the impact of raw material scarcities, capacity shortages, and high labor costs is clearly visible. Their development has all been amortized, and most possible cost improvements have been made.

"Learning curve"

Prices are firming for these products. For instance, small-signal, "metal can" transistors, ubiquitous little products used in almost every kind of electronic gear, dropped from 37 cents each in 1970 to 33 cents in 1971 to 25 cents in 1972. Last year, the price fell only 2 cents. For the semiconductor business, this is virtual stability.

On the other end of the product spectrum, the pricing of new, advanced technology products is different—and growing more so among modern pricing pressures. New semiconductor products tend to be priced closely to the manufacturing cost "learning curve," which correlates a steady increase in production and manufacturing experience with a steady decrease in product rejection rates.

Bernard T. Marren, executive vice-president of American Micro-Systems, Inc., cites as an example a typical new integrated circuit or "chip." The manufacturer's cost per wafer—the basic building block from which finished chips are produced—starts at about $25. Of that, perhaps one-third represents raw material costs, and the rest is labor. "You figure on losing 20 percent of your wafers in processing, which brings the cost up to $31," says Marren. Then from the surviving wafers, "you sort the good chips from the bad or defective." At a yield of 20 good chips per wafer, the cost for each chip runs $1.55. Assembly and packaging raise the final manufacturing cost to $2.38.

When the manufacturer gets to 80 good chips per wafer, his chip cost falls to 38 cents, and his manufacturing cost is about halved. At this stage, changes in raw material and even labor costs make little difference. "A 25 percent increase in raw material costs would add only about $2 to your wafer cost," Marren notes. "At a yield of 80, the chip cost would be raised only a penny."

Historically, the semiconductor industry prices for market share by anticipating the learning curve effect. "I want to keep my profit margins," says Marren. "But I also want that market share. So I predict future yields based on my experience with similar products in the past, and I price way out on the learning curve." On a product with heavy volume potential, the price may be several months farther along the learning curve than current costs. One example is the 1,024-bit random access memory (RAM) first introduced by Intel Corp. three years ago. This product, which has become the most popular semiconductor memory device for computers and other digital equipment, started out at a price of $28 per unit. It now sells for $3 to $4.

Future costs

One of today's hottest new semiconductor products, the 4,000-bit RAM had to provide a better value than the 1,024-bit RAM. So it could not start out at anything like the $28 level, at which Intel launched the 1,024-bit RAM. It had to sell for less than $15 if it was going to compete on a cost per function basis, even though it offers the bonus of reducing the number of components to be assembled for a given job. In fact, the 4,000-bit RAM is now being quoted at leass than $10 in large quantities, despite the fact that it would have to sell for more than $20 if the manufacturers were to cover all their costs.

Over the longer term, other forces and pressures promise to keep industry pricing in total flux. For one thing, says Wilfred J. Corrigan, executive vice-president of Fairchild Camera & Instrument Corp., labor and raw material costs are increasing much faster than ever, "which is affecting the more mature products that already are near the bottom of the learning curve." Offsetting this is an industry trend away from 2-inch silicon wafers toward 3-inch wafers, providing more chips per processing step and thus a lower chip cost. "It's like the pricing in any other industry today," says one Eastern electronics executive. "You simply take it one day at a time."

"Undeniably, there are, in many instances, pricing routines that are sometimes expressed as rules," the authors write. "But given the diversity of products that most of the companies sold, it was impossible to equate product policy and company policy in every area. Swift's dog food cannot be priced in the same way or under the same guides as fresh meat. Union Carbide's Prestone antifreeze requires a different type of pricing from the company's oxygen. Thus, there were few companies in a position to say, 'Our policy is to price our products according to a uniform procedure and target.' "

That has not changed today. While most prices reflect the same basic elements—cost, profit, demand, and competition—the weight and priorities assigned to each vary with the nature of the product (commodity or specialty), company (manufacturing, wholesale, or retail), market (consumer or industrial), corporate objectives, management style, and everything else that makes one company different from another. In the chemical industry, Du Pont tends to focus on higher margin specialty products. At first, it prices them high, then gradually lowers the price as the market builds and competition grows. Dow Chemical Co., which stresses lower margin commodity products, takes the opposite tack. It prices low, builds a dominant market share, and holds on for the long pull. As manufacturers, Dow and DuPont operate in a broad pricing milieu totally unlike that of the two other classes of business: wholesaling and retailing. All three classes use different pricing approaches, since they deal with different markets, different cost structures, and other variables.

* * * * *

"In the absence of any one ideal pricing formula," says an Eastern textile executive, "most well-managed companies are simply trying to improve the broader mechanism and organization that comes to bear on their particular formula." This means getting more and better pricing information, using it more effectively, and gaining more control. "After all," he adds, "the problem is not setting that initial list price. The problem is that discounts, special services, and other 'price shading' are making the list price almost meaningless. Except where major shortages exist, practically no one pays list anymore unless you're a consumer, and many times not even then. So how can a manufacturer know what his products are selling for?"

Depending upon the industry and company, price shading may knock anywhere from 5 to 20 percent or more off the price. Some of the most spectacular discounting, of course, comes into the auto business. At the dealer level, the retail "sticker" price on U.S.–made cars is only the top end of a bargaining spread that averages 17 percent on small cars, 21 percent on intermediates, 25 percent on large cars, and 21 to 25 percent on optional equipment. At the wholesale level, dealer sales bonuses and special allowances do the same thing.

More and more companies, however, are beginning to draw the line. Says J. Fred Weston, professor of economics and finance at UCLA and a long-time pricing authority: "In the past, many companies would publish a list price. Then their salesmen would shade prices all across the board, depending on market conditions, and tell the head office about it later. Now management itself is responding to the market before the salesman makes the sale, rather than afterward."

THE EFFECTS OF SHORTAGES

One example is Ducommun, Inc., a $190 million metals and electronics distributor in Los Angeles. "Two years ago," says Executive Vice-President Charles K. Preston, "we decided that since we couldn't raise our prices [because of controls], we'd concentrate on those items that would make us the best profit." So Ducommun boosted its salesmen's commissions 5 to 10 percent on its higher margin products, such as cutting tools and coated abrasives. "We've also given salesmen the rule," says Preston, "that we want no deviation from book price," unless authorized by management. Within its largest division, Ducommun has even created a price "czar" who consults with salesmen on any price changes. "We monitor the price on every order before the sale closes," says Preston.

* * * * *

At Fairchild, semiconductor salesmen have begun operating on price lists established by individual product marketing managers who must approve any special deals. "In the past," says Corrigan, "Fairchild salesmen were able to commit the company to pricing decisions. Today, the selling function no longer even reports to the division general managers who carry profit responsibility."

Like other semiconductor makers, Fairchild is also less willing to write contracts in "step-pricing" terms, a common procedure for passing along cost savings that come with volume production and steadily decreasing product rejection rates. Material shortages, of course, help stiffen the seller's backbone. "Up to a year or so ago, it often took two or three pricing go-arounds with a customer to finally land the contract," says one executive at GTI Corp., a semiconductor industry supplier. "Now, if the manufacturer is meeting his capacity levels, can demonstrate his capability of getting raw materials, and thus better assure on-time delivery, the customer is more willing to pay the suggested selling price, rather than bargain and perhaps lose out on the contract."

To guarantee delivery on ball bearings and other products that have steadily lengthening lead times, many customers are even willing to accept an escalator clause on their orders. This way, they pay the going price at time of shipment, rather than at the time of the order. Sometimes, the customer is not even told beforehand. "You get the stuff," grumbles one maker of logging equipment, "and you find the price is higher than was quoted." Adds a leading gear manufacturer: "Everybody we see is breaking every rule in the book. The price quoted to you when you place the order no longer means a thing. You won't take anybody to court over this. The courts would be jammed for years. So you sit down with your important suppliers and work it out."

As one example, he cites a new deferred pricing system, using standard indices. "You take today's factory price," he says, "and you quote that plus escalation tied to the wholesale price for ferrous and nonferrous metals—if that is what you are dealing in—and the Bureau of Labor Statistics index for machinery. The indices determine changes made at time of delivery." The problem, he adds quickly, "is that the marketing guys have to be retrained to sell this way, and purchasing people have to communicate faster and more fluently with the marketing people."

"UNBUNDLING" SERVICES

One of the biggest targets of pricing strategies is the jumble of so-called "free" services that have long inflated costs and distorted prices and profitability. Feeling the pressure of rising labor costs, many retailers, wholesalers, and manufacturers are now starting to "unbundle" these services and charge separately for them.

Grocery wholesalers, for instance, may pass through a straight invoice cost and then charge for delivery, packaging, or other onetime freebies. A growing number of department stores now charge extra for home delivery, gift-wrapping, and shopping bags. "This makes a good deal of sense," says Charles Goodman, marketing professor at the University of Pennsylvania's Wharton School. "People who don't want a service just shouldn't have to pay for it."

Norton Co., the big Worcester (Mass.) abrasives maker, took such thinking one step further. Under its pioneering "Norton Plan," introduced in 1965, the company's Grinding Wheel Division developed a contract distribution system that uses computers to calculate long-term usage trends and rates among major customers, and writes contracts at set prices. This cuts Norton's selling and handling costs, minimizes some of the peaks and valleys in its production cycle, and reduces inventory requirements both among Norton and its volume customers—allowing Norton to offer lower, long-range prices on larger sales.

A typical abrasive steel conditioning wheel, for instance, is priced regularly at $124.51, based on a bulk rate and subject to a 2 percent discount for cash prior to 30 days. Under the Norton Plan, the same wheel costs $98.03 or 21.3 percent less. Today, some 20 to 30 percent of the division's sales— excluding diamond products, which are not covered—fall within the plan.

"Under regular list pricing structures," says one university pricing expert, "I'm paying more because I don't need the technical services a company is offering. So I think about making the product myself or finding some little guy down the street to make it for me without the selling cost. If I'm Norton Co., I work out a pricing program, and I sell directly or use some other way to protect my market. If you are a price leader and you go to market with a lot of services, you must do this as your product becomes more mature or you'll lose a lot of volume."

Pricing of new products presents different problems, mainly because it is starting to pull in two different directions. One direction is toward "skimming," or charging as much as the traffic will bear. While this generates high initial profits, it also lures competition into the market and quickly drives prices down unless the skimmer has patent or other product protection. "Penetration pricing," on the other hand, relies on low prices to gain instant dominance in a market and to build a stronger long-range position of leadership.

Though opposite in their approach, both pricing strategies share the same basic requirement: an intensive analysis of the market. In the past, many consumer companies and nearly all industrial companies priced new products on the basis of cost, plus some predetermined markup, then adjusted the price to meet or anticipate competition. Now, more and more new product pricing is market- or value-oriented, rather than cost-oriented.

LESSON IN SKIMMING

Du Pont is one of the classic skimmers. The assistant director of Du Pont's Film Department elaborated on this philosophy in an antitrust case against Du Pont's cellophane in 1953: "The main competitive materials . . . against which cellophane competes are waxed paper, glassine, greaseproof, and vegetable parchment papers, all of which are lower in price than cellophane. We do not meet this price competition. Rather, we compete with these materials on the basis of establishing the value of our own as a factor in better packaging and cheaper distribution costs and classify as our logical markets those fields where the properties of cellophane in relationship to its price can do a better job."

Over the years, as Du Pont builds volume and competition rushes into the market, prices drop rapidly. Du Pont's Dacron, a polyester fiber, has slipped from $2.25 per pound when it was introduced in 1953 to today's 40-cent range. More recently, the price of Qiana, a five-year-old synthetic fiber with the look and feel of silk, has dipped 35 percent.

"We were using ingredients we never used before," says a Du Pont spokesman of the Qiana introduction. "And there was no point putting it into men's underwear." Instead, Du Pont launched Qiana in the high-fashion prestige market—with an initial price to match: $5.95 to $8.95 per pound, compared with $8 to $10 per pound for silk. "You get it into the very highest prestige garments to build a reputation and identity for it," says the Du Pont source. "We got the biggest designers and biggest names [Dior, Cardin, and Givenchy, for instance] to develop this identity." By now, Du Pont claims, the trademark is creating the appetite, so promotion costs and prices continue to drop. "Then to broaden your market," the Du Pont spokesman says, "you go into the next lower price category."

Or you can go the other way, getting customers to trade up to a higher-priced product. One of the shrewdest users of that tactic is the tire industry. In the early 1960s, the bias-ply tire was the industry's dominant product, selling for about $30. Then in 1965, B. F. Goodrich Tire launched the industry's first serious marketing campaign for a U.S.—made radial, selling in the $50 range. Consumers, however, were put off by the big price spread. So in 1968, tiremakers introduced an in-between product: the bias-belted tire, at about $40.

"We knew from experience that the premium-priced tire market is only so big," says Patrick C. Ross, president of Goodrich Tire. "So as the market shifted and the bias-belted tire became the popular tire, the step up to radials was not so great." Last fall, Goodrich moved up one more step, introducing the self-sealing "Golden Lifesaver" steel-belted radial, priced 15 to 20 percent above regular steel-belted radials.

Goodyear Tire & Rubber Co. is moving in the same direction. This summer, it will launch a national ad campaign for its new Customgard GT radials, priced at $75 to $85 each or about 5 percent higher than most other steel-belted radials. Instead of steel, Goodyear's new tires use Exten, a specially treated version of Du Pont's new Kevlar tire cord. While Kevlar costs about $2.85 per pound compared with 80¢ per pound for steel, it is billed as five times stronger than steel, which means far less belting is needed in each tire.

HOW HIGH TO PRICE?

The big imponderable, of course, is how high to price without pricing yourself right out of the market. The marketing landscape is littered with the mistakes of companies that priced the wrong product too high: Du Pont's Corfam imitation shoe leather, Cartrevision's home video recording system, a new type of sterile slag industrial incinerator from Dravo Corp., to name only a few.

An initial high price also leaves a new product exposed and vulnerable. Wella Corp. introduced its Wella Balsam hair conditioner at a hefty $1.98, compared with $1.19 for standard cream rinses. So Alberto-Culver Co. came in with Alberto-Balsam at $1.49, socked $621,000 into a big advertising sendoff (vs. $62,000 for Wella), and claims it surpassed Wella in only ten months. Today, Alberto claims 55 to 60 percent of the hair conditioner market. "We would have liked the profit margins that Wella had with its higher price," says Randy Irion, Alberto-Balsam's senior brand manager. "But we just couldn't get enough market penetration at $1.98."

Irion and other boosters of "penetration pricing" claim that a low price can unlock markets that may not even have been anticipated. This happened when electronic hand-held calculators broke through the $100 barrier and suddenly began moving from the industrial market into the far larger consumer market. "Nobody had any inkling that consumers would buy these things," marvels one retailer.

The same thing occurred when tiny Southwest Airlines recently came up with a $13 fare between Dallas and San Antonio, Tex. This was half the old fare. Braniff Airways quickly followed suit, and before long, air traffic between the two cities doubled, as businessmen and lower-incomers who previously drove between the two cities began flying. In this case, Southwest and Braniff actually changed some behavior patterns.

"In airlines and certain other industries where you have a heavy fixed cost, you are ahead if you can increase total revenue," stresses Richard W. Hansen, chairman of marketing at Southern Methodist University's School of Business. "Let's say you are operating at 35 percent of total capacity at a ticket cost of $26. If you can operate at 85 percent of capacity and charge $13, you are a lot better off." Southwest Airlines certainly is. The new fare helped the three-year-old carrier turn its first profit.

While corporate strategies continue grappling with the problems of modern pricing, they are the first to concede that they will probably never get it totally under control. "This is impossible, since costs are changing on one end of their business, competition and markets are changing on the other, and inflation keeps everything and everyone continually off balance," says Jerry Wasserman, senior consultant with Arthur D. Little, Inc. At the same time, Wasserman adds, "the whole role and function of marketing itself is in even greater flux than usual."

One of the latest shifts, of course, is the trend toward "de-marketing" of products. "For years, we were in a situation where we had a glut of supply relative to demand," says Southern Methodist's Hansen. "That's changing now in a lot of areas, and there is concern about what's going to happen to the marketing role. Rather than trying to increase consumption, some of these industries may take the tack that the oil companies and power utilities are taking: decreasing consumption. And maybe price is what they will use."

Then with a nod toward the idea of de-marketing—and toward the broader changes and ferment within the whole pricing function—Hansen adds with wry amusement: "I think we are in for an interesting period in marketing."

QUESTIONS

1. What forces make pricing more important and difficult in an inflation economy?
2. Are any of the firms discussed in the article using a simple cost-plus approach? If so, which? If not, why not?
3. Explain the pricing approach being used in the electronics industry example.
*4. What happens to "supersalesmen" (Reading 23) in times of shortages and rapidly rising prices? How about product managers (Reading 17)?

---

* Question relates concepts in this and other readings.

27
Flexible pricing

This article suggests that pricing executives are no longer relying so heavily on target-return pricing or follow-the-leader pricing. In an increasingly competitive marketplace, pricing executives are paying more attention to variations in demand. Further, they are recognizing that price reductions can win additional business, perhaps even an increased market share. The article also suggests that these aggressive pricing policies may lead to a greater concentration of industry and possibly to the need for new antitrust policies.

Scissored between soaring costs and sluggish demand at home and under intense competitive pressure from abroad, U.S. companies are overhauling ancient formulas for setting prices.

To fight Japanese inroads, Ford Motor Co. and General Motors Corp., in an unprecedented move, are charging less for their 1978 subcompacts on the West Coast than elsewhere in the country.

In a challenge to the industry's traditional price leaders, Armco Steel Co. last month announced plans to cut prices on four stainless steel products by an average of 5 percent.

In an industry long sheltered by government regulation of competition, airlines have been slashing prices to hold on to market shares.

In almost every consumer goods industry where producers had long believed that strong brand identification insulated their products from competition from cheaper makes, scores of famous names—Zenith, RCA, Singer, and even Sony Corp. of America—are being propelled headlong into a new world of fierce price competition.

The upshot is little short of a revolution in pricing practices that will have ramifications for capital spending, the inflation rate, industrial concentration, and the application of existing antitrust laws. Above all, though, an ability to adapt to the new pricing environment will characterize those companies that succeed in competing over the next decade.

The chief characteristics of the new price strategy are flexibility and a willingness to cut prices aggressively to hold market shares. On the way out the window are many of the pricing traditions of the U.S. industrial giants. Companies no longer try to hang on to fixed markups over cost through thick

Source: Reprinted with permission from *Business Week*, December 12, 1977, pp. 78–88. Copyright © 1977, McGraw-Hill, Inc.

and thin. The strong no longer hold the umbrella of high prices firmly over weaker competitors. And in many industries, customary price leadership—where competitors passively follow a big company that sets the price for all—is on its way out.

The new practices differ radically from the old in aim and concept. The traditional model for pricing by large industrial corporations was codified in the management system introduced at General Motors by Alfred P. Sloan in the 1920s. Pricing was essentially static. Companies set a price that they believed would provide a desired long-run "target rate of return" at a given production volume. Although management was obviously forced to deviate from this pricing ideal by competition, the aim nevertheless was to create a pricing structure that was programmed to change gradually and predictably and to stick to it. Price changes to meet competition were regarded as the exception rather than the rule. The list price on steel mill products, for example, rose less than 4 percent from 1950 to 1965; aluminum by about 3 percent. The prices of industrial commodities and crude materials fluctuated only slightly over these years. Even though price-cutting occurred at the fringes of the market, the corporate establishment looked on it with disdain as "chiseling" and sometimes disciplined the offender, as happened in steel in 1968, when several small companies tried to undercut the industry price.

Although this may seem like a strategy better suited to industrial pachyderms than the modern managers that Sloan was supposed to have inspired, it was, in fact, well-suited to the climate produced by the rapid growth of the first 2½ decades following World War II. To set a price that will be consistent with meeting profit targets over the long run, companies must be able to count on generally high levels of capacity utilization and predictability in the future course of costs and product demand. Although there were four recessions between 1945 and the end of the 1960s, companies in general found themselves in an atmosphere in which it made sense to gear business decisions, including pricing decisions, to long-run aims. Sloan-style pricing was an integral element in a business environment where companies confidently told securities analysts that they were aiming to iron out earnings fluctuations and were attempting to meet high and steady targets—such as Citicorp's famed 15 percent per year—for earnings growth.

THE NEW FLEXIBILITY

But in this decade, two recessions in five years, price controls introduced by a Republican Administration, and double-digit inflation have undermined the predictability and stability of growth as planning assumptions. And the restrictive policy reaction to inflationary forces—particularly in quadrupling of oil prices in 1974—sealed the doom of the old price strategy, by producing slow growth and excess industrial capacity around the world.

The initial business response was a confused attempt to pass on cost increases in an unthinking way—an effort to retain target rates of return but in an atmosphere requiring higher and higher prices. But with unused capacity around the world, there was just too little demand and too much competition to allow target return pricing to work. Indeed, 1975 and 1976 were marked by repeated retreats from announced industrywide price boosts in steel, paper, aluminum, and chemicals.

"Target pricing just does not prove to be as viable as it once was," says Robert F. Lanzillotti, dean of the University of Florida School of Business and a member of the commission that administered Phase II of President Nixon's price control program. "Firms are becoming much more flexible in their price thinking now." Businessmen acknowledge that the days of complacent attitudes toward pricing are over. "We were fat, dumb, and happy back in the 1960s," says a top executive of a major chemical company, "but now most companies have been so badly burned that it will be a long time before they commit themselves to a long-run pricing strategy."

Instead, companies throughout the U.S. economy, from mammoth chemical companies to small computer time-sharing complexes, are turning to a pricing strategy that is flexible in every respect. It is a strategy, says Norma Pace, chief economist at the American Paper Institute, that stresses pricing "product by product instead of the whole glob." While companies have always shown some willingness to adjust prices, or profit margins, on specific products as market conditions varied, this kind of flexibility is being carried to the state of a high art.

Long-term contracts that passed on cost increases from sellers to buyers flourished in the 1950s and 1960s. But they are now breaking down in a wide range of industries, including chemicals, where they have been a way of life, in favor of short-lived and more flexible—but far less predictable— arrangements.

Companies are taking several major steps to make their price policies bob and weave like a well-trained boxer dodging the blows of his opponent. They are juggling prices among products—raising some, lowering others—to get the maximum mix of sales and profits.

MARKETING AUTOS

In the automobile industry, for example, companies are "doing a balancing act in pricing that is highly dynamic," says an economist at one of the Big Three auto manufacturers. "And this means a more sensitive effort to assess the competitive relationship of products and the costs of making them." GM still dominates auto pricing and it uses long-range profit targets as a guide. Nevertheless, the auto industry is an excellent example of how a confluence of forces—government-mandated product standards, foreign competition, and worries over slow growth—is generating a new pricing strategy.

For auto makers, a special impetus to be flexible comes in part from an attempt to produce and market a product mix that will maximize profits while on average meeting federal gas mileage requirements. But equally important have been the squeeze from foreign competition and a general industry expectation of slower growth in car sales in the long run. Low-cost subcompact models, especially from Japan, such as Hondas, Toyotas, and Datsuns, have been taking an increasing share of the domestic market—the total import share had grown from less than 15 percent in 1976 to over 20 percent last September. Moreover, many auto economists say the market is near saturation with one car for every two Americans.

After raising prices last year on small cars, GM this year has slashed the price of its subcompact Chevrolet Chevette to head off foreign competition. More striking, though, is that GM and Ford have begun to price by geography, with geographic differences in prices exceeding traditional transportation cost differentials. Subcompact models—such as the Ford Pinto—were reduced 10 percent on the West Coast, where Japanese competition is the stiffest, and 6 percent in the rest of the country.

To offset the lower profit margins on lower-price, small cars, the industry is already raising the prices of large-size cars. The Cadillac Seville and Lincoln Versailles now sell for more than $14,000—four times the price of the lowest-price model. Ten years ago the top of the line was three times as costly as the lowest-price car. And some industry experts think this trend toward a wider pricing spread will intensify. "GM will be selling a $30,000 Cadillac by 1985," says Eugene F. Jennings, professor of management at Michigan State University.

Of course, such a pricing strategy is beyond the means of American Motors Corp., which does not build large-sized luxury cars. "I'm sure that GM, in its approach to small-car pricing, is awful damn glad it's got Cadillac Sevilles," says AMC Chairman Roy D. Chapin Jr.

In line with the new flexibility, manufacturers are now trying to build models in the low, medium, and high price ranges into each car size—small, intermediate, and full. By adding luxury appointments and optional equipment, companies are able to charge more, even for smaller-size cars. Chrysler Corp.'s intermediate-size Volaré, for example, now has stripped-down and luxury models as well as several special models, such as the high-performance Volaré Road Runner.

The airline industry has plunged into fierce competition as carriers break away from federally regulated, industrywide fares and initiate flexible pricing to maximize the use of seat space and airliners. Last summer Trans World Airlines Inc. began offering no-frills service on its Chicago to Los Angeles route, with discounts up to 43 percent off standard fare. Now the three other major airlines on that route—American, Continental, and United—have matched TWA's price cut. Flexible and more competitive pricing on domestic and international routes is fast becoming widespread.

THE END OF PRICE LEADERSHIP

Sharply rising energy costs, too, can impel companies to price flexibly. In the paper industry, for example, "companies now price, selectively to protect profit margins," says economist Pace. The industry is the economy's second-largest industrial consumer of energy. In contrast, prior to the 1973 oil embargo, paper companies were able simply "to price across the board in reaction to overall changes in the economy," says Pace.

The new environment is forcing companies into what would have been regarded as an act of corporate sacrilege only a few years ago: They are violating the price leader-price follower pattern. "The worst thing a company can do now is price identically to its competitors," says Gerard Badler, director of service programs at the Strategy Planning Institute, a nonprofit research center in Cambridge, Mass. "It should either price above or below the competition—anything to set itself apart—but it should never price equally."

Under target return pricing, the price for the industry was set by the industry leader—usually the company with the largest market share, such as a U.S. Steel Corp. or an International Business Machines Corp. Then the smaller companies fell in behind with identical prices. The system was designed to stave off price wars and "predatory" competition, which would force down prices and hurt all parties. Companies that deviated from this norm were chastised by discounting or shaving by the leaders. Price deviation was quickly disciplined. In the steel industry, for example, price discipline was so stringent "that in 1968 Bethlehem Steel came on as the price enforcer," says Eugene J. Frank, vice-president of Shearson Hayden Stone Inc. in Pittsburgh. In this case, Bethlehem announced formal price cuts. Within three months prices were raised back to the accepted industrywide level.

Now, however, smaller companies are taking bold steps to undercut the price leader. For example, while list prices of steel display a semblance of cooperation, companies are discounting prices of steel products more than ever. According to government sources, there is strong evidence that steel companies are offering substantial discounts under pressure from surging steel imports, which now account for nearly 20 percent of the total domestic market. "When this year's operating results are out, you're going to see that discounts of as much as 15 percent have been offered," say steel analyst Frank. "They are much bigger than expected." According to Frank, the large discounts have been offered in the Great Lakes market, where foreign imports have jumped by 73 percent this year.

Steel discounting does not always take the form of pure price reductions but often shows up in the elimination of inventory and freight charges or the knocking down of so-called "extra" charges for special cutting and treating of steel that normally are added to list prices. This kind of surreptitious price-shaving has gone on before, but now it is more intense than ever.

The only company that has publicly admitted to discounting is Armco Steel. Its big structural steel mill in Houston has taken a pounding from Gulf Coast imports, which now account for about 50 percent of the regional market. Last November the company announced a "foreign fighter" pricing campaign, shaving 20 percent off list prices and launching a splashy media effort against imported steel. Although the company suspended the discounts in the spring because the Japanese were still undercutting its prices, Armco revived the program this fall and recently announced that it would keep it running through next January. Now other steel makers reluctantly admit that they are meeting the Armco discount. Further, Armco last month announced actual price cuts on four stainless products—an average decrease of about 5 percent that will put pressure on its competitors to break their price rigidity.

Domestic steel companies are hoping that the so-called "reference pricing" system now being drawn up by the Treasury Dept. will protect them from Japanese competition. The reference price sets a minimum price below which Japanese steelmakers—who account for 50 percent of all steel imports—cannot sell products in the U.S. market. But reference pricing will help U.S. steelmakers only if the price is set near the current list price for steel. If it is set substantially lower, domestic companies will be forced to either cut prices or continue to lose business to the Japanese competition.

Even if reference pricing succeeds in protecting domestic steel companies from foreign price competition, it still may be too late to resuscitate price discipline. It is widely held that in the past companies would announce to the press their desire to stop price discounting as a way of signaling to the other companies to restore industrywide pricing. Right now industry executives admit they are having problems with such signals because companies have become so accustomed to the competitive environment.

In the chemical industry, price leadership is breaking down under pressure from several forces. Competition from foreign chemical companies, such as West Germany's giant Bayer, is growing steadily, and global demand is flagging. The result has been "a rash of temporary allowances on prices that breaks the industry discipline," says a chemical industry analyst.

Traditional patterns of price leadership also are breaking down in the glass container industry, with smaller companies moving to the fore in pricing. Last year, for example, Owens-Illinois Inc.—which is larger than its next five competitors combined—increased its list prices by 4½ percent. Fearing that the increase would hurt sales to brewing companies that were just beginning to switch to glass bottles, the smaller companies broke ranks and offered huge discounts. The action not only negated O–I's increase but served notice that the smaller companies were after O–I's market share. "In effect, the smaller companies became the price leaders in order to entice the brewers," says William A. Kerr, president of Kerr Glass Mfg. Corp. in Los Angeles.

REVISING THE RULES

Indeed, it is often a desperate financial condition that drives many small companies to break the follow-the-leader rule. "The small firms are always the first to feel a dwindling cash flow," says one economist, "so it comes as no surprise that they aren't afraid to go for the jugular."

Price decisions and product decisions are obviously interconnected. In the new environment, companies more than ever either are trying to carve out a niche where they can raise prices without sacrificing sales or cut prices and try to gain a larger market share with aggressive pricing. "We now find that loss of volume has profit implications as significant as price markups on each unit," says John J. Nevin, chairman of Zenith Radio Corp. Zenith was badly burned by Japanese competition in the TV–set market because it insisted on keeping prices up to protect profit margins. "We're making a more aggressive bid to make the maximum use of price to catch up with imports," says Nevin.

The key to securing a niche is for companies to distinguish their product from others on the market. Says the financial vice-president of a large data-processing company: "Because we can no longer depend on forward pricing, we try to find a proprietary enclave where our product has a unique application. This offers us a competitive alternative and helps protect our revenue stream from fluctuations." For this company, the solution lies in tailoring its data-processing services to customers' particular in-house computer requirements—such as inventory and production control. "We look harder now to find services that others just don't yet provide," says the vice-president.

Selecting the proper market segment has led many companies to centralize pricing decisions in corporate headquarters, taking the authority out of the hands of division heads and sales representatives. For example, at U.S. Elevator Corp., a subsidiary of Cubic Corp., top management now allows its salesmen to bid only on jobs priced under $100,000. All other bidding is handled by a headquarters "estimating group" that has doubled its staff in the last two years.

And to avoid cutthroat competition in the sluggish construction industry, says U.S. Elevator President George C. Tweed, "we try to find something to sell where we have a unique edge. Then pricing isn't quite so traumatic." Tweed has increased his service business by 40 percent in the last year and is now emphasizing so-called "special projects" such as shipboard elevators and nuclear-plant elevators. "The secret is seeking out business that nobody else wants," says Tweed.

ALONG THE "LEARNING CURVE"

The best example of a successful "market niche" pricing strategy is provided by the Hewlett-Packard Co. In the highly competitive pocket calculator market, where price-cutting is rampant, H–P has been able to thrive by offering high-priced products for a select segment of the market. H–P equips its products with special features and then offers its calculators at an average price higher than the industry average. To stay in the market with this strategy, H–P must continually vary its product line and offer new models as the competition rushes in to undercut H–P's price. So far, the strategy has been successful: H–P's pretax income has grown by a staggering 400 percent since 1967.

While H–P follows the market niche strategy, its major competitor follows a market share strategy. Texas Instruments Inc. employs a pricing system based on high sales volume for a limited product line. It is called "design-to-cost" planning and relies on the concept of the learning or experience curve. The concept holds that production costs will decline as output rises, partly because of economies of scale, but—more important—because machines and workers "learn" with time how to produce standard products faster. TI prices along its learning curve, which means steadily lower prices at higher levels of output for a relatively unchanging product. "We perform a careful study of the market to see how it expands as the price of the product is lowered," says Charles H. Phipps, TI's head of strategic planning and corporate development.

Pricing along the learning curve to maximize market share "has been a strategy of the Japanese for years in gaining a hold on U.S. markets," says Harvard Business School professor Steven C. Wheelwright. "They have used it in everything from steel, to textiles, to electronics." Now, U.S. companies are finally using this aggressive price strategy against the Japanese in the burgeoning new market for TV–set tape recorders. RCA Corp. made the first major price move in August when it set a suggested price of $1,000. Last month Zenith cut its suggested price to $995 from $1,295. Under pressure from these price cuts, Sony recently announced it would lower the price of its Betamax model by $200, to $1,095. However, most analysts agree that Sony will have to lower its price further to stay in the market.

Basic processing industries such as steel and chemicals have been the slowest to learn the market share strategy. But these are the industries that need it the most, according to marketing expert Bruce D. Henderson of Boston Consulting Group Inc. "These companies have been too concerned with earnings and short-term cash flow," he argues. "They have to be willing to give up short-run profits to gain market share."

Contending that "once market share shifts, it rarely shifts back," Henderson says that companies in these industries must build capacity faster than their competitors. "Once capacity is in place, the competition can't enter the market at the same price," says Henderson.

The problem, he says, is that companies in the past have followed a "pricing mythology," attempting to predict costs and pass them through to the consumer no matter how high they go. He cites the case of U.S. Steel, which "kept prices high enough to allow 10 to 12 smaller companies to take a substantial share of the market." As a result, Big Steel has watched its market share dwindle from 48 percent in 1910 to 34 percent in the mid–1950s and to 23 percent today.

Dow Chemical Co. offers the contrasting example of a mammoth company that prices aggressively. "This company is trying to price on a flexible basis, while U.S. Steel is trying to be the industry statesman and hold prices steady in good times and bad," says Henderson. Unlike U.S. Steel, Dow will not hesitate to slash prices when and where demand is slack and raise them as high as possible when and where demand is strong, he says.

According to the Strategy Planning Insitute (SPI), market share is a major determinant of profitability. SPI's computer analyses show that companies with larger market shares tend to have bigger profit margins. The reason, says SPI's Badler, is that "companies with larger market share realize economies of scale and are more clearly identified by customers."

PROFITS AND COST CONTROL

With financial support from 150 major corporations, including General Electric Co. and Control Data Corp., SPI has developed a computerized system, called profit impact of market strategy (PIMS), that pinpoints a company's market position. Then, depending on that position, SPI recommends an appropriate pricing strategy.

If excess capacity in the United States has contributed to the new price strategy, excess capacity abroad is making it vital to survival. Demand has been weak at home, but it has been moribund elsewhere in the industrialized West and in Japan. Growth rates in West Germany and Japan, for example, have slowed dramatically since the mid–1960s. The upshot is even more excess capacity in these countries than in the United States and intensification of industrial competition. Because the United States is the least unhealthy of these economies, foreign companies are rushing to capture ever-larger shares of its market.

Sustained periods of excess capacity have occurred before, most notably during the Depression of the 1930s. Then, in a highly protectionist atmosphere, the only real option that seemed open to industrial companies was to try to preserve what was left of profit margins by rigid adherence to target return pricing enforced by static follow-the-leader pricing patterns. While a huge deflation took place in agricultural, raw material, and service prices, industrial prices were characterized by a rigidity that was often noted and that was described in the voluminous report of the Temporary National Economic Committee.

But something new has been added to the pricing scene—if not to antitrust attitudes—since the 1930s. The growing sophistication of computer technology has provided the means for flexible pricing. Using computers, companies are now able to continuously monitor costs of inputs such as labor, raw materials, and energy across a wide range of product lines. In fact, computerized cost review has spread so fast that virtually all moderate-size companies use some kind of data-processing system for this purpose. U.S. Elevator, for example, initiated a cost-monitoring system earlier this year that follows daily and monthly cost fluctuations. The purchase price of every component or raw material is compared with its last purchase price and entered into a price book that the company president reviews daily. Every month a computer prints out how prices look in terms of 30-day periods.

And, 18 months ago, International Telephone & Telegraph Corp. began a system of cost review that provides the company's controller at New York headquarters with monthly cost monitoring for each of the company's divisions. The system tracks deviations of actual from budgeted production costs.

THE IMPACT ON FEDERAL POLICY

The new pricing strategy is almost certain to change the structure of U.S. business and force changes in government policy designed to foster competition, such as antitrust policy.

A giant company following a flexible price strategy aimed at effective competition with foreign producers can no longer be counted on to hold a high-price safety net under its weaker domestic competitors. In the past, says economist Lanzillotti, the giants in such industries as automobiles and steel preferred target return prices partly because these companies feared antitrust action if price-cutting forced smaller companies out of business. Now, as flexible prices gain steam, "it will make the positions of marginal companies like American Motors all the more precarious," he says. Indeed, AMC is already weakening under the new competitive pressure, even though the auto market in general has remained strong. The industry's smallest domestic producer recently announced the shutdown of its assembly plant in Kenosha, Wis., for one week because of declining sales. At the same time, both Ford and General Motors were working double shifts at their production plants.

What is happening in the auto industry is suggestive of what is almost bound to become a new trend toward more industrial concentration. As the U.S. industrial giants begin to price more efficiently to meet competition from the foreign industrial giants, it seems almost inevitable that the weaker, high-cost domestic producers will either fall by the wayside or be gobbled up in mergers. In effect, U.S. industry is being asked to choose between competing more effectively in a world of industrial giants, or hanging on to old price practices that allowed efficient and inefficient producers to coexist comfortably using price strategies that did not rile the antitrust enforcers.

In the case of the steel industry, economist Hendrik Houthakker, a former member of President Nixon's Council of Economic Advisers, says that the Justice Department may have to fundamentally change the way in which it approaches antitrust activity so that U.S. companies will be able to "achieve the economies of scale necessary to match the foreign competition."

Most companies appear to have decided to compete instead of coexist. And this could mean that the giants will soon be running into new battles with the Justice Department and the Federal Trade Commission, unless these agencies change their posture in a way that recognizes what life is really like in an internationally competitive world.

The new price strategy also appears to have some implications for policies designed to stabilize the economy. It is true that "profits inflation"—inflation caused by business attempts to push up profit margins in periods of declining demand—is less likely under flexible than under target rate of return pricing. But flexible pricing also means that any surge in demand is likely to lead to quicker and bigger price boosts than it has in the past, while lower demand will result in quicker price cuts. This strongly suggests that a flexible price economy is likely to be a relatively unstable economy.

But it is also likely to be a more vigorous economy. Companies that use flexible pricing to build market shares are apt to be more willing to undertake new capital spending projects, despite the presence of excess capacity, than are companies that are wedded to achieving hard and fast target rates of return. "Pricing feeds back into investment decisions in a powerful way," says Henderson of the Boston Consulting Group. "And the company with foresight to expand will gain the benefits of added market share."

The move to flexible pricing may eventually shake business investment out of the catatonic state it has been in for the past 2½ years.

The new competitiveness also makes business far riskier. Profits will be much more dependent on nimble decision-making than in the past. Companies in the same industry are much more likely to show diverse profit performance than any time during the past 25 years. It has been fashionable for commentators and economists to argue that U.S. executives have become averse to taking risks. This may still be a correct assessment of their psychology. But the new competitive atmosphere is likely to force companies that wish to be successful to take more risks, like it or not.

QUESTIONS

1. Why does it appear that many businesses are shifting to a more flexible approach to pricing?

2. What is likely to happen to General Motors' profitability if it is not able to sell $30,000 Cadillacs by 1985?

3. Will more flexible pricing benefit or harm a firm's customers? How about the economy?

4. Discuss the implications of more flexible pricing on small competitors who have been able to exist by pricing slightly below the "price leader" and not being excessively competitive or successful.

5. Compare the learning-curve approach to pricing with target-return pricing. Which is likely to lead to more aggressive competition? Do you feel that learning-curve pricing is wise for a company? Explain your answer with an example.

*6. Is learning-curve pricing compatible with Alderson's view (Reading 5) that firms should compete for a differential advantage?

---

* Question relates concepts in this and other readings.

Part 4

Marketing management in action

In addition to making decisions about the four Ps, the marketing manager must also develop a strategic plan for each market and a complete program if several plans are involved. The first two readings in Part 4 discuss the development of overall strategies in two important areas of marketing—product line management and multinational marketing. These readings stress the importance of a total view of the firm and its markets to strategic-level decision making.

Good management also requires an effective organizational structure, an information system to support the managers, and methods of evaluating the cost effectiveness and overall performance of marketing strategies. Three articles deal with these issues.

The final article in this part illustrates with a case example the effectiveness of good marketing strategies. Miller Brewing carefully considers the characteristics of beer consumption and how beer is seen by its target customers when it changes its strategies. In this way it more than tripled sales in a four-year period.

Marketing management in action

28
Planning product line strategy: A matrix approach

Yoram Wind and Henry J. Claycamp

This article suggests a five-step approach to product line evaluation and strategy planning. Wind and Claycamp feel that traditional product life cycle analysis does not go far enough in evaluating the competitive setting, profit considerations, and the fact that product sales are a function of the marketing effort of the firm and other environmental forces. They feel that analysis of existing products' performance, based on hard data on sales, market share, and profitability, can improve product line planning, while also providing management with an ongoing performance audit of its own and competitors' products.

Development of a strategic plan for the existing product line is the most critical element of a company's marketing planning activity. In designing such plans, management needs accurate information on the current and anticipated performance of its products. This information should encompass both (1) consumer evaluation of the company's products, particularly their strengths and weaknesses vis-à-vis competition (i.e., product positioning by market segment information); and (2) "objective" information on actual and anticipated product performance on relevant criteria such as sales, profits, and market share.

Whereas much has been written in recent years about the use of product positioning in strategic marketing planning,[1] little new information has been published about formal methods of using the product's actual and anticipated performance characteristics in terms of sales, profits, and market share as inputs to the design of a strategic marketing plan for the firm's existing product line. Several attempts have been made to use product sales (or, more explicitly, stage in the product life cycle) as a guideline for marketing strategy, including specific recommendations on items such as the type and level of

Source: Reprinted with permission from the *Journal of Marketing,* published by the American Marketing Association, vol. 40 (January 1976), pp. 2–9. At the time of writing, Yoram Wind was a professor of marketing at the Wharton School of the University of Pennsylvania and Henry Claycamp was vice president for marketing at the International Harvester Company.

[1] Yoram Wind, "The Perception of a Firm's Competitive Position," in *Behavioral Models of Market Analysis: Foundations of Marketing Action,* Francesco M. Nicosia and Yoram Wind, eds. (Hinsdale, Ill.: Dryden Press, in press).

advertising, pricing, and distribution.[2] Yet these recommendations have usually been vague, nonoperational, not empirically supported, and conceptually questionable, since they imply that strategies can be developed with little concern for the product's profitability and market share position.[3]

In the 1970s, some attention has been given to various aspects of sales, market share, and profitability as guidelines for marketing planning. Most notable of these efforts are the Marketing Science Institute's PIMS (Profit Impact of Market Strategy) project, which examines the determinants of profitability in the modern corporation,[4] and the Boston Consulting Group's product portfolio analysis.[5] These approaches do not, however, provide a comprehensive approach for product line planning based on all three measures—sales, market share, and profitability—which are integrally tied to positioning the product by market segment. The objective of this article is to outline such an approach, based on the development of a product evaluation matrix.

THE PROPOSED APPROACH

The proposed approach to strategic product line planning has two definitional phases followed by five analytical stages. The definitional phases relate to the determination of the strategic product/market area under consideration and the relevant measurement instruments. The analytical phases include: (1) determination of current and past trends for the product line in terms of industry sales, company sales, market share, and profit; (2) integration of these four scales into a single analytical framework, the *product evaluation matrix;* (3) projection of future performance given *(a) no* changes in marketing strategy or competitive or environmental conditions, and *(b)* a variety of alternative marketing strategies; (4) performance of additional diagnostic analyses to provide further guidelines for the firm's marketing strategies; and (5) incorporation of possible competitive actions and changes in environmental conditions into projection analysis.

---

[2] See, for example: Gosta Mickwitz, *Marketing and Competition* (Helsingfors, Finland: Centraltrykeriet, 1959); Jay W. Forrester, "Advertising: A Problem in Industrial Dynamics," *Harvard Business Review,* vol. 37 (March–April 1959), p. 100; Eberhard E. Schewing, *New Product Management* (Hinsdale, Ill.: Dryden Press, 1974); and Robert D. Buzzell et al., *Marketing: A Contemporary Analysis,* 2nd ed. (New York: McGraw-Hill Book Co., 1972).

[3] For an evaluation of the product life cycle literature, see: Rolando Polli and Victor J. Cook, "Product Life Cycle Models: A Review Paper," working paper, Marketing Science Institute, Cambridge, Mass., 1967; Rolando Polli and Victor J. Cook, "Validity of the Product Life Cycle," *The Journal of Business,* vol. 42 (October 1969), pp. 385–400; and William E. Cox, "Product Life Cycles as Marketing Models," *The Journal of Business,* vol. 40 (October 1967), pp. 375–84.

[4] Sidney Schoeffler, Robert Buzzell, and Donald Heany, "PIMS: A Breakthrough in Strategic Planning," working paper, Marketing Science Institute, Cambridge, Mass., 1974; and Bernard Catry and Michel Chevalier," Market Share Strategy and the Product Life Cycle," *Journal of Marketing,* vol. 38 (October 1974), pp. 29–34.

[5] The Boston Consulting Group, *Product Portfolio,* undated brochure.

The definitional phases

Phase A. Define the relevant universe in terms of the relevant strategic product/market area. This requires determination of:

1. *The product* of concern. The product definitions should be clear and unambiguous, and in all cases they should include the relevant subcategories of the product class at both the company and industry levels.

2. *The strategic market* for the given product and the key segments within it. Again, the more specific the definition is, the more operational the resulting analysis will be. For example, separating the domestic from the international market for automobiles (excluding trucks) can be the first step toward establishing the strategic market for automobiles. Within this broad strategic area, further segmentation can be undertaken, for example, by separating the commercial market from the private market. This can provide sharper focus and meaning to the analysis of the product life cycle of subcompact, compact, intermediate, standard, sport, and luxury automobiles.

Phase B. Establish the relevant measurement instruments in terms of units (e.g., dollar sales or unit sales), necessary adjustments (e.g., sales per capita), and time (e.g., quarterly or annually).

The analytical phases

Phase A. Determine and examine the current and past trends in product sales, market share, and profit position in each relevant strategic product/market area. Specifically, it is necessary to establish the following:

1. *Sales position* for the given product in the strategic market area. Two simple plots of industry and company sales against time are required, followed by the identification of the stage of the product in the classical product life cycle. Each product can be assigned to one of at least three product trend stages: decline, stable (which can in turn be separated into decaying and sustained maturity), and growth. The assignment of a product to one of these three or four categories can be based on the rule established by Polli and Cook[6] or on any other explicit criterion. A sample alternative criterion is:

If the annual sales trend over the past N years is:

Negative, assign to the *Decline* category.

0–10 percent increase, assign to the *Stable* category.

Over 10 percent increase, assign to the *Growth* category.

---

[6] The Polli and Cook approach is based on the percentage change in a product's real sales from one year to the next. Plotting these changes as a normal distribution with mean zero, they determined that if a product has a percentage change less than $.5\sigma$, it is to be classified as in the decline stage. Products with a percentage change greater than $.5\sigma$ were classified as being in the growth stage, and products in the range $\pm.5\sigma$ were considered to be stable. For the application of this approach, see Rolando Polli and Victor J. Cook, "Validity of the Product Life Cycle," *The Journal of Business*, vol. 42 (October 1969).

The determination of the specific criterion and number of categories is, of course, the responsibility of management, and it is likely to differ across industries and companies.

2. *Market share position.* The market share of the company's given product in the strategic product/market area should also be determined. As with the number of sales trend categories and the criterion for category assignment, it is also the responsibility of management to determine the number of market share categories and the assignment criterion. For illustrative purposes, three categories and their corresponding assignment rules are as follows:

If market share is less than 10 percent, assign to the *Marginal* category.

If market share is 10–24 percent, assign to the *Average* category.

If market share is over 25 percent, assign to the *Leading* category.

The market share figures that establish the three categories may, of course, vary from one strategic product/market area to another.

This stage assumes the availability of market share data. In many product areas, such data are available through services such as Nielsen or the Market Research Corporation of America (MRCA). In other areas, a firm may have to rely on expert estimates or relevant secondary sources.[7]

3. *Profit position.* The firm's profit position in the given strategic product/market area must be specified. Again, it is management's responsibility to establish explicit profit categories. These categories—whether based on return on sales, investment, or equity—should be stated explicitly, and at least three levels should be established to distinguish between *below target, target,* and *above target* profit performance.

The three separate analyses of sales, market share, and profitability result in the assignment of each product, in each of the market segments of any given strategic product/market area, into one category in each of the three areas. This is illustrated in Figure 1, which also includes the plotting of the past trends in company and industry sales. market share, and profitability.

Phase B. Once the unidimensional analysis suggested in Phase A is completed, it is necessary to combine the four unidimensional scales—for industry sales, company sales, market share, and profit—into a comprehensive scheme. The integration of the four dimensions into a single analytical framework constitutes the *product evaluation matrix,* which is presented in Figure 2. Positioning all products within this matrix, based on hard data on sales, market share, and profitability, is an essential input to all marketing decisions.

A more advanced approach might be one in which each of the four dimensions is presented as a continuous variable and not as a categorical one

---

[7] Louis W. Stern, "Market Share Determination: A Low Cost Approach," *Journal of Marketing Research,* vol. 1 (August 1964), pp. 40–45.

Figure 1
Establishing a product's sales, market share, and profit position (current and past trends)

ASSIGN PRODUCT TO ONE OF
THE FOLLOWING CATEGORIES: PLOT THE PAST TREND:

Sales   Sales trend

	Industry	Company
1. Decline	_____	_____
2. Stable	_____	_____
3. Growth	_____	_____

Market share   Market share

1. Marginal
   market
   position   _____
2. Average
   market
   position   _____
3. Leading
   market
   position   _____

Profitability   Profitability

1. Below
   target   _____
2. About
   target   _____
3. Above
   target   _____

that is based on some arbitrary decision rule. Yet, even the simple positioning of a product within this matrix provides clear understanding of the current position of the product on those dimensions that are most relevant for managerial control. Conducting such an analysis for all relevant segments of a product/market strategic area provides management with a summary auditing form that highlights the strengths and weaknesses of the firm's product line in all of its market segments.

This picture of product performance (based on current hard data) can be supplemented by a historical trend analysis of the changes in the product's

Figure 2
The product evaluation matrix: A hypothetical example tracing two products over three years

Industry sales	Market share	Decline			Stable			Growth		
	Profitability	Below target	Target	Above target	Below target	Target	Above target	Below target	Target	Above target
Growth	Leading									
Growth	Average								A₇₄	A₇₅
Growth	Marginal				A₇₃					
Stable	Leading									
Stable	Average									
Stable	Marginal									
Decline	Leading									
Decline	Average	B₇₄			B₇₃					
Decline	Marginal	B₇₅								

performance over time. Figure 2 also shows a hypothetical path for two products over a three-year period. Product A has been in a growth industry for these three years. In 1973, its company sales were at a stable level, but they did increase to the growth level in 1974 and 1975. Its market share position improved considerably from a marginal share in 1973 to an average share in 1974 and 1975. The major improvement, however, occurred with respect to its profit performance, moving from below target in 1973 to target in 1974 and above target in 1975.

Examination of the performance of hypothetical product B, however, reveals a bleak situation. The product is in a declining industry; its company sales decreased from 1973 to 1974; and while it maintained an "average market share" in 1973 and 1974, its share weakened to marginal in 1975. The only positive sign is that during these three years profits did not decline.

Phase C. Although the product evaluation matrix provides a useful tool for controlling the performance of the firm's product line and answering the question "Where are we?" it alone cannot serve as a guide for future marketing actions. To provide such a guide, the analysis must incorporate an orientation to the future and the anticipated impact of alternative corporate marketing strategies. This is achieved by the following two steps:

1.   Project the trend in sales, market share, and profitability assuming *no changes* in the firm's marketing strategies and no major changes in competitive actions and environmental conditions. This projection can be based on simple extrapolation of time series data or on any other forecasting procedure used by the firm. It should be done for each product in the strategic product/market area and should provide a range of possible results between the most pessimistic and most optmistic forecasts.

A simplified example of the current and projected positions of two hypothetical products is presented in the first eight columns in the upper panel of Figure 3. These data can then be transferred to the product evaluation matrix (the bottom part of Figure 3) to provide a clear picture of the anticipated trend in the position of each product. At this stage (even without engaging in conditional forecasting), the product evaluation matrix can start providing some useful guidance for the firm's product/marketing strategy for each of its products in the given strategic product/market area.

Product 1 is clearly a poor performer. It is in a declining industry, with declining sales, average market share, and below-target profitability, and if nothing is to change it is likely to stay in this situation (comparison of 1_C with 1_P). Product 2, on the other hand, is in a stable-industry and is expected to increase its sales (moving from a "decline" to a "stable" level in this category), while its market share position and profitability do not change (a move from 2_C to 2_P).

2.   Since the future performance of a product depends to a large extent on the firm's marketing efforts, a *conditional forecast* should be undertaken in which the sales, market share, and profit of each product are forecast under a variety of marketing strategies. Given a number of alternative marketing strategies, a separate forecasting analysis should be conducted for each and the results of the "best" strategy (according to the four dimensions) incorporated into the product evaluation matrix. If no dominant solution (i.e., "best" on all four dimensions) is revealed, all "best" strategies are to be incorporated into the matrix, as illustrated in Figure 3.

Product 1 has two alternative conditional forecasts. Forecast $1'_{CF}$ suggests no change in the sales position (it remains in a declining industry with decreasing company sales), worsening of market share (from average to marginal), but an improvement in profits from below target to target. A second marketing strategy, however, may result in position $1''_{CF}$, which enables the company to maintain an average market share, increase its sales (from "decline" to "stable" stage), but produces no improvement in its profit position, which remains below target. Assuming that only these two strategies are available, management should examine the trade-off between maintaining market share position but being below target on profits versus losing market share but achieving profit objectives.

Product 2, on the other hand, has a single "best" conditional forecast that moves the product from 2_C to 2_{CF}. This suggests that the marketing strategy

Figure 3
Incorporating sales, market share, and profit forecasts into the product evaluation matrix:
A hypothetical example

Product	Current position (C)				Unconditional projection(P)				Conditional forecast (CF)			
	Industry sales	Company sales	Market sales	Profita-bility	Industry sales	Company sales	Market share	Profita-bility	Industry sales	Company sales	Market share	Profita-bility
1	Decline	Decline	Average	Below target	Decline	Decline	Average	Below target	Decline	Decline	Marginal	Target
									Decline	Stable	Average	Below target
2	Stable	Decline	Average	Target	Stable	Stable	Average	Above target	Stable	Stable	Dominant	Target

Company sales		Decline			Stable			Growth		
Industry sales	Profita-bility Market share	Below target	Target	Above target	Below target	Target	Above target	Below target	Target	Above target
Growth	Dominant									
	Average									
	Marginal									
Stable	Dominant					2_{CF}				
	Average	2_C			2_P					
	Marginal									
Decline	Dominant									
	Average	1_C 1_P			$1''_{CF}$					
	Marginal		$1'_{CF}$							

Key: 1, 2 products.
C = Current.
P = Projected position.
CF = Expected position based on results of a conditional forecast analysis.

behind this forecast is likely to result in an improved market share position (from average for 2_P to dominant for 2_{CF}).

Phase D.　To provide further guidelines for the firm's marketing strategies within the strategic product/market area, management may want to make additional diagnoses. Among the more useful diagnostic analyses are those that relate to the competitive structure and the effectiveness of the marketing efforts of the firm. Some of this information may be obtained as a by-product of the conditional forecast analyses, but some may require special studies.

Some of the more useful diagnostic tools are those that focus on the product's competitive position—product positioning[8] and brand-switching matrices—and on the effectiveness of the various marketing strategies, that is, promotion, distribution, and price. These diagnostic analyses can be undertaken using simple graphical analysis (e.g., plotting advertising expenditures or number of outlets against sales or market share or profitability), or they may take advantage of any one of a number of appropriate multivariate statistical techniques, such as multiple regression analysis. Such an analysis could establish the relative importance of each of the pertinent marketing variables for determining the firm's sales, market share, and profits. This, in turn, could result in three critical equations—one for sales, one for market share, and one for profits—that, in the simplified linear case, would be of the form:

$$Y = a + b_1 A - b_2 P + b_3 D$$

Where:

Y = Sales, market share, or profits.

A = The appropriate measures of advertising and promotion (e.g., dollars spent on advertising).

P = The appropriate measure of price (e.g., actual price).

D = The appropriate measure of distribution (e.g., percent of effective distribution obtained).

b_1, b_2, b_3 = Parameter values, which are estimated separately for each equation.

Phase E. The analysis so far has not included an explicit consideration of competitive actions and changes in environmental conditions. To incorporate these factors into the analysis, a market simulation model is called for. Such a simulation can be developed for a given strategic product/market area and be based on four major phases, all of which should result in simulated information on sales, market share, and profit for each of a set of marketing alternatives. These four phases include analysis under the following conditions:

1. No competitive retaliation and no changes in any major environmental factors.
2. Competitive retaliation but no changes in environmental conditions.
3. Changes in environmental conditions but no competitive retaliation.
4. Competitive retaliation and changes in environmental conditions.

---

[8] Yoram Wind and Patrick J. Robinson, "Product Positioning: An Application of Multidimensional Scaling," in *Attitude Research in Transition*, Russell I. Haley, ed. (Chicago: American Marketing Association, 1972), pp. 155–75; and Yoram Wind, "A New Procedure for Concept Evaluation," *Journal of Marketing*, vol. 37 (October 1973), pp. 2–11.

Operationally, such a simulation may be based on a large-scale consumer study coupled with managers' subjective judgments. The consumer study should be aimed at establishing the following input base:

1. Consumers' utilities for various components of any marketing strategy (benefits sought). These utilities can be derived from a conjoint measurement analysis.[9]
2. Evaluation of the products of the firm and its competitors on the relevant benefits.
3. Assessment of the possible impact of different environmental conditions on consumers' utilities for the various benefits and their evaluations of the available product/brand offerings.

A market simulation based on this, a similar,[10] or even a different, structure[11] can serve both as a useful planning tool and as a way of generating inputs for the product evaluation matrix. In the latter context, the simulation can result in estimated sales and market share for any given product under a variety of alternative marketing strategies, anticipated competitive action, and alternative environmental conditions. To provide inputs on the anticipated profitability, it might be useful to couple the market simulation with an appropriate subjective risk analysis or simulation.[12] Thus, information on all four dimensions—industry sales, company sales, market share, and profits—can be incorporated into the product evaluation matrix in the same way that the information from the conditional forecast analysis was incorporated into the matrix, as illustrated in Figure 3.

CONCLUSIONS

A firm's major strategic product/market decision alternatives for its existing product line and the component products of that line in a given strategic product/market area are:

1. Do not change the product or its marketing strategy.
2. Do not change the product but do change its marketing strategy. This may involve a change in the type and level of advertising, distribution,

[9] Paul E. Green and Yoram Wind, *Multiattribute Decisions in Marketing: A Measurement Approach* (Hinsdale, Ill.: The Dryden Press, 1973); and Paul E. Green and Yoram Wind, "New Way To Measure Consumers' Judgment," *Harvard Business Review*, vol. 53 (July–August 1975), pp. 107–17.

[10] Yoram Wind, Steuart Joley, and Arthur O'Connor, "Concept Testing as Input to Strategic Marketing Simulations," in *Proceedings of the April 1975 AMA Conference*, Ed Mazze, ed. (Chicago: American Marketing Association, forthcoming).

[11] Philip Kotler, "Competitive Strategies for New Product Marketing Over the Life Cycle," *Management Science*, vol. 12 (December 1965), pp. 104–19.

[12] David Hergz, "Risk Analysis in Capital Investment," *Harvard Business Review*, vol. 42 (January–February 1964), pp. 91–106; and Edgar A. Pessemier and H. Paul Root, "The Dimensions of New Product Planning," *Journal of Marketing*, vol. 37 (January 1973), pp. 10–18.

and pricing strategies associated with a given positioning and given product attributes.

3. Change the product. This can involve product modifications either within the boundaries of the product's current market positioning or within a new positioning. Alternatively, it may involve no product modifications but rather a repositioning. In either case, a change in the associated marketing strategy is required.

4. Discontinue the product or the product line. This strategy may involve an interim product or product line "run out" (milking) strategy, pruning of the product line, or the immediate phasing-out of the product or the complete line.[13]

5. Introduce new product(s) into the line or add new product lines.

Traditional product life cycle analysis provides little guidance for making these decisions. It ignores the competitive setting of the product, the relevant profit considerations, and the fact that product sales are a function of the marketing effort of the firm and other environmental forces. The objective of this article was to propose a way of overcoming these shortcomings by taking these variables into account and hence providing management with the necessary product evaluation information for making the above decisions.

The results of experimentation with this approach in the International Harvester Company are encouraging, and the approach is now used on a regular basis in the preparation of all the firm's marketing plans. It is our belief that following the suggested approach (whether using the suggested criteria of sales, market share, and profitability, or others) may improve the strategic product/marketing decisions of industrial and consumer products companies.

The proposed approach requires five levels of analysis, each with an increasing specificity of guidance, for the firm's strategic marketing decisions. The first level is based on the evaluation of the product's current position with regard to industry and company sales, market share, and profitability, and it provides the vaguest and most limited guidance. The fifth level, on the other hand, provides detailed and specific guidance based on projected product position with regard to sales, market share, and profitability under alternative marketing strategies, anticipated competitive actions, and alternative environmental conditions. Table 1 summarizes these five levels of analysis.

Not every product/market situation requires the complete analysis at all five levels. Even in its simplest form (level 1) the product evaluation matrix goes well beyond traditional product life cycle analysis and offers valuable guidelines for product line management. Product performance information based on *hard data* on sales, market share, and profitability by strategic product/market units puts into context the commonly collected consumer-based positioning/segmentation information. The approach can also be

---

[13] Walter J. Talley, Jr., "Profiting from the Declining Product," *Business Horizons,* vol. 7 (Spring 1964), pp. 77–84; and Philip Kotler, "Phasing Out Weak Products," *Harvard Business Review,* vol. 43 (March–April 1965), pp. 107–18.

Table 1
Levels of analysis and specificity of guidance provided by the product evaluation matrix

Specificity of guidance	Nature of operation	Stage in the analysis
Lowest	1. Current product position on industry sales, company sales, market share, and profitability	A and B
	2. Projected product position on sales, market share, and profitability, assuming no major changes in the firm's marketing activities, competitive action, and environmental conditions	C-1
	3. Projected product position on sales, market share, and profitability under alternative marketing strategies (conditional forecast), assuming no major changes in competitive action and environmental conditions	C-2
	4. The above plus diagnostic insights into the competitive structure and the effectiveness of the firm's marketing activities	D
Highest	5. Projected product position on sales, market share, and profitability under alternative marketing strategies, anticipated competitive action, and alternative environmental conditions (based on computer simulation)	E

applied to competitive products, thus providing management with an ongoing performance audit of its own and competitors' products.

QUESTIONS

1. Explain briefly, in your own words, what is involved in each of the five analytical phases proposed by Wind and Claycamp.

*2. Explain what the authors' approach contributes beyond traditional product life cycle analysis (Reading 16).

3. The authors' approach is useful at International Harvester, but could it be useful (at reasonable cost) for a small firm? Explain your answer.

4. Would the approach be appropriate for not-for-profit organizations? If yes, explain why. If no, what modifications would have to be made to make it useful?

---

* Question relates concepts in this and other readings.

29
A conceptual framework for multinational marketing

Warren J. Keegan

Multinational marketing is different from domestic marketing in that a particular company operates simultaneously in two or more national markets with different environmental conditions. This may require only small changes in its strategic planning, or perhaps quite large ones. This article presents a framework to help multinational firms operate more effectively in a global economy consisting of 142 national markets.

A leading international businessman recently observed, "There is no such thing as a multinational market. We have domestic markets worldwide but no multinational markets. There are, to be exact, 142 national markets worldwide. Each one of these markets is unique in the sense that it is not exactly like any other market, and therefore each is a domestic market. Yet, any company which is marketing simultaneously in two or more national markets is involved in a process of international or multinational marketing."

The growing involvement in international marketing has created a need for a conceptual framework to guide practice and programs. What is multinational marketing? What dimensions, if any, distinguish multinational marketing from domestic marketing? How should marketers conceptualize the task of multinational marketing?

There are similarities and differences in all markets, domestic and foreign, but the concepts of marketing science are universally applicable. Basic marketing concepts such as the product life cycle and traditional marketing tools such as market segmentation are as applicable in Athens, Greece as they are in Athens, Georgia.

There are three basic dimensions of multinational marketing which differentiate it from domestic marketing. The first is environmental. Unlike his domestic counterpart, a multinational marketer must respond to many different national market environments. At the beginning of a company's international involvement, activities outside the home-country market are referred to as "foreign" marketing and require the management of the same activities as domestic marketing, but in an unfamiliar national environment.

Source: Reprinted with permission from the *Columbia Journal of World Business,* November 1972, pp. 67–76. At the time of writing, Warren Keegan was an assistant professor of business administration at the Columbia University Graduate School of Business.

One company's foreign market is, of course, another company's home or base environment. France is a foreign market to a U.S. manufacturer who has never operated there, but it is the home market for all French-based manufacturers. To a U.S. company with operations in France, the country may be simultaneously a "foreign" market to the U.S. headquarters and a "domestic" market for the company's French subsidiary. Over time, the U.S. company with operations in France may cease to think of France as a foreign market and consider it one of the company's market areas, no more "foreign" than an area in the United States. This occurs when French operations become truly integrated into the corporate operating structure, and the company has shifted in orientation from the binary domestic-foreign market concept set for operating markets to a unitary definition of operating markets in which they are all considered simply as "operating" markets. In such a company, "foreign" markets would simply be considered as markets in which the company has not yet established operations.

In a growing number of companies the concept of "foreign" is breaking down because of the growing involvement of the corporate headquarters in the company's marketing programs wherever they are located. ITT, for example, has product and functional specialists at headquarters who are responsible for marketing operations on a global basis. To these specialists, and to the president of ITT, there is no such thing as a "foreign" market in the psychological sense—there are markets in different parts of the world, at different stages of development, with different characteristics. Company operating units exist in each of these markets, and these units are expected to understand their own markets in depth. ITT knows as much about the French market for telecommunications equipment as it knows about the U.S. market.

A second dimension of multinational marketing which differentiates it from domestic marketing is the process of crossing national boundaries with a product, a price, or some aspect of an advertising, promotion or selling program. Crossing boundaries of sovereign nations requires passing through national controls which apply to goods and services. Some of these controls, such as tariffs and quotas, apply only to certain foreign-sourced goods. Others, such as safety regulations, apply to all goods regardless of origin. These terms of entry apply not only to products, but frequently to prices, advertising and other aspects of a marketing program. A multinational marketer must know what these terms are in each national market and incorporate them as parameters of his international marketing plan.

The third dimension of multinational marketing arises because a company markets its products simultaneously in more than one national environment. This results in issues and opportunities which are distinct from those associated with the crossing of national boundaries. A multinational marketer must evaluate and compare respective national market opportunities. He must decide who should perform marketing functions in the organization. For example, to what extent should marketing planning and control be autonomously performed by subsidiary management groups? To what extent should headquarters be involved in country marketing analysis, planning and control? To what extent should control and delivery of marketing services, such as marketing research and advertising creative work and management, rest at headquarters? To what extent can lessons gained in one market be applied in other national markets? To what extent can practices and techniques be applied across national boundaries? To what extent should products, prices, advertising, etc. be standardized to achieve global optimization of net profits? These are just a few of the questions raised when a company seeks to relate its activities in multiple nations to each other in ways that enhance the effectiveness of each national marketing program and the effectiveness of the total world marketing effort. Without a conceptual framework answers are difficult, if not impossible.

The major factors which constitute the environment of global marketing are depicted in Figure 1. At the center of the diagram is the company, defined in four major dimensions: its products, its marketing skills (particularly the marketing skills of product, communications, distribution, pricing and market-

Figure 1
The company in a world of clusters of national market environments

The Company

	Marketing skills
	Identifying global opportunities and threats
Products	Product development
	Advertising and promotion
	Distribution
	Pricing
	Research
Resources	Other skills
Manpower	Production
Financial	Research
Physical	Logistic
	Managerial
	Financial

Market cluster 1*
Market cluster 2*
Market cluster 3*
Market cluster 4*

* Note: The number of market clusters shown here is arbitrary. In any specific situation, the number of clusters used for operating and analytical purposes will depend upon the characteristics of the markets and the operating strategy of the company.

The objective in forming clusters is to maximize the within-cluster similarity of markets and the between-cluster differences on specific and weighted characteristics. These typically include such characteristics as location, income levels, market size, channel structure, language, communications infrastructure, etc. Each company must identify characteristics that are crucial to its own market success and weight these characteristics. The weights of characteristics may be different in clustering markets for operating purposes as opposed to analytical purposes. For example, for operating clusters, distance and proximity may be the most important market characteristics because of a need to minimize transportation and communications costs. In the same company, clusters developed for analytical purposes might ignore distance and proximity.

ing research management), other skills (production, R&D, financial and managerial skills), and its resources (manpower, financial and physical).

The company's products, skills and resources are the endogenous factors in the conceptual framework. The most important of these is the product(s) which a company offers in international markets. One useful way of looking at products internationally is to place them on a continuum of environmental sensitivity. At one end of the continuum are the environmentally insensitive products, that is products which do not require adaptation to differences in the economic and social environments of markets around the world. Typically, such products are industrial and are adapted to universal rather than local technology. A company with environmentally insensitive products will have to spend relatively little time finding out about the specific and unique conditions of local markets, since the product the company offers is basically universal. A computer line is an example of a relatively environmentally insensitive product.

At the other end of the continuum are those products which are highly sensitive to differences in economic, social and cultural, physical and governmental factors in national markets. The company in the business of marketing environmentally sensitive products will have to spend a great deal of time and effort to learn how its products interact with the environment of specific national markets. Convenience foods are an example of relatively environmentally sensitive products.

Skills are a second major category of endogenous resource. A primary skill of a multinational marketer is the ability to identify local opportunities and threats. When a company is entering international markets for the first time, the development of this skill is a first requirement. Since there are 142 different national markets, it is rarely feasible to study each of them in depth. In practice, a company must develop criteria for screening national markets in order to select those which present the greater opportunity. As a company grows internationally, an additional dimension arises: how best to allocate resources among existing markets.

Evaluating opportunities is not just a simple matter of finding the biggest existing market. Demand, competition and the degree of market difference from known markets are each important considerations. The first step in evaluating local opportunities is demand analysis. Two types of demand must be considered:

1. *Existing demand, or actual current sales in a market.* This consists of local production plus imports minus exports. Although such data are often lacking, various estimating techniques can be used.
2. *Latent demand.* This is demand which would exist if a desired product was offered at an acceptable price. In the United States latent demand has historically been tapped by new product developments, such as the Polaroid Land camera. The demand for instant photography already existed before this product was introduced.

The international company has a unique opportunity to tap latent demand by taking a product which it has marketed in one or more nations and introducing it to other national makets where the product has not previously been sold. If it chooses markets with enough similarity to those where it already has experience, it can apply that experience to the new market. Instead of marketing an entirely new product, the company is marketing a new international product. Skillfully done, this can substantially improve the chances of success as compared to those of new product introductions in a domestic market.

Demand levels for a product must be evaluated in the light of expected competition. The difficult choice is between large, often fast-growing competitive markets where the major challenge is the existing competition vs. smaller, less competitive markets. This is a strategic issue which must be resolved in the light of each company's appraisal of its best relative opportunity.

Another factor involved in the choice of new foreign markets is the degree of similarity existing between them and already-known markets. The greater the similarity to known markets the less there is to learn and the more applicable is previous experience. One of the reasons U.S. companies frequently begin their international market expansion in Canada and the United Kingdom is that these markets exhibit many characteristics in common with the U.S. market, not the least of which are language and the legal system.

In the end, a company must compare opportunities and threats involved in global expansion of markets to its own capabilities and decide on whether to expand; and if so upon a sequence of national markets entry. It must back this decision with a commitment of resources (people, money and facilities), the third endogenous factor in the conceptual framework.

Irrespective of the general nature of opportunities and threats, a company must have the skills to formulate successful marketing programs in each national market selected. Most companies find it necessary to assemble a national marketing staff as a part of each national subsidiary. These staffs are a major marketing resource of a global company.

The company exists in a world of 142 different national market environments. Each of these environments is unique. Yet each contains elements of commonality and similarity. The task of the multinational marketer is to recognize both similarities and differences. He can then respond to the unique dimensions of each market and still effectively transfer his marketing know-how to develop effective marketing programs. As a multinational organization develops, the transfer of know-how should shift first from a home-country to subsidiary pattern; then to an organic flow from within the multinational-country system. Regardless of the country of location, know-how and experience with potential applications elsewhere in the world should be exploited.

To break down the complexity of managing and coordinating large numbers of foreign subsidiaries, international managers have often adopted regional groupings which cluster countries exhibiting within-group similarities and between-group differences. The major dimension used has been physical proximity. Typical regional groupings would be the Americas, Europe, Asia and Africa, each combining countries that are reasonably similar in terms of broad environmental dimensions. Such regional groupings reduce the time and money costs of travel for the personnel involved.

These geographic groups, however, may be less useful for analytic purposes than groups or clusters based on other environmental dimensions. The marketer may find it more useful to cluster countries on the basis of market development as indicated by various economic, market and social measures. The clusters developed will depend upon the technique, the dimensions used and the weight assigned to each dimension. If stage-of-market development is specified as a major dimension, then the country clusters in Figure 1 would be based upon income. This would result in clusters of the respective high-, middle- and low-income countries of Europe, Asia, Africa and the Americas rather than geographic clusters.

Seven major dimensions of each national market environment are shown in Figure 2. These dimensions provide the exogenous influences or dimensions of a conceptual framework. Each of the dimensions is highly diverse from one part of the world to another. Stage-of-market development, for example, may be measured by per-capita GNP, which ranges from a low of $60 per annum in several African countries to the high in the United States of over $4,000. However, within this wide range of global per-capita GNP, there are clusters of countries at the bottom, in the middle and at the top which are sufficiently similar to provide a unifying influence.

Another important market characteristic is size as measured by total national income. The U.S. market, with over a trillion dollars in annual income, is enormous. Other industrialized countries with incomes on a per-capita basis quite similar or close to those in the United States are relatively small in the aggregate. A good example would be Sweden, whose per-capita GNP in 1969 was $3,553, but whose GNP was only $28 billion. At these extremes, the size of markets is a highly differentiating influence. The structure, information system and control system appropriate for the Swedish marketing organization would be grossly inadequate for an organization which obtains a comparable share of the U.S. market. A company which is simultaneously marketing in large and small markets cannot adopt a unified approach to both. If it did, it would find itself with organizations, information systems and control systems which were either inadequate or too elaborate for the size of the market.

Marketing facilities are highly varied. Television, for example, is unavailable in some markets such as South Africa, but it is the major advertising medium in Latin America. Food retailing is mainly via supermarkets in highly developed markets, but such outlets hardly exist in less-developed countries.

The legal environment, including tariffs, taxes, laws, regulations and codes, differs greatly from country to country. For example, companies marketing equipment used in the construction and building trades must face a

Figure 2
Major dimensions of a national market environment: Absolute and compared to other nations

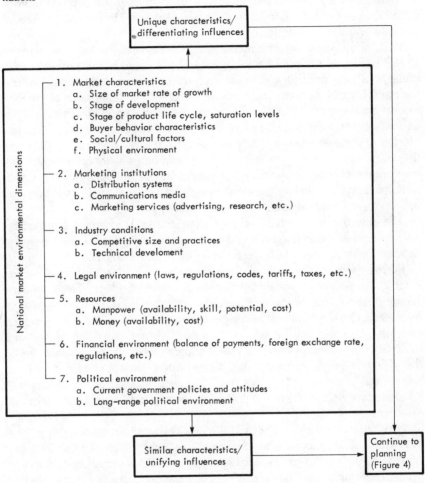

welter of codes and regulations which differ not only internationally but also within local political jurisdictions. The purpose sought by these regulations is not always a reliable guide to appropriate action. Consider, for example, the situation of a crane manufacturer. In many countries cranes must have a free-fall capability for instantly releasing their load in order to make the cranes safer. A crane with the capability of a free-fall displacement of its load is difficult to tip over. In other countries, however, there is a requirement that a crane *not* have a free-fall capability. This prohibition against free fall is also motivated by a desire to increase the safety of the crane operation. The rationale behind the prohibition of free-fall capability is that any crane with this capability is liable to lose its entire load accidentally and thereby cause an accident. Hence, any company that wishes to market this product internationally must be able to offer both types of crane—those with a free-fall capacity and those without.

Each of the seven major dimensions of the national market environments shown in Figure 2 should be analyzed and evaluated in the process of formulating a local marketing plan for each national market. At the same time, the multinational marketer must evaluate each of the dimensions of the local market environment in relationship to the rest of the world and in its relationship to a cluster of markets. The analysis should focus on the unique characteristics of the market which differentiate it from other national markets and the characteristics which it has in common with other national markets.[1] This environmental analysis of differentiating and unifying influences is the basis of a multinational marketing plan that integrates each national marketing plan into an overall multinational marketing strategy.

The objective of multinational marketing strategy is to optimize the utilization of company products, skills and resources on a global basis as opposed to national optimization, which results in a global suboptimization.[2]

Perceptive response to the unique characteristics of each national market is the major task of the local staff of each country subsidiary. This marketing group must do what domestic marketers do throughout the world—analyze their marketing environment and subsidiary capabilities and identify products and services which can be sold at a profit. Since the subsidiary is part of a multinational system, a major potential source of subsidiary capability lies in the ability of the subsidiary to tap the products, skills and resources of its parent and of other subsidiaries in the system. The subsidiary shares with headquarters responsibility for searching for applicable products, skills and resources.

Headquarters marketers bear the major responsibility in a multinational system to search for similar characteristics and unifying influences that provide opportunities to standardize elements of the global marketing program. There are major benefits of standardization, including cost savings in product development and manufacture, in packaging and in advertising and promotional programs. Another major advantage of identifying unifying features is the possibility of exploiting good ideas and people on a global basis.[3]

---

[1] See John Fayerweather, *International Business Management* (New York: McGraw Hill, 1969).

[2] It can be demonstrated that in any system of interdependent parts, the optimization of sub-systems makes it impossible to optimize the total system and, conversely, the optimization of the total system precludes the systematic optimization of sub-systems. See Russell L. Ackoff, *A Concept of Corporate Planning* (New York: Wiley Interscience, 1970).

[3] See, for example, Robert D. Buzzell, "Can You Standardize Multinational Marketing?" *Harvard Business Review,* November–December 1968.

One writer calls this "leverage."[4] There are three leverage opportunities for multinational marketers:

1. *Program transfers.* Multinational marketers can draw upon strategies, products, advertising appeals, sales management practices and promotional ideas that have been tested in several markets and apply them in comparable markets on a global basis. To the extent that a multinational company becomes successful in drawing upon its international experience in marketing programs it has an advantage over the purely domestic company, which draws upon its experience in only a single market.

2. *System transfers.* Again, to the extent that multinational marketers can identify similar characteristics in national markets they can use planning, budgeting and other successful marketing systems previously developed and tested in national markets.

3. *People transfers.* As marketers in multinational companies acquire the expertise required to identify the potentials and risks of national markets throughout the world it becomes increasingly possible to assign skilled marketing people across national boundaries. A manpower pool with international rather than national dimensions is thus available.

To exploit leverage opportunities the global company marketing staff must necessarily work together. Each marketing staff group in the global company illustrated in Figure 3 reports to a line manager responsible for a country, region, international division or the entire corporation. At the same time, there is a dotted-line relationship symbolizing coordination and involvement of marketing at all levels in the organization. A major purpose of this multilevel coordination and involvement is to identify leverage opportunities. In addition, this coordination insures that marketing analysis is worldwide and not divided into unrelated national assessments.

The endogenous and exogenous elements of this conceptual framework are related in Figure 4 to a suggested process of marketing analysis, planning and control. Key questions for each step of this process are suggested. The sequence consists of environmental analysis and company analysis leading to a strategic decision regarding marketing objectives and resources (people, money and facilities) which will be committed. These strategic decisions must then be expressed in operational plans, and the whole organization must be structured to fit their requirements. Finally, auditing and marketing control is necessary to insure that actual and desired results are as close together as possible.

---

[4] Ralph Z. Sorenson, associate professor of marketing at the Harvard Business School, first suggested the concept of multinational marketing leverage. Professor Sorenson is currently completing a study entitled *Multinational Marketing Leverages: A Study of Multinational Marketing Transfers within Nondurable Consumer Goods Firms.*

Figure 3
Marketing functional staff in a multinational company

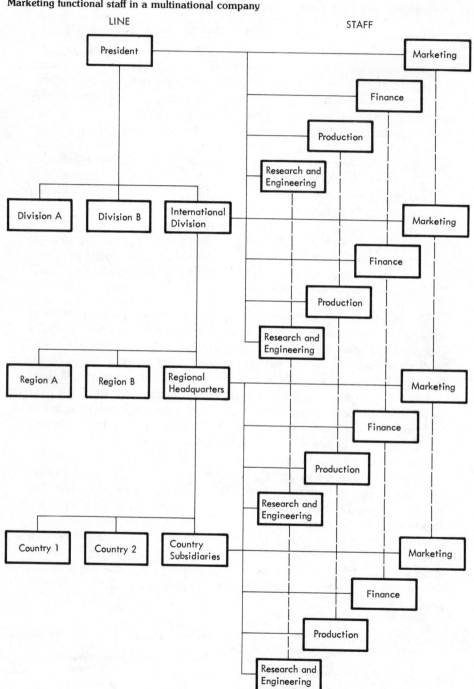

Figure 4
The multinational market management process

Key Questions for Analysis, Planning, and Control of Global Marketing

Environmental Analysis of National Markets (see Figure 2 for details of environmental dimensions)

Environmental analysis
1. What are the unique characteristics (see Figure 2 for characteristics) of each national market? What characteristics does each market have in common with other national markets?
2. Can we cluster national markets for operating and/or planning purposes? What dimensions of markets should we use to cluster markets?

Strategic planning
3. Who should be involved in marketing decisions?
4. What are our major assumptions about target markets? Are they valid?
5. What needs are satisfied by our products in target markets?
6. What customer benefits are provided by our product in target markets?
7. What are the conditions under which our products are used in the target markets?
8. How large is the ability to buy our products in target markets?
9. What are our major strengths and weaknesses relative to existing and potential competition in target markets?
10. Should we extend, adapt, or invent products, prices, advertising, and promotion programs for target markets?
11. What is the balance-of-payments and currency situation in target markets? Will we be able to remit earnings? Is the political climate acceptable?
12. What are our objectives given the alternatives open to us and our assessment of opportunity, risk, and company capability?

Strategic Planning

Structure
13. How do we structure our organization to optimally acheive our objectives, given our skills and resources? What is the responsibility of each organizational level?

Structure

Operational planning
14. Given our objectives, structure, and our assessment of the market environment, how do we implement effective operational marketing plans? What products will we market, at what prices, through what channels, with what communications, in which markets and market clusters?

Operational Planning

Controlling the Marketing Program

Controlling the marketing program
15. How do we measure and monitor plan performance? What steps should be taken to ensure that marketing objectives are met?

Multinational marketing management is one of the most dynamic areas in marketing today as the multinational corporations continue to extend their operations to the far corners of the world. The conceptual framework proposed relates the company to the global market environment and suggests a process for developing and implementing a global marketing plan.

QUESTIONS

1. What are the three basic dimensions of multinational marketing which differentiate it from domestic marketing?

2. Identify the major factors that Keegan suggests are important in the selection of foreign markets to be served. How do these differ from factors used to select domestic market segments?
3. Discuss the concept of leverage. Is this a concept that could be applied in domestic markets to help in developing effective marketing strategies?

30
Marketing information systems: A new dimension for marketing research

Richard H. Brien and James E. Stafford

A basic requirement for effective marketing decisions is adequate information. This article discusses the role that a marketing information system (MIS) could play in providing the necessary information. Brien and Stafford also show that a marketing information system is an expansion rather than a replacement for traditional marketing research.

Business enterprise in the United States is caught in an ironic dilemma: our economic system generates a massive volume of data daily, and the rate of information generation appears to be increasing exponentially; yet most managers continue to complain that they have insufficient, inappropriate, or untimely information on which to base operating decisions.

In 1958, Adrian McDonough observed: "Half the cost of running our economy is the cost of information. No other field offers such concentrated room for improvement as does information analysis."[1] Today, a decade later, the need for efficient information management is even greater, perhaps especially for marketing management since its job is to match the firm's products with dynamic markets. Marketing is inextricably caught up in the "Communications Revolution." The new era, "The Age of Information," will emphasize the information gathering and processing structure of the organization.

Source: Reprinted with permission from the *Journal of Marketing*, published by the American Marketing Association, vol. 33 (July 1968), pp. 19–23. At the time the article was published, Richard Brien and James Stafford were both assistant professors of marketing at the University of Houston.

[1] "Today's Office—Room for Improvement," *Dun's Review and Modern Industry*, vol. 73 (September 1958), p. 50.

It is the contention of this article that the problem of securing adequate decision information for marketing must, and now can, be seen from a broader perspective than previously has been the case. In seeking to establish a new outlook on a matter it is often helpful to cast the problem in new terms. The new perspective from which this inquiry will be launched is that of "managerial systems." The process of developing timely, pertinent decision data for marketing management can now be characterized more meaningfully, even if somewhat prematurely, as the functioning of a "marketing information system" rather than simply as "marketing research."

THE ROLE OF MARKETING RESEARCH

Where does research fit into the marketing management process? If the marketing concept—with its emphasis on integrated decision-making—were widely accepted and implemented, the answer would be fairly clear. Research would be used to analyze specified relationships in the various functional areas of marketing, but the emphasis would be on its use in a coordinated, systematic fashion in order to make the total marketing strategy of the firm more efficient. (See Figure 1.)

Research findings would serve at the outset as a basis for establishing objectives and formulating an apparently optimal plan. At this stage the role of research essentially would be *to predict* the results of alternative business decisions (for example, a "penetration" price versus a "skimming" price, or information dissemination through salesmen rather than through advertising). (See the "A" feedbacks in Figure 1.)

If the research effort were extended full cycle, periodic post hoc studies would be conducted *to evaluate* the execution of specific aspects or phases of the marketing program ("B" feedbacks in Figure 1). In this role, research would provide the basis for control, modification, or redirection of the overall program.

Control and modification (or redirection), in sum, represent *reformulation*, and the "B" feedbacks (evaluative) in fact would become "A" feedbacks (formulative), for the succeeding stage of the marketing program. This condition simply underscores the fact that marketing management is an ongoing process, or—in the newer terminology—a dynamic system.

Formulative and evaluative information can also come *from inside the firm*, notably from the accounting department. This information flow typically is not considered part of "marketing research." It is definitely an integral part, however, of a marketing information system.

Under the marketing concept, research should also help to anticipate new profit opportunities for the firm in the form of new products or services (the "C" feedback in Figure 1). In many U.S. industries—especially consumer goods industries—the rate of product innovation, the rate of new product failure, and the cost of new product failure are all extremely high and still rising. To survive in such dynamic markets the firm must try to develop a

Figure 1
The marketing management process and information flow

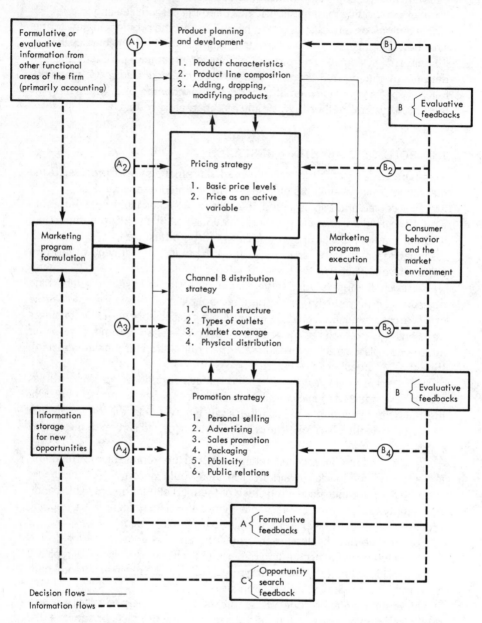

Decision flows ————
Information flows — — —

sensitivity to changes in consumer behavior and in the conditions that influence behavior, both of which create opportunities for successful new products.

It is meaningless to talk of a new product without considering at the same time the related marketing decisions (the rest of that product's marketing mix) that will have to be made. This consideration would bring the cycle back to the formulative role of research (the "A" feedbacks), suggesting again that marketing research really *should be a coordinating agent*. Each marketing decision should be thought of as an input in the dynamic system, and research should be used as an agent to assist in phasing the inputs. The common goal of the decision inputs is the profitable satisfaction of consumer needs or wants; this brings the matter back to the marketing concept, and the package seems reasonably complete. In fact, if marketing research and the marketing concept had this kind of relationship in widespread practice, the case for marketing information systems would be considerably weakened.

RESEARCH BY FITS AND STARTS

A recent survey revealed that unfortunately there is still considerable confusion and wide divergence of opinion regarding the definition and managerial implications of the marketing concept.[2] Especially disappointing was the failure of many companies to cite customer-orientation and integrated decision-making as important aspects of the concept. One of the consequences of this narrow view has been the evolution of marketing research somewhat "by fits and starts."

A widely used definition of marketing research is "the systematic gathering, recording, and analyzing of data about problems relating to the marketing of goods and services."[3] Unfortunately, the research procedure has tended to be unsystematic, to emphasize data collection per se instead of the development of decision-pertinent information, and to concern itself with isolated problems almost on an ad hoc basis. "There is a widespread failure to visualize marketing research as a continuing process of inquiry in which executives are helped to think more effectively."[4]

TOWARD MARKETING INFORMATION SYSTEMS

The systems approach to marketing management is breathing new life into marketing research. The emphasis that systems theory places on interaction and integration in the decision-making process makes it clear that the par-

---

[2] Martin L. Bell, *Marketing: Concepts and Strategy* (Boston: Houghton Mifflin Company, 1966), p. 10.

[3] Committee on Definitions of the American Marketing Association, Ralph S. Alexander, Chairman, *Marketing Definitions: A Glossary of Marketing Terms* (Chicago: American Marketing Association, 1962), pp. 16–17.

[4] Joseph W. Newman, "Put Research into Marketing Decisions," *Harvard Business Review*, vol. 40 (March–April 1962), p. 106.

ticularistic, "brush-fire" approach that has characterized traditional marketing research is rapidly becoming obsolete. What is needed is "a *marketing intelligence* system tailored to the needs of each marketer. Such a system would serve as the ever-alert nerve center of the marketing operation."[5]

The "nerve center" concept is the theme used by Philip Kotler, who has drafted a blueprint for a new organizational unit within the firm, the Marketing Information and Analysis Center (MIAC).[6] MIAC represents a complete overhaul and expansion of the marketing research department into a comprehensive executive marketing information service.

Definition of MIS

Despite minor variations in terminology, it is clear that many of the critics of the narrow view of the role of marketing research are advocating a common concept—"the concept of careful search to generate a flow of ideas and information which will help executives make better decisions."[7]

The notion of a sustained flow of decision-information leads to the term, "marketing information system," defined as follows:

> A structured, interacting complex of persons, machines, and procedures designed to generate an orderly flow of pertinent information collected from both intra- and extra-firm sources, for use as the bases for decision-making in specified responsibility areas of marketing management.

It will be helpful to take a closer look at the essential components of the definition: first, a *structured, interacting complex.* The important notion here is that the marketing information system is a carefully developed master plan for information flow, with explicit objectives and a home in the formal organization. Successful information systems will not evolve spontaneously within the organization, nor will they result if their creation is left exclusively to information technicians. Donald Cox and Robert Good point out that a characteristic common to each of the companies that so far has had success with its marketing information system is the *support of top management.*[8]

A marketing information system is a structured, interacting complex of *persons, machines, and procedures,* requiring the coordinated efforts of many departments and individuals, including:

Top management.
Marketing management, brand management.

[5] Lee Adler, "Systems Approach to Marketing," *Harvard Business Review,* vol. 45 (May–June 1967), p. 110.

[6] Philip Kotler, "A Design for the Firm's Marketing Nerve Center," *Business Horizons,* vol. 9 (Fall 1966), p. 70.

[7] Same reference as footnote 4, p. 106.

[8] Donald F. Cox and Robert E. Good, "How to Build a Marketing Information System," *Harvard Business Review,* vol. 45 (May–June 1967), p. 149.

Sales management.
New product groups.
Market research personnel.
Control and finance departments.
Systems analysts and designers.
Operations researchers, statisticians, and model builders.
Programmers.
Computer equipment experts and suppliers.[9]

It is clear that in traditional management terms both line and staff personnel inevitably will be involved in any marketing information system.
Decision-makers will have to be a great deal more precise in specifying their
information needs, and a complete crew of information specialists will be
called upon to satisfy them.

What is not clear is the determination of the most effective organization
pattern for implementing and administering the system. In fact, the organization problem is probably the greatest deterrent to the more rapid and widespread diffusion of the information systems concept. The question, like many
others in the area of organization structure, is not generically answerable;
each firm's system will have to be tailor-made.

One of the major factors that makes it meaningful to talk of information
systems is the tremendous improvement since World War II in information
handling *technology and machinery*. The building of the first primitive computer, only slightly more than two decades ago, has been designated the
beginning of a revolution in the information sciences.

There has been some confusion, however, about the relationship between
computers and information systems. They are not synonymous; nor is either
the sine qua non of the other. The system is the structure and procedure of
the entire organization's communicative process; the computer is a processing
device that may or may not be included in the information system.

The consideration of the use of computers has, however, forced many
organizations to pay explicit attention to their information systems. "The
flexibility and power of the new tool, as well as its great cost, has caused many
managers to think for the first time of formally planning their information
flows and processing functions."[10]

Business information systems include many machines other than the computer, and some of them promise to have an impact on future systems that
will rival the computer's influence. In particular, data copying, storage, and
retrieval machines have greatly expanded management's information processing capability.

It is estimated that in 1966 some half a million duplicating machines

---

[9] Same reference as footnote 8.

[10] Frederick G. Withington, *The Use of Computers in Business Organizations* (Reading,
Mass.: Addison-Wesley, 1966), p. 3.

spewed out 400 billion copies.[11] At the same time, a new document storage system was developed permitting the storage of up to 500,000 single-page documents on a single 7,200-foot reel of videotape. This means that roughly 20,000 articles or chapters from books could be stored on one reel, with a retrieval time measured in seconds.

But the physical capacity to generate and process fantastic volumes of data at very high speed is an asset only if the types of data to be gathered and the sources from which they are to be elicited are carefully prescribed. The definition of a marketing information system alleged that it is *designed to generate an orderly flow of pertinent information collected from both intra- and extra-firm sources.*

Computer-based reporting systems

Internal information includes fundamental records of costs, shipments, and sales and any analyses of these that can be made to measure the firm's performance (distribution cost analysis, market shares by product and region, and the like). The computer and more progressive accounting departments that see their role as the provision of management information rather than as simply "scorekeeping" have been two of the most important contributors to the integration of such data, on a regular basis, into the marketing information flow.

Many companies are experimenting with "computerized marketing information" in an attempt to shorten the delay between the performance of their products in the market and the receipt of performance reports. In doing so, they stand to sharpen their strategy by gaining valuable lead-time over their competitors.

One producer and nationwide marketer of consumer goods gets monthly reports on 3,000 key accounts 20 days earlier than before, thanks to computer-based reporting systems. Each account is compared with its performance at the same point in time during the previous year and with the company's current total volume in the particular market zone. Also provided are gross daily tabulations for each package size of each brand by geographic district.

When the doors open each morning at another company, a major grocery products manufacturer, marketing management has a complete sales analysis and inventory position as of closing time the previous day. The data are fed by teletypewriter from the company's sales offices and warehouses to a central computer which analyzes the day's orders. In addition, each salesman is required to "mark sense" his daily call reports and send them in to headquarters each evening for computer analysis. Once accumulated, these reports on the in-store impact of frontings, shelf positions, and point-of-sale materials

---

[11] E. B. Weiss, "The Communications Revolution and How It Will Affect All Business and All Marketing," a special issue reprinted from *Advertising Age* (Chicago: Advertising Publications, Inc., 1966), p. 22.

provide marketing management with an up-to-date retail product-movement picture.[12]

Integrating research into the MIS

The most important notion in these examples is that a timely, basic data flow has been established to chart the firm's progress and raise warning signals when there is a marketing malfunction. Such a framework will make additional data needs much clearer, allowing special supplementary information to be collected, *as needed,* from external sources through surveys, panels, or experiments. At this point, then, the proper order will have been established: *the need for conducting "marketing research" and the technique to be used will be determined in the context of specific managerial information requirements.*

Such an approach will help assure that any data gathered are *pertinent,* another important aspect of the definition of a marketing information system. It is perhaps a more grievous sin to collect unnecessary or redundant information than it is to fail to collect any data at all about a particular matter. Superfluous information costs money to develop and wastes decision-makers' time; it represents a serious misallocation of managerial resources. It must be remembered, the definition asserts, that the data generated are to be used as *the bases for decision-making in specified responsibility areas of marketing management.*

Thus, the questions of the types of data the information system is to generate and the sources from which it is to elicit the data really can be answered only in the framework of a careful designation of the organizational decision-structure and the specification of the information requirements for the decision process. In fact, according to many organizational theorists, information processing and decision-making are inseparable in practice. A decision occurs only on "the receipt of some kind of communication, it consists of a complicated process of combining communications from various sources and it results in the transmission of further communications."[13]

Mr. Paul Funk, executive vice-president of McCann/ITSM, contends that marketing information management is the basic business of business: "Only by putting together an overall construction of the total marketing process; only by identifying—and in most instances by visualizing—interrelationships, information flows, concurrent and sequential work patterns and critical decision points can one truly grasp control of the bewildering and complex range of activities engaged in by the present-day major cooperation."[14]

The pursuit of marketing information systems, then, really involves much

---

[12] Same reference as footnote 11, pp. 13–14.

[13] John T. Dorsey, Jr., "A Communication Model for Administration," *Administrative Science Quarterly,* vol. 2 (December 1957), p. 309.

[14] "Why Industrial Marketers Aren't Using Computers," *Industrial Marketing,* vol. 51 (November 1966), pp. 88–89.

more than expanding and automating the data gathering process. It is an inextricable part of the larger pursuit of more efficient forms and methods of organization for marketing management.

We are running late

There is ample evidence that marketing decision-making is becoming more complex, making the need for a systematic approach to information management all the greater. First, there is a growing complexity of the areas that have to be managed, largely a function of the tendency toward larger scale enterprise. Second, as expanded marketing effort takes the firm across existing environmental frontiers, whether geographic, economic, or social (or, more likely, all three), the information needs of the enterprise are substantially compounded. It is highly likely that the most crucial constraint currently imposed on the growth of international marketing, for example, is the dearth of pertinent decision-information.

But perhaps the most compelling argument for marketing information systems is the "Information Explosion" itself. The world's store of knowledge has allegedly doubled during the past decade and is expected at least to double again in the next decade.

Information, including management information, is growing by the microsecond and even nanosecond. We cannot turn off the flow. We had therefore better learn to control it—and we are already running late. [15]

QUESTIONS

1. Define briefly, in your own words, what is meant by a marketing information system.
2. Explain how a marketing information system could fit into the marketing management process.
3. How does a marketing information system differ from the traditional marketing research activity of the firm?
*4. Would an MIS have a different role to play in inflationary times? Explain. (See Reading 26.)

---

[15] Howell M. Estes, "Will Managers Be Overwhelmed by the Information Explosion?" *Armed Forces Management*, vol. 13 (December 1966), p. 84.
* Question relates concepts in this and other readings.

31
Profitability analysis by market segments

Leland L. Beik and Stephen L. Buzby

The contribution approach to cost accounting can relate products, channels, and other marketing components to the profitability of market segments. Using the techniques discussed in this article, a marketing manager can plan and control decisions for the component being analyzed and also make collateral adjustments in other elements of the marketing mix.

By tracing sales revenues to market segments and relating these revenues to marketing costs, the marketing manager can improve and control his decision making with respect to the firm's profit objective.

First expressed by Smith in 1956, the concept of market segmentation has since been elaborated in many different ways.[1] It has recently been defined by Kotler as ". . . the subdividing of a market into homogeneous subsets of customers, where any subset may conceivably be selected as a market target to be reached with a distinct marketing mix."[2] The underlying logic is based on the assumption that:

. . . the market for a product is made up of customers who differ either in their own characteristics or in the nature of their environment in such a way that some aspect of their demand for the product in question also differs. The strategy of market segmentation involves the tailoring of the firm's product and/or marketing program to these differences. By modifying either of these, the firm is attempting to increase profits by converting a market with heterogeneous demand characteristics into a set of markets that although they differ from one another, are internally more homogeneous than before.[3]

Source: Reprinted with permission from the *Journal of Marketing,* published by the American Marketing Association, vol. 37, (July 1973), pp. 48–53. At the time this article was published, Leland Beik was a professor of marketing at The Pennsylvania State University, and Stephen Buzby was an assistant professor of marketing at the University of Indiana.

[1] Wendell R. Smith, "Product Differentiation and Market Segmentation as Alternative Marketing Strategies," *Journal of Marketing,* vol. 21 (July 1956), pp. 3–8; and James F. Engel, Henry F. Fiorillo, and Murray A. Cayley, eds., *Market Segmentation: Concepts and Applications* (New York: Holt, Rinehart and Winston, Inc., 1972).

[2] Philip Kotler, *Marketing Management,* 2d ed. (Englewood Cliffs, N.J.: Prentice-Hall, Inc., 1972), p. 166.

[3] Ronald E. Frank, "Market Segmentation Research: Findings and Implications," in *Applications of the Sciences in Marketing Management,* Frank M. Bass, Charles W. King, and Edgar A. Pessemier, eds. (New York: John Wiley & Sons, Inc., 1968), p. 39.

The concept of market segmentation may be used for strategic alignment of the firm's productive capacities with its existing and potential markets. By analyzing market needs and the firm's ability to serve those needs, the basic long-run policies of the firm can be developed. Through choice of target segments, competition may be minimized; through selective cultivation, the firm's competitive posture may be greatly improved.

For both strategic and tactical decisions, marketing managers may profit by knowing the impact of the marketing mix upon the target segments at which marketing efforts are aimed. If the programs are to be responsive to environmental change, a monitoring system is needed to locate problems and guide adjustments in marketing decisions. Tracing the profitability of segments permits improved pricing, selling, advertising, channel, and product management decisions. The success of marketing policies and programs may be appraised by a dollar and cents measure of profitability by segment.

Managerial accounting techniques have dealt with the profitability of products, territories, and some customer classes; but a literature search has revealed not one serious attempt to assess the relative profitability of market segments.[4] Although the term "segment" has a history of use in accounting, this use implies a segment of the business rather than a special partitioning of consumers or industrial users for marketing analysis. Even when classifying customers, accounting classes are formed by frequency and size of order, location, credit rating, and other factors, most of which are related to controlling internal costs or to assessing financial profit.[5]

After indicating the value for marketing decision making, this article will delineate a framework for cost accounting by market segments. An industrial product example is constructed to demonstrate the process and to spell out the features of the contribution approach to cost accounting as applied to accounting for segment profitability. Further discussion extends the concept to a consumer situation and specifies difficulties that may attend full-scale application of the technique. The expectation is that the technique will better control marketing costs and improve marketing decisions.

MARKET SEGMENTATION AND ITS UTILITY

To have value for managerial judgments, Bell notes that market segments should: (1) be readily identified and measured, (2) contain adequate potential, (3) demonstrate effective demand, (4) be economically accessible, and (5) react uniquely to marketing effort.[6] For present purposes, the key criterion for choosing the bases for segmenting a given market is the ability to trace

---

[4] Closest to the present analysis and perhaps the best summary of the state of the art is Charles H. Sevin, *Marketing Productivity Analysis* (New York: McGraw-Hill Book Company, 1965).

[5] Robert B. Miner, "Distribution Costs," in *Marketing Handbook,* Albert W. Frey, ed. (New York: The Ronald Press Company, 1965); see especially pp. 23 · 17 and 23 · 32.

[6] Martin L. Bell, *Marketing: Concepts and Strategy,* 2d ed. (Boston: Houghton Mifflin Company, 1972), p. 185.

sales and costs to the segments defined. Allocating sales and costs is the most stringent requirement and limitation of profitability accounting as used to support marketing decisions.

Among the many possible bases for market segmentation, the analysis can be accomplished using widely recognized geographic, demographic, and socioeconomic variables.[7] Many of these, such as geographic units and population or income figures, provide known universe classifications against which to compare company sales and cost performance. Other bases of segmentation such as buyer usage rate, expected benefits, or psychological or sociological characteristics of consumers typically require research to match their distribution, directly or indirectly, with company sales and costs.

Given proper segmentation, separate products (or channels or other elements of the marketing mix) can serve as the primary basis for cost and revenue allocation. Knowledge of profit by segments then contributes directly to decisions concerning the product line and adjustment of sales, advertising, and other decision variables. The process is illustrated in the following industrial example.

A matrix system can be developed as part of marketing planning to partition segments for profitability analysis.[8] A company with lines of computers, calculators, and adding machines might first divide its market into territories as in the upper section of Figure 1. The cell representing adding machines in the eastern market might next be sorted by product items and customer classes. The chief product preference of each company class is noted by an important benefit segmentation within the cells of the lower section of Figure 1.

Figure 1
Matrix breakdown by products and segments

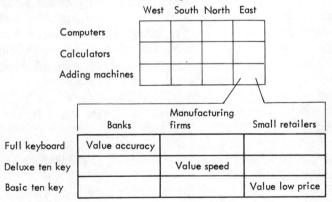

[7] See William M. Weilbacker, "Standard Classification of Consumer Characteristics," *Journal of Marketing,* vol. 31 (January 1967), p. 27.

[8] See William J. E. Crissy and Robert M. Kaplan, "Matrix Models for Marketing Planning," *MSU Business Topics,* vol. 11 (Summer 1963), p. 48. The matrix "targeting" treatment is also familiar to readers of basic marketing texts by E. J. McCarthy or G. D. Downing.

Since the segments react differently to product variations and other marketing activities, it is advantageous to isolate profit by product for each market segment. Using this information, the marketing manager can specifically tailor product policies to particular market segments and judge the reaction of segments to increased or decreased marketing efforts over time. Decision adjustments and control of marketing costs interact to improve product line management directly and other decisions indirectly.

In theory, segment profitability analysis is worthwhile only where decisions adjusting the marketing mix add incremental profits that exceed the costs of the extra analysis. In practice, information concerning the profitability of marketing decisions has been so sparse that the analysis is likely to be profitable where allocations to market segments are approximate and fail to approach theoretical perfection.

MARKETING COST ANALYSIS

In its simplest form, marketing cost analysis relates the cost of marketing activities to sales revenues in order to measure profits. A profit and loss statement must be constructed for any marketing component (e.g., product, channel) being analyzed. The approach consists of dividing the firm's basic costs (e.g., salaries, rent) into their functional categories (e.g., selling, advertising). The functional category amounts are then assigned within the appropriate marketing classifications.

The actual form of the profit and loss statements will depend upon the nature of the company being analyzed, the purpose of the marketing analysis, and the records available. The form of statement will also depend upon the accounting technique used to assign costs to the marketing components under study. One might use a full-cost approach, assigning both direct and indirect costs across the marketing classifications on the best available bases. Alternatively, one might use a direct-cost approach and assign direct costs only, avoiding arbitrary assignment of fixed or overhead costs. Most marketing sources have utilized the full- and direct-cost approaches.

A third costing approach is better suited to the needs of the marketing manager and the requirements of analysis by market segments. Essentially, it is an adaptation of the contribution approach to preparing financial statements.[9] Table 1 presents a simplified illustration of how the contribution approach can be adapted to break out product profitability for adding machines in the eastern market.

First, all of the variable nonmarketing costs have been assigned to products. These costs represent nonmarketing dollar expenditures which fluctuate, in total, directly in proportion to short-run changes in the sales volume of a

---

[9] See Charles R. Horngren, *Cost Accounting: A Managerial Emphasis*, 2d ed. (Englewood Cliffs, N.J.: Prentice-Hall, Inc., 1967); and Ralph L. Day and Peter D. Bennett, "Should Salesmen's Compensation be Geared to Profits?" *Journal of Marketing*, vol. 26 (October 1962), pp. 6–9.

Table 1
Product productivity analysis—contribution approach

	Company total	Full keyboard	Deluxe 10-key	Basic 10-key
Net sales	$10,000	$5,000	$3,000	$2,000
Variable manufacturing costs	5,100	2,500	1,375	1,225
Manufacturing contribution	$ 4,900	$2,500	$1,625	$ 775
Marketing costs				
Variable:				
Sales commissions	450	225	135	90
Variable contribution	$ 4,450	$2,275	$1,490	$ 685
Assignable:				
Salaries—salesmen	1,600	770	630	200
Salary—marketing manager	100	50	25	25
Product advertising	1,000	670	200	130
Total	$ 2,700	$1,490	$ 855	$ 355
Product contribution	$ 1,750	$ 785	$ 635	$ 330
Nonassignable:				
Institutional advertising	150			
Marketing contribution	$ 1,600			
Fixed-joint costs:				
General administration	300			
Manufacturing	900			
Total	$ 1,200			
Net profits	$ 400			

given product. Similarly, variable marketing costs have been deducted to produce variable product contribution margins identical to those which would result from a direct-costing approach.

The remaining marketing costs have been broken down into two categories—assignable and nonassignable. The assignable costs represent dollar expenditures of a fixed or discretionary nature for which reasonably valid bases exist for allocating them to specific products. For example, the assignment of salesmen's salaries in Table 1 might be based on Sevin's recommendation to use "selling time devoted to each product, as shown by special sales-call reports or special studies."[10] The marketing manager's salary could be assigned on the basis of personal records indicating the amount of time devoted to the management of each product. Product advertising would be assigned by reference to the actual amount spent on advertising each product.

The use of the actual dollar level of sales was purposely avoided in choosing the allocation bases for the assignable costs in Table 1. Horngren, among

---

[10] Same reference as footnote 4, p. 13.

others, has stated that when dealing with fixed or discretionary costs, "The costs of efforts are independent of the results actually obtained, in the sense that the costs are programmed by management, not determined by sales."[11]

The nonassignable marketing costs represent dollar expenditures of a fixed or discretionary nature for which there are no valid bases for assignment to products. Consequently, institutional advertising has not been assigned to the products to avoid confounding the product profitability margins which would result from the arbitrary allocation of this cost. Since the primary purpose is calculating marketing-related product contribution margins, the remaining nonmarketing costs can be taken as a deduction from the total marketing contribution margin to produce a net profit figure for the firm.

Although the preceding example was purposely simplified, the framework is sufficiently flexible to handle different objectives and more complex problems. If the firm in Table 1 were a single-product firm, for example, the three customer classes (banks, manufacturers, and retailers) could easily be substituted for primary emphasis in place of the products. The analysis would differ only through variations in the treatment of fixed, variable, and assignable costs required by the new objective. That assignability changes with objective may be illustrated by the fact that product advertising costs can often be assigned to products but rarely to customer classes.

To aid in handling more complex problems, a discussion of common bases for assigning a wide range of marketing costs may be found in Sevin.[12] In some instances, the approach can be further improved by application of mathematical programming to assign costs to the marketing components.[13] Budgetary data and marketing lags could also be introduced to upgrade the analysis.[14]

COSTING BY SEGMENTS

In particular, the framework of the contribution approach may be applied to costing by segments. Table 2 extends the product analysis of Table 1. Recall that the segments are partitioned by territorial, customer class, and product benefit criteria although the primary customer class names are used to identify segments in the table. Instead of tracing the sales of each product to all three customer classes, one simplifying device is to identify the primary benefit sought by a customer class as segment sales and to combine sales of the given product to the other customer classes as nonsegment sales. For example, sales of the full-keyboard adding machine to banks become seg-

---

[11] Same reference as footnote 9, p. 381.

[12] Same reference as footnote 4, chapter 2.

[13] William J. Baumol and Charles H. Sevin, "Marketing Costs and Mathematical Programming," in *Management Information: A Quantitative Accent,* Thomas Williams and Charles Griffin, eds. (Homewood, Ill.: Richard D. Irwin, Inc., 1967), pp. 176–90.

[14] Richard A. Feder, "How to Measure Marketing Performance," in *Readings in Cost Accounting, Budgeting, and Control,* 3d ed., W. Thomas Jr., ed. (Cincinnati, Ohio: South-Western Publishing Co., 1968), pp. 650–68.

Table 2
Segment productivity analysis—contribution approach

	Company total	Full keyboard Bank segment	Full keyboard Non-segment	Deluxe 10-key Manu-facturing segment	Deluxe 10-key Non-segment	Basic 10-key retail segment
Net sales	$10,000	$3,750	$1,250	$2,550	$450	$2,000
Variable manufacturing costs	5,100	1,875	625	1,169	206	1,225
Manufacturing contribution ..	$ 4,900	$1,875	$ 625	$1,381	$244	$ 775
Marketing costs						
Variable:						
Sales commissions	450	169	56	115	20	90
Variable contribution	$ 4,450	$1,706	$ 569	$1,266	$224	$ 685
Assignable:						
Salaries—salesmen	1,600	630	140	420	210	200
Salary—marketing manager ...	100	38	12	19	6	25
Product advertising	1,000	670	–0–	200	–0–	130
Total	$ 2,700	$1,338	$ 152	$ 639	$216	$ 355
Segment contribution	$ 1,750	$ 368	$ 417	$ 627	$ 8	$ 330
Nonassignable:						
Institutional advertising	150					
Marketing contribution	$ 1,600					
Fixed joint costs:						
General administration	300					
Manufacturing..............	900					
Total	$ 1,200					
Net profits	$ 400					

ment sales, while sales to large manufacturing firms or to retailers are non-segment sales. This device is appropriate where nontarget sales are expected to be minimal; otherwise more columns can be added to the table.

Where sales revenues can be traced directly to customers, customer classes, and territories and where marketing costs can be similarly traced, the analysis is straightforward. Where the less tangible benefit segmentation is used, sales analysis or marketing research must measure the degree to which benefits are related to each customer class. If sales analysis shows that banks purchase 75 percent of the full-keyboard sales because they value accuracy, while manufacturers and retailers account for the remaining 25 percent, both revenues and sales commissions may be prorated accordingly. This allocation is employed in Table 2.

To illustrate a few marketing implications, it might be noted that over one-half of the full-keyboard profit contribution actually comes from non-segment sales rather than from the primary target segment. The nonsegment profitability results in part from low personal selling and absence of advertising costs. An opportunity possibly exists in further promotion, perhaps to large manufacturing firms. Had the table completed the analysis for purchases of full-keyboard machines by manufacturers and retailers, the actual segment of opportunity could be pinpointed. If institutional or other possible sales proved substantial during further classification, a new segment of opportunity might be identified.

Quite obviously, the eastern banking segment has a low profit contribution considering the level of marketing effort expended. Table 2 deals with one sample area and product class, and a comparison with other area banking segments might prove enlightening. Perhaps marketing costs could be reduced in the eastern segment if sales were up to par. Or if sales were comparatively low, marketing effort (price, personal selling, advertising) could be reallocated to meet competition more effectively.

Similar analysis can be applied to the manufacturing and retailing segments of Table 2, and to the territories and products not incorporated in the present illustration. The advantage over standard sales analysis is that a profit rather than a volume measure is applied and that variations in marketing costs and sales response are taken into account.

MARKETING PRODUCTIVITY: CONSUMER SEGMENTS

The previous example has been simplified so that minimum tables serve to explain the technique. Segment analysis becomes complex as more than two or three criteria are used for partitioning and as additional criteria are considered for different classes of marketing decisions. A further example adds realism and extends the concept to a consumer situation.

A company that sells snowmobiles is likely to have some special channel problems. To control channel management, meteorological data permit primary and secondary snow belts to be mapped across the United States and Canada. Sales analysis or research could show how to allocate purchases among consumers in major metropolitan, city, town, and rural areas. Further analysis could determine patronage among department stores, automotive dealers, farm equipment dealers, marinas, and other classes of outlets. Sales to resorts for rentals might be included as a segment or analyzed separately. Finally, the several analyses could map sales into geographical units. Segmenting by snow conditions, population density, outlets patronized, and dwelling area and then allocating revenues and costs to the segments would point outlet selection and channel adjustments toward the more profitable outlets in favorable population and snow-belt locations.

By collecting and analyzing warranty card information, snowmobile purchasers could be classified as to family life cycle, social status, or other variables. This data would probe the profit potential of appealing to young families, selected social classes, or possibly even to hunters, sailing enthusiasts, and other outdoors people. Dates on the warranty cards would help adjust the timing of promotions in advance of the snow season or to balance the pre-Christmas advertising in line with purchase habits of its customer segments. Having targeted promotion on the basis of past data, current warranty card information, and revenue and cost information, the profitability of each target segment could be determined.

Analyzing the profitability of advertising or price decisions involves special problems in tracing sales and costs. If segments have been defined on tangible bases, say area and dealer patronage, the difficulty might be overcome by setting up an experiment.[15] Variations of advertising messages, local media, and possibly price would serve as treatments in segments matched to control other variables. Recording segment revenues and treatment costs would constitute a profit measure of selected advertising and/or price decisions. Experiments may thus be used with segment cost analysis to plan corporate marketing programs.

MANAGERIAL IMPLICATIONS

Given responsible means of partitioning market segments, major elements of the marketing mix may be segregated for analysis using the contribution approach to cost accounting. An example has been employed to show how segment profitability can be measured for items in a product line, thereby contributing directly to product management decisions. By analyzing the profit and loss statements for the costs of other marketing efforts, additional adjustments can be made in other decisions such as personal selling and advertising. A further example has indicated how channel and other marketing management problems can be similarly gauged by a profit measure for a consumer product and consumer segments.

Several major problems have to be met in applying costing techniques to market segments. One difficulty is choosing productive bases for segmentation, and limiting analysis to a manageable number of bases is another. Although some bases are obvious from experience, they remain product specific, and criteria for choice are not fully developed. Another major problem is obtaining data for the less tangible modes of segmentation, particularly data that permit assignment of sales revenues and costs in accord with each base used for segment definition.

Recognizing and solving problems, however, often leads to further improvements. For example, many of the behavioral applications to marketing imply use in segment analysis but are difficult to relate to other marketing variables on any basis other than judgment. As limitations of source data are overcome, profit accounting by segments may add to the marketing utility of behavioral advances.

Costing by market segments promises improvement in marketing efficiency by way of better planning of expenditures and control of costs. Upon documenting reasons for today's soaring marketing costs, Weiss comments

---

[15] Same reference as footnote 4, chapters 6, 7, and 8.

over and over that marketing costs are resistant to sophisticated cost analysis and that marketing cost controls are inadequate in modern corporations.[16] Although not calculated to stem such pressures as inflation, cost accounting by market segments can control selling, advertising, packaging, and other marketing costs in relation to profit potentials. Perhaps even greater value stems from the potential ability to fine-tune product offerings and other marketing decisions to the requirements of well-defined consumer segments. As part of the material regularly supplied to marketing managers, market segment profitability analysis could easily become a key component of marketing information systems of the future.

QUESTIONS

1. Briefly explain the authors' procedure for calculating the profitability of market segments.

2. Could the process discussed by Beik and Buzby be used to help select target markets? Why or why not?

*3. Is the Beik and Buzby approach really any different from the total cost approach discussed by Lewis (Reading 22)? Explain.

---

[16] E. B. Weiss, "Pooled Marketing: Antidote for Soaring Marketing Costs," *Advertising Age*, vol. 43 (November 13, 1972), pp. 63–64.

* Question relates concepts in this and other readings.

32
Conducting and using a marketing audit

John F. Grashof

---

*This article describes how to conduct a marketing audit.
This is still an art, requiring much judgment, but an organized approach can be helpful. Grashof presents a
checklist of factors to consider and forms which can help
organize the evaluation process.*

Over the past several years, many firms have come to realize the necessity of
"keeping tabs on" and evaluating various functions within the firm. These
control efforts often take the form of audits. For example, many firms conduct
management audits to assess their management structures and the strengths
and weaknesses of their managers and other employees. The accounting
profession conducts audits of financial records for purposes of internal control
as well as for the protection of outside investors and lenders. And, during the
last couple of years, increasing attention has been given to the social audit, an
evaluation of the firm's degree of social responsibility.

With the increasing recognition of marketing, and particularly marketing
strategies, as central to the success of all businesses more attention has been
given to the evaluation of this category of a firm's activities. In response to the
need for evaluation, more and more academicians and practitioners are calling for marketing audits.[1] "A marketing audit," suggests Martin Bell, "is a
systematic and thorough examination of a company's marketing position."[2]
More formally, Abe Shuchman defines a marketing audit as:

. . . a systematic, critical, and impartial review and appraisal of the total marketing
operation: of the basic objectives and policies and the assumptions which underlie
them as well as the methods, procedures, personnel, and organization employed to
implement the policies and achieve the objectives.[3]

Source: An original contribution. At the time of writing, John Grashof was an associate
professor and chairman of the Department of Marketing of Temple University.

[1] Philip Kotler, *Marketing Management: Analysis, Planning and Control,* 2d ed. (Englewood
Cliffs, N.J.: Prentice-Hall, Inc., 1972), p. 774.

[2] Martin L. Bell, *Marketing: Concepts and Strategies,* 2d ed. (Boston: Houghton Mifflin Co.,
1972), p. 428.

[3] Abe Shuchman, "The Marketing Audit: Its Nature, Purposes, and Problems," *Analyzing
and Improving Marketing Performance,* Report no. 32 (New York: American Management Association, 1959), p. 13.

MARKETING AUDITS: WHY, WHEN, WHAT, AND WHO

Are marketing audits really necessary?

Marketing audits are necessary for a number of important reasons, not the least of which is the complex and continually changing environment of the modern corporation. As the marketplace, the competitive scene, and the economic and political climates change, the firm should study its marketing activities to determine what, if any, changes should be made.[4] The marketing audit can be a viable approach to structuring the evaluation of strategies in a meaningful way. By examining the firm's strategies relative to its competitors and the market, and with respect to internal consistency, the audit can highlight strengths and weaknesses.

Audits are typically evaluations of past behavior and present practices, and marketing audits do perform this function. However, marketing audits can reveal not only present weaknesses, but also may identify potential problems and, thus, may play an important role with respect to future planning.[5] Marketing managers are typically more concerned that the goals and directions of their marketing efforts are correct than they are that their past performance has been good.[6] Through a critical evaluation of the objectives of the firm, and the plans and programs designed to meet these objectives, the marketing audit serves a role similar to a pro forma or forecasted income statement.

How often should a marketing audit be conducted?

Most authors suggest that audits be conducted on a periodic basis. The length of time between audits may vary among firms, but audits should be a routine part of the planning process of a firm. Audits, in addition to those normally scheduled, may be conducted as desired by management, but such additional audits should not replace those regularly scheduled.

Shuchman suggests that audits can be profitably conducted in extremely good times, and may be absolutely necessary in times of crisis.[7] For example, American bicycle manufacturers were largely unprepared for the sudden upsurge in sales that occurred in the early 1970s. The combined impacts of increased concern for physical fitness and the growing environmental problems led to the rediscovery of the bicycle by many adults. Failure to anticipate the increasing sales trend left the industry saddled with a child-oriented product line and insufficient production facilities. Thus, the door was opened for an influx of foreign imports. Apparently, the U.S. firms had been lulled into complacency by years of steady, profitable sales. Had these firms been con-

---

[4] Shuchman, "Marketing Audit," p. 15.

[5] Ibid., pp. 12–14.

[6] Bell, *Marketing*, p. 429.

[7] Shuchman, "Marketing Audit," pp. 15–16.

ducting periodic marketing audits, it is likely that they would have been better prepared for the rapid increase in sales.

What is the best way to approach a marketing audit?

There are a variety of approaches to conducting a marketing audit. One decision that must be made is whether to examine generally the whole range of marketing activities or to look at one section in detail. Richard Crisp defines these as the horizontal and vertical audits:

The *horizontal* audit examines all of the elements that go into the marketing whole, with particular emphasis upon the relative importance of these elements and the 'mix' between them. It is often referred to as a 'marketing mix' audit. The *vertical* audit singles out certain functional elements of the marketing operation and subjects them to thorough, searching study and evaluation.[8]

Which approach is best for a particular firm at a point in time must be determined by that firm. The choice will depend on a number of factors, including where the firm is experiencing success and where it is having problems. However, in those cases where the firm selects a vertical audit it must not completely ignore evaluation of the mix aspect of its marketing program.

An alternative view of the components of a marketing audit is presented by Kotler, Gregor, and Rodgers.[9] They identify six components of an audit as follows:

1. *Marketing environment audit.* An evaluation of the uncontrollable variables which surround and impact upon the firm, and the marketing institutions and agencies with which the firm interacts, including customers, suppliers, ad agencies, and dealers and distributors.
2. *Marketing strategy audit.* A consideration of the marketing strategies of the firm, given the opportunities available to them, the resources they have available, and the guidance provided by top-management objectives.
3. *Marketing organization audit.* A study of the marketing organization, the structure through which the resources of the firm are applied to achieve its objectives. The audit will consider whether the organization is appropriate, given the objectives, and effective, given the resources of the firm.
4. *Marketing systems audit.* An examination of the nature of the system by which the marketing managers obtain the information they need for

---

[8] Richard D. Crisp, "Auditing the Functional Elements of a Marketing Operation," *Analyzing and Improving Marketing Performance,* Report no. 32 (New York: American Management Association, 1959), pp. 16–17.

[9] P. Kotler, W. Gregor, and W. Rodgers, "The Marketing Audit Comes of Age," *Sloan Management Review,* vol. 18 (Winter 1977), pp. 25–43.

decision making, as well as the quantity and quality of information that the system makes available.

5. *Marketing productivity audit.* An attempt to understand, through an examination of accounting data, the costs and revenues associated with specific elements of the firm's activities, such as customers or products. The objective is to understand which of the firm's activities are contributing to profits and which are not profitable.

6. *Marketing function audits.* A detailed investigation into specific functional activities of the firm's marketing program, such as its distribution system or its sales force. These are conducted at the suggestion of an auditor, with the agreement of management, when specific problems are noted.

The six components listed above are semiautonomous. That is, they can be conducted independently of each other, depending on the specific problems a firm is having or the objectives of the audit. A complete marketing audit of a firm would include all six components.

Who should conduct the marketing audit?

The selection of an individual or team to be responsible for conducting the marketing audit can obviously have a significant impact on the quality of the completed evaluation. The auditor should be unbiased, experienced, and knowledgeable about the company and industry. Crisp lists six alternative sources of auditors.

1. *Self-audit.* A company can ask the executive who is directly in charge of an activity to appraise its strengths and weaknesses.

2. *"Audit from across."* A company can assign persons in a related activity on the same functional level to prepare an audit of the neighboring activity.

3. *"Audit from above."* The audit can be conducted by the executive to whom the manager reports.

4. *Company auditing office.* The company can establish an office with the responsibility for conducting all company marketing audits.

5. *Company task-force audit.* The company can appoint a team of company executives with varied backgrounds and experience to conduct the audit.

6. *Outside audit.* The company can hire an outside individual or agency to conduct the marketing audit.[10]

Crisp feels that the sixth alternative, the outside audit, is usually the best choice. The outside agent is able to be more objective since he is not examining his own or a co-worker's performance and since he is not so likely to be subjected to pressure from superiors or co-workers.

---

[10] Crisp, "Auditing the Functional Elements," pp. 41–44.

CONDUCTING A MARKETING AUDIT

Conducting a marketing audit and the subsequent strategy evaluation is a three-step process, as outlined in Figure 1. Step 1 consists of the accumulation of a great many facts concerning the firm's marketing program. Step 2 is the evaluation of the information gathered in Step 1 with respect to the firm

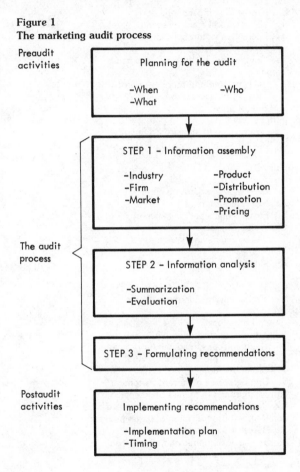

Figure 1
The marketing audit process

Preaudit activities

Planning for the audit

–When   –Who
–What

STEP 1 – Information assembly

–Industry   –Product
–Firm   –Distribution
–Market   –Promotion
                –Pricing

The audit process

STEP 2 – Information analysis

–Summarization
–Evaluation

STEP 3 – Formulating recommendations

Postaudit activities

Implementing recommendations

–Implementation plan
–Timing

and its competition and the internal consistency of the firm's marketing program. The third and final step is the development of a set of recommendations based on the analysis conducted in Step 2.

Step 1: Information assembly

The information-assembly step of a marketing audit is the most time-consuming and may be the most frustrating. A detailed examination of a firm's marketing program involves a great deal of data, and a comprehensive

Table 1
Checklist of areas to be examined in a marketing audit

I. THE INDUSTRY
   A. Characteristics
      1. Size (in units produced, dollar sales)
      2. Number of firms
      3. Nature of competition
      4. Geographical concentration
      5. Interaction with other industries
      6. Product life cycle
      7. Government and societal constraints
   B. Trends
      1. Sales volume and number of firms
      2. Geographic localization
      3. Size of firms
   C. Firm's Position
      1. Size relative to industry leaders
      2. Market strength
      3. Leader or follower
II. THE FIRM
   A. History
      1. Growth and expansion
      2. Financial history
      3. Past strengths and weaknesses
   B. Goals and Objectives
   C. Current Strengths and Weaknesses
      1. Market
      2. Managerial
      3. Financial
      4. Technical
      5. Market information mechanisms
III. THE MARKET
   A. General Structure
      1. Number of customers
      2. Geographical spread and/or grouping
      3. Breadth of product use
      4. Urban vs. rural
      5. Demographics of current customers
   B. Firm's Approach to Market Segmentation
      1. Degree to which firm has segmented the market
      2. Degree of specification of target markets
      3. Bases of segmentation used
         a. Socioeconomic and demographic
         b. Psychographic
         c. Geographic
         d. Use patterns
   C. Segments Identified by the Firm
      1. What are characteristics?
      2. Degree of difference among segments
      3. What segments have been selected by the firm as target markets?
   D. Has the Firm Considered Factors Which Affect the Market?
      1. Income effects
      2. Price and quality elasticity
      3. Responsiveness to marketing variables
      4. Fashion cycles
      5. Seasonality

Source: Based in part on an outline for a marketing audit developed by B. J. La Londe, James R. Riley Professor of Marketing and Logistics, The Ohio State University.

Table 1 (*continued*)

IV. THE PRODUCT
    A. List the Company's Products
        1. Strengths
        2. Weaknesses
        3. Distinctive features
    B. Competitive Position
        1. Price and quality relative to competitors
        2. Market share
        3. Patents or trademarks
    C. Product Policy
        1. Written or verbal
        2. Product line width and depth
        3. New product policy
        4. Product deletion policy
V. DISTRIBUTION
    A. Channels of Distribution
        1. Description of channel(s) used
        2. Institutions in each channel
        3. Basis for selection of institutions used
    B. Distribution Policy
        1. Extent and depth of market coverage
        2. Role of distribution in marketing mix and marketing plans
    C. Physical Distribution
        1. PD organization within firm
        2. Customer service level policy
        3. Inventory
            a. Number of locations of stock
            b. Type of warehouse (i.e., public vs. private)
            c. Planned and actual inventory levels
        4. Transportation
            a. Product shipment terms
            b. Mode of transportation used
            c. Type of carrier
                (1) Common
                (2) Contract
                (3) Private
VI. PROMOTION
    A. Goals of Promotional Activities
        1. Advertising
        2. Personal selling
        3. Sales promotion
    B. Promotion Blend
    C. Advertising
        1. Budget in dollars and per cent of sales
        2. Tasks assigned to advertising
        3. Evaluation procedures
    D. Personal Selling
        1. Organization of sales force
        2. Sales force management
        3. Tasks assigned to the sales force
VII. PRICING
    A. Goals and Role of Pricing in the Marketing Mix
    B. Approach Used to Set Prices
        1. Basis on which prices are set
        2. Flow of pricing decisions within the firm
    C. Prices Compared with Competitors
    D. Trade Discount and Allowances
    E. Financing and Credit Arrangements

listing of the information required for a marketing audit would be lengthy. Seven major areas which affect a firm's marketing program need to be examined. They are:

1. The industry.   5. Distribution.
2. The firm.   6. Promotion.
3. The market.   7. Pricing.
4. The product.

Table 1 outlines these general areas and lists a few of the more important factors to be studied under each.

Step 2: Analyzing the audit information

Once the information concerning the industry, the firm, and its marketing programs has been gathered, the audit team needs to analyze this information to obtain a more complete picture of the firm's marketing activities. Often, effectiveness of a firm's marketing program hinges not on the individual activities that it undertakes but, rather, on the way in which these activities fit together into a comprehensive marketing mix. As a starting point, a summary judgment should be made concerning the extent to which the firm embraces and follows the dictates of the marketing concept. Following this summary evaluation, other, more specific analyses can be made of particular aspects of the firm's marketing activities.

One analysis that the auditors should carry out is a comparison of the firm with its competitors. Throughout the information-gathering step of the marketing audit, the audit team has been collecting data not only about the subject firm but about the activities of its competitors. This information should now be tied together to develop a comprehensive picture of the marketing program of the firm and the marketing operations of its competitors. These two should then be compared in a side-by-side evaluation.

Table 2 presents a possible format for such an evaluation. Some of the judgments will be difficult, but the process of trying to accomplish such an analysis will be beneficial to the auditors and the firm. While a firm need not, indeed probably should not, be doing exactly the same thing as its competitors, such an evaluation does point out where their activities are the same and where they are different. Where they are the same, they should be examined for possible changes that would give the firm an advantage over the competitors. Where they are different, each difference should be evaluated to determine whether it is a strength or a weakness. Such side-by-side evaluation can mean much to a firm in identifying competitive strengths and weaknesses and in developing suggestions for ways to make its marketing programs relatively stronger.

In addition to the comparative analysis of the firm's marketing program and that of its competitors, the market offerings of the firm should be evaluated with respect to each market segment it is attempting to serve. In analyz-

Table 2
Suggested format for comparative evaluation of firm and competitors

	Description of factor for		
Factor*	The firm's approach	Major competitors' approach	Differences
1. Market			
Has the market been segmented?	(Highly, somewhat, or not segmented)		
What is segmentation based on?	(Demographics, psychographics, or benefits; specific attributes)		
Size of market served	(Local, regional, or national)		
2. Product			
Quality level	(High, medium or low quality)		
Width and depth of product line	(Broad, medium, or narrow; deep, moderate, or thin)		
Is the firm an innovator?	(Typically innovator, typically follower)		
Brand strength in market	(Brand unrecognized, recognized, preferred, or insisted upon)		
Market penetration	(Largest, average, or small market share)		
Goods class of products	(Industrial or consumer goods; subclasses)		
3. Distribution			
Direct or indirect distribution?	(Direct or indirect; number of intermediaries)		
Type of middlemen used	(Handles own distribution or uses others; specific type of middlemen used)		
Degree of market coverage	(Intensive, selective, or exclusive)		
Service level	(Best in market, average, poorest)		
Physical distribution system	(One central warehouse or field warehouse system; public or private transportation and/or warehouses)		
4. Promotion			
Amount of advertising	(Percent of budget; total dollars)		
Target of promotion	(Consumers for pull strategy or middlemen for push strategy)		
Type of appeal	(Factual, emotional, humorous)		
Type of media	(Print, broadcast; local, national)		
Promotion blend	(Percent advertising vs. personal selling)		
Organization of sales force	(By territory, division, product line; company sales staff or manufacturers' agents)		
Functions of sales force	(Technical design, customer systems design, nontechnical)		
5. Pricing			
Price level	(High, medium, or low price)		
Terms and/or discounts	(Strict or liberal; better, same, or less than industry)		
Use of price competition	(Price major competitive weapon, competes on other bases)		

*The factors listed are suggestions and are not intended to be exclusive or exhaustive. Further, the descriptors for each of the factors are only suggestive.

ing the market, each segment was identified along with those factors which cause persons in the segment to buy the firm's product versus the product of a competitor. The degree of congruence between the factors which are important in a segment's purchase decision and the marketing offering of the firm should be evaluated. Further, the trends in specific aspects of the behavior of market segments should be evaluated with respect to proposed changes in the firm's market offerings. Such an evaluation will help to ensure that the firm is adjusting to the changing needs of the market it serves. For example, a marketing audit might have shown the U.S. auto companies the shift in consumers' preferences toward smaller, more economical cars. Had the strength of this trend been identified earlier, the U.S. companies might not have suffered as much as they did from imported car competition.

In evaluating the firm's offerings to the several market segments it serves, the internal consistency of the marketing mix should be given close scrutiny. While a firm's marketing mix is made up of many different aspects, there are strong relationships among these aspects. For example, products which are considered to be convenience goods in the consumer goods classification system should have intensive distribution, whereas products that are in the shopping goods categories may need only selective or perhaps even exclusive distribution. This was relevant for the Elgin Watch Company, a prestigious manufacturer of high-quality men's products. The company suffered irreparable damage when the U.S. Time Company began selling inexpensive Timex watches as convenience goods. A marketing audit could have helped Elgin revise its marketing strategy to compete effectively with Timex. By identifying the shift in goods class of wristwatches for a large segment of the population, an audit might have given Elgin the information necessary to make better decisions.

One approach to such an evaluation is to select several control points or factors which have been identified as being critical to the firm's marketing program. Potential control points include product attributes such as quality and number of special features, distribution considerations such as number and type of retail outlets and service level along the channel, promotional appeals used and media selected, and pricing policies. The performance of the firm with respect to each control point can then be evaluated. Deviations should be noted, and those that are significant will be points about which suggestions for improvement need to be made.[11]

Evaluation of a firm's marketing strategies can be made even more valuable if the control points selected are tied to characteristics of the target markets selected. Table 3 suggests one approach to such an evaluation.

To be used most effectively, an approach such as that suggested by Table 3 requires that the dimensions of the firm's approach and the target market characteristics be similar. With similar dimensions considered in both col-

[11] Mark E. Stern, *Marketing Planning: A Systems Approach* (New York: McGraw-Hill Book Co., 1966) pp. 131–36.

Table 3
One approach to firm vis-à-vis target market strategy evaluation

Strategy aspect	Target market characteristics	The firm's approach
1. Product		
Quality level	(The firm's quality level should match that desired by the target market)	
Features/options	(Those of the product should be those desired by the target market)	
Services offered	(Such as delivery, installation, and repair)	
Guarantee	(Consistent with the desires of target market?)	
Selection offered	(Consistent with variability within target market?)	
2. Distribution		
Store type	(Characteristics of retail outlets must be consistent with desires of target market)	
Market coverage	(Be consistent with target market's view of product; i.e., intensive if convenience good)	
Channel structure	(Provide services desired by target market)	
3. Promotion		
Type of appeal	(Firm's message must be consistent with what will affect the target market)	
Media used	(Must be media that reach target market)	
Personal sales effort	(Self-service vs. sales aid vs. high-pressure salesperson)	
4. Price		
Price level	(Consistent with target market; also consistent with product quality and promotional appeals)	
Discount structure	(Meet needs of target market; i.e., quantity discounts if customers buy in quantity)	
Price as competitive factor	(Use price if major factor in purchase decision, and vice versa)	

Note: The strategy aspects and characteristic descriptors listed are only examples and are not intended to be exhaustive. The approach is based on the concept of identifying those factors that are determinants of purchase behavior *for the target market selected* and comparing the firm's market offerings to the needs of the target market.

umns, congruence and discrepancy between the firm's marketing strategy and the characteristics of the target market are easily seen. For example, a firm might select as a target market stereo enthusiasts who want good quality sound and are willing to build kits in order to save money (target market characteristics) but offer only poor quality kits that are extremely difficult to assemble (the firm's marketing approach). Listing these factors on a form such as Table 3 would make the discrepancy more obvious.

Step 3: Developing recommendations

Once the analysis of the information about the firm's marketing programs has been completed, the audit team should complete its activities by making specific recommendations regarding the firm's marketing program. The recommendations should be based on the strengths and weaknesses of the firm's activities, as identified in Step 2 of Figure 1. If the analysis was done well, such recommendations will often be relatively simple to make because discrepancies become quite obvious.

In making recommendations, the audit should be concerned more with how the firm's marketing program can be modified to improve it in the future rather than pointing the finger at poor performance in the past. While management errors should be identified, it should be done from the point of view of not making the same mistakes twice rather than a "witch hunt" to single out poor performers. This approach will establish confidence in managers concerning the value of an audit and the ability of an audit to help them.

CONCLUSION

A marketing audit is often a time-consuming and perhaps expensive project. However, the benefits which result from such a comprehensive evaluation of a firm's past programs and present activities often more than justify the time and money invested. Further, the insights gained can be profitably applied to future planning of the firm's marketing activities. The improved future planning that can be accomplished as a result of a marketing audit may be just the edge needed to provide a breakthrough opportunity for the firm.

Marketing audits should be a regular part of the firm's planning process. The audits should be conducted by experienced and knowledgeable people who are in a position to be unbiased in their evaluation of the firm and the industry. The firm may choose to examine either the whole range of its marketing activities at a general level or examine part of its activities in depth. In either case, the audit should concentrate on the marketing mixes of the firm with respect to the industry in which it operates, its competitors, and, most importantly, the market segment(s) which the firm is attempting to serve.

QUESTIONS

1. What is a marketing audit? Why is it needed?
2. List and briefly explain the three steps that are involved in conducting a marketing audit.
3. Try to complete Table 3 for one of the cases in your textbook. Then make the appropriate recommendations.
*4. Would a marketing audit be more important during inflationary times? Would the procedures have to be changed? Explain. (See Reading 26.)

---

* Question relates concepts in this and other readings.

33
Miller's fast growth upsets the beer industry

After Philip Morris bought the Miller Brewing Company in 1970, it began to market beer the way it handles cigarettes. Miller adopted a segmentation strategy and began to introduce new products and to use strong promotional campaigns to reach selected markets. As a result, Miller sales tripled between 1972 and 1976.

When Philip Morris Inc. purchased Miller Brewing Co. in 1970 and a year later brought in John A. Murphy as its president, it hardly seemed a natural fit. After a decade with Philip Morris in which he rose to executive vice president of international operations, Murphy had a background clearly in tobacco. Even his Irish heritage seemed out of place in an industry still dominated by old-line German families. Now, however, Murphy gives every impression that he likes the beer business almost as much as he enjoys quaffing its products and chain-smoking his company's cigarettes. "Every Irishman dreams of going to heaven and running a brewery," jokes Murphy.

The combination of cigarettes and beer has indeed been a heaven on earth for both Murphy and Miller Brewing. But the Philip Morris–Miller combination is having quite the opposite effect on the nation's 48 other brewers. While Murphy's affability has already made many of those brewers his friends, they have become wary of his determination to dominate the U.S. brewing industry.

Not since Anheuser-Busch Inc. took over the industry lead in the late 1950s from the present runner-up, Jos. Schlitz Brewing Co., has a single brewer had such a dramatic effect on its competitors. Ranked seventh five years ago, Miller was the industry's sleeper—a brand with broad potential appeal but no marketing pizazz. With razzle-dazzle marketing techniques and the input of money at a dizzying pace, Philip Morris has more than tripled Miller's beer sales since 1972 [see Figure 1]. This year [1976] Miller may edge out Pabst Brewing Co., for third place in industry sales.

This performance has so stunned brewers that Murphy's talk about making Miller No. 1 is no longer considered idle chatter. Even August A. Busch III, who took over the chief executive post at Anheuser from his father last year, is reacting—revving up the "King of Beers" for its first serious competitive challenge in years. In fact, the 39-year-old Busch, who talks more like a street fighter than a fourth-generation member of brewing's royalty, seems bristling

Source: Reprinted with permission from *Business Week,* November 8, 1976, pp. 58–62, 67. Copyright © 1976 by McGraw-Hill, Inc.

Figure 1

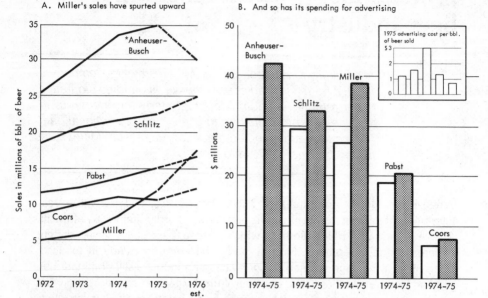

A. Miller's sales have spurted upward

B. And so has its spending for advertising

* Anheuser-Busch sales were affected by a 95-day strike in the second quarter of 1976.
Data: Part A, *Modern Brewery Age, Business Week* estimate; Part B, company figures except for Miller, which is estimate of Wertheim & Co.

for a fight not only to maintain but even to expand his company's 23 percent market share despite Miller's challenge. Says Busch: "Tell Miller to come right along, but tell them to bring lots of money."

Already it is clear that the Anheuser-Miller clash could trigger a vicious industry battle. It should also accelerate a revolution that is changing the competitive framework of the beer business—one of the nation's oldest consumer product industries and one that has passed through much of the 20th century without being changed by it.

Among the other factors that are altering the U.S. brewing industry and how it does business:

A massive addition to capacity by the nation's largest brewers. This is bound to create such overcapacity and heated competition that the number of brewers could be reduced from 49 today to 15 by 1980, putting almost 90 percent of the market into the hands of just five companies—Anheuser, Miller, Schlitz, Pabst, and Adolph Coors Co. These five have squeezed the regional brewers by expanding their collective share of the market from 53 percent in 1971 to 69 percent today.

A basic change in the way beer is marketed. Production efficiency and price promotion once were the keys to growth in brewing. But Miller has

successfully followed the Procter & Gamble formula, and beer marketing strategy is shifting to market segmentation, new-product proliferation, and heavy advertising—concepts that are doctrines in other consumer product fields but that have been largely ignored by most U.S.
brewers.

An unexpected slowdown, starting last year [1975], in the growth rate of
beer consumption. This could hasten the demise of smaller brewers and
put the new marketing orientation to a stiff early test. It may also encourage brewers to diversify aggressively for the first time.

The most serious challenge from government that the brewers have faced
since Prohibition. While the challenge has erupted on a number of fronts,
the most immediate threat is posed by a handful of federal agencies and
a couple of grand juries that are investigating the big brewers for allegedly making kickbacks to major customers and for suspected predatory pricing.

Strong, aggressive companies such as Anheuser and Miller may emerge
as winners from all this turmoil. But it spells nothing but trouble for most of
the brewing industry. Already, heightened competition has kept most brewers
from raising prices sufficiently to compensate for cost increases in packaging
and raw materials of 40 percent or more in 1974 and 1975. As a result, the
aftertax margins of even the largest publicly held brewers have dropped from
about 6 percent five years ago to 3.5 percent last year. In that same period,
their returns on equity fell from 15 percent to 10 percent.

With cost pressures easing somewhat, and with the aid of a 95-day strike at
Anheuser, most brewers are reporting improved profits this year. But in view
of the battle that is developing, the investment community senses that the
recovery may be short-lived. Despite better profits, the price/earnings ratios
of U.S. brewers still languish in the 10-to-1 range or lower, well below the
multiples of 30 or more a few years ago. "If everyone goes out to move the
capacity they are building, returns in this business have got to tumble," says
William K. Coors, chairman of Coors. Adds Emanuel Goldman, senior
analyst with Sanford C. Bernstein & Co.: "You have to search to find a
positive factor in brewing."

ENTER PHILIP MORRIS

The biggest single reason for such industry gloom is the challenge from
Miller. Before its acquisition by Philip Morris in 1970, Miller could not challenge anyone. While brewing's leaders were growing at 10 percent a year,
twice the industry's overall growth rate, Miller's sales remained flat. Then
came PM, loaded with excess cash from a profitable cigarette business and
looking to exploit in other areas a highly tuned marketing expertise that had
lifted it from sixth to second place in the tobacco business. Because it was

making net profits larger than those of industry leader Anheuser, PM's entry into the business caused immediate concern.

The concern was well founded. After spending a couple of years sizing up Miller's problems and replacing its management with executives from its tobacco operations and other consumer industries, PM shifted Miller into high gear. The results have been astonishing. Miller's sales leaped from 5 million barrels in 1972 to an estimated 18 million barrels this year. In that same period, its market share jumped from 4 percent to 12 percent.

By the end of the year, PM will have trebled Miller's beer-making capacity to 20 million barrels a year. And the company last summer broke ground on what eventually will be a monster brewery to turn out 10 million barrels a year at Eden, N. C. That, along with other planned plant expansions, will boost Miller's total capacity to 40 million barrels by 1980, about the same capacity as Anheuser's.

"By 1980 there are going to be at least 20 million barrels of beer sales that Anheuser, Schlitz, Pabst, and Coors thought they would get that Miller will sell instead," predicts Peter W. Stroh, president of eighth-ranked Stroh Brewing Co. in Detroit. Adds consultant Robert S. Weinberg, former corporate planning vice-president for Anheuser: "Two words have changed this industry completely—Philip Morris."

THE TOBACCO APPROACH

How Miller did it is almost as important as what Miller did because its methods are now being emulated by other brewers. Essentially, Miller's new managers borrowed the classic consumer marketing techniques that had brought PM success in the cigarette business and produced the nation's leading tobacco brand, Marlboro. The approach calls for dividing up the U.S. beer market into demand segments, producing new products and packages specifically for those segments, and then spending with abandon to promote them.

With notable exceptions such as Anheuser, most brewers have ignored this type of standard consumer marketing, relying instead on only one brand of beer. "Until Miller came along, the brewers operated as if there was a homogeneous market for beer that could be served by one product in one package," observes consultant Weinberg.

It did not take Miller's Murphy long to recognize that High Life—the single product the company had when PM took over—was not only not enough but was also aimed at the wrong beer-drinking market. Sold for years as the champagne of beers, High Life was attracting a disproportionate share of women and upper-income consumers who were not big beer drinkers. "A lot of people drank the beer, but none of them in quantity," says Murphy.

Under Murphy, advertisements for High Life began featuring young people riding in dune buggies and oil drillers sipping on a cool one after squelching an oil blowout. Explains Murphy: "We repositioned the product to attract the real beer drinker."

Figure 2

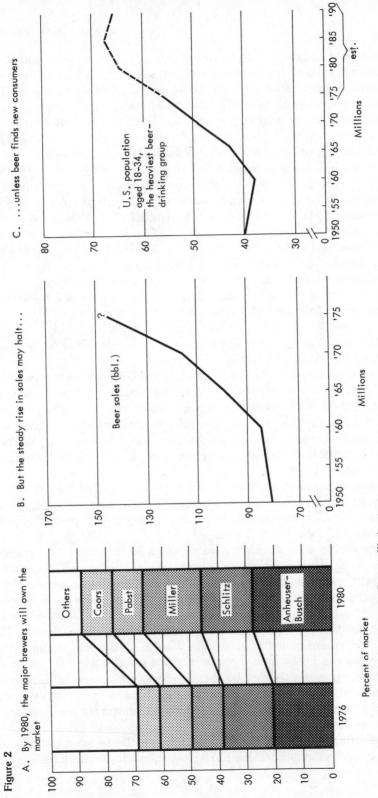

A. By 1980, the major brewers will own the market

Others
Coors
Pabst
Miller
Schlitz
Anheuser–Busch

1976   1980

Percent of market

B. But the steady rise in sales may halt...

Beer sales (bbl.)

170
150
130
110
90
70
0

1950 '55 '60 '65 '70 '75

Millions

C. ...unless beer finds new consumers

U.S. population aged 18–34, the heaviest beer–drinking group

80
70
60
50
40
30
0

1950 '55 '60 '65 '70 '75 '80 '85 '90
est.

Millions

Data: Census Bureau, Treasury Department; *Business Week* estimate.

Then Miller began opening up new market segments, beginning in 1972 with the introduction of a 7-ounce pony bottle, an idea that had failed earlier for several regional brewers. Miller's new product turned out to be a favorite of women and older people, who thought the standard 12-ounce size was simply too much beer to drink. The pony beer bottle had benefits even for the big beer drinker. "On a hot summer day," explains Murphy, "you can finish it without fearing that some of the beer in the bottom will get warm."

This year Miller will sell an estimated 2.5 million barrels of beer in 7-ounce bottles, about 15 percent of this year's volume and equal to half of all the beer Miller sold in 1972. But the pony's success was only a stage-setter for Miller's big marketing coup, the introduction of lower-calorie Lite beer (see *Business Week,* October 13, 1975).

First marketed nationally in early 1975, Lite now stands to become the most successful new beer introduced in the United States in this century. That is not saying a whole lot, though: In recent decades the U.S. brewing industry has had few new product winners. The major exceptions are Anheuser's Michelob and a few new malt liquors. The record shows a much longer list of disappointments, including Schlitz's Encore, Budweiser's Malt Liquor, Hamm's fruit-flavored beers, Carling's Tubor, Meister Brau's Lite (now owned by Miller), and Rheingold's Gablinger.

Like Miller's Lite, both Meister Brau's Lite and Gablinger were low-calorie beers. But they turned out to be disasters largely because they were marketed as diet drinks to diet-conscious consumers who do not drink beer in the first place. By contrast, Miller's heavy advertising program for Lite features sports personalities who offer the message that Lite, with one-third fewer calories, offers the big beer drinker an opportunity to drink as much beer as before without feeling so filled.

More than a few brewers laughed at what they insisted was Miller's attempt to enter a market that did not exist. But this year Miller will sell an estimated 5 million barrels of Lite, equal to its entire beer production four years ago, and the laughter has ceased.

While its first new products were designed to fill voids in the market, Miller's latest experiment is aimed squarely at challenging Michelob—Anheuser's most profitable product. Michelob is slightly heavier than Anheuser's Budweiser and sells for about 25 cents a six-pack more. Sales of Michelob have been growing at more than 30 percent a year, and the brand is virtually unchallenged in the so-called super-premium beer market. But under an agreement with Löwenbräu Munich, Miller this spring began test-marketing a Lowenbrau that it brews domestically and sells at a price 25 percent higher than Michelob's. Sensing Miller's first major assault against his company, Busch snaps: "This is Lowenbrau made in the United States not the beer imported from Europe, and the consumers are not going to be fooled by that little game."

Clearly much of Miller's success thus far rests on the fact that, unlike many family-owned breweries, Miller is run by managers who were not raised in the brewing business. "Other brewers are so convention-bound that they often don't experiment," says consultant Weinberg. "Philip Morris comes into this business with no rulebook and no prejudices."

BIG SPENDING, SMALL PROFIT

Marketing prowess is not the only key to Miller's meteoric rise in the U. S. beer business. Cigarette money is another. By 1980 Miller will have spent $850 million on plant expansion in addition to the $227 million that Philip Morris paid to buy the Milwaukee brewer. Much of that will come from PM's tobacco profits.

Miller's advertising expenditures seem profligate to many other brewers. Last year Miller spent an estimated $3 a barrel on advertising, nearly three times the industry average. This season it surprised everyone by booking the lion's share of major sporting events that brewers love to sponsor. Included in the Miller lineup: the World Series, ABC Monday night football, CBS pro football, college football, professional basketball and tennis, and the Indianapolis 500.

Because of its heavy expenditures, Miller's unprecedented growth in market share has not produced comparable profits. The company made only a total of $34 million in operating profits in the last five years, and when interest charges are deducted for the capital that PM has poured into it, Miller has lost an estimated $30 million for PM in that time. To many threatened brewers, this use of PM's cigarette profits (now 2½ times Anheuser's profits) to bankroll Miller's no-profit grab for market share is unfair competition. And some believe it may be unlawful.

"I suspect that there will be a lawsuit against Miller," says Robert A. Uihlein Jr., chairman of Schlitz, "because it is definitely taking profits from one business and sticking them into another business to gain market share by selling below cost. The law prohibits predatory pricing, and the question now is whether someone might try to interpret it to block what Miller is doing."

Others wonder whether Miller will be able to continue increasing its market share when PM finally calls on it to make a profit. They remember the scare when a predecessor company of Canada's Carling O'Keefe Ltd. bought tiny Carling Brewing Co. in the mid-1940s and poured huge sums of money into expanding the Carling Black Label brand in the United States. Subsidized by a very profitable Canadian brewing operation, Carling vaulted from 53rd place in the U.S. beer market to fourth by 1960. But after deducting interest on the money its parent was providing, Carling was not making a profit in those years of growth. Now Carling languishes in 11th place after losing $9 million last year.

"Somewhere down the pike, Miller is going to have to face economic realities, and when it is constrained to make a profit, market share growth may be more difficult," predicts Eugene B. Peters, president of Schlitz.

Experts who have been watching Miller closely, however, believe that

PM's big investment will pay off handsomely in a few years. This year Miller will nearly treble last year's $28 million operating profit. And after the interest on PM money is deducted from that, the year's net income will wipe out all of PM's earlier losses on Miller.

STEPPING UP THE COMPETITION

Though they were caught off guard by Miller's drive for top position in the U.S. brewing industry, the other major brewers now are moving to prevent Miller from growing further at their expense. All have started major capacity expansions. In addition to Miller's 25 percent expansion next year, Schlitz will start up the first one-third of a giant 6 million-barrel brewery in Syracuse, N.Y., next month, and Anheuser will bring on a new 3.7 million-barrel California brewery next spring. Meanwhile, Pabst and Coors are expanding their capacity by about 10 percent, and aggressive regionals such as Stroh and G. Heileman Brewing Co., of La Crosse, Wis., are also planning expansions to gain the economies of scale that bigger brewers enjoy.

In the next five years, more than 50 million barrels of new capacity will be made available, adding almost 30 percent to the industry's present total capacity. And some 18 million barrels of that capacity will come on stream in the United States in 1977, the largest single expansion in the industry's history. Since next year's 10 percent expansion will be three times as large as the most bullish projection of next year's growth in demand, it is bound to cause painful overcapacity. "I wonder how we are ever going to sell all this beer," muses William T. Elliott, president of C. Schmidt & Sons Inc., of Philadelphia.

The glut is likely to bring either massive price discounting or massive advertising, or both. Either way, many brewers are going to be seriously hurt, and the ax will fall first on the weaker regionals. The reason is basic economics. The secret to the growth of national brewers has not been the market share they took away from each other through improved marketing techniques but, rather, the market share they took from regionals by building more sophisticated production facilities.

In the mid-1960s, the majors began constructing super breweries that were more than double the size of anything built previously and that cut labor costs in half by taking advantage of technological improvements, particularly in packaging. This allowed the majors to cut the price spread between their premium beers and the popular-priced beers of the regionals from 25 cents per six-pack to as little as 10 cents. Tough pricing by the majors helps explain why beer prices in the late 1960s and early 1970s rose only 2 percent a year, half the growth rate of consumer prices overall. It also explains why the brewers' ranks in the last decade were trimmed from 118 to 49.

Given the enormous expansions of the majors, the industry may now be entering the final stage of consolidation that could wipe out most of the remaining regionals and leave only about 15 brewers in business by 1980.

While a few regionals, such as Stroh, Heileman, and Olympia Brewing Co., of Olympia, Wash., are given a good chance of making the grade, many large brewers privately concede that others, such as Rheingold Breweries (owned by Chock full o' Nuts), Schmidt, F. & M. Schaefer Brewing, of New York City, and Falstaff Brewing, of San Francisco, will have difficulty staying alive. Says Henry B. King, president of the U.S. Brewers Association: "I know half a dozen brewers who would sell out tomorrow if they could find a buyer."

While Miller's surge and the current round of capacity expansions will hurt the regional breweries most, it will also hurt some of the largest brewers for the first time. "There aren't that many weak regionals left from which the majors can take barrelage," says Edwin S. Coombs Jr., president of Seattle-based Rainier Cos. "That means the nationals are going to have to start taking market share from each other."

In fact, the battle of the big brands may already be under way. Preparing for its new California brewery, Anheuser last year increased its market share in California from 20.6 to 24.3 percent largely by taking it away from Coors, whose share dropped four points, to 36 percent. Coors, in turn, moved into the southern two-thirds of Texas, its first major territorial expansion in two decades, and has increased its share of the Texas market from 17.6 percent a year ago to 29 percent now. In Texas, Coors grew mostly at the expense of Schlitz, which fell four points to 29.6 percent. But Schlitz has fought back: It has become the fastest-growing brand in the Mountain States, where Coors boasts a dominant 40 percent market share.

Now that the efficient brewers with similar economies are pitted against one another, price promotion has become a much less important sales tool. "The companies that made it big in this business did so because they built big and the key to growth was productive efficiency," observes Schlitz's Peters. "Now the key to growth is marketing."

THE MARKETING SHOWDOWN

Already the major brewers are copying Miller's marketing strategies. Anheuser, Schlitz, and Pabst, for example, have introduced 7-ounce bottles to sell against Miller's pony bottle. Last year Schlitz introduced its own light beer. And later this year Anheuser, which pioneered market segmentation with Michelob and the popular-priced Busch Bavarian, will also start test-marketing a new light beer. "We could see more new products introduced in the next five years than we have seen in all this century," predicts Peters.

To sell their new beer products, companies are loosening the purse strings on advertising. The industry's media expenditures last year jumped 17 percent, and they could increase an additional 25 percent next year.

If marketing is now the key to the beer business and if the developing battle causes casualties among the national brewers, few experts think Anheuser and Miller will be among the losers. Observes John Maxwell, director of Maxwell Associates, a Richmond (Va.) investment banking concern:

"The early signs are that both Busch and Miller will be among the winners because they have the best marketing talent."

It is likely that Coors will also be a winner, although it has not advanced much further than the Adam Smith school of marketing. William Coors himself jokes freely about his company's paltry advertising expenditures, which are half the industry's average. And while other brewers are bringing out new products, Coors still insists that one product is enough to grow on.

But Coors has a big advantage in that it sells beer in only 20 percent of the U.S. market, and its product possesses a certain mystique. Moreover, that mystique seems strongest on the fringes of Coors's present market boundaries, which helps explain why it moved into command when it entered south Texas last year. When Coors moved into Montana this month, it got its usual wild reception: 2,000 applicants applied for the 10 distributorships it offered.

Thus, while Coors may lose some of its 40 percent market share in the 12 states where it now operates, it may compensate in the next few years by doubling its sales territory. "We have a built-in safety valve," says a confident William Coors. "If we need to sell more beer, all we have to do is expand our market."

If any of the top five brewers are vulnerable, Pabst and Schlitz are the most likely. While sales of Pabst have been growing recently at a reasonable rate, the company has shown little of the marketing aggressiveness its strong balance sheet might warrant. It is considered to have the most conservative expansion plans of all the big brewers, and its newer products (including a popular-priced beer called Red, White, and Blue and a super-premium called Andeker) have gone nowhere. Pabst's greatest vulnerability probably is to acquisition; both a food company and a tobacco company have been rumored to be suitors.

Schlitz has a different kind of problem. It lost momentum in 1974 and 1975, when its sales growth rate dropped from 12 to 4 percent and profits plummeted 42 percent. Partly because of a strike at Anheuser, Schlitz's sales and profits both look much better this year, but a real reversal may be hard to sustain. Chairman Uihlein claims that the trouble started when Schlitz led the beer price inceases of 1974. But some competitors cite another reason for the company's loss of pace. Schlitz indulged too long in price promotions in the early 1970s, they say, cheapening its brand image.

Whatever the reason, Schlitz now faces an uphill struggle. Two months ago it suspended its top marketing executives and admitted that it was under government investigation for alleged marketing malpractices. And even Uihlein concedes his company has more debt than he would like, which may explain why Schlitz is not hurrying to match Miller's expansion moves.

As a result, many believe Miller may supplant Schlitz as the second-largest beer company in the United States in a few more years. "If Miller continues to throw money into this business the way it has," concedes Schlitz President Peters, "it will eventually overtake both Schlitz and Busch because we are looking at the bottom line, and obviously Miller is not."

A FADING THIRST FOR BEER

Even as the competition among the big brewers heats up, the industry is faced with another problem that will spare no one—the decline in growth of demand for beer in the United States. From 1970 through 1974, beer consumption grew at a healthy 4.6 percent annual rate; now it is growing at only half that rate.

The recession and two consecutive years of 10 percent increases in beer prices—the first major increases in more than two decades—are part of the explanation. But while a consumer-spending recovery will boost soft-drink sales by an estimated 8 to 12 percent in 1976, the brewers will be lucky to get a 2.5 percent increase. This is puzzling because it comes when the brewers are putting new marketing strategies into action to step up beer sales.

Moreover, the rate of increase in demand for beer could slow even more in the decade ahead. Beer consumption grew an impressive 48 percent in the United States in the past decade partly because the number of people in the 18-to-34 age bracket grew 37 percent, far faster than the total population. This is traditionally the beer-drinking group; it drinks more than 50 percent of all beer sold. As the post–World War II babies outgrow this age in the 1980s, the growth in the beer-drinking age group will flatten. That spells real trouble for the breweries and could force even more rapid change.

For one thing, it is likely to spur the search for products that appeal to people who traditionally have not drunk much beer. Part of Miller's success with Lite and its 7-ounce bottle is that both fit the wish of older consumers and particularly women for beers that are less filling. "These people won't die at age 34 in the 1980s, and they won't stop consuming alcohol," asserts Busch. "They will merely be getting older, and that's why we'll be looking in the future for beers that are less filling and that have different tastes from those we are selling to today's younger market."

Still, the prospect of slower growth in demand for beer has set brewers to thinking about diversification, a strategy long ago adopted by other consumer product industries but resisted by the breweries. Even Schlitz and Anheuser, the largest and most diversified of U.S. brewers today, still get more than 90 percent of their income from beer—an almost unbelievable percentage for companies with respectively $2 billion and $1.1 billion in annual sales.

Busch expects this to change. "The point is approaching," he says, "when our growth will be constrained by the industry's growth. And since we'll then have more dollars than we can invest in brewing, we'll start putting them in other businesses."

Meanwhile, though, the U.S. brewing industry also faces another menace: challenges from government on several fronts. One issue is the nonreturnable can or bottle. In recent years, the industry has fought off federal and state legislation that would require a returnable deposit of 5 cents or more per bottle. The brewers insist that such laws would force them to spend $3 billion to convert their packaging lines from the aluminum can to the returnable bottle. And they have had solid backing from organized labor in the container industry in fighting such legislation. But they may have more trouble with the voters than with the legislators: Four states will hold referendums next week on this issue, and polls show that voters may overwhelmingly support deposits.

CHARGES OF KICKBACKS

The biggest and most immediate governmental challenge, however, is to certain marketing practices in the beer industry. Already the Securities and Exchange Commission, the Treasury Department, and the Justice Department are investigating possible payoffs and other illegal kickbacks by brewers to big retail customers to induce them to buy their brands. Regional brewers claim that kickbacks and other marketing malpractices of the majors are partly responsible for the demise of the smaller brewers.

An even more important break for the regionals could come through charges of predatory pricing. Smaller brewers have long argued that the big brewers sell below cost in some areas to gain market share and subsidize their losses with profits from areas where they are already dominant. The key case could be the lawsuit that Pearl Brewing Co. has brought against Anheuser and Schlitz. Pearl claims that, partly because of predatory pricing by both majors, its share of the Texas market has fallen from 23 percent in 1966 to a mere 6 percent today.

At the same time, the big brewers are wondering what is in store for them as a result of a three-year study that has been completed, but not yet released, by the Federal Trade Commission. The FTC reportedly has looked into charges of predatory pricing as part of an effort to understand the rapid recent consolidation in the brewing business.

Whatever the outcome of these investigations, there is little doubt that the next few years could bring big changes in the U.S. brewing industry. Competition may be fairer, but it will be no less intense. And the number of competitors will dwindle. "The next five years will be crucial in determining whether you remain in this business or not," says E. Lee Birdsong, president of Pearl Brewing. "And that goes not only for us but for brewers who are a lot larger."

QUESTIONS

1. What was the major factor behind the growth of Miller Brewing Company after Philip Morris bought it? Was it simply the amount of advertising dollars spent, or were other factors important as well?
2. Why was Miller successful with a low calorie beer when others had not been?
3. Why are some brewers expanding plant capacity at a time when the rate of increase in total consumption is only a very modest 2.5 percent?
4. Identify how the government has or may have an impact on the operation of the brewing industry. Are any market opportunities being created by present or potential government regulation?

Part 5

Marketing reappraised

Marketing contributes a great deal as an activity of the firm, both within the organization (micro-marketing) and in society as a whole (macro-marketing). Nevertheless, marketing's critics maintain that it could accomplish more or cost less, or both.

The first article in Part 5 discusses what consumerism means for marketers in a positive way. It considers both micro- and macro-level matters and suggests that consumerism offers marketing managers not only challenges but opportunities as well.

The other articles in this part are concerned with the basic structure of our economic system, in particular whether it should be market directed or central planned. The article on the optimum number of gasoline service stations is really concerned with the broader issue of how far an economic system should go in satisfying its consumers. Subsequent articles describe experiences with market-directed and planned economies. One argues for more planning for the U.S. economy while others suggest less, relying more on a market-directed system. These important matters affect not only marketing managers but the performance and operation of our whole macro-marketing system. Your own and society's decisions on these matters will affect your future as a producer and a consumer.

34
What consumerism means for marketers

Philip Kotler

Consumerism is not a new phenomenon, and Kotler argues that the current movement was inevitable and will be enduring. Further, it could be beneficial, promarketing, and profitable. He feels the real challenge for business is developing products and marketing practices that combine short- and long run consumer values. This leads him to advance a new concept of societal marketing to replace the marketing concept.

In this century, the U.S. business scene has been shaken by three distinct consumer movements—in the early 1900s, the mid—1930s, and the mid—1960s. The first two flare-ups subsided. Business observers, social critics, and marketing leaders are divided over whether this latest outbreak is a temporary or a permanent social phenomenon. Those who think that the current movement has the quality of a fad point to the two earlier ones. By the same token, they argue that this too will fade away. Others argue just as strongly that the issues which flamed the latest movement differ so much in character and force that consumerism may be here to stay.

In retrospect, it is interesting that the first consumer movement was fueled by such factors as rising prices, Upton Sinclair's writings, and ethical drug scandals. It culminated in the passage of the Pure Food and Drug Act (1906), the Meat Inspection Act (1906), and the creation of the Federal Trade Commission (1914). The second wave of consumerism in the mid—1930s was fanned by such factors as an upturn in consumer prices in the midst of the depression, the sulfanilamide scandal, and the widely imitated Detroit housewives strike. It culminated in the strengthening of the Pure Food and Drug Act and in the enlarging of the Federal Trade Commission's power to regulate against unfair or deceptive acts and practices.

The third and current movement has resulted from a complex combination of circumstances, not the least of which was increasingly strained relations between standard business practices and long-run consumer interests. Consumerism in its present form has also been variously blamed on Ralph

Source: Reprinted with permission from the *Harvard Business Review*, May—June 1972, pp. 48–57. Copyright © 1972, the President and Fellows of Harvard College. At the time of writing, Philip Kotler was a professor of marketing at Northwestern University.

Author's note: I wish to thank Professor Fred Allvine for his helpful and incisive comments during the writing of this article.

Nader, the thalidomide scandal, rising prices, the mass media, a few dissatisfied individuals, and on President Lyndon Johnson's "Consumer Interests
Message." These and other possible explanations imply that the latest
movement did not have to happen and that it had little relationship to the real
feelings of most consumers.

In this article, I shall discuss the current phenomenon and what it portends
for business. In so doing, I shall present five simple conclusions about consumerism and largely focus my discussion on these assessments. Consider:

1. *Consumerism was inevitable.* It was not a plot by Ralph Nader and a
handful of consumerists but an inevitable phase in the development of our
economic system.

2. *Consumerism will be enduring.* Just as the labor movement started
as a protest uprising and became institutionalized in the form of unions,
government boards, and labor legislation, the consumer movement, too, will
become an increasingly institutionalized force in U.S. society.

3. *Consumerism will be beneficial.* On the whole, it promises to make
the U.S. economic system more responsive to new and emerging societal
needs.

4. *Consumerism is promarketing.* The consumer movement suggests
an important refinement in the marketing concept to take into account
societal concerns.

5. *Consumerism can be profitable.* The societal marketing concept
suggests areas of new opportunity and profit for alert business firms.

These assessments of consumerism are generally at variance with the views of
many businessmen. Some business spokesmen maintain that consumerism
was stirred up by radicals, headline grabbers, and politicians; that it can be
beaten by attacking, discrediting, or ignoring it; that it threatens to destroy the
vitality of our economic system and its benefits; that it is an antimarketing
concept; and that it can only reduce profit opportunities in the long run.

WHAT IS CONSUMERISM?

Before discussing the foregoing conclusions in more depth, it is important
to know what we mean by "consumerism." Here is a definition: *Consumerism is a social movement seeking to augment the rights and power of
buyers in relation to sellers.* To understand this definition, let us first look at a
short list of the many traditional rights of sellers in the U.S. economic system:

Sellers have the right to introduce any product in any size and style they
wish into the marketplace so long as it is not hazardous to personal
health or safety; or, if it is, to introduce it with the proper warnings and
controls.

Sellers have the right to price the product at any level they wish provided
there is no discrimination among similar classes of buyers.

Sellers have the right to spend any amount of money they wish to promote the product, so long as it is not defined as unfair competition.

Sellers have the right to formulate any message they wish about the product provided that it is not misleading or dishonest in content or execution.

Sellers have the right to introduce any buying incentive schemes they wish.

Subject to a few limitations, these are among the essential core rights of businessmen in the United States. Any radical change in these would make U.S. business a different kind of game.

Now what about the traditional *buyers' rights?* Here, once again, are some of the rights that come immediately to mind:

Buyers have the right not to buy a product that is offered to them.

Buyers have the right to expect the product to be safe.

Buyers have the right to expect the product to turn out to be essentially as represented by the seller.

In looking over these traditional sellers' and buyers' rights, I believe that the balance of power lies with the seller. The notion that the *buyer has all the power he needs because he can refuse to buy the product is not deemed adequate* by consumer advocates. They hold that consumer sovereignty is not enough when the consumer does not have full information and when he is persuasively influenced by Madison Avenue.

What additional rights do consumers want? Behind the many issues stirred up by consumer advocates is a drive for several additional rights. In the order of their serious challenge to sellers' rights, they are:

Buyers want the right to have adequate information about the product.

Buyers want the right to additional protections against questionable products and marketing practices.

Buyers want the right to influence products and marketing practices in directions that will increase the "quality of life."

Consumer proposals

The "right to be informed," proposed by President Kennedy in his March 1962 directive to the Consumer Advisory Council, has been the battleground for a great number of consumer issues. These include, for example, the right to know the true interest cost of a loan (truth-in-lending), the true cost per standard unit of competing brands (unit pricing), the basic ingredients in a product (ingredient labeling), the nutritional quality of foods (nutritional labeling), the freshness of products (open dating), and the prices of gasoline (sign posting rather than pump posting).

Many of these proposals have gained widespread endorsement not only from consumers but also from political leaders and some businessmen. It is hard to deny the desirability of adequate information for making a free market operate vitally and competitively in the interests of consumers.

The proposals related to additional *consumer protection* are several, including the strengthening of consumers' hands in cases of business fraud, requiring of more stafety to be designed into automobiles, issuing of greater powers to existing government agencies, and setting up of new agencies.

The argument underlying consumer protection proposals is that consumers do not necessarily have the time and/or skills to obtain, understand, and use all the information that they may get about a product; therefore, some impartial agencies must be established which can perform these tasks with the requisite economies of scale.

The proposals relating to *quality-of-life* considerations include regulating the ingredients that go into certain products (detergents, gasoline) and packaging (soft drink containers), reducing the level of advertising and promotional "noise," and creating consumer representation on company boards to introduce consumer welfare considerations in business decision making.

The argument in this area says that products, packaging, and marketing practices must not only pass the test of being profitable to the company and convenient to the consumer but must also be life-enhancing. Consumerists insist that the world's resources no longer permit their indiscriminate embodiment in any products desired by consumers without further consideration of their social values. This "right" is obviously the most radical of the three additional rights that consumers want, and the one which would constitute the most basic challenge to the sellers' traditional rights.

CONSUMERISM WAS INEVITABLE

Let us now consider in greater depth the first of the five conclusions I cited at the outset of this article—namely, that consumerism was inevitable. Consumerism did not necessarily have to happen in the 1960s, but it had to happen eventually in veiw of new conditions in the U.S. economy that warranted a fresh examination of the economic power of sellers in relation to buyers.

At the same time, there are very good reasons why consumerism did flare up in the mid–1960s. The phenomenon was not due to any single cause. Consumerism was reborn because all of the conditions that normally combine to produce a successful social movement were present. These conditions are structural conduciveness, structural strains, growth of a generalized belief, precipitating factors, mobilization for action, and social control.[1] Using these six conditions, I have listed in Exhibit 1 the major factors under each that contributed to the rise of consumerism.

---

[1] These conditions were proposed in Neil J. Smelser, *Theory of Collective Behavior* (New York: The Free Press, 1963).

Exhibit 1
Factors contributing to the rise of consumerism in the 1960s

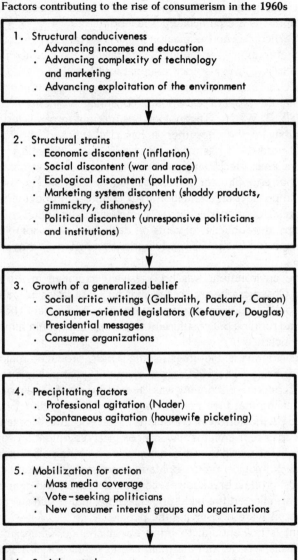

1. Structural conduciveness
   . Advancing incomes and education
   . Advancing complexity of technology
     and marketing
   . Advancing exploitation of the environment

2. Structural strains
   . Economic discontent (inflation)
   . Social discontent (war and race)
   . Ecological discontent (pollution)
   . Marketing system discontent (shoddy products,
     gimmickry, dishonesty)
   . Political discontent (unresponsive politicians
     and institutions)

3. Growth of a generalized belief
   . Social critic writings (Galbraith, Packard, Carson)
     Consumer-oriented legislators (Kefauver, Douglas)
   . Presidential messages
   . Consumer organizations

4. Precipitating factors
   . Professional agitation (Nader)
   . Spontaneous agitation (housewife picketing)

5. Mobilization for action
   . Mass media coverage
   . Vote-seeking politicians
   . New consumer interest groups and organizations

6. Social control
   . Business resistance or indifference
   . Legislative resistance or indifference

Structural conduciveness refers to basic developments in the society that eventually create potent contradictions. In the latest consumer movement, three developments are particularly noteworthy.

First, U.S. incomes and educational levels advanced continuously. This portended that many citizens would eventually become concerned with the quality of their lives, not just their material well-being.

Second, U.S. technology and marketing were becoming increasingly complex. That this would create potent consumer problems was noted perceptively by E. B. Weiss: "Technology has brought unparalleled abundance and opportunity to the consumer. It has also exposed him to new complexities and hazards. It has made his choices more difficult. He cannot be chemist, mechanic, electrician, nutritionist, *and* a walking computer (very necessary when shopping for fractionated-ounce food packages)! Faced with almost infinite product differentiation (plus contrived product virtues that are purely semantic), considerable price differentiation, the added complexities of trading stamps, the subtleties of cents-off deals, and other complications, the shopper is expected to choose wisely under circumstances that baffle professional buyers."[2]

Third, the environment was progressively exploited in the interests of abundance. Observers began to see that an abundance of cars and conveniences would produce a shortage of clean air and water. The Malthusian specter of man running out of sufficient resources to maintain himself became a growing concern.

These developments, along with some others, produced major *structural strains* in the society. The 1960s were a time of great public discontent and frustration. Economic discontent was created by steady inflation which left consumers feeling that their real incomes were deteriorating. Social discontent centered on the sorrowful conditions of the poor, the race issue, and the tremendous costs of the Vietnam war. Ecological discontent arose out of new awarenesses of the world population explosion and the pollution fallout associated with technological progress. Marketing system discontent centered on safety hazards, product breakdowns, commercial noise, and gimmickry. Political discontent reflected the widespread feelings that politicians and government institutions were not serving the people.

Discontent is not enough to bring about change. There must grow a *generalized belief* about both the main causes of the social malaise and the potent effectiveness of collective social action. Here, again, certain factors contributed importantly to the growth of a generalized belief.

First, there were the writings of social critics such as John Kenneth Galbraith, Vance Packard, and Rachel Carson, that provided a popular interpretation of the problem and of actionable solutions.

---

[2] "Marketers Fiddle While Consumers Burn," *Harvard Business Review,* July–August 1968, p. 48.

Second, there were the hearings and proposals of a handful of Congressmen such as Senator Estes Kefauver that held out some hope of legislative remedy.

Third, there were the Presidential "consumer" messages of President Kennedy in 1962 and President Johnson in 1966, which legitimated belief and interest in this area of social action.

Finally, old-line consumer testing and educational organizations continued to call public attention to the consumers' interests.

Given the growing collective belief, consumerism only awaited some *precipitating factors* to ignite the highly combustible social material. Two sparks specifically exploded the consumer movement. The one was General Motors' unwitting creation of a hero in Ralph Nader through its attempt to investigate him; Nader's successful attack against General Motors encouraged other organizers to undertake bold acts against the business system. The other was the occurrence of widespread and spontaneous store boycotts by housewives in search of a better deal from supermarkets.

These chance combustions would have vanished without a lasting effect if additional resources were not *mobilized for action.* As it turned out, three factors fueled the consumer movement.

First, the mass media gave front-page coverage and editorial support to the activities of consumer advocates. They found the issues safe, dramatic, and newsworthy. The media's attention was further amplified through word-of-mouth processes into grass-roots expressions and feelings.

Second, a large number of politicians at the federal, state, and local levels picked up consumerism as a safe, high-potential vote-getting social issue.

Third, a number of existing and new organizations arose in defense of the consumer, including labor unions, consumer cooperatives, credit unions, product testing organizations, consumer education organizations, senior citizen groups, public interest law firms, and government agencies.

Of course, the progress and course of an incipient social movement depends on the reception it receives by those in *social control,* in this case, the industrial-political complex. A proper response by the agents of social control can drain the early movement of its force. But this did not happen. Many members of the business community attacked, resisted, or ignored the consumer advocates in a way that only strengthened the consumerist cause. Most legislative bodies were slow to respond with positive programs, thus feeding charges that the political system was unresponsive to consumer needs and that more direct action was required.

Thus all the requisite conditions were met in the 1960s. Even without some of the structural strains, the cause of consumerism would have eventually emerged because of the increasing complexity of technology and the environmental issue. And the movement has continued to this day, abetted by the unwillingness of important sections of the business and political systems to come to terms with the basic issues.

IT WILL BE ENDURING

As we have seen, observers are divided over whether consumerism is a temporary or a permanent social phenomenon: some people argue that the current consumer movement will pass over; others argue that it differs substantially from the two earlier movements. For example, the ecology issue is here to stay and will continue to fuel the consumer movement. The plight of the poor will continue to raise questions about whether the distribution system is performing efficiently in all sectors of the economy. There are more educated and more affluent consumers than ever before, and they are the mainstay of an effective social movement. The continuous outpouring of new products in the economy will continue to raise questions of health, safety, and planned obsolescence. Altogether, the issues that flamed the current consumer movement may be more profound and enduring than in the past.

No one can really predict how long the current consumer movement will last. There is good reason to believe, in fact, that the protest phase of the consumer movement will end soon. The real issue is not how long there will be vocal consumer protest but rather what legacy it will leave regarding the balance of buyers' rights and sellers' rights.

Each of the previous consumer movements left new institutions and laws to function in behalf of the consumer. By this test, the victory already belongs to consumers. Sellers now must operate within the new constraints of a Truth-in-Lending Law, a Truth-in-Packaging Law, an Auto Safety Law, an Office of Consumer Affairs, an Environmental Protection Agency, and a greatly strengthened Federal Trade Commission and Federal Food and Drug Administration.

It is no accident that such laws and institutions come into being when the demonstration and agitation phase of the consumer movement starts to dwindle. It is precisely the enactment of new laws and creation of new institutions that cause the protest phase to decline. Viewed over the span of a century, the consumer movement has been winning and increasing buyers' rights and power. In this sense, the consumerist movement is enduring, whether or not the visible signs of protest are found.

IT CAN BE BENEFICIAL

Businessmen take the point of view that since consumerism imposes costs on them, it will ultimately be costly to the consumer. Since they have to meet more legal requirements, they have to limit or modify some of their methods for attracting customers. This may mean that consumers will not get all the products and benefits they want and may find business costs passed on to them.

Businessmen also argue that they have the consumer's interests at heart and have been serving him well, and that customer satisfaction is the central tenet of their business philosophy. Many sincerely believe that consumerism is politically motivated and economically unsound.

The test of beneficiality, however, lies not in the short-run impact of consumerism on profits and consumer interests but rather in its long-run impact. Neither consumerism nor any social movement can get very far in the absence of combustible social material. Protest movements are messages coming from the social system that say that something is seriously wrong. They are the body politic's warning system. To ignore or attack protest signals is an invitation to deepening social strains. Protest movements are social indicators of new problems which need joint problem solving, not social rhetoric.

The essential legacy of consumerism promises to be beneficial in the long run. It forces businessmen to reexamine their social roles. It challenges them to look at problems which are easy to ignore. It makes them think more about ends as well as means. The habit of thinking about ends has been deficient in U.S. society, and protest movements such as consumerism, minority rights, student rights, and women's rights have a beneficial effect in raising questions about the purposes of institutions before it is too late.

Beyond this philosophical view of the beneficial aspects of protest movements may lie some very practical gains for consumers and businessmen. Here are four arguments advanced by consumerists:

1. Consumerism will increase the amount of product information. This will make it possible for consumers to buy more efficiently. They may obtain more value or goods with a given expenditure or a given amount of goods with a lower expenditure. To the extent that greater buying efficiency will result in surplus purchasing power, consumers may buy more goods in total.

2. Consumerism will lead to legislation that limits promotional expenditure which primarily affects market shares rather than aggregate demand. Consumer games, trading stamps, and competitive brand advertising in demand-inelastic industries are largely seen as increasing the costs of products to consumers with little compensating benefits. Reductions in the level of these expenditures, particularly where they account for a large portion of total cost, should lead to lower consumer prices.

3. Consumerism will require manufacturers to absorb more of the social costs imposed by their manufacturing operations and product design decisions. Their higher prices will decrease the purchase of high social cost goods relative to low social cost goods. This will mean lower governmental expenditures covered by taxes to clean up the environment. Consumers will benefit from a lower tax rate and/or from a higher quality environment.

4. Consumerism will reduce the number of unsafe or unhealthy products, which will result in more satisfied, healthier consumers.

These arguments are as cogent as contrary arguments advanced by some business spokesmen against responding to consumerism. This is not to deny that many companies will inherit short-run costs not compensated by short-run revenues and in this sense be losers. Their opposition to consumerism is understandable. But this is not the basis for developing a sound long-run social policy.

IT IS PROMARKETING

Consumerism has come as a shock to many businessmen because deep in their hearts they believe that they have been serving the consumer extraordinarily well. Do businessmen deserve the treatment that they are getting in the hands of consumerists?

It is possible that the business sector has deluded itself into thinking that it has been serving the consumer well. Although the marketing concept is the professed philosophy of a majority of U.S. companies, perhaps it is more honored in the breach than in the observance. Although top management professes the concept, the line executives, who are rewarded for ringing up sales, may not practice it faithfully.

What is the essence of the marketing concept?

The marketing concept calls for a *customer orientation* backed by *integrated marketing* aimed at generating *customer satisfaction* as the key to attaining long-run profitable volume.

The marketing concept was a great step forward in meshing the actions of business with the interests of consumers. It meant that consumer wants and needs became the starting point for product and market planning. It meant that business profits were tied to how well the company succeeded in pleasing and satisfying the customer.

Peter F. Drucker suggested that consumerism is "the shame of the total marketing concept," implying that the concept is not widely implemented.[3] But even if the marketing concept as currently understood were widely implemented, there would be a consumerist movement. Consumerism is a clarion call for a *revised marketing concept*.

The main problem that is coming to light rests on the ambiguity of the term *customer satisfaction*. Most businessmen take this to mean that *consumer desires* should be the orienting focus of product and market planning. The company should produce what the customer wants. But the problem is that in efficiently serving customers' desires, it is possible to hurt their long-run interests. Edmund Burke noted the critical difference when he said to the British electorate, "I serve your interests, not your desires." From the many kinds of products and services that satisfy consumers in the short run but disserve or dissatisfy them in the long run, here are four examples:

1.   Large, expensive automobiles please their owners but increase the pollution in the air, the congestion of traffic, and the difficulty of parking, and therefore reduce the owners' long-run satisfaction.

2.   The food industry in the United States is oriented toward producing new products which have high taste appeal. Nutrition has tended to be a secondary consideration. Many young people are raised on a diet largely of potato chips, hot dogs, and sweets which satisfy their tastes but harm their long-run health.

---

[3] "The Shame of Marketing," *Marketing/Communications,* August 1969, p. 60.

3.   The packaging industry has produced many new convenience features for the American consumer such as nonreusable containers, but the same consumers ultimately pay for this convenience in the form of solid waste pollution.

4.   Cigarettes and alcohol are classic products which obviously satisfy consumers but which ultimately hurt them if consumed in any excessive amount.

These examples make the point that catering to consumer satisfaction does not necessarily create satisfied consumers. Businessmen have not worried about this so long as consumers have continued to buy their products. But while consumers buy as *consumers,* they increasingly express their discontent as *voters.* They use the political system to correct the abuses that they cannot resist through the economic system.

The dilemma for the marketer, forced into the open by consumerism, is that he cannot go on giving the consumer only what pleases him without considering the effect on the consumer's and society's well-being. On the other hand, he cannot produce salutary products which the consumer will not buy. The problem is to somehow reconcile company profit, consumer desires, and consumer long-run interests. The original marketing concept has to be broadened to the societal marketing concept:

The societal marketing concept calls for a *customer orientation* backed by *integrated marketing* aimed at generating *customer satisfaction* and *long-run consumer welfare* as the key to attaining long-run profitable volume.

The addition of long-run consumer welfare asks the businessman to include social and ecological considerations in his product and market planning. He is asked to do this not only to meet his social responsibilities but also because failure to do this may hurt his long-run interests as a producer.

Thus the message of consumerism is not a setback for marketing but rather points to the next stage in the evolution of enlightened marketing. Just as the *sales concept* said that sales were all important, and the original *marketing concept* said that consumer satisfaction was also important, the *societal marketing concept* has emerged to say that long-run consumer welfare is also important.

IT CAN BE PROFITABLE

This last assessment is the most difficult and yet the most critical of my five conclusions to prove. Obviously, if consumerism is profitable, businessmen will put aside their other objections. It is mainly because of its perceived unprofitability that many businessmen object so vehemently.

Can consumerism be profitable? Here my answer is "yes." Every social movement is a mixed bag of threats and opportunities. As John Gardner observed, "We are all continually faced with a series of great opportunities brilliantly disguised as insoluble problems." The companies that will profit from consumerism are those in the habit of turning negatives into positives. According to Peter F. Drucker: *"Consumerism actually should be, must be, and I hope will be, the opportunity of marketing. This is what we in marketing have been waiting for."*[4]

The alert company will see consumerism as a new basis for achieving a differential competitive advantage in the marketplace. A concern for consumer well-being can be turned into a profitable opportunity in at least two ways: through the introduction of needed new products and through the adoption of [a] companywide consumerist orientation.

NEW OPPORTUNITIES

One of the main effects of consumerism is to raise concerns about the health, safety, and social worthiness of many products. For a long time, *salutary criteria* have been secondary to *immediate satisfaction criteria* in the selection of products and brands. Thus when Ford tried to sell safety as an automobile attribute in the 1950s, buyers did not respond. Most manufacturers took the position that they could not educate the public to want salutary features but if the public showed this concern, then business would respond.

Unfortunately, the time came but business was slow to respond. Consumer needs and wants have been evolving toward safety, health, and self-actualization concerns without many businessmen noticing this. More and more people are concerned with the nutritiousness of their foods, the flammability of their fabrics, the safety of their automobiles, and the pollution quality of their detergents. Many manufacturers have missed this changing psychological orientation of consumers.

Product reformulations

Today, there are a great many opportunities for creating and marketing new products that meet consumer desires for both short-term satisfaction and long-term benefits.

Exhibit 2 suggests a paradigm for thinking about the major types of new product opportunities. All current products can be classified in one of four ways, using the dimensions of immediate satisfaction and long-run consumer interests. As this exhibit shows, *desirable products* are those which combine high immediate satisfaction and high long-run benefit, such as tasty, nutritious breakfast foods. *Pleasing products* are those which give high immediate satisfaction but which may hurt consumer interests in the long run, such as cigarettes. *Salutary products* are those which have low appeal but which are also highly beneficial to the consumer in the long run, such as low-phosphate detergents. Finally, *deficient products* are those which have neither immediate appeal nor salutary qualities, such as a bad-tasting patent medicine.

---

[4] Ibid., p. 64.

Exhibit 2
Classification of new product opportunities

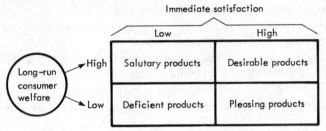

The manufacturer might as well forget about deficient products because too much work would be required to build in pleasing and salutary qualities. On the other hand, the manufacturer should invest his greatest effort in developing desirable products—e.g., new foods, textiles, appliances, and building materials—which combine intrinsic appeal and long-run beneficiality. The other two categories, pleasing and salutary products, also present a considerable challenge and opportunity to the company.

The challenge posed by pleasing products is that they sell extremely well but they ultimately hurt the consumer's interests. The product opportunity is therefore to formulate some alteration of the product that adds salutary qualities without diminishing any or too many of the pleasing qualities. This type of product opportunity has already been seized by a number of companies:

Sears has developed and promoted a phosphate-free laundry detergent which has become a big selling brand.

American Oil and Mobil Oil have developed and promoted no-lead or low-lead gasolines.

Pepsi-Cola has developed a one-way plastic soft drink bottle that is degradable in solid waste treatment.

Various automobile manufacturers are redesigning their engines to reduce their polluting levels without reducing their efficiency.

Various tobacco firms are researching the use of lettuce leaf to eliminate the health hazards of tobacco leaf in cigarettes.

Not all of these product reformulations will be successful. The new product must incorporate the salutary qualities without sacrificing the pleasing qualities. Thus new low-phosphate detergents must continue to wash effectively, or almost as effectively, as the former high-phosphate detergents. New low-lead or no-lead gasolines must continue to give efficient mileage and performance.

In addition, the company must be skilled at marketing the new products. The company faces difficult questions of what price to set, what claims to make, and what to do with the former product. In the case of low-lead gasoline, initial sales have been disappointing because of several factors, not the least of which is that it was priced at a premium and discouraged all but the most devoted environmentalists from buying it. The environmental appeal is strong, provided that the new product performs about as well as the old product and is not priced higher.

Salutary products, such as noninflammable draperies and many health foods, are considered "good for the customer" but somehow lack pleasing qualities. The challenge to the marketer is to incorporate satisfying qualities in the product without sacrificing the salutary qualities. Here are examples:

Quaker Oats has been reviewing desirable nutrients and vitamins and formulating new breakfast cereals around them.

Some food manufacturers have created new soybean-based products, in each case adding pleasing flavors that appeal to the intended target groups.

Fabric manufacturers are trying to create attractive draperies out of new synthetic, noninflammable materials.

Thus new product opportunities may be found by starting with appealing products and trying to add salutary qualities, or starting with salutary products and trying to add appealing qualities. This will become more important as more people show a concern for their environment and demand desirable products. There is already a sizable market segment made up of environmentalists who are ready to buy any product that has a salutary stamp. The alert company can even specialize in this market by commiting itself to creating and assorting products of high environmental appeal.

Consumerist orientation

A second way to respond profitably to consumerism is to become one of a growing number of companies that adopt and implement a thoroughgoing concern-for-the-consumer attitude. This goes beyond the occasional introduction of a few new products that combine pleasing and salutary qualities. It goes beyond an enlarged public relations campaign to appear as a "we care" company. To be effective, it involves management commitment, employee education, social actions, and company investment. A few companies have moved into a total consumerist orientation and have earned high consumer regard in the process. Here are two illustrative examples:

Giant Food, Inc., a leading supermarket chain in the Washington, D.C. area, actively introduced unit pricing, open dating, and nutritional labeling. According to a spokesman for the company, "These actions have improved Giant's goodwill immeasurably and have earned the admiration of leaders of the consumer movement."

Whirlpool Corporation has adopted a large number of measures to improve customer information and services, including a toll-free complaint service and improved product warranties. According to Stephen E. Upton, Whirlpool Vice President, "Our rate of increase in sales has tripled that of the industry. Our interest in the consumer has to be one of the reasons."

Obviously, such companies believe that these measures will increase their consumer goodwill and lead in turn to increased profits. The companies in each industry that adopt a consumerist orientation are likely to earn the early advantage and reap the rewards. If the profits are forthcoming, others will rush in and imitate the innovators. But imitation is often not as effective as innovation. Consumerism may well turn out to be an opportunity for the leaders and a cost for the laggards.

CONCLUSION

Consumerism was born for the third time in this century in the middle 1960s as a result of a complex combination of circumstances, not the least of which was increasingly strained relations between current business practices and long-run consumer interests. To many businessmen, it came as a shock because they thought the economic machinery, creating the highest standard of living in the world, was beyond consumer complaint. But the movement was inevitable, partly because of the success of economic machinery in creating complex, convenient, and pleasing products.

My assessment is that consumerism will be enduring, beneficial, promarketing, and ultimately profitable. Consumerism mobilizes the energies of consumers, businessmen, and government leaders to seek solutions to several complex problems in a technologically advanced society. One of these is the difference between serving consumer desires efficiently and serving their long-run interests.

To marketers, it says that products and marketing practices must be found which combine short-run and long-run values for the consumer. It says that a societal marketing concept is an advance over the original marketing concept and a basis for earning increased consumer goodwill and profits. The enlightened marketer attempts to satisfy the consumer *and* enhance his total well-being on the theory that what is good in the long run for consumers is good for business.

QUESTIONS

1. Was consumerism "inevitable"? Explain.
2. Evaluate Kotler's view that consumerism:
   a. Will be enduring.
   b. Can be beneficial.

    c. Is promarketing.
    d. Can be profitable.
3. Provide a new illustration for each of Kotler's four new-product opportunities.
*4. Compare and contrast Kotler's societal marketing concept and Lazer's social marketing concept (see Reading 1).

* Question relates concepts in this and other readings.

35
How many service stations are too many?

Richard D. Lundy

Lundy analyzes a very difficult question for any economy—how much consumer satisfaction (in goods and services) should be provided. This must be decided explicitly in a planned economy, while in a market-directed economy the decisions of many producers and consumers decide the matter. In either case, critics may find fault if too much or too little is provided for consumers as a whole or for specific market segments.

    Perhaps the title would be better phrased as "How much is too much?" Lundy shows that the answer to this question is not easy. It is important to note that the article applies not only to gasoline service stations but more broadly to the number of brands in a product category, the quality built into competing products, and so on. In other words, it is concerned with how well consumers should be satisfied by a macro-marketing system.

I. TOO MANY FOR WHAT?

As of June 1948, some 3,881,500 business firms were operating in the United States. Of these, 1,771,000, or 45.6 percent, were retailers. Both figures represented new highs. Recovering sharply after a setback suffered during the war, the business population grew rapidly from 1944 to 1947 and

Source: Reprinted with permission from Richard D. Lundy, *Theory in Marketing* (Homewood, Ill.: Richard D. Irwin, Inc., 1950), pp. 321–33. At the time of writing, Richard Lundy was a graduate student at the Wharton School, University of Pennsylvania.

then leveled off. By the end of 1947, the number of firms in operation virtually equaled the number calculated by the United States Department of Commerce as "normal" or "expected" on the basis of the prewar relationship between the business population and the general level of business activity.[1]

Statistics of this sort have long evoked two contradictory responses from observers of business. One is based upon a faith in the social desirability of having the business of this country in the hands of numerous free and independent businessmen. It leads to programs for the encouragement and protection of small business. The other response depends upon an emphasis on technical efficiency, especially in marketing institutions. It believes that goods and services would be produced and distributed more cheaply if society could rid itself of large numbers of small, weak, and badly managed firms. Observers who take this point of view are the ones who ask, in particular: "Are there too many retailers?" Usually they mean this as a rhetorical question, to which the answer is a self-evident affirmative.

If the question is considered seriously as a question, however, the answer ceases to seem obvious. One soon discovers that "too many" is a term not easily or precisely defined. Its meaning depends upon the objectives one thinks retailing should achieve, and one soon must ask: "Too many for what?"

The present essay summarizes the results of an attempt to determine whether, even with this addition, the question lends itself to a single meaningful answer. Attention has been centered upon the service station as a type case of retailer. The author has first set up certain assumptions as to the objectives service stations are supposed to achieve. Where possible, he has then estimated the number of stations required to achieve these objectives, as of 1946. The results have some interest for their own sake and may be helpful in suggesting how one may go about measuring the extent to which the number of retailers is too large, too small, or about right to accomplish the purposes for which they are established and maintained.

II. BASES OF MEASUREMENT

The service station may be considered to have three basic functions in the community:

1. Like any other retail enterprise, the service station supplies certain needs of the consumer. It has the function of providing service for the motorist in keeping with what he can and will pay.

2. To the operator, the service station is a way of making a living. In return for rendering to the consumers the services they want, he expects personal benefits. To him, the function of the service station is to yield a satisfactory money profit.

---

[1] *Survey of Current Business*, vol. 28 (November 1948), pp. 12–13.

3. In addition to performing these functions for specific individuals, the service station operates in a social setting toward which it has responsibilities. To justify its existence in the social picture, it must do more good than harm; it must in some sense add value to the community.

Provision of direct service to the consumer, of profit to the operator, and of general benefit to the community are, then, the functions of the service station. In relation to each of these functions, the term "optimum number" has an entirely different meaning. To the consumer, the optimum number is a problem of services performed at convenient locations for reasonable prices without a serious threat of monopoly. To the dealer, it is a problem of earning profits and maintaining a market position. To the community, it means a source of employment and taxes, an effective choice among alternative uses of land, and an interest in community appearance.

Measured against each of these functions, the optimum will come out differently. The degree of overcapacity or undercapacity present in the actual market will vary as the basis of measurement varies.

In the actual community, judgments will be based upon a combination of these various viewpoints. Only by integrating them in some workable fashion can the observer achieve the results most desirable to all. However, the difficulties inherent in integration are great, and all that will be attempted here is to study each phase of the problem independently for whatever light it may throw upon the overall question.

Thus limited, the problem to be solved is either to measure separately the contribution a given number of service stations makes toward fulfilling each of the three functions described, or, alternatively, to determine how many stations would be required to perform these functions at any specified level of adequacy. For present purposes, the second alternative is accepted, and measurement is attempted against four tests of adequacy:[2]

1. The minimum number of stations needed to provide the physical supply of gasoline that consumers must have in their tanks, with no consideration of convenience or amenities.
2. The number of stations needed to provide maximum convenience for consumers.
3. The number of stations needed to maximize net profit for the individual stations.
4. The number of stations needed to produce the optimum positive effect on the welfare of the communities in which they are located.

III. MINIMUM NUMBER OF STATIONS REQUIRED FOR PHYSICAL SUPPLY

The absolute minimum number of service stations is set by the bare physical job of putting gasoline into the tanks of the motor vehicles in the United

---

[2] The present analysis has also been restricted to the work of the service station as a distributor of gasoline alone.

States. If the amount of gasoline consumed is taken as given, then the number of stations required will be fixed by the capacity of a service-station pump and the number of pumps per station. For any given number of pumps per station, the number of stations will be a minimum under the following conditions, which represent no inconsiderable degree of austerity for consumers and operators:

1. All stations operate twenty-four hours during every day in the year.
2. All supply tanks in the stations are refilled as needed without interruption of service to consumers.
3. The customers' automobiles are lined up one behind the other, so that no time is lost between cars.
4. Each customer arrives at the station with his tank empty and has it filled to capacity.
5. Only one brand is offered for sale, and that in a single grade.
6. Consumers will move their residences, if necessary, to be near a station that can serve them. Presumably, the extreme limit of the distance from a station at which any consumer will locate is something less than the mileage he can travel from station to home and back on one tankful of gasoline.
7. Population so distributes itself that the amount of gasoline sold by the various stations is equalized.
8. Once the population is thus distributed, there are no further shifts, although individuals may replace or be replaced by others in the groups assigned to particular stations.
9. Consumption of gasoline is steady throughout the year, with no seasonal or other fluctuations.

Under these rigorous conditions, the minimum number of service stations that could have met the 1946 consumption of 30,039,823,000 gallons of gasoline is set by making two more assumptions: that each station has three pumps, and that each pump dispenses gasoline at the rate of ten gallons per minute.[3] On this basis, the United States in 1946 "needed" only 1,906 three-pump service stations, or a total of 5,718 pumps. For purposes of comparison, it may be noted that in 1946 there actually were approximately 215,000 service stations and approximately 180,000 retailers of other types who sold gasoline. There were approximately 1,500,000 gasoline pumps in the country.[4]

---

[3] The figures for the 1946 consumption of gasoline include all gasoline-consuming equipment; American Petroleum Institute, *Petroleum Facts and Figures* (New York: 1947), pp. 18–19. The rate of operation of the average pump was established at ten gallons per minute on the advice of the American Petroleum Institute.

[4] These estimates were made for the writer by the research staff of a large oil company. The retailers other than service stations proper include vehicle dealers, garages, repair shops, parts and accessories dealers, and country general stores. Approximately 120,000 pumps were operated by fleet owners and others to provide gasoline for their own vehicles rather than for resale. The remaining 1,380,000 average 3.5 pumps per gasoline retailer.

The figure of 1,906 stations represents the extreme minimum number possible in 1946 only on the further supposition that the conditions imposed would not themselves act to reduce consumption. Because consumption almost certainly would be reduced in these circumstances, 1,906 stations cannot be taken as a "workable minimum" for the distribution of 30,039,823,000 gallons of gasoline. For such a figure, it is clear, some of the conditions must be relaxed. It is interesting to note how rapidly the numbers rise as conditions are relaxed.

Operation for twenty-four hours each day in the year presumably is physically feasible for filling stations; but allowances must be made for unavoidable interruptions. There will be some nonpumping time between the moment when one car's tank has been filled and the moment when the next has been pulled into place. This nonpumping time includes time for taking the nozzle out of the tank, replacing the cap, making change, resetting the pump's gauge, waiting for the change of cars, removing the cap of the new car, and inserting the nozzle. If one allows only thirty seconds for these operations and ninety seconds to fill a fifteen-gallon tank, there will be a 25 percent time loss per car, or a loss of six hours per day. As a result, the number of stations must be increased by one-third to 2,542.

A system of refilling underground tanks that avoids interfering with service to consumers is quite feasible. Therefore, this assumption requires no modification. However, a steady stream of cars, each arriving with an empty fifteen-gallon tank to be filled to capacity, is not likely to make even a remote approach to workability, and thirty seconds between cars is obviously too little. If we assume that the average buyer takes five gallons and if we allow for a two-minute interval between cars throughout the twenty-four hours, the number of stations needed rises to 19,060.

How far will a consumer really drive to obtain gasoline? If the station is so far from his home that he would use his entire tankful in one round trip, then the gasoline would have no utility to him. Assuming that he insists upon having at least two-thirds of this gasoline for uses other than that of getting the gasoline itself, we put a limit of approximately fifty miles (or one hundred miles per round trip) upon the distances drivers who have their tanks filled will go for gasoline.[5] Although consumers would suffer considerably less hardship with the 19,060 stations permitted under the loosening of assumptions thus far than with the 1,906 stations set as the absolute minimum, a good deal of movement of consumers would still be necessary to make sure that each station had its full quota of customers within the fifty-mile radius.

If consumers are not to move at all, the number of stations required presumably will rise still further. It is now necessary to assume that a service station exists within fifty miles of every consumer, no matter where he may be. Furthermore, we can no longer assume that every station is used to

---

[5] This assumes that the consumer gets twenty miles to the gallon in his trips to and from the station.

capacity before another is installed. This would be true even if the three-pump station were taken as an average rather than as a uniform standard for every station, so that, in sparsely settled areas, stations could have a single pump and elsewhere more than three.

An approach to estimating the number of stations required under this standard could be made by using data on the physical areas of the various counties and the number and basic location of the automobiles in each. Since such a computation lies beyond the resources of the author of this essay, he must rest content with the guess that consumers could be thus served only by a further substantial rise in the number of stations.

Admission of seasonal variation in the use and purchase of gasoline would add still more to the number of stations required to give minimal service to consumers. Day-to-day and hour-to-hour variations would also increase the number, especially if these vary sharply from one location to another. This is true because a peaking of service at some times, with appropriate expansion of facilities, means idle equipment and staff at other times. Hence, in areas where previous computations have assumed that there are enough consumers to keep all the stations completely busy twenty-four hours a day, additional facilities would be needed to carry the peak loads. Here, again, the precise number of stations required could be determined only by laborious computations that lie beyond the writer's resources.

Since there has been no effort to compute the number of stations made necessary by reintroduction of a population scattered without regard to the convenience of service stations and wide fluctuations in consumption, it is not possible to say how close the relaxation of conditions thus far has carried the minimal number of stations to the number actually operating. The author's guess is that minimal and actual would still be rather far apart, since the number last computed (19,060 stations) could be doubled to take care of the scattered population, doubled again to allow for fluctuations in consumption, and still fall well under 100,000, as compared with the actual number—345,000.

Before we can assume that the difference of 285,000 represents "waste," we must remember at least one other fact. In practice, gasoline is only one of many products and services sold by most distributors. A station as a whole is not idle because no one is pumping gasoline, and it is by no means certain that the lowest cost for gasoline itself would be achieved if gasoline were singled out for separate handling in order to keep the pumps fully occupied within the limits prescribed.

IV. NUMBER OF STATIONS REQUIRED TO GIVE MAXIMUM CONVENIENCE TO CONSUMERS

At the opposite extreme from the austere economy assumed at the beginning of Section III is a situation that makes very little demand upon the consumer for foresight or exertion in buying. The consumer unquestionably attaches considerable value to what is vaguely called "convenience." The larger this element of service is in his purchase from the service station, the less meaningful become criteria for numbers of service stations worked out by reference solely to the physical task of getting gasoline into automobile tanks. Since the desire for additional sorts and amounts of service is extensible virtually without limit, a maximum can be set only by arbitrary definition. Accordingly, for purposes of the present analysis, maximum convenience will be assumed to exist when the following conditions are met:

1. Service stations are located at intervals of one mile along all streets and roads, so that no consumer is ever more than half a mile from a station.
2. Along sections of streets or highways where crossing over would involve hazard for the motorist, service stations are located at intervals of one mile on both sides.
3. There are enough stations to serve all cars in the country within any one consecutive hour, allowing six minutes per car. This service is to be provided without any motorist's having to travel more than half a mile to the nearest station, no matter where he may be, or to cross over anywhere along busy highways.
4. All stations operate twenty-four hours every day in the year.
5. Every consumer has a choice among three brands of gasoline at each station.

Presumably, the first test of convenience for a consumer is that a station be always close at hand, so that he need never go a great distance if he runs out of gasoline. He wants a station within a few minutes' driving range of any point to which he may go, preferably in the direction he is already traveling; and he wants to use as little as possible of his gasoline in driving to and from the station itself. If stations are placed at one-mile intervals on all roads, streets, and highways, we shall assume that this test of convenience is met satisfactorily. On this basis, approximately 3,450,000 stations will be needed.[6]

It has been observed that, in fast-moving traffic along busy highways and on congested streets, motorists very seldom cross traffic to reach a service station. Often they cannot do so with reasonable safety or without violating traffic regulations. The remedy for this inconvenience is to construct stations on both sides of the busier thoroughfares. Some 950,000 miles of streets and highways that carry 86 percent of the traffic[7] can be counted as the "busy" ones for present purposes. Construction of stations on both sides of these sections at intervals of one mile would add 950,000 stations and raise the total required to 4,400,000.

---

[6] Figures on road mileage are from D. G. Kennedy, *The Role of the Federal Government in Highway Development,* printed for the use of the U.S. Senate Special Committee on Post-war Economic Policy and Planning, 78th Congress, 2d Session (Washington, D.C.: Government Printing Office, 1944).

[7] Ibid.

To provide maximum convenience, all stations must be open all the time, so that any consumer can buy gasoline whenever and wherever the need (or the whim) seizes him. Furthermore, there must be sufficient stations to take care of all consumers at the same time if they simultaneously get the impulse to buy. For present purposes, "the same time" will not be interpreted literally but will be taken to mean within any one continuous hour during the twenty-four. Since a three-pump station can serve three vehicles at a time, it can provide service in the one peak hour, at six minutes per vehicle, for thirty vehicles. The absolute minimum number of stations required under this standard in 1946 to serve 34,000,000[8] motor vehicles would have been 1,133,333. This total is substantially smaller than the totals already required to meet the preceding two conditions of geographic distribution.

In practice, even 4,400,000 stations would probably be too small a number. It has been assumed that stations would be located at uniform intervals along all highways and streets, but it cannot be assumed that customers would be so distributed at all times as to have each station accessible to its quota of thirty peak-hour vehicles. At particular hours, some stations would have few customers, or none, whereas others would have many more than thirty. In order to meet the requirement that all cars can be served within any one-hour period, wherever they may be, additional stations would be needed at any location if the stations already provided for find themselves with more than thirty customers to serve in any hour. How many more stations would be needed could be determined only by traffic counts throughout the country. These, again, call for resources far beyond those of the present writer.

If recognition is to be given by every station to brand preferences of consumers, still more stations would be needed. With three pumps available, each station could offer three brands. Additional brands could be provided for only by increasing the number of pumps or the number of stations at locations already specified. If the stations set up under preceding assumptions differed among themselves as to brands carried, some individual customers would find that they were not at all times within half a mile of the particular brand they wanted or that they could not be served within the one-hour peak specified. Thus would arise the phenomenon of "four stations on every corner," to which critics of marketing often refer.

Furthermore, even if customers were satisfied with three brands, since each station is limited to one brand per pump, additional pumps or stations would be required at particular locations unless each station's customers divided their trade precisely in thirds among the various brands. Exactly how many additional stations would be made necessary by enlarging the number of brands could be determined only if the distribution of customer preferences among brands were known.

Except for enlarging the number of brands, the conditions here set up

---

[8] American Petroleum Institute, op. cit.

make no allowance for establishing a vigorous competition among retailers. If the strict definition of "competition" used by economists of the monopolistic-competition school were adhered to, there would have to be so many stations at each location that no one of them could exert any influence upon its particular local market. This would raise the total number of stations to levels considerably more fantastic than those already reached in the present analysis. For practical purposes, the number already provided could be expected to produce a reasonably good approximation to the results of pure and perfect competition.

The present analysis has paid no attention to costs and their effects, through prices, upon consumption. It has simply been assumed that consumption would remain as it is. In fact, of course, if 4,400,000 service stations operating 24 hours a day were to divide the total sales among themselves, many would do so little business that their unit costs would rise enormously. Consumers would have to compromise between their desires for convenience and limitations on their purchasing power.

We may conclude that, large though it is in absolute terms, the number of service stations operating in this country is considerably smaller than would be necessary to meet what we have called the standard of maximum convenience to consumers. Not less than 4,400,000 stations would have been required by this standard in 1946, and the number might well have run above 5,000,000. Although many consumers might welcome this degree of service, they obviously cannot afford the cost. The strength of their desires and of their pocketbooks is such, however, as to pull the number of stations operated far away from the minimum required by physical supply and well over into the area of convenience.

V. NUMBER OF STATIONS REQUIRED TO MAXIMIZE PROFITS

The third test of adequacy looks to the service station as a device by means of which the operator makes an income rather than as a device by which consumers are served. Here, effectiveness is measured by the closeness of the actual situation to that in which returns to the individual stations would be maximized. If those who manage to get into the business maximize their individual profits, it makes no difference, under this standard, whether the aggregate profit of all the stations operating is maximized or not.

A full analysis of what would be required to meet this standard is impossible in the absence of much information about demand and supply factors in thousands of localities. It will throw light on the problem under analysis, however, if an effort is made to determine the number of stations required to achieve the following conditions:

1. The maximum gallonage per station operating.
2. The maximum price for each gallon.
3. The minimum expenditure for costs and expenses.

If continuous operation every minute of every day is maintained by a station, it will achieve its maximum output of 10,939,050 gallons per year, allowing only for minimum necessary time losses, as in Section III. Naturally, each station operating, to achieve this maximum gallonage, must have enough customers to consume the amount pumped.

Seasonal, weekly, daily, and hourly fluctuations would have to be eliminated. If the station's output were geared to either average or peak consumption during the year, it would be idle part of the time, thereby preventing the attainment of maximum output. In other words, if all stations operating are to operate at capacity all year, their total output cannot exceed the annual total computed by extending throughout the year the rate of consumption reached in the poorest period. This low point in consumption is ordinarily reached in February.[9] The largest number of stations that could have been kept fully occupied during 1946, then, was the February consumption multiplied by 12 and divided by the individual station's capacity. This gives a total of 2,127 stations. Such a number would give each station operation at 100 percent of its capacity but would, of course, leave a good deal of consumer demand unsatisfied.

Further analysis indicates that even 2,127 stations is too high a number for the purpose sought. In order to satisfy the conditions laid down, each station must be guaranteed enough customers to maintain continuous operation at full capacity. This would require that there be no change in the motorist population in any area once stations had been located, and probably would mean leaving some consumers out entirely. The stations would operate only in territories having a sufficient number of customers to take their full output. Areas without such populations would have to do without gasoline. Here, again, only detailed and laborious computations would tell how many stations could operate; but the number must be smaller than 2,127. Each station would be designed to achieve minimum costs at its location. Since customers would not transfer from one station to another, costly competition would not exist.

Each operator, having a complete monopoly in dealing with his particular segment of consumers, could charge each individual customer a price just below that which would drive him away from the use of gasoline. It might be, of course, that revenue per station operating would increase if the volume of gasoline sold were reduced below the amount that would keep each of 2,127 stations operating at capacity. In that event, the number of stations operating might have to be reduced still further. In no event would more than 2,127 stations be called for, since the 1946 consumption was achieved at much less than monopoly prices.

As to expenses of operation, it can be assumed that the conditions set forth would reduce them to a minimum. Costs of competitive selling would be eliminated by the absence of competition. As to other costs, with each station

---

[9] American Petroleum Institute, op. cit., pp. 18–19.

operating at full capacity, its unit costs should be as low as they could go. This assumes, of course, that the three-pump station specified is just large enough but not too large to keep expenditures at their minimum when operations are at capacity. If this assumption is modified in practice, the number of stations required could go either up or down, according to the facts as regards the relationship between size and cost.

VI. NUMBER OF STATIONS REQUIRED TO MAXIMIZE WELFARE

As to the effects of the number of stations upon the social values they add to their communities, there seems to be no workable way to measure them quantitatively, even though it is possible to set up lists of ways in which the stations ought to contribute to community welfare. Thus, one could say that service stations:

1. Should carry their fair share of the group costs of community life through payment of taxes.
2. Should provide a fair share of the employment needed by the community's labor force.
3. Should contribute to the most effective use of the community's land.
4. Should enhance the physical beauty of the community.
5. Should contribute to protecting the safety of the people in the community, especially from fire and traffic hazards.

There is no convenient index by which to determine what a particular station is contributing in each of these particulars. Furthermore, even if the contributions made could really be measured, one would still find it difficult, perhaps impossible, to correlate the contributions made with the number of stations operated. One cannot even assume that there is a consistent relationship between number of stations operated and contributions to welfare.

Case studies, community by community, could perhaps determine the number of stations that would be of most benefit in some ways at given times and under given circumstances. They might, for example, be able to decide whether additional stations would absorb the unemployed or merely shift workers from other and possibly more useful jobs; whether closing down stations would release workers to more useful tasks or merely throw them out of work. They could make decisions as to the probable effects of increasing or decreasing the number of stations upon land utilization, community appearance, and safety.

In the absence of case studies of this sort, there is no readily apparent answer to the question as to whether service stations are too numerous or not numerous enough to maximize their contribution to community welfare. All one can say with conviction is that no evidence bears very heavily in either direction.

CONCLUSION

The answer to the question, "How many service stations are 'too many'?" turns out to be, then, a very wide range of numbers insofar as a quantitative solution is possible. If the criterion of adequacy is to maximize the profits of individual station operators, anything more than approximately 2,000 stations would have been too many in 1946. Correspondingly, if the criterion of adequacy is to pump a given quantity of gasoline over a given period of time, through as few pumps as possible, without regard to what the consumer wants from the retailer other than the physical product gasoline, then anything more than 1,900 or 2,000 stations in 1946 would have been hard to justify. On the other hand, four million or even five million stations might have been necessary to provide gasoline plus maximum convenience for consumers.

The 393,000 retailers of gasoline and the 1,500,000 pumps in operation in 1946, it is thus evident, may have been either far too many or far too few. In a society organized to give the consumer as little service as possible and to squeeze out of him as high a profit as possible for the station from which he buys, the number operating in 1946 was excessively large. The number of stations fell very far short indeed, however, of what would be required for a consumer's paradise where everything possible was done to reduce the energy and foresight he must himself exercise if he is always to have gasoline for his automobile tank exactly where and when he wants it with no more than a few moments' delay.

QUESTIONS

1. How many service stations are too many?
2. How many brands of cake mix are too many?
3. What criteria should be used to evaluate the adequacy of the number of outlets for a given service, or the number of brands of a given item? To what extent do the objectives of the societal system impact on the criteria selected?
*4. How many service stations would be "desirable" using the concepts introduced by Kotler (Reading 34)?

---

* Question relates concepts in this and other readings.

36
Would you want your son to marry a marketing lady?

Richard N. Farmer

The question of ethics in marketing, the nature of business practices under a market-directed system, and the benefits and drawbacks of having alternatives are considered in this article. A decade ago Richard Farmer wrote an article in which he asked: "Would you want your daughter to marry a marketing man?" He ended that article with: "If that nice young man who has dates with your daughter turns out to be a marketing major, what would you do? I would chase him off the premises fast. Who wants his daughter to marry a huckster?" Over the years he has changed his opinion, as well as the gender of the marketing person.

Ten years ago, I was brave enough to ask, "Would you Want Your Daughter to Marry a Marketing Man?"[1] This article got me into a lot of trouble, as clearly most marketing people strongly disagreed with my answer. I noted that there were really two major criticisms of modern marketing: (1) that marketing was unethical, and (2) that it was irrelevant to major world needs. The fact that these charges had little to do with technique, competence, or even the fact that most marketing people are quite ethical people personally, I argued, was beside the point. Until marketing people got more involved in what was of real importance in the world, the field would probably continue to be severely criticized everywhere.

Ten years have gone by, and much has happened. Marketing itself, along with all business fields, has made major strides in perfecting itself. Yet we have experienced wars, recessions, student revolts; we have seen countries turning Marxist, and even a few going Capitalist. We have seen the rich get relatively richer, while the world's poor, though gaining a bit, are growing relatively poorer. And the same nasty problems that plagued us in 1967 are still around. Poverty, sex and race discrimination, uneven economic development, and population pressures all are still very much with us. Ecological concerns have mounted enormously, and now we feel a new critique that

---

Source: Reprinted with permission from the *Journal of Marketing*, published by the American Marketing Association, vol. 41 (January 1977), pp. 15–18. At the time of writing Richard Farmer was chairman of the Department of International Business, Indiana University, Bloomington.

[1] Richard N. Farmer, "Would You Want Your Daughter to Marry a Marketing Man?" *Journal of Marketing*, vol. 31 (January 1967), pp. 1–3.

marketing pushes silly consumption while scarce resources are running out. Whether all this is really so or not doesn't deter the critics.

The same old ideologies are still struggling in the same old areas. Those who thought that marketing is unethical still think that way, and those who preach the virtues of free enterprise and all that goes with it are still firm in their beliefs. Pundits argue that the world is generally drifting away from these freedoms, while others optimistically note that free enterprise is still around and very vigorous. But a decade is too short to spot any really long-term trends. We are still vacillating between (1) our liberal, Judeo-Christian, Marxist ethics, which regard pushing soap as vulgar and, believe it or not, unclean; and (2) our pragmatic observation that if you really want to get rich as a country or world, sell the damn soap.

In short, nothing much has changed in terms of the broad debate. But much has happened in terms of evolution toward clearer perceptions of basic issues. We are beginning to see more clearly the options we face; and just as it was true ten years ago, it is true now that marketing is right in the center of the controversy.

CHANGES, GOOD AND BAD

Winston Churchill once remarked that democracy is a terrible system. About all you could say for it was that it was better than any alternatives. Marketing in a free enterprise economy sits in the same uncomfortable position. It may be unethical and irrelevant, but it just happens to be better than any alternatives. We have had plenty of experience with the options in the form of Marxist states, both Communist and Socialist, in the past ten years, and we also have had plenty of opportunities to watch market-oriented economies function.

The marketing people win hands down if wealth and extra income is what you want. Such improbable countries as South Korea, Japan, Hong Kong, Singapore, the Ivory Coast, and Taiwan, which have in effect gone the total marketing route, are among the fastest growing economies of the world. What they do is to find out what the world wants, and then produce it. The nice results are 10 percent-plus real economic growth rates. Japan is so good at this that it is rapidly catching up with everyone, and now is among the top five nations of the world in terms of per capita real income. Thirty years ago, it was one of the poorest countries in the world.

The oil-producing countries, which market oil everywhere and use the money to import what they need, have done even better. Abu Dhabi [United Arab Emirates] is probably still the richest country per capita in the world (who has data?), and this wealth all came from merely doing what marketing people have been saying for centuries. Find out what is needed, produce it, and sell it everywhere at the best price you can get. Indeed, these countries have been so successful at our game that some thinkers have wondered if it really was such a good idea to let brilliant Saudi Arabians such as Mr. Yemani attend Harvard Business School. Perhaps they learn too much too fast!

The real losers in the past ten years have been the Marxist countries that tossed aside market economies and went into planning with a vengeance. North Korea, Burma, Cambodia, and Albania may have many virtues, but they are awfully hard to find. Nothing much happens in such places, and nothing ever will. Eastern Europe, with its more developed Communist states, is also a real loser, no matter what the glowing propaganda statements say. The problem in such places is to figure out how to lock up the locals so that they cannot escape from the worker's paradise. The Marxist alternative is a grim, grey, dull, stifling situation where no one has any fun. They don't have much income either, in spite of what the governments say.

In the end, those places that have stayed with free markets, soap peddling, lousy TV commercials and all the rest, are the winners in the economic game. Unethical they may be, but in a broader sense they are most ethical of all. That extra income generated by the soap peddlers, used car salesmen, and other market-oriented hustlers can, and does, go into buying better education, medical care, churches and mosques, and, just maybe, happiness. Perhaps by default, marketing people have demonstrated that their game is the best of all. It's a terrible game, really, but what else do you have?

Not surprisingly, over 10 percent of all of our graduate students in our best business schools are foreigners, mainly from poorer countries, and many of these young people are majoring in marketing. The word is spreading, slowly but surely; and since nothing else really works all that well, perhaps we shall see much more interest in applying good marketing concepts worldwide in the future. The part of marketing that outsiders pay no attention to, such as logistics and physical distribution, have actually become so respectable that even the wilder-eyed UN types have enthusiastically adopted their principles. And it is good that they have, since the real gains possible in poorer countries stemming from better warehousing, transport systems, and similar developments can be very large.

American marketing practitioners and scholars have also helped spread the word, including entering areas where marketing men previously feared to tread. The multinational corporations have done more than anyone to show that good management, including very importantly marketing, really pays off, and they have done this so well that they have scared many poorer countries to death. Everyone hates multinationals, but they produce, so they are tolerated and even encouraged in many countries. Most of the discussion about how to control these monsters focuses on political control and obtaining their technology and industrial know-how, but few complain about their superb marketing or grasp that it is the major reason for their success.

The very fact that MNCs exist overseas provides the best possible marketing lessons to the rest of the world, and locals everywhere watch and learn. One odd result is that good marketing in all of its dimensions is better practiced in such countries as Spain, France, and Japan than it was ten years ago. If you can't beat them, join them.

Scholars and even a few practitioners have cautiously explored such fields as marketing of birth control devices and more nutritious foods. If you can sell soap, why not sell something socially useful? There is much to be done along these lines, but at least marketing people are asking the right questions, and few would object on scholarly or ethical grounds. The general field of marketing is much more powerful than most marketing people realize, and investigators are beginning to find new territories to explore.

BACK AT THE HOME FRONT

Just about everything we tried in the United States that ignored marketing has not worked very well in the past ten years. We have had a war on poverty, and the net result of this experience is that national income has shifted its distribution slightly to the top third of all income recipients. We tried all sorts of social experiments, including much educational reform, and the net results seem to be that students learn slightly less than they used to. The whole counterculture thing came and went, and all that seems to remain are a bunch of small business entrepreneurs selling honey, health food, and leather belts in the classic tradition.

One irony of the whole counterculture is that the real winners were those extremely efficient drug pushers, who knew a lot about marketing. Another is that in the end the successful communes ended up selling something. But after ten years of sound and fury, our social problems are still with us. Like Marxism, the government planning option just doesn't work all that well. Indeed, the American government option is ultimately the same as Marxism.

One practice the government forced on the private sector was the hiring of a significant number of minorities and women, a healthy innovation. In the narrow WASP business culture of 1967, too many first-rate people were excluded from the game before they could begin. Conservatives mumble about unqualified blacks and women getting the breaks, but we have had a payoff from this program. There are indeed some highly capable people around who are not WASPs, and they are appearing with increasing frequency in marketing jobs and other places as well. Our graduate schools of business now often have over 40 percent female enrollments, along with 10 percent other so-called minorities; and with all those foreigners included, the WASP males are now in the minority. Plenty of marketing departments, both in companies and universities, are now more efficient simply because more good people can get into the game. And more is to come.

Indeed, there is much more tolerance around generally in marketing than there used to be. The older image of the up-tight WASP executive in the three-piece suit is fading fast, to be replaced by just about anything that works. We have been forced to think more about what we really want to do, not about what is "right" in some vague ethical sense. And as we move this way, much of the criticism about reactionary marketing types exploiting the public may also fade.

It is becoming difficult to find stereotypes to poke fun at, when the salespersons I meet are bearded males, blacks with Afros, and women of all ages, along with more traditional types. It is even tougher to find some stereotype when I discover the best people can be any of these diverse types. And when serious economic development scholars start talking about market segments for birth control pills, and government people talk about using effective advertising to peddle rapid transit rides, I find it even more difficult to figure out who the villains really are.

THE WINNERS BY DEFAULT

In the end, marketing may win by default. Nothing else works; so, with a sigh, we turn to the experts who raise the relevant questions. What do people really want? How can we convince them to want desirable things? If we provide the things they want, we get fantastic motivation, so our societies become much more wealthy and productive as well. Buried in all of those excellent tools and techniques of marketing are the keys to whatever we want to do, whatever it may be, so outsiders keep cautiously nosing around the profession, often calling it something else, since the faint aura of moral decay still lingers.

We are all ethical men and women, or try to be. And for 2,000 years now, the Judeo-Christian morality has pushed us in the direction of love and brotherhood. Moslems and other non-Westerners have much the same ethical biases, so worldwide we agree generally on what should be. And what should be is a world that avoids human greed, and that is peaceful, tranquil, and decidedly uninterested in marketing. It makes us feel good to see love and brotherhood, while greed, corruption, and exploitation upset us. We go to church on Sunday and hear these words. What has come out of our religious and ethical heritage is not the trappings of the faiths, but rather the general feeling that somehow we should be nice to each other.

But sadly, we are still humans, full of messy greeds and aggressions. Marketing, without really realizing it, drifted right into the middle of this problem. Marketing essentially deals with greed and selfishness and base human desires. It is realistic, which gets the field into even more trouble, since no one interested in true ethics is really interested in reality. We prefer not to face what we really are, but rather dream of what we could be. I suspect that most of the vicious criticisms of marketing and its ethics stem from this frantic effort to avoid what we really are. Better to plan and dream along the lines of what we should be rather than face the awful truth.

But such dreams and plans do not work well, so in the end we get back to marketing, because no other discipline has what we need to get where we want to go. As the world wends its precarious course between the Marxist and

Capitalist solutions, marketing, by its very nature, is stuck right in the dead center of all the fuss. Sorry about that, but it is true.

People now talk about the collapse of values and the need to build some new philosophical synthesis about what we are and what we should be. Our old gods have failed, and we do not know what to do. We do not want to return to rapacious Capitalism, but the Marxist gods are feeble too, and the government planning gods are not doing the job in all countries. I suspect that if anyone does build a new synthesis, good old marketing, with all its concepts, subfields, and hang-ups, will be a significant part of it. This will occur simply because marketing *works*, and any realistic vision of the future will have to be workable above all else. But in a very basic sense, marketing excites all the base human instincts too, which is precisely why this new synthesis will be so hard to come by.

So my son has a date, and it turns out that this young lady is majoring in marketing. She's perceptive and intelligent, so she will go far. As my son points out, she'll probably make a lot more money than he will. And maybe, just maybe, she will do something highly creative and even moral in a field long abused for being immoral. Above all, that future has to *work*! Do I want my son to marry a marketing lady? Well, you see, it's this way . . .

QUESTIONS

1. Why has Farmer changed his position regarding marketing? In his opinion, has it become ethical where it was unethical, and relevant where it was irrelevant?

2. Identify the important changes in marketing practice that Farmer observed in the ten years between the two articles discussed here.

3. Farmer refers in several places in the article to our Judeo-Christian heritage and morality. What does this have to do with his criticisms and favorable comments about marketing?

37
Laissez-faire, planning and reality

Arthur Schlesinger, Jr.

The author of this article feels that more planning and government regulation of our economy are necessary to deal with the urgent problems facing us. Schlesinger faults the conservatives for naive reliance on the "marketplace," which he says has failed.

In recent weeks [1975] the main lines of President Ford's thinking about the economy have emerged with commendable clarity. In the name of "maximum freedom for private enterprise," he is proclaiming a crusade against the awful state of "regulatory bondage" in which, as he sees it, the American government is holding the oppressed and helpless American businessman. "I hear your cries of anguish and desperation," he told one audience of capitalists, as if they were inmates of a Soviet forced labor camp. "I will not let you suffocate." If only he had shown comparable sympathy for Solzhenitsyn!

Inveighing against "the mistaken, stupid idea that regulation protects people," the President argues that the public interest can be served best "through the market place" and proposes de-regulation as a primary goal of national policy. As for inflation, his solution for that, he recently acknowledged, is mass unemployment. "As you bring down the inflation," he has said, "We [an interesting pronoun] may have to suffer for a short period of time higher unemployment than we like." He has called for the partial denationalization of atomic energy, with the future production of enriched uranium turned over to private ownership (apparently under terms that guarantee profits to the private owners). The "critical choice" in the months ahead, he tells us, is between a "free" economy and "an economy whose vital decisions are made by politicians while the private sector dries up and shrivels away."

A certain amount of this may be discounted as the pre-campaign oratory of a man who has a natural concern about heading off Ronald Reagan. But enough of it corresponds to what we know about Gerald Ford as a Congressman to suggest that he probably is, on this range of questions, personally the most conservative President since Herbert Hoover. One doubts whether Eisenhower or even Nixon had Mr. Ford's gallant confidence that the unregulated market place is a sure guarantee of full employment, stable prices, decent wages and working conditions, protection for the consumer and truth

---

Source: Reprinted with permission from *The Wall Street Journal*, July 30, 1975, p. 10. At the time of writing, Arthur Schlesinger, Jr., was Albert Schweitzer Professor of the Humanities at the City University of New York and a member of *The Wall Street Journal*'s Board of Contributors.

in the securities markets. One must call this confidence gallant because it runs squarely against the evidence of history. It was, of course, the sad but indisputable fact that the unregulated market place achieved none of these things, which got the national government into the business of regulation in the first place.

MARKET PLACE FAILURES

And it is also the fact that the unregulated market place is patently unable to deal with urgent problems in our day. It has manifestly failed, for example, to control inflation while avoiding mass unemployment. Friedrich von Hayek, the high priest of laissez faire, admitted the other day that, under his creed, "We cannot avoid substantial long-term unemployment." Ford's own economists expect high unemployment till the end of the decade. Nor can the unregulated market place contain the administrative power over prices exerted by concentrated industries. Nor can the unregulated market place cope with problems like oil that are essentially political rather than economic in character. Nor can the unregulated market place bring about the reconstruction and expansion of our mass transit system which would be both helpful in re-employment and essential in the conservation of energy. Nor can the unregulated market place meet the nation's needs for health care, education, housing, welfare, solvent cities and environmental protection.

It is the obvious impotence of the unregulated market place in face of the hard problems of our time which has led some members of Congress—notably Senators Hubert Humphrey and Jacob Javits—to introduce the Balanced Growth and Economic Planning Act of 1975. This bill springs in part from a group called the Initiative Committee for National Economic Planning; and I must declare my own interest, for I was among those who signed that committee's statement. More formidable signers include economists like J. K. Galbraith, Wassily Leontief and Robert R. Nathan, labor leaders like Leonard Woodcock of the UAW, Arnold Miller of the Mine Workers and Jerry Wurf of the Federation of State, County and Municipal Employes and, it should be noted, business leaders like Robert McNamara, Stanley Marcus, Philip Klutznick, Robert Roosa of Brown Brothers Harriman, William F. May of American Can, W. Michael Blumenthal of Bendix, J. Irwin Miller of Cummins Engine, Arjay Miller of the Stanford Business School and Alfred C. Neal of the Committee for Economic Development.

The Humphrey-Javits bill would be regarded as innocuous in any other highly industrialized country. It would create an Economic Planning Board in the Executive Branch, establish procedures for industry and labor participation in the setting of economic targets and provide for congressional approval or disapproval of all plans developed by the board. The essence of the planning would be the gathering of information, the estimation of national resources and requirements and the coordination of national policies. There would be no enforcement authority, no interference with the making of private decisions, no revision of the pattern of ownership, no action except on the basis of legislation. The bill, in short, would give the nation the analytical, though not the enforcement, machinery to do for itself what every large corporation does every day in the way of advance planning.

Our radicals are naturally suspicious of all this. They recall that the idea of national planning received its first powerful endorsement in this country before World War I from George W. Perkins of J. P. Morgan and Company. They recall the summons to national planning during the depression by men like Gerard Swope of General Electric and Henry I. Harriman of New England Power. They recall Joseph P. Kennedy writing in 1936, "An organized functioning society requires a planned economy. . . . Planned action is imperative, or else capitalism and the American scheme of life will be in serious jeopardy." They remember how business took over the NRA in the early New Deal, as it has taken over nearly all the regulatory agencies that cause President Ford such distress.

In view of all this, it is astonishing to note the hysteria the Humphrey-Javits bill has provoked in fundamentalist business circles. Walter B. Wriston of Citicorp has called it "a program designed to destroy the free-market system and with it our personal liberty." Wriston even challenges the proposition that "government regulation of goods and services is a legitimate function of government." Thomas A. Murphy of General Motors predicts that "inevitably someone—maybe all of us—would lose some freedom." This overkill is, I say, astonishing, except for those venerable enough to remember the same hysteria with which business leaders in other days fought Social Security, unemployment compensation, stock exchange regulation, the guarantee of bank deposits, food stamps, the Employment Act of 1946—fought, indeed, all the forms of government intervention which, by saving business in 1975 from a ghastly collapse in the style of 1929–32, permit savants like Wriston and Murphy to run on so about the beauties of the market place. If those earlier attacks on government regulation had succeeded, one shudders to think what real trouble the nation would be in today.

HISTORY'S SPECIAL RELISH

I do not believe that national planning is a panacea. The left wing fear that business will capture the planning mechanisms is not without substance. The European and Japanese experience in national planning reveals problems as well as achievements. In addition, the failure of economic (and all other types of) foresight is a salient fact of life. History outwits us all, and does so all the time, and seems to take special relish in outwitting businessmen and economists.

Still, when laissez-faire zealots object that planning will infallibly get us into a mess, one can only comment that it is hard to imagine a greater mess than the refusal to plan has got us into already: the worst inflation in a generation, the highest unemployment in 35 years, the worst decline in real output in nearly 40 years, the worst deficit in the balance of payments ever, the worst peacetime budgetary deficits ever, the worst energy shortages ever, the worst crises in municipal finance ever. Is more of this the glorious future that Ford, Wriston, Murphy and the rest are holding out to the American people?

And it is sheer irresponsibility to denounce the mild Humphrey-Javits measure as contemplating, in Wriston's phrase, an "economic police state." It was the same sort of irresponsibility that led most Americans to stop paying any attention to the self-righteous and self-serving wails of business leaders in the 1930s. If the American businessmen want W. H. Whyte to write a sequel to his sterling book of 1952, "Is Anybody Listening?," Wriston and Murphy are pointing out the direction in which they should go. It is almost as irresponsible for an American President to pretend that the country can get along without government regulation. For the reality is that we will continue to have government regulation—and that we will not lose our freedom.

Joseph P. Kennedy's question of 40 years ago is still to the point: "Should we try to have a balance between regulation and individualism, or should we revert to an uncontrolled individualistic scheme." The answer is self-evident: We must strive for a better balance—a balance that will enable us to meet some of the problems the unregulated market place can never meet—and stop confusing our minds and dissipating our energies by trying to transform manageable differences over degree into a religious war.

QUESTIONS

1. How much planning does Schlesinger seem to be proposing? Is it possible to have only a "little" planning, or is it a yes or no question? Explain.

2. Does Schlesinger support planning on the basis of the success of planning? If so, how does he know it will continue? If not, how does he know it will work any better than the marketplace?

3. Suggest what criteria could be applied to a "problem area" to help decide whether regulation (or more regulation) is needed to achieve the "better balance" Schlesinger calls for.

38
Still no consumer clout in U.S.S.R.

Philip Caputo

In this very brief look into the consumer goods world of the U.S.S.R., Caputo discusses some of the problems in a centrally planned economy. While the government may order the system to "rescue the people from shortages, shoddy goods, and surly service," there is no guarantee that such will happen. Why?

MOSCOW—In the latest of a long line of government decrees aimed at improving the lot of the Soviet consumer, the Kremlin has ordered the Soviet bureaucracy to rescue the people from shortages, shoddy goods, and surly service.

The decree, published in the Communist Party newspaper Pravda, recently took up two columns of the paper's front page and was published the same week that Pravda's sister newspaper, Izvestia, ran a story about an old man named Vassily Alexandrovich.

Vassily did not rate page one, but the story of his problems illustrates why official decrees are not going to bring about the salvation of the Soviet consumer—a perennially neglected creature.

The 74-year-old Alexandrovich's story centers around a private plot—no, not a conspiracy, but a plot of ground he bought in a central Russian village. Izvestia described it as so barren that not even weeds could be made to grow on it. Nevertheless, Alexandrovich, a retired factory worker, put his back into it and soon was growing potatoes for the local market.

This kind of small-scale, private enterprise is allowed in the Soviet Union, and is sometimes encouraged by more liberal officials in the government. And for good reason. Although private plots take up only 4 percent of the arable land in the U.S.S.R., they produce one third of the country's meat, eggs, and vegetables, and one half of its potatoes.

State and collective farms, though they occupy the remaining 96 percent of farmland, produce the other two-thirds. The lesson is clear: Peasants work harder and produce more when they work for themselves. It is a lesson that has been learned by President Leonid Brezhnev.

A pragmatist, Brezhnev appears to be concerned about critical food shortages that, according to unconfirmed reports, have provoked distur-

---

Source: Reprinted with permission from the *Chicago Tribune,* August 27, 1977, p. 9. At the time of writing Philip Caputo was the Moscow correspondent for the *Chicago Tribune.*

bances in several outlying cities. Officials in the Ukraine, Brezhnev's native region, were reported to have complained bitterly and openly about the lack of meat and other products in local stores.

It is thought here that the Soviet president and party leader is worried about the possibility that the chronic scarcities may become serious enough to try even the immense patience of the Russians and set off the kind of demonstrations that shook the Polish government last year [1976].

But Brezhnev has been opposed by orthodox hard-liners who feel that encouraging private agricultural enterprise will weaken the ideological foundations of the socialist system. Or, to put it another way, the entrenched bureaucrats are not worried about providing food and other items to the consumer, but about losing the absolute power they wield over the country's economy.

Which leads back to Vassily Alexandrovich. Some party dogmatists in his town, ignoring Brezhnev's calls to help private farmers, punished the old man for his display of initiative by plowing up and ruining his potato crop.

Undaunted, he turned to growing hothouse cucumbers. Because the local collective farmers were either too lazy or too unconcerned to produce these vegetables, Alexandrovich became the town's sole supplier. He grew prosperous and built a new, brick house to replace the tumbledown log shack he had moved into.

Alexandrovich's enterprise was rewarded with a denunciation. Party hacks and the local press branded him a "speculator and pernicious individual." There were calls to bring him to account as an example to others who might be tempted by the lure of hard work and private gain.

Izvestia, the second most important newspaper in the world's largest Communist state, ironically came to his defense, and urged local authorities to leave people like Alexandrovich alone.

Whether they do or not, his case is a microcosm of why the Soviet system is chronically unable to meet the needs and wants of the consuming public. An authoritative West European economic report recently described the problem as one that "lies in the Soviet system."

Transforming the U.S.S.R.'s economy from a 19th-century one oriented toward heavy industry and weapons to a modern one oriented toward domestic demands will require radical social and economic reforms, the report said.

These reforms have not been made, it added, because of "a rigid, centralized traditional planning and decision-making system whose principal aim is not to bring about progress, but to preserve the established socio-economic structure."

The results can be seen on paper and on the streets of most Russian cities. The shelves in state stores here are almost empty of fresh vegetables and fruits in the winter. Shoes are shoddily made and expensive, with some pairs selling for as much as 25 to 40 rubles [$33.50 to $53.60], or the equivalent of five to ten days' pay for the average Russian worker. Meat, reflecting a 20 percent decrease in hog production and a mere 1.7 percent increase in cattle production in the 1971–75 five-year plan, is extremely scarce.

So are household utensils, radios, television sets, paper, tableware, and dishes. "You see now why we have such a low crime rate," quipped a Soviet economist. "There's nothing to steal."

The average Russian therefore spends a great deal of his or her time shopping for essentials. For many, grocery shopping is a daily ordeal because, according to Soviet statistics, roughly 40 percent of the country's families do not own refrigerators.

Despite some advances on the consumer front in the past decade, the queue remains a feature of Soviet life. Long lines of shoppers can be seen standing outside most stores here and in other cities. Russians often join a line without even knowing what's on sale in the shop. They assume it is valuable—otherwise there wouldn't be a line. Leningrad, Russia's second largest city, has professional queue-standers: People who stand in a line, then sell their place to someone else for a couple of rubles before moving on to the next line.

The Soviet automobile industry has also run into trouble. Several years ago, it was decided to step up passenger car production to make available a product that would give Soviet citizens an incentive to work harder. The state planning committee [Gosplan] promised that 800,000 passenger cars would be on sale in 1975. Things did not quite work out that way. Although 1975 production met the five-year plan's objective—1.2 million—most of those were exported or used to replace official automobiles.

According to Western analysts, the failures in the Soviet consumer industries are largely due to the glacial pace of modernization in this country. Vast imports of Western technology have helped somewhat, but even that cannot bring about significant results until the structure of the Soviet economy is changed. Russia, in short, needs another revolution, a technological one.

QUESTIONS

1. Discuss the message of the story of Alexandrovich. How would the story be different if Alexandrovich lived in the United States?

2. What "radical social and economic reforms" would be needed to transform the U.S.S.R.'s economy into a "modern one oriented toward domestic demands"?

*3. The U.S.S.R. does have some "balance" of planned and free market activities. Is a U.S.S.R.—type planned economy what Schlesinger (Reading 37) has in mind?

---

* Reading relates concepts in this and other readings.

39
Let's get back to the competitive market system

C. Jackson Grayson, Jr.

For years, some economists and historians have been pre-dicting the eventual collapse of capitalism in the United States and the emergence of a perfectly planned, government-regulated economy. We have already reached the stage where private enterprise has surrendered many of its freedoms to public authority. Our free-market system may simply collapse. Grayson argues that this should be a concern not only for business and labor leaders but also for each individual who wants to preserve a way of life that is worth caring about.

For almost 15 months during Phase II of the Economic Stabilization Program, I served as the chairman of the Price Commission.* Exercising control over most of the nation's price system, I saw this complex, capitalist economy from a most unusual observation post.

From this experience, and from what has happened since, I am personally convinced that our economic system is steadily shifting from a private enterprise, free-market economy to one that is centrally directed and under public control.

Price and wage controls such as we have experienced in Phases I through IV have helped to extend the degree of public control and to accelerate the rate of change. At some point—and I predict that at the present rate, this point may be reached in about 15 to 20 years—the essential characteristics of a competitive, private enterprise system (nonregulated prices, profit motive, risk taking, collective bargaining) will no longer make up the economic engine that drives our system.

I am not saying that there is and will continue to be public regulation of the

Source: Reprinted with permission from the *Harvard Business Review*, November–December 1973, pp. 103–12. Copyright © 1973, the President and Fellows of Harvard College. At the time of writing, C. Jackson Grayson, Jr., former head of the Phase II Price Commission, was dean of the School of Business Administration at Southern Methodist University.

*Editors' note: Phases I, II, III, and IV refer to a wage and price control program during the Nixon administration. The phases were designed to control inflation in the period following the Vietnam conflict and to help the economy move to stable growth. The Price Commission was the agency empowered to evaluate and approve wage and price increases in a broad range of areas, including negotiated labor contracts and the pricing of industrial and consumer goods. The allowable increases were generally in the range of 5 to 6 percent, and larger increases were seldom permitted.

private enterprise system. Since 1930, we have had that—a mixed public-private system. But, in the 1970s, the pendulum of the mix has been swinging further, and faster, toward central control.

Call it what you will—managed capitalism, socialism, a planned economy, a postindustrial state—the end result will be the virtual elimination of the free-market system as we now know it. There will be no signposts or traffic lights. We will simply shift over to another kind of system.

The resulting system will probably not have widespread public ownership of production and distribution; but it will have public control. General Motors will not die; but neither will it remain a capitalistically motivated and directed enterprise. Rather, it will operate as an organization designed to implement *public* economic, political, and social policy.

Impetus for this trend has not come from a group of revolutionists, and only partly from leftists, liberals, youth, intellectuals, and socialists. Instead, it has come from the public at large, from the Congress, and, perhaps most surprisingly, from the actions of many labor and business leaders.

I feel that this current threat to our free, competitive economy should seriously concern us, not only because I strongly believe in that system, but also because of the effect its loss would have on the social character of the United States.

In this article I attempt to identify what the current shifts away from freedom are and why they are a cause for alarm, and to suggest courses of action that businessmen, labor leaders, and legislators could take to help reverse the clear and present trend.

WARNING SIGNS

The trends I see can be summarized as follows:

Business and labor are too often seeking to reduce rather than to encourage competition in their markets.

Continuing price and wage controls are leading the public to believe that central planning and control are superior, mandatory, and desirable.*

Americans, in distrusting the market system, are demanding more economic benefits from the federal government and are seeking ways to insulate themselves from the impact of economic change.

In addition, international economic interdependencies are complicating our privately controlled market system. As recent balance-of-payments and exchange-rate problems demonstrate, closed economies are a thing of the past. Inflation can be exported and imported, increasing the call for more centrally coordinated economic policies between and inside nations.

Editors' note: These controls, which have since been dropped, still existed in 1973.

Business seeks protection

Consciously and unconsciously, businessmen themselves are adding to the probability of greater centralization of economic control by seeking ways to reduce market competition—the very keystone on which the capitalist system rests.

Normally, competition is curtailed either by private monopoly power or by government protection. It is still unclear whether large corporations have sufficient power to control markets, reduce competition, and "administer" prices. Our internal studies at the Price Commission did not provide any evidence that prices were being administered by corporations. But, clearly, we did not have sufficient time to make a full study of this issue.

We did have time, however, to observe innumerable instances in which business turned to government to seek forms of assistance which, in effect, would reduce competition—for example, asking for imposition of subsidies and tariffs, occupational licensing, fair trade laws, and import quotas.

Excerpts from letters written to me at the Price Commission by businessmen serve as illustrations:

"I do not advocate any program of isolation, but I do think it is good business for us to protect our national economic situation in the face of stiff and competitive foreign trade." (A steel company)

"We need government protection because we can't compete against the big companies." (A consumer goods company)

"If you break our fair trade laws, the market will be chaotic." (A cosmetics company)

"We can't survive if you let cheap products in from foreign countries." (A shoe manufacturer)

"We must have minimum milk prices if we are to have an orderly market." (A dairy products company)

"If we allow liquor prices to fluctuate freely, competition will be ruinous and the Mafia might move in." (An alcoholic beverages company)

Another way some businesses are hampering the free-market system is by not using the age-old competitive tool of reducing prices as a way to increase their sales.

Again, to quote from my 1972 mail:

"In all my years in business, I have never reduced prices to hurt a competitor." (A retail food supplier)

"Why did I raise my prices? My competitor did. I always go up when he does." (A chemical company)

Of course, this attitude is not shared by all businessmen. After the Price Commission authorized a cost-justifed price increase, one businessman told me, "You gave us a price increase. I wish the market would."

My point, however, is that far too few companies are exploring market flexibility by reducing prices. And yet, when we ordered some companies to reduce prices because they had violated regulations, several reported that they experienced increased volume and a higher total profit.

But the reluctance to reduce prices is also understandable. Several heavy-industry companies reported that they feared competing too aggressively on price because they would capture a larger market share, drive out smaller companies, and be subject to Justice Department or competitor antitrust suits. Efficient stevedoring companies argued they would drive out smaller businesses if they held prices down. And after the Russian wheat sale drove flour prices up, small bakeries urged us to force large bakeries to raise their bread prices.

The threat of continuing price controls has compounded the price-reduction problem. Many companies report hesitancy to reduce prices for fear of being caught with a low "base price" in future freezes and phases. This was clearly demonstrated in Phase III, when freeze "talk" actually accelerated price increases.

Finally, I was surprised to find that the majority of businessmen with whom I talked wanted Phase II controls continued. The most commonly stated reason was fear of union power. The argument was that the balance of power has swung so far toward the unions that businessmen feel they can no longer negotiate successfully. Accordingly, they choose price controls over wage disputes; they prefer regulation to the problems freedom poses.

So does labor

In the model of the free market, it is axiomatic that competitive behavior is required not only of business but also of labor. There must be competition in wages as well as in prices. More and more, however, it's not turning out that way.

Like big business, big labor tries to use government or private power to protect itself against such natural effects of competition as layoffs, disloca-tions, wage reductions, and advancement by competition.

Whether labor has too much power was not an issue we studied at the Price Commission during the control period. But many instances in which noncompetitive labor prices were driving costs up were reported to us as justifications for price increases—featherbedding in railroads and docks, re-strictive work rules in construction and shipping, and rules barring more efficient methods in construction and printing.

An October 1971 staff report of the Bureau of Domestic Commerce esti-mates such extra costs in construction at $1 billion of $3 billion annually, in railroads at $700 million to $1.2 billion, in printing at $400 million to $600 million, in supermarkets at $250 million to $400 million, and in trucking at $275 million to $400 million.

These restrictive, noncompetitive work practices are usually defended by labor on humanitarian grounds. Without judging the merit of that position, I can definitely say that these practices drive costs up and usually result in higher unit labor costs, higher domestic prices, and reduced competitive abilities aborad.

Just as business often does not see price reductions as necessary and competitive, so labor does not see wage levels as connected to successful or unsuccessful competition in the free-market system. Nor does labor see the natural relationship between productivity and the wages that a company can afford to pay. Companies report mounting pressure from labor for increased compensation, regardless of the productivity of individual workers or of the nation as a whole. Labor's typical demands include increased minimum wage levels, "catch-up" wage increases, fixed productivity rates, tandem wage agreements, and annual pay increments.

For example, in late 1971, workers in the coal industry, which has had productivity decreases in recent years, received nearly a 14 percent wage increase settlement. The Price Commission, in one of its most important decisions, ruled that this practice would lead to further cost-push inflation and, despite the 14 percent wage settlement, allowed the coal industry to submit only a 5.5 percent wage cost as justification for price increases. This practice was then followed for all companies throughout Phase II.

As a result of this "5.5 rule," two things happened. Some companies suffered reduced profits. But other companies bargained harder at the table because they knew they could not "pass on" more than 5.5 percent. In fact, some companies reported privately that they were pleased with the rule because it gave them a bargaining weapon greatly needed to withstand labor's pressures.

There is little question that if labor settlements, on the average, rise faster than overall productivity, the result will be inflation, unemployment, or both. Our 5.5 percent limitation was an attempt to crack into the wage-productivity imbalance by forcing price increases to reflect no more than the long-term national productivity gain of 3 percent, plus a 2.5 percent inflation goal. The 5.5 percent was a national procrustean bed that served a crunching purpose in the short run.

We've also heard arguments by labor that economic justice demands wages be increased—a growing egalitarian ethic that wages be based on need rather than on competitive reality.

But those who argue this line sometimes end up taking contradictory positions, as was illustrated during the debate over the minimum wage. At the same time that many labor leaders and members of Congress were loudly protesting price increases in Phase II, they were also fighting equally hard for increased minimum wage levels and extended coverage. Without entering into the merits of the economic justice argument, the commission computed that the various proposed bills on the minimum wage before Congress in

1972 would have increased the Consumer Price Index anywhere from 0.3 to 0.8 percent. Since no productivity gains would have ensued, the increased costs would have either come out of profits or been passed on in prices.

In summary, I can only point out to labor and to business that any time they seek, through private market power or government help, to reduce the effects of competition, they invite the danger of permanent central control over the economic system. Without competition, public controls may become not an option, but a necessity.

Wage-price controls distort

True, wage-price controls help attack inflation in the short run by (1) reducing inflationary expectations, (2) intruding on discretionary market power of business and labor, and (3) influencing the timing of price and wage decisions.

But, by their very design, such controls interfere with the market system and hasten its move toward a permanent central one. I can spot seven ways this occurs.

First, wage-price controls lead to distortions in the economic system, which can be minimized only in the short run. The longer controls are in, the harder it is to discern real from artificial signals. No matter how cleverly any group designs a control system, distortions and inequities will begin to appear. It happened in European control programs; it was beginning to happen in Phase II.

For instance, lumber controls were beginning to lead to artificial middle-men, black markets, and sawmill shutdowns. Companies trapped with low base-period profit margins were beginning to consider selling out to those with higher base periods, sending their capital overseas, or reducing their efforts. Instances of false job upgrading—which were actually "raises" in disguise—were reported on a scattered but increasing basis. To keep away from profit-margin controls, companies were considering dropping products where costs, and thus prices, had increased. And shortages of certain products (e.g., molasses and fertilizer) were appearing because artificially suppressed domestic prices had allowed higher world prices to pull domestic supplies abroad.

Exceptions and special regulations can handle some of these distortions, but the task grows more difficult as each correction breeds the need for another.

Second, during controls, the public forgets that not all wage-price increases are inflationary. In a changing, competitive economy, wage and price increases occur because of real consumer demand shifts and supply shortages. The resulting wage and price increases signal to business, "Make more"; or to labor, "Move here"; or to the public, "Use less."

Controls interfere with the signaling mechanism. A good example of how an artificially suppressed price-signal leads to eventual shortages is natural gas. Similar examples can be found in labor where suppressed wages do not attract labor to areas in which there are shortages of skills or of workers.

But with wage-price controls in place, the public believes that all increases are inflationary—almost antisocial—and the clamor is for no, or very small, increases.

The sense of the statement, "You can eliminate the middleman, but not his function," applies equally to our economic system. We live in a world of scarce resources, and, as much as some would like to repeal the laws of supply and demand, it can't be done. Some system must allocate resources, we hope to the most efficient use for society. If wage-price controls, other government regulatory rules, or business labor monopolies prohibit the price system from performing its natural function, then another rationing system (central planning and control) must be used. You can eliminate the price system, but not its function.

Third, during a control period, the public forgets what profits are all about. Even before wage-price controls, the public believed profits were "too high," even though they have actually declined in the past few years, from 6.2 percent of GNP in 1966 to 3.6 percent in 1970, and increasing only to 4.3 percent in 1972. And, with profit increases raised to the top of the news during the recovery of 1972 and early 1973, the negative public sentiment against profits increased. Why? The control system itself heightened the public's negative attitude toward profits at a time when capital regeneration, the fuel of the capitalist engine, was already alarmingly low.

Fourth, wage-price controls provide a convenient stone for those having economic or political axes to grind, particularly those interested in promoting a centralized economic system. For example, in 1972, Ralph Nader argued that automobile companies should not be allowed to raise their prices to reflect style changes. Others argued that price increases should not be given to companies that employ insufficient numbers of minorities or pollute. Nor should wage increases go to uncooperative unions.

Fifth, wage-price controls can easily become a security blanket against the cold winds of free-market uncertainties. They tell people what the limits are; they help employers fight unions, and union leaders to placate demands for "more" from their rank and file. The controlled tend to become dependent on the controllers and want regulations continued in preference to the competition of a dynamic market. At the same time, the controllers themselves can become so enamored with their task that they also don't want to let go. The public begins to fear what will happen when controls are ended, and seeks continuance. Witness the recent fears of moving from Phase II to Phase III, and the public (and Congressional) pressure for the freeze to replace Phase III. Even Wall Street seems terrified at the thought of returning to supply and demand in the market. All of this proves that it is much easier to get into controls than to get out.

Sixth, under controls, business and labor leaders begin to pay more attention to the regulatory body than to the dynamics of the marketplace. They inevitably come to the same conclusion, summed up by one executive: "We know that all of our sophisticated analysis and planning can be wiped out in the blink of a Washington controller's eye."

Seventh, and most dangerous, wage-price controls misguide the public. They draw attention away from the fundamental factors that affect inflation—fiscal and monetary policies, tax rates, import-export policies, productivity, competitive restrictions, and so on. The danger is that attention will become permanently focused on the symptom-treating control mechanism rather than on the underlying problems.

The public voice

The public is also adding to the probability of more central control of our economic system. I can cite several basic attitudes at work to explain this phenomenon:

Increasing loss of faith in the ability of both business and labor leaders to operate our economic system.
Increasing expectation of greater economic benefits.
Intensified search for stability and egalitarianism.

In recent years poll after poll has quantified the growth of these trends in public opinion. For instance, over the last seven years, Louis Harris and Associates has been asking the public about its degree of confidence in the leadership of our institutions, and has made these discoveries:

Corporate executives share with bankers and educators the largest loss in public respect, declining from 55 percent in 1966 to 27 percent in 1973.
Confidence in labor leaders shrank from 22 to 15 percent in the same time period.[1]

And a 1971 Opinion Research Corporation study revealed that 62 percent of the public favored governmental controls over prices, 60 percent of all stockholders believed competition could not be counted on to keep prices "fair," and fully one third of the public believed that Washington should set ceilings on profits.[2]

In general, my personal mail and my experience in numerous interviews with newspaper editorial boards and others confirmed that the public feels there should be more, not less, control of business and labor. And Congress reflects this mood in asking for more controls, tighter regulations, and more public agencies. Time and again, when I was testifying before congressional committees, I was told that we had to have more controls because the private

---

[1] Louis Harris, "The Public Credibility of American Business," The Conference Board Record, March 1973, p. 33.

[2] Thomas W. Benham, "Trends in Public Attitudes toward Business and the Free Enterprise System," White House Conference on the Industrial World Ahead (Washington, D.C.: Government Printing Office, February 1973).

enterprise system "didn't work." Such a sentiment does not make me optimistic about continued public support for our free enterprise economy.

Nevertheless, the growth in the public's disenchantment with the private enterprise system has been matched by an increase in the public's demands on that system. The public wants, for instance, higher pay for teachers, policemen, and women; a clean environment; better schools and medical care—and all without increases in prices or taxes.

At various Price Commission public hearings and in meetings with public groups and congressmen, I heard demands for increased pollution controls but, at the same time, for lower transportation prices, increased health benefits but lower hospital costs, increased mine safety but lower coal prices, decreased insecticide usage but lower food prices, protected forests but lower lumber prices, and so on. The demands are outrunning what we, as a society, can afford.

We cannot have it all ways without increased productivity. And, more and more, the public is not willing to wait for the market to provide remedies but is seeking centralized solutions to obtain the desired benefits now.

Finally, the move toward a central system is being aided by the public's desire to make people the same, both in ability and in susceptibility to economic change. The market system is conceived on the concepts of competition, monetary reward, excellence, and change. The current attitude stresses stability, cooperation, egalitarianism, and income equality enforced by a central authority.

"Can we be equal and excellent too?" queries John Gardner in the subtitle to his book Excellence—a question which he discusses extensively but does not answer.[3] Everyone might like both, but the competitive system is built on the notion that those individuals and institutions outperforming others are not and should not be rewarded equally. But now, more people are seeking and getting protection, through tax reform, income redistribution plans, promotion by seniority, and so on, against "differences" generated by the operation of the competitive system.

And society's insistent cry for economic stability poses two dilemmas for our capitalistic system.

First, if the business cycle can be sufficiently dampened by government policies to avoid the unpleasant by-products, we might also run the risk of removing some of the essential features of capitalism, principally the ability of the capitalist system to adapt to changing circumstances and to encourage risk taking. That is, if we remove the valleys do we not also remove the "mountains of incentive" for risk and change?

Second, the goal of "maximum employment" has been interpreted to mean low unemployment, and the arguments have centered on definitions of "low" (3 percent, 4 percent, 5 percent) and "unemployment." But stimulating demand to achieve low unemployment risks inflation. And moderating demand to reduce inflation risks high unemployment.

[3] New York: Harper & Row, 1961.

This unemployment-inflation trade-off is becoming more difficult to manage centrally. If low unemployment is government's primary goal, as it has been in recent years, inflationary pressures are created and fixed incomes become vulnerable. In turn, there are more cries for wage-price controls and greater planning.

Central economic planning holds a great deal of logical appeal for many economists, intellectuals, and businessmen. They conclude that, if businesses plan, governments should—or that somebody should be in charge of the economy.

While their arguments are appealing, to date no one in any society has been able to come up with a central planning model that is more efficient and effective than the seemingly uncoordinated actions of the marketplace. I do not believe it is possible to construct one. In the Price Commission, almost every time we tried to adjust our economic system to correct one problem, two or three more were created, and the more we felt the temptation to "control."

In the end, I believe that any extended control system would disrupt the free-market system. At worst, the market would break down; at best, it would be highly ineffective and subject to bottlenecks, quotas, and black markets. The trade-offs in our extremely large and highly interdependent economy are too complex to be done efficiently on a centralized basis. And then there is the question of who would supply the value judgments for the operations of such a system. Why not return to the one planning system we have that *works*— the price system.

POINT OF NO RETURN?

What does this all add up to? Where are we headed? Is our private enterprise system actually doomed?

There are many who have said *yes*. Karl Marx predicted that capitalism would destroy itself; Joseph A. Schumpeter flatly stated that capitalism cannot survive;[4] and Robert L. Heilbroner concluded: "The change [away from capitalism] may require several decades, perhaps even generations, before becoming crystal clear. But I suggest that the direction of change is already established beyond peradventure of doubt."[5] Even "Adam Smith" observed in *Supermoney* that "the consensus is moving away from the market as decision maker and from the business society."[6]

Clearly, the factors I have cited *are* carrying us further and further away from the market system and toward a central economic one. I cannot prove we have gone or will go "too far," but I can point to figures substantiating the trend: our national income accounts show a shift in governmentally directed

---

[4] *Capitalism, Socialism and Democracy,* 3d ed. (New York: Harper & Row, 1962), p. 61.

[5] *Between Capitalism and Socialism* (New York: Vintage Books, 1970), p. 31.

[6] New York: Random House, 1972, p. 266.

expenditures from 15 percent in 1930 to about 40 percent today. And the federal proportion has risen from 5 percent to 26 percent in the same period.

I am *not* saying, however, that the private enterprise system is doomed, nor that continuance of the trend toward central control is inevitable and irreversible. Nor do I feel that government has no role in the economic-allocation system. It clearly does and should. I believe, rather, that we are very near the point where further centralization will change our present system into one that can no longer perform its function efficiently.

I view this trend with alarm because I favor retaining the very powerful features of the market system. I hold this position, not out of blind faith in an ideology, but for these reasons:

Demonstrated economic superiority. The economic record clearly reads that the U.S. free-market, private enterprise system has produced the highest standard of living in history and has demonstrated a remarkable ability to adapt to changing conditions.

Political freedom. The principles of democracy and personal freedom are most compatible with a decentralized market system.

Personal experience. I have witnessed the difficulties of trying to allocate resources by centrally directed price controls. These difficulties have convinced me that it is impossible to improve on the system in which billions of daily market decisions by the public determine our resource allocations.

Before some brand me a chauvinistic throwback to Social Darwinism, let me quickly add these points.

I am aware that our present system has competitive imperfections on both the price and the wage sides. It has never been, and never will be, as theoretically competitive as Adam Smith's description. Government vigilance and action are required to prevent the natural monopolistic tendencies of the system.

I am also aware that there are social problems and inequities in our present system which need correction, and that the central government should play a role in this task.

The difference between the centralists and myself is that I do not think the best solution is always to increase the size of the central system. *Rather, it is in a better functioning of our private competitive system and a better quality, not quantity, of public control.* The question remains: How can this be accomplished?

Backing up

It is obvious from the foregoing that I strongly believe the trends toward a centralized, or government-controlled, economy should be halted. I believe the survival of almost our total economy is at stake.

Businessmen, labor leaders, government legislators, and administrators have the power to slow or alter the trends I've cited. By doing so, we may be falsely labeled right-wingers or reactionaries, but we should not be daunted. If a goodly number of us do not try to stop the present trends, we may, even within this decade, end up with an economy we cannot manage.

Recommendations on how to halt the present trends are discussed below. I do have one comment that applies to all of them. I do not believe, as some free-enterprisers do, that any of the suggestions I make should do away with the social achievements of the past 40 years. I believe that much, if not most, of the social legislation passed by the U.S. Congress protects the unprotected and provides social equity in economic terms that are consonant with the spirit of our political life and the protection of the individual by law. I deeply believe in equity.

I do not believe, however, in inequity. It is the inequities, rigidities, bureaucratic stiflings, and actual absurdities that we must attack. But again it is a question of how.

Selective deregulation.   Obviously, not all regulation in the public interest should cease—for example, in the areas of safety, product quality, pollution, and health. But many economists can make a good list of those regulations that are interfering excessively with the competitive model, such as subsidies, quotas, tariffs, and competition-limiting labor and business practices referred to earlier in the article.

Monopolistic vigilance.   Both business and labor have innate tendencies to seek monopolistic positions, and therefore they must be restrained. The same message also goes for professions (e.g., medicine and law) and trades (e.g., accounting and investment) that build up anticompetitive practices in the name of "professionalism."

The Sherman, the Robinson-Patman, and the Clayton acts, all designed to bring about these goals, were written many years ago. Each needs continued enforcement and should be examined for revisions and oversights in its application.

Three-branch overhauls.   Just as physical systems need periodic checks and overhauls, so do our social institutions. Government is no exception. Many of our procedures and institutions at the local, state, and federal level were designed for an agrarian society with slow communications and an isolated domestic economy.

At a minimum, I suggest a regularized public review, say, every three years, of the organizational and administrative procedures of government.

Political involvement.   We live not just in an economy but in a *political* economy. Our economic system does not operate according to the classical laws of supply and demand but through the interaction of power and politics with economics. If business and labor leaders wish to steer the system in the direction they believe best, they cannot simply deplore, fume, curse, and hire a Washington lawyer or lobbyist. They must get directly involved by holding public office, personally visiting regulatory bodies and Congress, participating in citizens' affairs groups, and allocating time for employees to participate in local, state, and national politics.

Public advocacy. Related to the need for political involvement is the need for public advocacy of all views about our economic system. Those supporting increases in government's role are currently more vocal than are the advocates of the private enterprise system. The reason, I suspect, is that advocacy of private enterprise is often ridiculed as mossback in viewpoint, anti-intellectual, socially insensitive, and on the side of vested interests and "fat cats."

Nevertheless, those believing in the private enterprise system must speak out, not bombastically but intelligently. Every avenue should be utilized— speeches, articles, participation in local affairs, appearances at schools, employer-employee discussions, and so forth.

Economic education. If people are to make intelligent choices about the nature of our economic system, they must understand more economics. My experience at the commission has convinced me that economic understanding in this nation is low, much lower than it should be for people to make wise choices.

Education to promote understanding should begin with our young people and extend through adult life, emphasizing not a partisan view but a clear presentation of various economic fundamentals and systems.

Better economic tools. The economic policy tools of taxation, budget, and monetary supply, by which government manages the overall economy, are very crude and require overhauling. The econometric models are weak, the implementation process rigid, and the needed data often not available. For instance, decisions were made in Phase II with a frightening paucity of economic information. At the very least, this situation could be corrected by funding the many excellent economic research organizations to enable them to come forward with recommendations for the Congress and the President.

Business schools. Business schools should turn out students who understand both the strengths *and* the weaknesses of the private enterprise system, as well as its responsibilities to society. Too often, technicians are being graduated who are narrow professionals and blind ideologists.

One particular recommendation is that more schools encourage entrepreneurs. The entrepreneur is the lifeblood—the innovator, creator, pusher—of the private enterprise system; without him, the system will tend to become change-resistant and bureaucratic.

Department of Economic Affairs. Part of President Nixon's proposed departmental reorganization program is the creation of a new Department of Economic Affairs. In the Price Commission, we saw numerous instances in which the dispersal of economic policy matters in various parts of government inhibited the formulation of an integrated and consistent program.

I support the proposed new department, which would gather together under one head the economic branches of various departments and agencies, e.g., Transportation, Commerce, Labor, the Small Business Administration, and others.

Productivity.   A strong, increasing productivity is one of the best preventives against inflation and one of the strongest assets of a private enterprise system. Therefore, business and labor must work together to shore up our lagging productivity, particularly as we shift to a more service-oriented, and hence lower-productivity, economy. Government can also help in this area through policies that stimulate capital investment and R&D.

In addition to the National Commission on Productivity in Washington, there should be a private sector productivity institute, like those in Japan, Germany, and Israel, which would be a clearinghouse of information and source of help and education.

A DIFFERENT KIND OF ROAD

My recommendations advocate continuation of a private enterprise, free-market system with these essential features:

The price system.
Private ownership.
Collective bargaining.
The profit motive.
Freedom of entry.

Capitalism is more than a system of economic voting by buying a can of peas. It is also a system of values and attitudes, a way of life that permits individual motivation, excitement, personal freedom, variety, and excellence. I do not see these attributes flourishing in centrally planned and controlled systems.

Yet I am not denying a role to central government. Government can help to ease transitions caused by change through stimulating or contracting the economy and informing the public of the cost and benefits of various alternatives, e.g., pollution control versus higher prices, caribou protection versus energy supply, unemployment versus inflation. Government also has the extremely important function of setting and monitoring the rules of the economic game through antitrust laws, product-quality standards, pollution controls, and so on. These restrictions are set principally to keep competition alive and to protect the general public.

The key issue is at what point do such activities and restrictions on the private enterprise system inhibit it to the point of rendering it effectively inoperative?

The tug between laissez-faire and state regulation has been going on for centuries. They are contradictory, but both are valid approaches and applicable under appropriate conditions. Yet neither is of universal application for all purposes.

We seem to advance by overaccentuation of one principle at a time, like a sailing vessel that is first on one tack and then on another, but is making to windward on both. It is important, therefore, not to hold too long on the same tack, not to believe too strongly that either principle is absolute and universal.

For the real danger is that people will strive for the triumph of a particular philosophy and will refuse to consider the limits of proper application of their particular point of view. In the heat of debate, the advocate often asserts extreme opinions and demands action more drastic than he would call for if he reflected more calmly.

I submit that what we must do is seek the balance between these opposing principles, realizing that it is almost as impossible to frame a comprehensive and universally applicable economic system as it is a political one. In making our Constitution subject to amendment, our forefathers showed they were aware that the best solution will not be found in one principle but in a set of ideas determined by experiment and observation of practical results. And it is extremely likely that the chosen path will not be the same forever, but will shift from time to time.

Phase IV could be a return trip to the relatively free-market system and, I hope, a reversal of the trend I have observed. It could be an opportunity for labor and business to demonstrate that the private sector can manage the market and fight inflation without further government intervention. If not— then I don't think that either labor, business, or the public will like the controls that will be imposed on our freedoms in the future. And we will have helped to build our own cages.

This is not a pessimistic view, for, as Schumpeter stated, a report that a ship is sinking is not defeatist. It is only defeatist if the crew sits and drinks. They can also rush to man the pumps.

In every sense it's up to each of us.

QUESTIONS

1. Why does Grayson feel that we should "get back" to a competitive market system? Who and what forces are pulling the other way?

2. Would the changes suggested by Grayson be a step forward or backward toward meeting the societal goals of the United States? Whose goals?

3. What impact would Grayson's suggestion have on the relative importance and use of price in marketing mixes? Is this wise from a profit point of view?

*4. Is Kotler's proposal for a more socially responsible marketing concept (Reading 34) compatible with Grayson's position?

---

* Question relates concepts in this and other readings.